SIEGECRAFT II

SIEGECRAFT II

NO FORTRESS IMPREGNABLE

HAROLD A. SKAARUP

ISBN: 978-1-63795-733-2   (Paperback Edition)
ISBN: 978-1-63795-734-9   (Hardcover Edition)
ISBN: 978-1-63795-732-5   (E-book Edition)

Because of the dynamic nature of the Internet, any Web addresses or links contained in this book may have changed since publication and may no longer be valid.

The views expressed in this work are solely those of the author and do not necessarily reflect the views of the publisher, and the publisher hereby disclaims any responsibility for them.

The information presented here has been gleaned from a great number of living and historical sources, many of whom were participants in the sieges described. They were there, I was not, and an individual eyewitnesses view is often open to many interpretations. You must choose for yourself what to believe in these accounts, and remember that it is your right to do so.

E Tenebris Lux and Ex Coelis.

Book Ordering Information

Phone Number: 315 288-7939 ext. 1000 or 347-901-4920
Email: info@globalsummithouse.com
Global Summit House
www.globalsummithouse.com

Printed in the United States of America

Dedication

To the currently serving members of the Allied Forces of the North Atlantic Treaty Organization (NATO), the Canadian Armed Forces, North American Aerospace Defense Command (NORAD), United States Northern Command (USNORTHCOM), United States Space Command (USSPACECOM), and the United Nations (UN) Security Forces currently deployed, thank you. Grant we keep the peace.[1]

---

[1]   The author has had the honour of serving in uniform alongside the soldiers, sailors, and airmen of these outstanding organizations.

Epigraph

"Whoso sheddeth man's blood, by man shall his blood be shed."[2]

"The great struggles of the 20th century between liberty and totalitarianism ended with a decisive victory for the forces of freedom – and a single sustainable model for national success: freedom, democracy, and free enterprise. In the 21st century, only nations that share a commitment to protecting basic human rights and guaranteeing political and economic freedom will be able to unleash the potential of their people and assure their future prosperity. People everywhere want to be able to speak freely; choose who will govern them; worship as they please; educate their children - male and female; own property; and enjoy the benefits of their labor. These values of freedom are right and true for every person, in every society - and the duty of protecting these values against their enemies is the common calling of freedom-loving people across the globe and across the ages."[3]

---

[2] *The Holy Bible*, King James Version, Thomas Nelson Inc., Camden, New Jersey, 1970, *Genesis, Chapter 9, verse 6*, p. 6.

[3] The White House, Washington, 20 September 2002, W01081-02*: The National Security Strategy of the United States of America*, p. 1.

Table of Contents

List of Illustrations

32. The fall of the walls of Jericho, ca 1400 BC.
33. Medieval Castle under siege.
34. Crusader fortress Krak des Chevaliers, Northwest Syria.
35. British First World War Mk. IV (Male) Tank with a fascine.
36. 13th century CE illustration showing a medieval siege in France.
37. Roman watchtower on the lower Danube frontier, c113 AD.
38. Roman fortress reconstruction, Saalburg Main Gate (Porta Praetoria), Germany.
39. Roman castle of Iciniacum near Theilenhofen in Bavaria Germany.
40. Musée Mémorial de la Ligne Maginot du Rhin, Maginot Line Casemate, south of Strasbourg, France.
41. Model of the Fortress of Megiddo, 1457 BC.
42. A wheeled siege engine, 9th century BC bas-relief of an Assyrian attack, found in the palace of Ashurnasirpal II (883-859 BC), at Nimrud.
43. Mykonos vase depicting the Trojan Horse.
44. Triumphant Achilles dragging Hector's body around Troy, from a panoramic fresco of the Achilleion by Franz Matsch.
45. Engraving of a 13th century catapult throwing Greek fire.
46. The Catapult, painting by Sir Edward Poynter.
47. Roman Mangonel.
48. Ballista siege engine, engraving.
49. Roman Ballista with Roman soldiers.
50. Roman one talent *ballista* (26 kg weight projectile).
51. Medieval Ballista, drawing.
52. Trebuchet, Middle Ages.
53. Siege tower, engraving.
54. Belfry.
55. Medieval Siege Tower.
56. Bohemond of Taranto mounts the rampart of Antioch, engraving by Gustave Doré.
57. The process of sapping in the 17th century, engraving.
58. Engraving of a Counter Ram in operation.
59. Rams in operation.
60. Romans under the cover of their shields in an assault formation known as a "tortoise."
61. Roman Onager in action.
62. Roman Javelin catapult.
63. Catapult drawing from the *Dictionary of French Architecture from 11th to 16th Century*.
64. Boudicca statue, London.
65. The destruction of Jerusalem by the Romans, under the command of Titus, AD 70. Painting by David Roberts.
66. Aerial view of the fortress of Masada, Israel.
67. The Goths at the Battle of Mons Lactarius during the Gothic War, 535-553. Painting by Alexander Zick.
68. Raiding Huns attack a Roman Villa. Roche Grosse.
69. Engraving of Ostrogoths entering Rome.
70. Fury of the Goths, depicting the Battle of the Sabis, 57 BC, painting by Paul Ivanovitz.
71. Statue of Charlemagne, 19th century, Louvre, Paris, France.
72. Imperial Coronation of Charlemagne, painting by Friedrich Kaulbach, 1861.
73. The Storming of Ipswich by the Danes, painting by Lorentz Ipplich.

114. Sultan Mehmed II and the Ottoman Army approaching Constantinople with a giant bombard, painting by Fausto Zonaro.
115. The Dardanelles Gun, a very heavy 15th-C bronze muzzle-loading cannon of type used by Turks in the siege of Constantinople in 1453.
116. Sultan Mehmed II's entry into Constantinople, painting by Fausto Zonaro.
117. The surrender of Granada, 1492, painting by Pradilla.
118. Siege of Rhodes, 1522, engraving by Guillaume Caoursin.
119. Gate of Saint Athanasiou, Rhodes.
120. Bombard-Mortar of the Knights of Saint John of Jerusalem, Rhodes, 1480-1500.
121. The English Post, the scene of heaviest fighting on Rhodes.
122. Kolossi Castle, Cyprus.
123. Fort Saint Angelo de la Valette on the Birgu peninsula.
124. Detailed Map of the Siege of Malta, a fresco by Egnazio Dante.
125. Lifting of the Siege of Malta, painting by Charles Philippe Lariviere.
126. The Last Days of Tenochtitlan, Conquest of Mexico by Cortez", a 19th-century painting by William de Leftwich Dodge.
127. Coevorden citadel diagram, and a painting of the re-capture of Coevorden, December 1672, as part of the Franco-Dutch War.
128. Siege of Groningen, engraving.
129. Fort Bourtange, Netherlands, diagram, and aerial view.
130. Vauban's system of attack, diagram.
131. Fortress Charle Roy, France, diagram of the plan of attack, 1693.
132. Plan of Geneva, Switzerland, fortifications in 1841.
133. Oliver Cromwell at Dunbar, painting by Andrew Carrick Gow 1881.
134. Map of the siege of Newark (6 March 1645 – 8 May 1646).
135. Siege of Vienna, contemporary 1529 engraving of clashes between the Austrians and Ottomans outside Vienna by Bartel Behmam.
136. Siege of Vienna, 1683, painting.
137. Chittorgarh Fort.
138. The legendary "Malik-i-Maidan" Gun, reported to be the largest piece of cast bronze ordnance in the world.
139. Siege of Londonderry, 13 April 1689, engravings.
140. The armed merchant ships *Mountjoy* and *Phoenix* break through the defensive boom to relieve the Siege of Derry.
141. Sébastien Le Prestre de Vauban.
142. Blaise François, Comte de Pagan, engraving.
143. Besançon fortifications designed by Vauban.
144. Ravelin Peter (1708) and access bridge, Petersberg Citadel, Erfurt, Germany.
145. Blaye Citadel, plan view, 1752.
146. The fortification of Lille, France, designed by Vauban in 1709.
147. The Citadel of Lille, detailed view, designed by Vauban in 1709.
148. The Citadel of Arras, plan view of the fortifications designed by Vauban.
149. Ville-franche-de-Conflènt fortification.
150. Fortress of Belfort, plan view of the fortifications designed by Vauban.
151. Fortress of Landau, plan view of the fortifications designed by Vauban. This fortress came under siege in 1702.
152. Neuf Brisach, France, plan and aerial views of the fortifications designed by Vauban.

187. Turret formations in a portion of the Maginot Line.
188. Fort Eban Emael.
189. German DFS 230 Troop carrying glider and German paratroops.
190. Australian troops, Tobruk, 13 Aug 1941.
191. Russians soldiers in the trenches, defending Leningrad with a 7.62-mm DP-27 machine gun.
192. RCAF Lockheed CC-130 Hercules dropping Canadian paratroopers.
193. Vietminh soldiers in trenches at Dien Bien Phu, 1954.
194. 2nd Battalion, 173rd Airborne Brigade, destroying enemy bunkers after assault on Hill 875, near Dak To, Vietnam, 1967.
195. Twin apartment buildings burning in the centre of Sarajevo after being hit by Serbian gunfire during the siege in 1992.
196. Russian tanks destroyed during the battles in Grozny in 1996.
197. Author Photo.
198. Four Leaders of the First Crusade, engraving by François Guizot.
199. Godfrey of Bouillon enters Jerusalem, engraving.
200. Fort Ticonderoga, aerial view; and "The storming of Fort Ticonderoga, 1775", painting by Frederick Remington.

Foreword

It has been said that the taking of a fortress depends primarily on the making of a good plan to take it, and the proper implementation and application of the resources to make the plan work. Long before a fortress has been besieged and conquered, it must have been out thought before it can be outfought. This book outlines some of the more successfully thought out sieges and demonstrates why it is that no fortress is impregnable.

A siege can be described as an assault on an opposing force attempting to defend itself from behind a position of some strength. Whenever the pendulum of technology swings against the "status quo," the defenders of a fortification have usually been compelled to surrender. We must stay ahead of the pendulum, and not be out-thought long before we are out-fought, for, as it will be shown in this book, "no fortress is impregnable."

US Navy Captain (retired) Scott Lewis

Acknowledgements

I would like to thank US Navy Captain (retired) Scott Lewis, who knew the story of the long bow, and for taking the time to write the foreword to this book.

There are a great number of friends, military historians and colleagues who have guided me throughout my military career, all of whom I would like to thank. Most of their names are too far numerous to list here, but suffice it to say that I had the great privilege to serve in the company of many of Canada's finest soldiers and alongside a great number of soldiers in Allied nations including NATO, NORAD and the UN. I would specifically choose to mention the outstanding paratroopers of the Canadian Airborne Regiment, formerly of CFB Edmonton and CFB Petawawa. I also had the honour to serve with the extremely professional Commanders, staff and soldiers of HQ 4 Canadian Mechanized Brigade and 1 Canadian Division Forward based in Lahr, Germany.

During my military education and training I have walked the battle grounds of Normandy and Waterloo, and the Great War killing fields of Vimy Ridge, Verdun and the Vosges mountains. I have stood on the Horns of Hattin in Israel, where Saladin defeated the Crusaders before the Second Crusade, and I have had the privilege to guard the line with the UN in Cyprus and to serve with the NATO-led Peace Stabilization Force (SFOR) in Sarajevo, Bosnia-Herzegovina. I had the honour to serve with the Kabul Multinational Brigade (KMNB), in Kabul, Afghanistan, from January to August 2004 alongside some of the more than 40,000 Canadian Forces personnel who also served there, and with allied nations from more than 40 different countries in theatre, all working to make our world a safer place.

I am greatly indebted to colleagues and instructors I served with at the Combat Training Center at CFB Gagetown, and the Intelligence Schools at CFB Borden and CFB Kingston, as well as the great number of highly dedicated Canadian and American military personnel from all branches of the service in NORAD. All are outstanding warriors and comrades and it was a great privilege to serve in their company. None will be forgotten.

My father Aage C. Skaarup served with the RCAF at 3 (F) Wing, Zweibrucken, Germany, (1959-1963), and he took our family castle hunting often throughout our time there. This generated a huge interest for me in exploring and examining these historic time capsules. When I joined the Army, I had the extraordinary privilege of serving with HQ CFE in Lahr from 1981 to 1983, and with 4 CMBG based at CFB Lahr, from 1989 to 1992. Because of these postings, I have often returned to visit the castles I explored with my parents and brother Dale, and have taken my wife Faye and sons Jonathan and Sean to see them as well. I have explored, photographed, painted pictures and documented castles from one end of Europe to the other, and you will find a number of historical entries describing some of them in this book.

While working as a volunteer at the New Brunswick Military History Museum at 5 Canadian Division Support Base Gagetown, New Brunswick, I was motivated to produce a book on all the historic artillery preserved in Canada. This resulted in the production of the book *"Shelldrake - Canadian Artillery Museums & Gun Monuments"*, (iUniverse.com, Bloomington, Indiana, 2012). A tremendous number of military historians, researchers and friends assisted with the explorations and research that helped me to put these books together. In the process, I found myself digging into the history of the fortifications and the sieges these cannon were employed in throughout Canada and overseas. This continues to take up our family time, and is in fact, a lifelong journey of learning and exploring.

This book is designed to be an aide-memoire, to aid in answering basic questions on the subject of a number of historic sieges throughout the history of the world we presently live in.

Doug Knight, a retired RCEME Officer and a volunteer with the Canadian War Museum, has been a mentor and guide. His knowledge of Canada's cannon, much of it presented in his book, *Guns of the Regiment*, (Service Publications, Ottawa, 2016), is my go-to reference. I am not a gunner, just an interested retired Army Officer and amateur historian. What I do have, is a collection of colleagues and friends with similar interests who provide invaluable help when it comes to identifying cannon and related artifacts, and a generous willingness to find answers to interesting questions.

Terry Honour and Maxwell J. Toms in Ottawa have been stellar in their support (and gloriously super aggressive in chasing down "new finds"). We share what we discover and in so doing, help to preserve our military history.

The cross-referencing of data here, has resulted in a great many surprising and often wonderful new discoveries, and often led to contacting world-renowned subject-matter experts on cannon and sieges. Ruth Rhynas Brown provided detailed references for historic cannon in many instances. My mother, Beatrice Skaarup, now age 90, has been extremely enthusiastic in acting as a spotter for me on what she calls "gun hunts". She loves to explore.

Harold Wright, a member of the Friends of the New Brunswick Military History Museum association and an esteemed historian in the Saint John community has been a significant contributor for numerous projects we have worked on. (He has also gotten me involved in many public speaking engagements on military history over the years).

When you have access to such incredibly knowledgeable people, the windows on the military history world open like the doors of an immense cathedral – and it is my privilege to know some of them.

To round out the circle, I need to confirm that there have been many contributors too numerous to name, who assisted in the hunt for the castles and the background to the sieges included in this book, and who helped to provide and update the data presented here. Many of the photos in this book have been sourced from the Library and Archives Canada files and from the generous contributors to Wikipedia. Please credit them as annotated. Any errors found here are mine, and any additions, updates, corrections or amendments to this list of historic sieges would be most welcome and may be e-mailed to the author at hskaarup@rogers.com.

Thank you to all who gave their support, time, assistance and expertise on the fortifications, sieges and battles found here, your patience and assistance has been invaluable. This book is a small sample of our military history – and should serve to explain the reason why I think "no fortress is impregnable".

Introduction

(Pierpont Morgan Library, New-York)
Illustration of a Medieval trebuchet in action during the First Crusade (1095–1099). The illustration is from a book made for King Louis IX (or Saint Louis) of France in 1250.

A siege is a military blockade of a city, or fortress, with the intent of conquering by attrition, or by a well-prepared assault. This derives from *sedere*, Latin for "to sit". Siege warfare is a form of constant, low-intensity conflict characterized by one party holding a strong, static, defensive position. Consequently, an opportunity for negotiation between combatants is not uncommon, as proximity and fluctuating advantage can encourage diplomacy.

A siege occurs when an attacker encounters a city or fortress that cannot be easily taken by a quick assault, and which refuses to surrender. Sieges involve surrounding the target to block the provision of supplies and the reinforcement or escape of troops (a tactic known as "investment"). This is typically coupled with attempts to reduce the fortifications by means of siege engines, artillery bombardment, mining (also known as sapping), or the use of deception or treachery to bypass defenses.

Failing a military outcome, sieges can often be decided by starvation, thirst, or disease, which can afflict either the attacker or defender. This form of siege can take many months or even years, depending upon the size of the stores of food the fortified position holds.

The attacking force can circumvallate the besieged place, which is to build a line of earthworks, consisting of a rampart and trench, surrounding it. During the process of circumvallation, the attacking force can be set upon by another force, an ally of the besieged place, due to the lengthy amount of time required to force it to capitulate. A defensive ring of forts outside the ring of circumvallated forts, called contravallation, is also sometimes used to defend the attackers from outside.

Ancient cities in the Middle East show archaeological evidence of having had fortified city walls. During the Warring States era of ancient China, there is both textual and archaeological evidence of prolonged sieges and siege machinery used against the defenders of city walls. Siege machinery was also a tradition of the ancient Greco-Roman world. During the Renaissance and the early modern period, siege warfare dominated the conduct of war in Europe. Leonardo da Vince gained as much of his renown from the design of fortifications as from his artwork.

Medieval campaigns were generally designed around a succession of sieges. In the Napoleonic era, increasing use of ever more powerful cannon reduced the value of fortifications. In the 20th century, the significance of the classical siege declined. With the advent of mobile warfare, a single fortified stronghold is no longer as decisive as it once was. While traditional sieges do still occur, they are not as common as they once were due to changes in modes of battle, principally the ease by which huge volumes of destructive power can be directed onto a static target. Modern sieges are more commonly the result of smaller hostage, militant, or extreme resisting arrest situations. (Duffy, Christopher. *Siege Warfare: Fortress in the Early Modern World, 1494–1660.* Routledge and Kegan Paul, 1996)

BEFORE FORTRESSES

Since the beginning of time, man has sought to defend himself and his family by finding a shelter or building a strong fortification. In equal measure and determination there have been those who have sought to overcome these defenses, which generally consisted of three different methods of protective works. The earliest and most simple field fortifications often consisted of stakes, stones, ditches, abatis (an obstacle comprised of cut trees with their branches facing the enemy), and other common obstacles constructed just before a battle began and which were primarily only intended for temporary or immediate use during a battle. The techniques used often mirrored the basic techniques used by early hunters, who built obstacles whose design and implementation were derived from simple but effective pits and traps which had been used to catch animals. As attack methods grew in sophistication, more ingenious ideas and methods of defense came to be employed.

Sharpened stakes joined together to form a palisade came into increasing use, as well as traps set with a chevaux-de-frise (medieval defensive anti-cavalry measure consisting of a portable frame (sometimes just a simple log) covered with many projecting long iron or wooden spikes or spears). Improvements in the use of metallurgy contributed to the tools available to the defender, including such devices as the caltrop (shown above), a metal device which was formed from four iron spikes joined in the form of a tetrahedron shape. Many of these devices would be thrown on the ground forward of a defensive position with the object of causing the attacker's horse to stumble or fall, so unhorsing the rider or knight and rendering them more vulnerable in their cumbersome armor on the ground.

(Library of Congress Photo cwpb.02598)

Chevaux-de-frise used in the defence of the Confederate Fort Mahone at the Siege of Petersburg, Virginia, fought from 15 June 1864, to 2 April 1865, during the American Civil War. The campaign consisted of nine months of trench warfare in which Union forces commanded by Lieutenant-General Ulysses S. Grant assaulted Petersburg unsuccessfully and then constructed trench lines that eventually extended over 30 miles (48 km) from the eastern outskirts of Richmond, Virginia, to around the eastern and southern outskirts of Petersburg. Petersburg was crucial to the supply of Confederate General Robert E. Lee's army and the Confederate capital of Richmond. Numerous raids were conducted, and battles fought in attempts to cut off the Richmond and Petersburg Railroad. Many of these battles caused the lengthening of the trench lines. Lee finally gave in to the pressure and abandoned both cities in April 1865, leading to his retreat and surrender at the Appomattox Court House. The Siege of Petersburg foreshadowed the trench warfare that was common in the First World War, earning it a prominent position in military history.

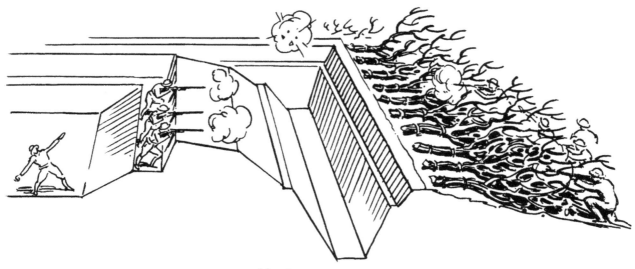

Abatis arrangement.

The use of stakes led in turn to the construction of more complex fortifications made of wood, as well as the idea of making them portable. William the Conqueror's Norman troops, for example, brought prefabricated wooden castles with them when they landed in England in 1066, and the first thing they did on arrival was to erect one of them on the beach. The aim of these fortifications, and the reason they were initially effective, was to divide an attacker's attention between trying to overcome them while simultaneously trying to keep his own forces protected.

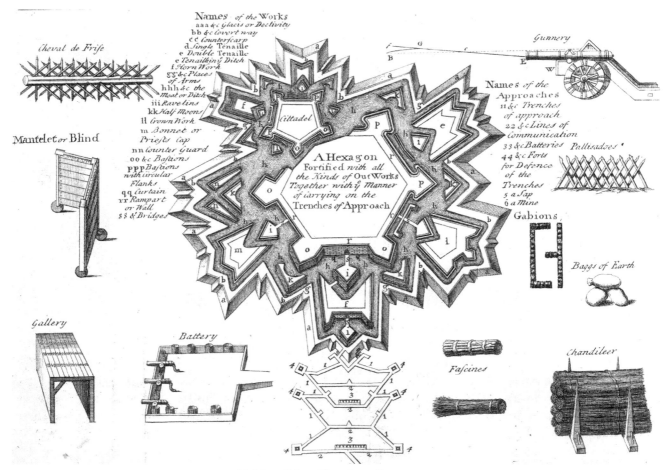

Table of fortification diagrams.

Fortifications, both temporary and long-term, have helped to decide the outcome in several very famous battles, including those at Crécy in 1346, Poitiers in 1356, and Agincourt in 1415.[4]

---

4 26 Aug 1346 Battle of Crécy. The English defeat the French. First known use of gunpowder weapons in battle in Europe (by the English), although guns may have been used at Metz in 1324, or at Algeciras in 1342. The English chose the battle site, their strength 20,000, the French strength 60,000. Beginning about 6 PM in rain, the battle went through the night. English archers stopped the French knights in the mud in 15 or 16 waves, leaving 1,542 dead French knights and Lords and between 10 and 20,000 men. English losses were 200, including 2 knights. The French had good cavalry, but atrocious leadership. Since the time of Crécy, infantry has remained the primary element of the ground combat forces.

19 Sep 1356 Battle of Poitiers. The French are defeated by an Anglo-Gascon force at Maupertuis, near Poitiers. Fought during the Hundred Years War. Edward the Black Prince with 7,000 troops vs. the French led by King John II with 16,000 men.

In each of these specific battles, English archers fired their arrows from behind a protective shield of sharpened wooden stakes angled to face the assaulting French knights. Since the idea was effective, it remained little changed for centuries, and in fact variations on wooden stakes were used in Vietnamese defense works in the 1960s and 70s.

25 Oct 1415 Battle of Agincourt. Fought during the Hundred Year's War between Henry V of England with 1000 knights and men-at-arms and some 5000 archers, against Charles VI of France and 20,000 French forces. The English won, losing 1600 casualties vs. 7000 casualties for the French.

The renewed English invasion of 1415 found France ruled by a mad king, Charles VI. From his conquest of Harfleur on 22 Sep, Henry V marched northward toward Calais with his English army. Unable to cross the lower Somme because of flooding and French defenses, the English had to swing inland to cross above Amiens. This detour enabled a French army of 20,000 men under the constable Charles d'Albret and the Marshal Jean Bouciquaut II to interpose itself between the invaders and Calais. Henry had no choice but to fight. At the village of Agincourt, 33 miles northwest of Arras, he chose a position between two patches of woods that narrowed the front to 1,200 yards. Sending his horses to the rear, he deployed his men-at-arms in three divisions abreast, each supported by a group of archers on either flank. To his front lay ploughed fields, heavy with mud after a week of rain.

The French, with most of their numerical superiority lost on the cramped front, also dismounted, and deployed in three lines in depth. Little use was made of their crossbowmen or heavy cannon. At eleven o'clock on 25 Oct the English opened the battle by advancing their archers to bring the longbows within killing range (about 250 yards). The French first line, led by a cavalry spearhead, plodded forward through the mud. Although suffering terrible casualties from English arrows, they reached Henry's front ranks, only to be repulsed when the archers exchanged their bows for axes and swords. Then the second line, under the Duc d'Alencon, pressed forward to continue the deadly hand-to-hand struggle. It, too, was finally beaten back, leaving the duke dead on the field, and many wounded, as well as able-bodied, prisoners in the hands of the English. At this moment, the French camp followers broke into Henry's camp, seeking plunder. Believing himself attacked in the rear while the third line of the enemy stood intact on his front, the king ordered the massacre of all prisoners. This led to the deaths of much of the remaining warrior arm of the French nobility.

After extinguishing the threat to their rear, the English braced to meet a new assault. But the French third line, shaken by the heaps of corpses to their front, recoiled without making an effective charge. The battle had ended in less than three hours with 7,000 French casualties. D'Albret was dead and Bouciquaut a prisoner. English losses were reported no higher than 1,600. At odds larger than 3 to 1, England had won one of the great victories of military history.

With the way now open Henry marched on to the English base at Calais, reaching there on 16 Nov. Buoyed by the dramatic victory at Agincourt, he returned two years later to launch a systematic conquest of all Normandy.

(Chapter CXXIX of Jean Froissart's Chronicles, 15th century)

BATTLE OF CRÉCY, 1346

The Battle of Crécy took place on 26 August 1346 in north-east France between a French army commanded by King Philip VI and an English army led by King Edward III. The French attacked the English while they were traversing northern France during the Hundred Years' War resulting in an English victory and heavy loss of life among the French.

The English army had landed in the Cotentin Peninsula on 12 July. It had burnt a path of destruction through some of the richest lands in France to within 2 miles (3 km) of Paris, sacking many towns along the way. The English then marched north, hoping to link up with an allied Flemish army which had invaded from Flanders. Hearing that the Flemish had turned back, and having temporarily outdistanced the pursuing French, Edward had his army prepare a defensive position on a hillside near Crécy-en-Ponthieu. Late on 26 August the French army, which greatly outnumbered the English, attacked.

During a brief archery duel a large force of French mercenary crossbowmen was routed by Welsh and English longbowmen. The French then launched a series of cavalry charges by their mounted knights. These were disordered by their impromptu nature, by having to force their way through the fleeing crossbowmen, by the muddy ground, by having to charge uphill, and by the pits dug by the English.

The attacks were further broken up by the effective fire from the English archers, which caused heavy casualties. By the time the French charges reached the English men-at-arms, who had dismounted for the battle, they had lost much of their impetus. The ensuing hand-to-hand combat was described as "murderous, without pity, cruel, and very horrible". The French charges continued late into the night, all with the same result: fierce fighting followed by a French repulse.

Other accounts report that Genoese crossbowmen had led the assault, but they were soon overwhelmed by King Edward's 10,000 longbowmen, who could reload faster and fire much further. The crossbowmen had then retreated, and the French mounted knights attempted to penetrate the English infantry lines. In charge after charge, the horses and riders were cut down in the merciless shower of arrows. At nightfall, the French finally withdrew. Nearly a third of their army lay slain on the field, including King Philip VI's brother, Charles II of Alencon (1297-1346); his allies King John of Bohemia (1296-1346) and Louis of Nevers (1304-46); and some 1,500 other knights and esquires. King Philip was wounded but survived. English losses were considerably lower.

The English then laid siege to the port of Calais. The battle crippled the French army's ability to relieve the siege; the town fell to the English the following year and remained under English rule for more than two centuries, until 1558. Crécy established the effectiveness of the longbow as a dominant weapon on the Western European battlefield.

King John at the Battle of Poitiers, painting by Eugène Delacroix.

BATTLE OF POITIERS, 1356

The Battle of Poitiers was a major English victory in the Hundred Year's War. It was fought on 19 September 1356 in Nouaillé, near the city of Poitiers in Aquitaine, western France. Edward, the Black Prince, led an army of English, Welsh, Breton and Gascon troops, many of them veterans of the Battle of Crécy. They were attacked by a larger French force led by King John II of France, which included allied Scottish forces. The French were heavily defeated; an English counterattack captured King John II along with his youngest son and much of the French nobility.

The effect of the defeat on France was catastrophic, leaving Dauphin Charles to rule the country. Charles faced populist revolts across the kingdom in the wake of the battle, which had destroyed the prestige of the French upper-class. The Edwardian phase of the war ended four years later in 1360, on favourable terms for England.

Poitiers was the second major English victory of the Hundred Year's War. Poitiers was fought ten years after the Battle of Crécy (the first major victory), and about half a century before the third, the Battle of Agincourt (1415). The town and battle were often referred to as *Poictiers* in contemporaneous recordings.

Morning of the Battle of Agincourt, 25th October 1415. (Painting by Sir John Gilbert)

BATTLE OF AGINCOURT, 1415

The Battle of Agincourt was one of the English victories in the Hundred Year's War. It took place on 25 October 1415 (Saint Crispin's Day near Azincourt, in northern France. England's unexpected victory against the numerically superior French army boosted English morale and prestige, crippled France, and started a new period of English dominance in the war.

After several decades of relative peace, the English had renewed their war effort in 1415 amid the failure of negotiations with the French. In the ensuing campaign, many soldiers died from disease, and the English numbers dwindled; they tried to withdraw to English-held Calais but found their path blocked by a considerably larger French army. Despite the disadvantage, the following battle ended in an overwhelming tactical victory for the English.

King Henry V of England led his troops into battle and participated in hand-to-hand fighting. King Charles VI of France did not command the French army himself, as he suffered from psychotic illnesses and associated mental incapacity. Instead, the French were commanded by Constable Charles d'Albret and various prominent French noblemen of the Armagnac party. This battle is notable for the use of the English longbow in very large numbers, with the English and Welsh archers comprising nearly 80 percent of Henry's army.

(US Army Photo)
"Dragon's teeth", concrete tanks traps from the Second World War on the Siegfried Line, Germany.

Early fortifications could be by-passed and "picketed" - a term we use in present day service when a commander directs his mechanized formation of tanks and armoured vehicles to surround and guard a defended enemy position while the rest of the military formation presses on to its objective. In ancient times, the way to prevent a fortress from being outflanked was to build a continuous wall, such as the 400-mile long Limes Germanicus constructed by the Romans across southern Germany in the 2nd century; the Byzantine Wall erected to protect Constantinople; or the more than 5000-mile long Great Wall of China; and the complicated concrete defenses of France's Maginot Line.[5]

---

[5]   98 AD: Trajan reinforces the Roman wall on the Rhine known as the Limes Germanicus. 117-138 AD: Hadrian's Limes constructed, followed by additions from138-161 by Antonius Pius. Limes abandoned c260 AD.

(Jakob Halun Photo)
Great Wall of China, Jinshanling.

The drawbacks to these extended lines of defensive walls were many, including the labor, time and expense required to build them, and more so, the troops required to man them to maintain the defenses which is reason for their construction in the first place. Constant patrolling was required as well as regular rotations of the personnel manning the signal towers and garrisons stationed at intervals along these walls. Eventually, siege techniques were designed to overcome even the most elaborate walls and complexes of fortifications. For practical purposes, early defensive strongpoints evolved to a form of closed ring or "enceinte" to use the French term.

Enceintes protected fortresses, citadels, castles and in some cases entire cities and came to serve as a point of refuge for the population in the surrounding area. The earliest indication of this practice is the stone fortifications which encircled the city of Jericho, which date to about 7000 BC.[6] The Sumerian cities of Ur and Lagash in Mesopotamia have foundations which braced impressive structures dating back to 3500 BC. These buildings rose high above the irrigated flood-plain of the Tigris and Euphrates Rivers. The Egyptians may have built similar fortifications in the era of the Old Kingdom (2500-1500 BC).[7]

---

[6] Excavations by archaeologists at Jericho on the west bank of the Jordan River note that its approximately 3,000 citizens of that period (7,000 BC) enclosed their town with a free-standing stone wall 6' thick, 22'high and running almost 900 yards around it. It was defended with a tower 24' across and the fortifications were completely surrounded by a ditch 26' wide and 9' deep. Martin H. Brice, Stronghold, *A History of Military Architecture*, B.T. Batsford Ltd., London,1984, p.33.

[7] Egypt was divided into Lower and Upper Egypt. Lower Egypt refers to the area north of Memphis, and Upper Egypt traditionally refers to the area south of Memphis, which is the opposite of the way it seems they should be on the map. Upper Egypt is both upriver and uphill from Lower Egypt.

Sargon of Akkad (2371-2316 BC) destroyed the city of Kazalla and made a specific point of wrecking the walls of cities he captured. His warriors rushed the cities gates or they built a sloping rampart of earth as high as the city wall and swarmed over them taking the cities by storm.[8] Assyrian reliefs depicting siege warfare indicate it was in use at least as early as 850 BC, and by that time the basic principles of fortress construction such as making use of loopholes for shooting arrows, curtain walls, crenellation, parapets, reinforced gates and towers projecting from walls were well understood.

Although many medieval fortresses consisted of castles rather than of town walls (many of which were built over foundations and stonework dating back to Roman times), there were very few new elements added. Medieval castles were generally centered on massive stone towers, keeps or donjons. These were often surrounded by multiple layers of curtain walls that had covered galleries, buttresses, parapets, crenellation, machicolations, flanking towers, sally ports, and protected gates incorporated into their design and construction. The designs evolved continuously over the lifetime of each fortress or castle, with ditches and moats being added where possible, particularly in Northwestern Europe because of the abundance of water. The primary difference in medieval castles over their primitive predecessors was their function. A castle was used to dominate the countryside it surveyed, which meant many were sited on strategically chosen spurs of hills overlooking all approaches, which gave additional warning and protection. To overcome them, an attacker had to be inventive and utilize increasingly sophisticated methods of siegecraft and siege engines.

Siege warfare may have been practiced in Sumer as early as the third millennium BC. Based on ancient reliefs, the Assyrian army that destroyed the Biblical Kingdom of Israel and nearly did the same to Judea, already possessed a considerable array of apparently effective siege engines. They made use of ropes which had been attached to hooks, crowbars, scaling ladders, rams, and siege towers. They constructed mantelets which were basically wagons mounted with armor in front and which could be pushed close to the walls while providing cover for the archers. They also undermined the Hebrew defenses with tunnels and mines.

---

[8]   Ibid, p. 34.

Assyrians using siege ladders in a relief of attack on an enemy town during the reign of Tiglath-Pileser III 720-738 BCE from his palace at Kalhu (Nimrud). (British Museum collection, gypsum relief on loan to the Getty Villa)

Subterfuge was also used. Thutmose III's General Thot pretended to be abandoning a long siege at Jaffa in Palestine, by offering the defenders 200 baskets or sacks of supplies and tribute. Once they had been brought inside the walls, a soldier emerged from each container. These men then formed up and captured the gates, which allowed the Egyptian army waiting outside to gain access and to seize the rest of the city.[9]

The battering ram was one of the earliest inventions to overcome fortifications, and its use dates from at least 2500 BC. By 2000 BC, it was a normal implement of warfare. The ability to fasten large spear

---

[9]   Ibid, p. 35.

blades to the front end of long wooden beams allowed engineers to pry stones loose from the walls until a breach was achieved. The Hittites used the technique of building an earthen ramp to a low spot in the wall on which they then rolled large, covered battering rams into place to attack the wall at its thinnest points. The Assyrians built wooden siege towers taller than the defender's walls and then used archers to provide covering fire for the battering ram crews working below. The Assyrians also perfected the use of the scaling ladder by using short ladders to mount soldiers with axes and levers who dislodged the stones in the wall at midpoint. Longer ladders were used to bring combat forces over the higher walls.[10]

Most of the early siege engines were made of wood, often in combination with leather and on occasion wickerwork to provide protective coverings for the attackers. In later years, iron plates were attached to them to provide additional armor for the sides of towers and covered siege devices exposed to a defender's fire. Iron was relatively scarce in medieval times and was used mainly for the heads of battering rams and of course for the nails, rivets, axles, and hinges between moving parts that a good number of these devices required. Virtually all the medieval siege engines were powered by man or beast.

In the Bible in the book of 2 Chronicles, King Uziah of Judea made use of stone throwing engines to protect Jerusalem:

"Uzziah built towers in Jerusalem at the corner gate, and at the valley gate, and at the turning of the wall, and fortified them. Also he built towers in the desert…(and) had a host of fighting men, that went out to war by bands under the hand of Hananiah, one of the king's captains…2,600 chiefs (with) 307,500 that made war…And Uziah prepared for them throughout all the host shields, and spears, and helmets, and habergeons, and bows, and slings to cast stones. And he made in Jerusalem engines, invented by cunning men, to be on the towers and upon the bulwarks, to shoot arrows and great stones withal."[11]

More details on the use of mechanical siege engines will be found in a later chapter. The storage of energy and the use of technology to launch missiles against a determined defender changed the face of war. A new kind of warrior was required in the form of engineers with technical expertise and professionalism. Mathematical calculations in the use of mechanical siege devices became the norm from about 200 BC until the dark ages, when they appear to have been forgotten for a period until they re-emerged in the middle ages.[12]

About 1050 AD, both the Christian and Muslim world began to reintroduce siege machines into warfare, and by the time of the Crusades these weapons sometimes numbered in their hundreds. Onagers, mangonels, petriers, arbalasts, ballistae and catapults such as trébuchets led to fundamental changes in the nature of siege warfare until the age of gunpowder ushered in the next stage in the level of fire with effect.[13]

---

[10] Internet: http://www.au.af.mil/au/awc/awcgate/gabrmetz/gabr000d.htm.

[11] *The Holy Bible*, King James Version, Thomas Nelson Inc., Camden, New Jersey, 1970, *2 Chronicles, Chapter 26, verses 9-15*, p. 341.

[12] 410 AD: Beginning of the Dark Ages for the people of Europe, when the Army of Alaric the Visigoth captured and sacked Rome. Dark because of the apparent lack of light shed in those times by contemporary historians. The walls of Rome had been constructed 271-281 AD, restored 395 AD, and held out against Alaric in 408 AD, when the invaders were bought off. In 410 AD, slaves opened the gates and Alaric's troops stormed in. 476-814 AD: Period considered to be the Middle Ages.

[13] The manufacture of gunpowder in the 17th century involved extracting and refining the saltpeter from earth found in decomposing organic matter such as the kind found in cattle sheds, sheep pens and dung heaps. It was then blended with charcoal and brimstone, and then the mixture was milled finely, in a relatively simple but dangerous process. Paul Johnson, *Castles of England, Scotland, and Wales*, Weidenfeld and Nicolson, London,1989, p. 168.

No one side has a monopoly on the employment of useful ideas and weapons for attack and defense, and so it is that the development of enceintes and the siege engines to break them appears to have moved along at the same pace. Outthinking the opposing side became a major problem for the commander. The capture of a well-designed and constructed castle or fortress from the 14th century onwards, for example proved to be an extremely difficult task as will be shown in detail later in these records. Finding a weak spot would prove to be the key, and this was rarely simple. Reconnaissance and good intelligence gathering would prove to be that essential key, permitting the successful commander to find and exploit the weakness in his opponent's position. The result would basically depend on a well-coordinated plan based on a sound assessment of the best method of attack. A good commander who is supported by an excellent staff and the right resources is often in a better position to outthink his opponent, leading him to outfight and defeat him.

This book will contain examples of sieges, both successful and unsuccessful, demonstrating that no matter how securely a fortress or defensive position is constructed and defended, eventually a good plan and a determined besieger can overcome it. One way or another, time, willpower and determined effort will be brought together in sufficient quantity and quality to bring a siege or a defence to a successful conclusion. It will be argued through the examples presented in this book that ultimately, "no fortress is impregnable."

Major (Retired) Harold A. Skaarup
Former Honorary Lieutenant-Colonel for 3 Intelligence Company, Halifax

Introduction

Siegecraft – the word brings to mind great hosts of crusaders smashing the walls of medieval castles using catapults flinging great stones against them, while flaming arrows flash through the air against attackers and defenders in peril. One can hear the sounds of horns coming to relieve the defenders, or see the walls crumbling as the besieged look on in horror when their defenses fall against the hammering war machines driven by a powerful and unrelenting foe. Stories, visions and history such as these of so-called impregnable fortresses being battered into submission, led me to examine the ruins and remains of several hundred medieval and modern castles and battlefields over the course of my military career, particularly during a number of tours of duty overseas. The information you will find here will be used to capture a number of the most famous as well as a few of the more obscure battles where effective Siegecraft – or the lack of it, decided the outcome for those who believed their fortresses were impregnable.

(Roman Geber Photo)

Château Gaillard ruins viewed from the west. The keep is on the right and the ruins of the outer bailey (an open space surrounded by a wall inside the castle, aka a ward), including remains of some of the towers, are on the left.

The strange scallop-shaped walls of the inner defenses of Richard Coeur-de-Lion's fortress at Château Gaillard, for example, continue to exist (albeit it ruins) to this day along the historic Loire River West of the city of Paris, and are well worth a visit by both historians and general tourists alike.

(Zairon Photo)
Ossuary, Douaumont, Départment of Meuse, Region of Grand Est, France.

Much further to the east of the city of lights you will find the remains of the French fortresses of Verdun. There, one may view a giant ossuary which holds the bones of many of the dead soldiers (German and French) which continue to surface more than 87 years after the combatants were buried beneath the surface in the incessant shelling that took place there in 1915. Some 750,000 soldiers never went home from that battle alone.

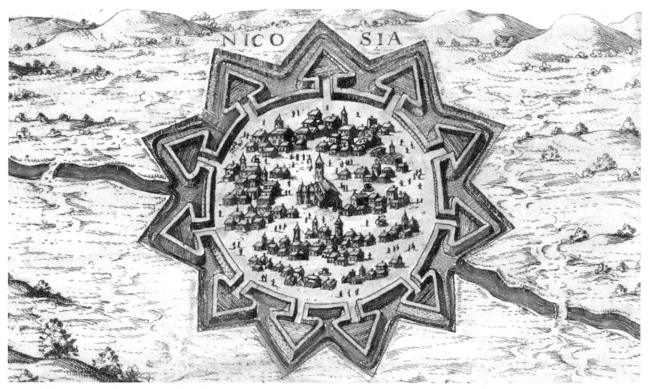

Plan view of the star fortifications in Nicosia, Cyprus in 1597, created by Giacomo Franco.

I have walked the battle grounds of Normandy and Waterloo, and the Great War killing fields of the Vimy Ridge, Verdun and the Vosges mountains. I have stood on the Horns of Hattin in Israel, where Saladin defeated the Crusaders before the Second Crusade, and had the privilege to guard the line with the UN in Cyprus and with the NATO-led peace stabilization force in Sarajevo, Bosnia-Herzegovina. I spent time in Kabul along with some of the more than 40,000 Canadian Forces personnel who also served there, and we saw what happens when good advice is ignored and the positive effects when it is followed.

My observations of these events of the past, and the battles of the Gulf Wars and the terrorist attacks on America in recent times, are that no fortress is impregnable. I have specifically included the siege at Dien Bien Phu because of the use of paratroopers in the operation. When the embattled defenders ran short of manpower, they called on their headquarters staffs to send in reinforcements. Hundreds of rear-area staffs volunteered to go in, and most of them found themselves making their first parachute jumps as they did so.

In our present time, there are often politically short-sighted reasons that several countries feel their military forces and defence networks do not need to be maintained. There is no quicker way to increase the vulnerability of your "fortress," than to let your military arm be depleted to the point where it will be ineffective when you need it. Those who do so, will clearly find their homelands unsafe and insecure, and highly vulnerable to attack – and there will always be some group or other who hopes to gain power over the weak. Paratroops are only one of many links in an army's necessary suit of chainmail. It is the spirit, élan, and professionalism of these kinds of dedicated soldiers that will ensure a successful outcome to a defense or attack. To let such people be lost to the exigencies of political expedience is to diminish the chances of survival for the nations who make such decisions.

SIEGE OF JERICHO, C1405/1406 BC

The fortifications at Jericho under the command of a Canaanite, were located on a plain just west of the Jordan River at the site of Tel es-Sultan in present day Israel. In 1405 BC, they were successfully besieged by Hebrew forces under the command of Joshua. The Hebrew destruction of Jericho cleared the first major obstacle to settlement in the "Promised Land". The twelve tribes of Israel had left Egypt in a mass exodus 40 years earlier. On their approach to Jericho, the Hebrews initially engaged in a battle with the Amorite Kings Sihon and Og, defeating their forces (Joshua 2:9b-10). This victory gave them clear access to the Jordan River north of the Dead Sea. An earthquake blocked the riverbed upstream, facilitating an easy crossing for them.

Joshua sent two of his scouts (spies) into Jericho, even though they should have been visible as the Hebrews would have been within 8 km (5 miles) from the city at their river crossing. They were hidden by an Innkeeper named Rahab and escaped capture. Jericho was a well-established town built around the spring of Ain es-Sultan, in the Plain of Jericho, with excellent crops well-watered, but surrounded by barren land. Modern excavations of the site indicate Jericho was defended by a 4 to 5 metre (1-15 feet) high retaining wall topped with a mud brick wall 7 to 8 metres (20-26 feet) high and 2 metres (6 feet) thick. A second wall of mud bricks was raised outside the retaining wall. Rahab lived between the walls.

Joshua had instructed his soldiers to form up and walk to city's walls and march around them and then return to the river site. They were to do this for six days, and no sound was to come from the marchers. This may have led the defenders to think they might escape an eventual assault, although each day they manned the walls, prepared for it. The soldiers paraded in full battledress and carried the Ark of the Covenant in their processions around the walls. The orders changed on the seventh day, and the parade encircled the city walls seven times. The soldiers halted after the last circuit, faced the walls, their priests blew trumpets made of ram's horns, and all shouted simultaneously. The walls suddenly collapsed, likely due to a well-timed earthquake similar to the one that had dammed the Jordan River the previous week. The crumbled walls would have facilitated easy access to the inner city, which the Hebrews quickly took advantage of putting all in the city to the sword (Joshua 6:20-21).

(Lithograph by Julius Schnorr von Carolsfeld)

After looting the city of its treasures, the Hebrews burned it. With Jericho destroyed, the Hebrews launched into the remainder of Canaan. Joshua divided the lands his army captured, among the twelve tribes of Israel.

SIEGE OF LACHISH, C701 BC

The Assyrian Siege of Lachish led to the conquest of the town in 701 BC. The siege is documented in several sources including the Bible, Assyrian documents and in the Lachish relief, a well-preserved series of reliefs which once decorated the Assyrian king Sennacherib's palace at Nineveh. Several kingdoms in the Levant ceased to pay taxes for the Assyrian King Sennacherib and as a result he set out on a campaign to re-subjugate the rebelling Kingdoms, among them the Jewish King, Hezekiah. After defeating the rebels of Ekron in Philistia he set out to subjugate Judah and in his way to Jerusalem he came across Lachish, the second most important among the Jewish cities.

The battlefield was the walled city of Lachish, situated on a hill. The northern part of the hill is steeper than the southern side and due to that the gate is situated there. On top of the fact that the hill as of itself is quite high, the wall further makes the city hard to breach. Inside the city itself there was a castle with significant walls.

The Assyrian Army was the most effective force of its time and was divided mostly into three different categories, Infantry, which included both close-combat troops using spears, and archers. There were also hired mercenaries throwing stones (slingers). The infantry was highly trained and worked alongside military engineers in order to breach sieges. In regard to cavalry, Assyrian cavalry were among the finest in the ancient middle east and included both close-combat cavalry units with spears and mounted archers which could both use the agility of the horses alongside long-range attacks. Chariots, which were not used as much in sieges as in regular land engagements.

The Jewish military force was insignificant compared to the professional and massive Assyrian army and mostly included local militias and mercenaries. There were barely any cavalrymen and chariots in the Jewish army which mostly included infantry, either for close combat (spearmen) or long-range combat (archers), they were also significantly less organized.

Due to the steepness of the northern side of Lachish the Assyrian Army attacked from the south, where the Jewish defenders situated themselves on the walls. The Jewish defenders threw stones and shot arrows at the advancing Assyrians; the Assyrians started shooting arrows and stones themselves, creating a skirmish between the two armies. Meanwhile Assyrian military engineers built a ramp to the east of the main gate where Assyrian and Jewish troops began engaging in close combat. The Assyrians meanwhile brought siege engines to the ramp and broke the wall; the Jewish defenders could not hold the Assyrian army and retreated, with some attempting to escape from the other side of the hill.

The city was captured by the Assyrians, its inhabitants led into captivity and the leaders of Lachish tortured to death. The town was abandoned but resettled after the return from Babylonia. Assyrian reliefs portraying the siege of Lachish clearly show battering rams attacking the vulnerable parts of the city. The siege and capture of the town of Lachish, one of the fortress towns protecting the approaches to Jerusalem, is unique in that it is mentioned in the Bible (II Kings 18; II Chronicles 32)(Micah 1:13) and in the Annals of the Assyrian king, Sennacherib.

Illustration of Assyrian relief of Tiglath-Pileser III besieging a town. The British Museum has a set of relief carvings which depict the siege, showing Assyrian soldiers firing arrows, and sling stones, and approaching the walls of Lachish using mudbrick ramps. The attackers shelter behind wicker shields and deploy battering rams. The walls and towers of Lachish are shown crowded with defenders shooting arrows, throwing rocks and torches on the heads of the attackers. The relief also shows the looting of the city, and defenders being thrown over the ramparts, impaled, having their throats cut and asking for mercy. A bird's eye plan of the city is shown with house interiors shown in section. After he captured the second most important city in Judah, Sennacherib encamped there and then sent his Rabshakeh (Chief of the Princes) to capture Jerem. (Finkelstein, Israel, and Nadav Na'aman. 2011. *The Fire Signals of Lachish: Studies in the Archaeology and History of Israel In the Late Bronze Age, Iron Age*)

Assyrian reliefs depicting siege warfare indicate it was in use at least as early as 850 BC, and by that time the basic principles of fortress construction such as making use of loopholes for shooting arrows, curtain walls, crenellation (a pattern along the top of a parapet (fortified wall), most often in the form of multiple, regular, rectangular spaces in the top of the wall, through which arrows or other weaponry may be shot, especially as used in medieval European architecture), parapets (a low protective wall along the edge of a roof, bridge, or balcony), reinforced gates and towers projecting from walls were well understood.

SIEGE OF JERUSALEM, C721 BC

In approximately 701 BCE, Sennacherib, King of Assyria, attacked the fortified cities of Judah, laying siege on Jerusalem, but failed to capture it. In 721 BCE, the Assyrian Army captured the Israelite capital at Samaria and carried away the citizens of the Kingdom of Israel (Samaria) into captivity. The virtual destruction of Israel left the southern kingdom, Judah, to fend for itself among warring Near Eastern kingdoms. After the fall of the Northern Kingdom, the kings of Judah tried to extend their influence and protection to those inhabitants who had not been exiled. They also sought to extend their authority northward into areas previously controlled by the Kingdom of Israel. The latter part of the reign of Ahaz, and most of that of Hezekiah were periods of stability during which Judah was able to consolidate both politically and economically. Although Judah was a vassal of Assyria during this time and paid an annual tribute to the powerful empire, it was the most important state between Assyria and Egypt.

When Hezekiah became king of Judah, he initiated widespread religious changes, including the breaking of religious idols. He re-captured Philistine-occupied lands in the Negev desert, formed alliances with Ashkelon and Egypt, and made a stand against Assyria by refusing to pay tribute. In response, Sennacherib attacked Judah, laying siege to Jerusalem. Sources from both sides claimed victory, the Judahites (or Biblical author(s)) in the Tanakh, and Sennacherib in his prism. Sennacherib claimed the siege and capture of many Judaean cities, but only the siege, not capture, of Jerusalem.

The Hebrew account Sources from both sides claimed victory, the Judahites (or Biblical author(s)) in the Tanakh, and Sennacherib in his prism. Sennacherib claimed the siege and capture of many Judaean cities, but only the siege, not capture, of Jerusalem.

The story of the Assyrian siege is told in the Bible books of Isiah, Chronicles and Second Kings. As the Assyrians began their invasion, Hezekiah began preparations to protect Jerusalem. In an effort to deprive the Assyrians of water, springs outside the city were blocked. Workers then dug a 533-metre tunnel to the Spring of Gihon, providing the city with fresh water. Additional siege preparations included fortification of the existing walls, construction of towers, and the erection of a new, reinforcing wall. Hezekiah gathered the citizens in the square and encouraged them by reminding them that the Assyrians possessed only "an arm of flesh", but the Judeans had the protection of Yahweh.

According to Second Kings 18, while Sennacherib was besieging Lachish, he received a message from Hezekiah offering to pay tribute in exchange for Assyrian withdrawal. According to the Bible, Hezekiah paid three hundred talents of silver and thirty talents of gold to Assyria, a price so heavy that he was forced to empty the temple and royal treasury of silver and strip the gold from the doorposts of Solomon's temple. Nevertheless, Sennacherib marched on Jerusalem with a large army. When the Assyrian force arrived, its field commander Rabshakeh brought a message from Sennacherib himself. In an attempt to demoralize the Judeans, the field commander announced to the people on the city walls that Hezekiah was deceiving them, and Yahweh could not deliver Jerusalem from the king of Assyria. He listed the gods of the people thus far swept away by Sennacherib then asked, "Who of all the gods of these countries has been able to save his land from me?"

During the siege, Hezekiah clad himself in sackcloth out of anguish from the psychological warfare that the Assyrians were waging. The prophet Isaiah took an active part in the political life of Judah. When Jerusalem was threatened, he assured Hezekiah that the city would be delivered, and Sennacherib would fall. The Hebrew Bible states that during the night, an angel of YHWH brought death to 185,000 Assyrians troops. Hezekiah had shut up all water outside the city so thirst and the fatigue of a long and tiring campaign possibly could have forced the Assyrians to retreat. It is also a possibility that a disease spread throughout the camp and killed many Sennacherib's men. When Sennacherib saw the destruction wreaked on his army, he withdrew to Nineveh. Jerusalem was spared destruction.

The Bible's suggestion that Jerusalem was victorious rather than defeated, is corroborated by the Jewish historian Josephus. He quotes Berossus, a well-known Babylonian historian, that a pestilence broke out in the army camp. According to Herodotus, though, field mice chewed at the leather of their weapons and rendered them useless. It is more likely that the mice described by Herodotus were the cause of the pestilence described by Berossus. Nevertheless, as all of these are expansions on the Bible's account, adding Midrash, none are independent witnesses. In any case, most scholars agree that Sennacherib suffered a humiliating defeat while besieging Jerusalem, and that he went back to Nineveh, never to return. "Like Xerxes in Greece, Sennacherib never recovered from the shock of the disaster in Judah. He made no more expeditions against either the Southern Levant or Egypt."

The Syrian account is taken from Sennacherib's Prism, which details the events of Sennacherib's campaign against Judah, was discovered in the ruins of Nineveh in 1830, and is now stored at the Oriental Institute in Chicago, Illinois. The account dates from about 690 BCE. The text of the prism boasts how Sennacherib destroyed forty-six of Judah's cities, and trapped Hezekiah in Jerusalem "like a caged bird." The text goes on to describe how the "terrifying splendor" of the Assyrian army caused the Arabs and mercenaries reinforcing the city to desert. It adds that the Assyrian king returned to Assyria where he later received a large tribute from Judah. This description inevitably varies somewhat from the Jewish version in the Tanakh. The massive Assyrian casualties mentioned in the Tanakh are not mentioned in the Assyrian version, but Assyrian government records tend to commonly take the form of propaganda claiming their own invincibility, with the result that they rarely mention their own defeats or heavy casualties. There is speculation that the accounts of mass death among the Assyrian army in the Tanakh might be explained by an outbreak of cholera (or other water-borne diseases) due to the springs beyond the city walls having been blocked, thus depriving the besieging force of a safe water supply.

After he besieged Jerusalem, Sennacherib was able to give the surrounding towns to Assyrian vassal rulers in Ekron, Gaza and Ashdod. His army was still in existence when he conducted campaigns in 702 BCE and from 699 BCE until 697 BCE, when he made several campaigns in the mountains east of Assyria, on one of which he received tribute from the Medes. In 696 BCE and 695 BCE, he sent expeditions into Anatolia, where several vassals had rebelled following the death of Sargon. Around 690 BCE, he campaigned in the northern Arabian deserts, conquering Dumat al-Jandal, where the queen of the Arabs had taken refuge.

When Marduk-apla-iddina continued his rebellion with the help of Elam, in 694 Sennacherib took a fleet of Phoenician ships down the Tigris River to destroy the Elamite base on the shore of the Persian Gulf. While he was doing this the Elamites captured Ashur-nadin-shumi and put Nergal-ushezib, the son of Marduk-apla-iddina, on the throne of Babylon. Nergal-ushezib was captured in 693 BCE and taken to Nineveh, and Sennacherib attacked Elam again. The Elamite king fled to the mountains and Sennacherib plundered his kingdom, but when he withdrew the Elamites returned to Babylon and put another rebel leader, Mushezib-Marduk, on the Babylonian throne. Babylon eventually fell to the Assyrians in 689 BCE after a lengthy siege. (Sayce, Archibald Henry. *The Ancient Empires of the East.* Macmillan)

A never-ending series of sieges of Jerusalem continued over many centuries.

SIEGE OF JERUSALEM, 597 BC

The first Siege of Jerusalem carried out by Nebuchadnezzar II, King of Babylon, took place in 597 BC. In 605 BC, he defeated Pharaoh Necho at the Battle of Carchemish, and subsequently he invaded Judah. According to the Nebuchadnezzar Chronicle, King Jehoiakim of Judah rebelled against Babylonian rule, but Nebuchadnezzar captured the city and installed Zedekiah as ruler.

To avoid the destruction of Jerusalem, King Jehoiakim of Judah, in his third year, changed allegiances from Egypt to Babylon. He paid tribute from the treasury in Jerusalem, giving up some temple artifacts and some of the royal family and nobility as hostages. In 601 BC, during the fourth year of his reign, Nebuchadnezzar unsuccessfully attempted to invade Egypt and was repulsed with heavy losses. The failure led to numerous rebellions among the states of the Levant which owed allegiance to Babylon, including Judah, where King Jehoiakim stopped paying tribute to Nebuchadnezzar and took a pro-Egyptian position. Nebuchadnezzar soon dealt with these rebellions. According to the Nebuchadnezzar Chronicle, he laid siege to Jerusalem, which eventually fell on 2 Adar (16 March 597 BC).

The Chronicle states: In the seventh year (of Nebuchadnezzar, 598 BC) in the month Chislev (November/December) the king of Babylon assembled his army, and after he had invaded the land of Hatti (Syria/Palestine) he laid siege to the city of Judah. On the second day of the month of Adar (16 March) he conquered the city and took the king (Jeconiah) prisoner. He installed in his place a king (Zedekiah) of his own choice, and after he had received rich tribute, he sent forth to Babylon.

Jehoiakim died during the siege, possibly on 22 Marcheshvan (10 Dec 598 BC), or during the months of Kislev, or Tevet. Nebuchadnezzar pillaged the city and its Temple, and the new king Jeconiah, who was either 8 or 18, and his court and other prominent citizens and craftsmen, and much of the Jewish population of Judah, numbering about 10,000 were deported to Babylon. The deportation occurred prior to Nisan of 597 BC, and dates in the Book of Ezekiel are counted from that event. A biblical text reports, "None remained except the poorest people of the land". Also, taken to Babylon were the treasures and furnishings of the Temple, including golden vessels dedicated by King Solomon. (2 Kings 24:13-14)

The events are described in the Nevi'im and Ketuvim sections of the Old Testament. The first deportation was the beginning of the Jewish Diaspora (or exile). (2 Kings 24:10-16) Nebuchadnezzar installed Jeconiah's uncle, Zedekiah as a puppet-king of Judah, and Jeconiah was compelled to remain in Babylon. The start of Zedekiah's reign has been variously dated within a few weeks before, or after the start of Nisan 597 BC.[14]

SIEGE OF JERUSALEM, 589 BC

The second Siege of Jerusalem carried out by Nebuchadnezzar II, King of Babylon began in 589 BC. In 586 BC, after completion of the eleventh year of Zedekiah's reign, Nebuchadnezzar broke through Jerusalem's walls, conquering the city. After the fall of Jerusalem, the Babylonian general, Nebuzaraddan, was sent to complete its destruction. Jerusalem was plundered, and Solomon's Temple was destroyed in the summer of 587 or 586 BC. The city was razed to the ground, and only a few people were permitted to remain to tend to the land. Zedekiah and his followers attempted to escape but were captured on the plains of Jericho and taken to Riblah. There, after seeing his sons killed, Zedekiah was blinded, bound, and taken captive to Babylon, where he remained a prisoner until his death. (2 Kings 25:1-7, Chronicles 36:12, and Jeremiah 32:4-5)

SIEGE OF SARDIS, 547 BC

The Siege of Sardis (547-546 BC), was the last decisive conflict after the Battle of Thymbra, which was fought between the forces of Croesus of Lydia and Cyrus the Great, when Cyrus followed Croesus to his city. He laid siege to it for 14 days, and then captured it.

---

[14] Horn, Siegfried H. *The Babylonian Chronicle and the Ancient Calendar of the Kingdom of Judah.* Andrews University Seminary Studies, V 1.

In the previous year King Croesus of Lydia, impelled by various considerations, invaded the kingdom of Cyrus the Great, hoping to quell the growing power of Achaemenid Persia; to expand his own dominions; and revenge the deposition of his brother-in-law Astyages. He thought he was certain of success, deluded by the ambiguous assurances of the apparently reliable oracle of Apollo at Delphi. Croesus crossed the Halys and met Cyrus at Pteria in Cappadocia, but after a drawn-out battle against superior forces in which neither side obtained the victory Croesus resolved to fall back for the winter, summon new allies, and renew the war reinforced in the next spring. In the interim, he disbanded his army and returned to Sardis, expecting Cyrus to hang back after the sanguinary battle in Cappadocia. But the energetic Cyrus, as soon as he heard that Croesus' forces were dispersed, crossed the Halys and advanced with such speed that he had arrived at the Lydian capital, Sardis, before Croesus had any word of his approach. Undaunted, Croesus mustered his available troops and met Cyrus in the Battle of Thymbra outside the walls. Cyrus was victorious, having contrived to deprive the Lydians of their last resource, their cavalry (in which the Lydians allegedly surpassed all other nations at the time), by frightening off their horses with the sight of his camels. The remnants of the Lydian army were driven within the city and promptly besieged.

Croesus was still confident in his chances because Sardis was a well-fortified city consecrated by ancient prophecies to never be captured. Additionally, he had sent for immediate aid from Sparta, the strongest state in Greece and his firm ally, and he hoped to enlist the Egyptians, the Babylonians, and others in his coalition against Persia as well. Unfortunately for him, the Spartans were then occupied in a war with neighboring Argos, and neither they nor any other of Croesus' allies would assemble in time.

Cyrus offered large rewards to the first soldiers who should ascend the battlements (top of a protective wall); but repeated Persian attacks were repulsed with loss. According to Herodotus, the city ultimately fell by the agency of a Persian soldier, who climbed up a section of the walls which was neither adequately garrisoned, nor protected by the ancient rites which had dedicated the rest of the cities' defenses to impregnability; the steepness of the adjoining ground outside the walls was responsible for this piece of Lydian Hubris. Hyroeades, the Persian soldier, saw a Lydian soldier climbing down the walls to retrieve a dropped helmet, and tried to follow the example. The success of his ascent set the example to the rest of Cyrus' soldiers and these swarming over the exposed wall and the city was promptly taken.

Cyrus had previously issued orders for Croesus to be spared, and the latter was hauled a captive before his exulting foe. Cyrus' first intentions to burn Croesus alive on a pyre were soon diverted by the impulse of mercy for a fallen foe, and according to ancient versions, by divine intervention of Apollo, who caused a well-timed rainfall. Tradition represents the two kings as reconciled thereafter; Croesus succeeded in preventing the worst rigors of a sack by representing to his captor that it was *his*, not Croesus' property being plundered by the Persian soldiery.

The kingdom of Lydia came to an end with the fall of Sardis, and her subjection was confirmed in an unsuccessful revolt in the following year, promptly crushed by Cyrus' lieutenants. The Aeolian and Ionian cities on the coast of Asia Minor, formerly tributaries of Lydia, were likewise conquered not long after, establishing the circumstances for Greco-Persian animosity, which would last till the outbreak of the Persian Wars in the succeeding century. (Herodotus. *The Histories*, Penguin Books, 1983)

SIEGE OF NAXOS, 499 BC

The Siege of Naxos (499 BC) was a failed attempt by the Milesian tyrant Aristagoras, operating with support from, and in the name of the Persian Empire of Darius the Great, to conquer the island of Naxos. It was the opening act of the Greco-Persian Wars, which would ultimately last for 50 years.

Aristagoras had been approached by exiled Naxian aristocrats, who were seeking to return to their island. Seeing an opportunity to bolster his position in Miletus, Aristagoras sought the help of his overlord, the Persian king Darius the Great, and the local satrap, Artaphernes to conquer Naxos. Consenting to the expedition, the Persians assembled a force of 200 triremes under the command of Megabates.

The expedition quickly descended into a debacle. Aristagoras and Megabates quarreled on the journey to Naxos, and someone (possibly Megabates) informed the Naxians of the imminent arrival of the force. When they arrived, the Persians and Ionians were thus faced with a city well prepared to undergo siege. The expeditionary force duly settled down to besiege the defenders, but after four months without success, ran out of money and were forced to return to Asia Minor.

In the aftermath of this disastrous expedition, and sensing his imminent removal as tyrant, Aristagoras chose to incite the whole of Ionia into rebellion against Darius the Great. The revolt then spread to Caria and Cyprus. Three years of Persian campaigning across Asia Minor followed, with no decisive effect, before the Persians regrouped and made straight for the epicentre of the rebellion at Miletus. At the Battle of Lade, the Persians decisively defeated the Ionian fleet and effectively ended the rebellion. Although Asia Minor had been brought back into the Persian fold, Darius vowed to punish Athens and Eretria, who had supported the revolt. In 492 BC therefore, the first Persian invasion of Greece, would begin because of the failed attack on Naxos, and the Ionian Revolt. (Herodotus. *The Histories*, Penguin Books, 1983)

SIEGE OF ERETRIA, 490 BC

The Siege of Eretria took place in 490 BC, when the city of Eretria on Euboea was besieged by a strong Persian force under the command of Datis and Artaphernes. The siege lasted six days before a fifth column of Eretrian nobles betrayed the city to the Persians. The city was plundered, and the population enslaved on Darius's orders. The Eretrian prisoners were eventually taken to Persia and settled as colonists in Cissia.

After Eretria, the Persian force sailed for Athens, landing at the bay of Marathon. An Athenian army marched to meet them and won a famous victory at the Battle of Marathon, thereby ending the first Persian invasion. (Herodotus. *The Histories*, Penguin Books, 1983)

SIEGE OF SYRACUSE, 397 BC

The Siege of Syracuse in 397 BC was the first of four unsuccessful sieges Carthaginian forces would undertake against Syracuse from 397 to 278 BC. In retaliation to the Siege of Motya by Dionysius of Syracuse, Himilco of the Magonid family of Carthage led a substantial force to Sicily. After retaking Motya and founding Lilybaeum, Himilco sacked Messana, then laid siege of Syracuse in the autumn of 397 BC after the Greek navy was crushed at Catana.

The Carthaginians followed a strategy which the Athenians had used in 415 BC and were successful in isolating Syracuse. A pestilence broke out in the Carthaginian camp in the summer of 396 BC, which killed most of the troops. Dionysius launched a combined land and sea attack on the Carthaginian forces, and Himilco escaped with the Carthaginian citizens after an underhand deal with Dionysius. The surviving Libyans were enslaved, the Sicels melted away while the Iberians joined Dionysius. Dionysius began expanding his domain, while Carthage, weakened by the plague, took no action until 393 BC against Syracusan activities. (Kern, Paul B. *Ancient Siege Warfare*. Indiana University Publishers. 1999)

SIEGE OF PELIUM, 335 BC

The Siege of Pelium was undertaken by Alexander the Great against the Illyrian tribes of what is modern-day Albania. It was critical for Alexander to take this pass as it provided easy access to Illyria and Macedonia, which was urgently needed to quell the unrest in Greece at this time in Athens and Thebes. This was an important point of demarcation in Alexander's early reign, as it established him among the Danubian tribes to the north as a serious monarch to be reckoned with, just as he would later establish this precedent for the Greek city states under his hegemony. Taking this place allowed Alexander to march his army to southern Greece quickly, which would eventually result in the total destruction of Thebes.

News of the Illyrian revolt under Cleitus the Dardanian, and King Glaukias of the Taulantii first reached the ears of Alexander while he was campaigning on the Danube against some of the northern tribes that his father, Philip II of Macedon had previously reduced to a satisfactory level of subjection, although not outright submission. As this area had been far from the Greek theatre of operations, Phillip had been satisfied with the level of subjection he had reduced them to.

Alexander was immediately concerned about the news of this revolt, as the settlement of Pelium itself occupied one of the most important passes between Illyria and Macedonia. As a result of this, Alexander would have to make a long march around a mountain range to the south, and then into Illyria. In addition to this, without access to this crucial pass, Alexander could be cut off from Greece, which had freshly revolted, and would eventually do so again, with aid of the Great King. The loss of this pass, and the resultant long march would give the Greek city states to the south ample time to prepare for Alexander's arrival while he was reducing the Illyrians.

An ally of Alexander offered aid to him by protecting his flank from Illyrian tribes while he marched towards Pelium. Langarus, of the Agrianians, made frequent incursions into the country of the Autariatae, and managed to put them on guard sufficiently to allow Alexander to march by in relative peace. Having successfully made this march, Alexander arrived to find Cleitus the Dardanian in control of Pelium and awaiting the arrival of King Glaukias with reinforcements. When Alexander arrived, Cleitus reportedly sacrificed three boys, three girls, and three black rams before meeting the Macedonians.

Alexander arrived with 15,000 soldiers and determined to attack Pelium at once, as he hoped to take the place out of hand before King Glaukias could arrive and reinforce Cleitus. The first thing Alexander did upon arriving was set up the Macedonian camp. The Macedonians found that not only was Pelium itself held, which commanded the plateau, but the heights surrounding the Plain of Pelium was held in force. Upon completing the camp, Alexander resolved to attack the troops of Cleitus that were surrounding the heights. This he did with some effect, and because of this assault the Illyrians retreated within the walls of Pelium. Alexander then attempted to take the town by assault, but failing in this, he started to erect circumvallation (a line of fortifications, built by the attackers around the besieged fortification facing towards an enemy fort, designed to protect the besiegers from sorties by its defenders and to enhance the blockade), and contravallation (a second line of fortifications outside the circumvallation, facing away from an enemy fort. The contravallation protects the besiegers from attacks by allies of the city's defenders and enhances the blockade of an enemy fort by making it more difficult to smuggle in supplies), around Pelium. This, however, was interrupted by the arrival of Glaukias and his reinforcements the next day, which compelled Alexander to retreat from the heights that he had captured the day before.

Having been forced back into the plain itself by King Glaukias, Alexander was in now a perilous situation. He was outnumbered by the Illyrians, who were free to gather supplies. Not only that, but Alexander was anxious to take Pelium quickly before Thebes and Athens could seriously consider imperiling Macedonian hegemony. Therefore, not only did Alexander have pressing issues elsewhere, but the Illyrian forces were determined to annihilate Alexander's forces and could afford to wait.

Being short of supplies, Alexander sent Philotas, one of his lieutenants, out to forage for materials. King Glaukias witnessed this force leaving and pursued and attacked the foragers. However, Alexander was, with some difficulty, able to fend off the attackers and extricate his hypaspists, Agrianians and bowmen.

Seeking to seize his line of retreat before putting his shoulder to the siege, Alexander decided to attack the heights that commanded the defile through which he had come. This defile was small, and only four men could march through it abreast. He drew up some of his infantry and cavalry in front of the settlement of Pelium itself to defend this maneuver from being attacked by a sortie from Cleitus. He then drew up his phalanx, one hundred and twenty men deep, with 200 cavalry on either flank, and arranged his soldiers to perform close-order drills down on the plain, in full view of the Illyrians, in complete silence. As Peter Green describes:

"At given signals the great forest of sarissas would rise to the vertical 'salute' position, and then dip horizontally as for battle-order. The bristling spear-line swung now right, now left, in perfect unison. The phalanx advanced, wheeled into column and line, moved through various intricate formations as though on the parade-ground - all without a word being uttered. The barbarians had never seen anything like it. From their positions in the surrounding hills they stared down at this weird ritual, scarcely able to believe their eyes. Then, little by little, one straggling group after another began to edge closer, half-terrified, half-enthralled. Alexander watched them, waiting for the psychological moment. Then, at last, he gave his final pre-arranged signal. The left wing of the cavalry swung into wedge formation and charged. At the same moment, every man of the phalanx beat his spear on his shield, and from thousands of throats there went up the terrible ululating Macedonian war-cry - 'Alalalalai!' - echoing and reverberating from the mountains. This sudden, shattering explosion of sound, especially after the dead stillness which had preceded it, completely unnerved Glaucias' tribesmen, who fled back in wild confusion from the foothills to the safety of their fortress."[15]

The Macedonian forces took the heights overlooking Pelium. During this engagement, not a single Macedonian armored soldier was killed. However, deaths among light troops were usually not reported, and it is unknown whether any were killed in this instance.

There were still some Illyrian light infantry on the heights that commanded the ford, and it was critical for Alexander to seize these heights to gain control of the entire plain. Before engaging in battle, Alexander decided to re-establish his camp on the far side of the river near the ford to ensure the security of both his operations and his camp. However, in the process of doing so he ran the danger of being engaged in the rear while his troops were crossing the river. The Illyrians indeed attacked him, perceiving his army to be retreating. So, he ordered his troops to turn around to simulate an advance, while initiating a charge with his companion cavalry. Meanwhile, he also ordered his archers to turn around and fire their arrows from mid-stream. Having gained a place of relative security on the far side of the river, Alexander was able to freely supply his army and await reinforcements. Before reinforcements arrived, however, Macedonian scouts reported that they observed the Illyrians becoming careless in protecting the settlement, as they thought Alexander was in retreat.

Acting on this intelligence, Alexander awaited the arrival of night, and then rushed ahead without awaiting the crossing of his complete force, leading his archers, his shield-bearing guards, the Agrianians, and the brigade of Coenus as the leading unit. He then rushed down upon the defenders with his Agrianians and archers, who were formed in phalanx formation. Many of the Illyrians were still asleep and were taken completely by surprise. A great slaughter followed; many of the Illyrians were also captured.

As a result of this siege, Alexander gained Pelium, and built a fresh outpost there, as the Illyrians had burnt the settlement that had previously been situated there. The Illyrians begged for terms, and Alexander was happy to accept their submission and allow them to swear fealty to him anew. Having

---

[15]   (Green, Peter, *Alexander of Macedon, 356-323 B.C.* University of California Press, 1991)

completed his conquest, Alexander had established himself as a new monarch to be revered and was now free to march south to Boeotia and deal with the threat from Thebes and Athens. (Dodge, Theodore Alexander. New York, NY: Da Capo, 1890).

SIEGE OF MILETUS, 334 BC

The Siege of Miletus was Alexander the Great's first siege and naval encounter with the Achaemenid Empire. This siege was directed against Miletus, a city in southern Ionia, which is now located in the Aydin province of modern-day Turkey. It was captured by Parmenion's son, Nicanor in 334 BC.

(The capture of Miletus, engraving by Andre Castaigne)

SIEGE OF HALICARNASSUS, 334 BC

The Siege of Halicarnassus was fought between Alexander the Great and the Achaemenid Persian Empire in 334 BC. Alexander, who had no navy, was constantly being threatened by the Persian Navy. It continuously attempted to provoke an engagement with Alexander, who would not oblige them. Eventually, the Persian fleet sailed to Halicarnassus, to establish a new defense. Ada of Caria, the former queen of Halicarnassus, had been driven from her throne by her younger brother Pixodarus of Caria. When Pixodarus died, Persian King Darius had appointed Orontobates satrap of Caria, which included Halicarnassus in its jurisdiction. On the arrival of Alexander in 334 BC, Ada, who was in possession of the fortress of Alinda, surrendered the fortress to him.

Orontobates and Memnon of Rhodes entrenched themselves in Halicarnassus. Alexander had sent spies to meet with dissidents inside the city, who had promised to open the gates and allow Alexander to enter. When his spies arrived, however, the dissidents were nowhere to be found. A small battle resulted, and Alexander's army managed to break through the city walls. Memnon, however, now deployed his catapults, and Alexander's army fell back. Memnon then deployed his infantry, and shortly before Alexander would have received his first defeat, his infantry managed to break through the city walls, surprising the Persian forces. Memnon, realizing the city was lost, set fire to it, and withdrew with his army. Strong winds caused the fire to destroy much of the city.

Alexander committed the government of Caria to Ada; and she, in turn, formally adopted Alexander as her son, ensuring that the rule of Caria passed unconditionally to him upon her eventual death. During her husband's tenure as satrap, Ada had been loved by the people of Caria. By putting Ada, who felt very favorably towards Alexander, on the throne, he ensured that the government of Caria, as well as its people, remained loyal to him. (Cartledge, Paul. *Alexander the Great: The Hunt for a New Past.* Woodstock, NY; New York: The Overlook Press, 2004)

SIEGE OF TYRE, 332 BC

Island fortifications pose several logistical siege difficulties for an attacker. In 332 BC, Alexander the Great chose to conduct an attack against the important island of Tyre, sited roughly half a mile off shore.[16] This island was protected by high, two-mile long wall constructed of heavy stone, which ran around it, and also protected by a strong navy.

---

[16] Alexander the Great (356-323 BC). Alexander's father Philip II (382-336 BC) was the king of Macedon. Philip II married Olympias, the wild, witch-like daughter of the king of Epirus. According to Plutarch in his Life of Alexander (2.3-4) when newly wed, Philip came upon his wife asleep with a serpent by her side. He was filled with revulsion and feared her as an enchantress. Alexander, born of their union, was a fair-skinned handsome youth, quick to anger. He studied under Aristotle, the most celebrated philosopher of his time and had Leonidas as a tutor, a man of stern temperament. Alexander thus became a great lover of all kinds of knowledge and always placed Homer's Iliad alongside of his dagger under his pillow when he slept. Alexander's faithful companion in both battle and the hunt, was his horse, Bucephalus. Plutarch (6.1-4) records that Alexander was barely fifteen years of age when he tamed this tempestuous and unruly steed. Bucephalus was brought before Philip by a Thessalian who demanded an exorbitant sum of thirteen talents in exchange. No sooner did an attendant attempt to mount him, than the horse reared up and tossed him to the ground. As the horse was being led away, Alexander exclaimed that he would be able to mount him. Philip mocked his son and asked him what sum he would pay in case he was unhorsed. Alexander replied that he would pay his father the full price of the horse. On hearing this, the king and his attendants burst out into loud laughter. Unabashed, Alexander ran to the horse and turned him directly towards the sun, for the youth had observed that Bucephalus was afraid of the motion of his own shadow. He

Naval Action during the Siege of Tyre.

Tyre was of strategic importance to Alexander the Great.[17] He initially attempted to seize it by subterfuge, claiming he wished to enter Tyre in order to sacrifice to Heracles. At that time, Alexander was convinced that once Tyre was his, all the Phoenician ships would desert the Persian king and come over to his side.

---

then led the horse forward, stroking him gently, and with one nimble leap, mounted him, let him go at full speed and galloped away. Philip and his attendants looked on in wonder. When Alexander dismounted, according to Plutarch (6.5), Philip embraced him and said, "O my son, look thee out a kingdom equal to and worthy of thyself for Macedonia is too small for thee."

[17] 356-323 BC: Alexander the Great unraveled the legendary Gordian Knot by cutting it with his sword. Between 336-323 BC, Alexander III mobilizes The Great Army, comprised of light mobile columns & light cavalry bowmen. He was wounded in 327 BC during an assault on the citadel of Malli in India, when a scaling ladder broke under him. Having seized Taxila, which was at that time a major centre of Brahman culture, Alexander vanquished the

Confident in the fortifications of their island city, the Tyrians objected. Alexander prepared a plan of siege that involved joining the island fortress to the mainland by an artificial isthmus, thus turning Tyre into a peninsula over which he could bring his powerful siege engines up to the city's walls.[18]

During the 7-month long siege which followed, Alexander had his engineers construct a causeway to the island. A strait of four "stadia" separated the island city from the mainland and it was exposed to southwest winds. Alexander ordered large stones and tree trunks from the mountains of Lebanon to be brought down to the coast and cast into the sea. As long as the building of the mole went on near the mainland, the work went on smoothly, but as his men went into deeper water and came closer to the city, they came under a volley of arrows shot by archers positioned on the walls. At the same time, the Tyrians sent warships which sailed up on either side of the workers, mocking and harassing them. This causeway was destroyed several times before Alexander finally succeeded. To do so, Alexander eventually came to understand that the island couldn't be taken unless he had ships to counter the Tyrian navy and enable him to control the sea.

Alexander ordered two towers to be built on the mole and had them equipped with siege engines. The towers were covered with hides and skins so they could withstand fire darts launched by the Tyrians. In response, the Tyrians filled a large horse-carrying transport ship with dry boughs and other combustible materials. They fixed two masts on the ship's prow, each with a projecting arm from which was suspended a cauldron filled with bitumen, sulphur, and other highly inflammable materials. The stern of the vessel was loaded with stone and sand, which in turn elevated the bow so that it could be easily driven over the mole to reach Alexander's towers. The Tyrians then waited for a favorable wind to blow towards the mole, and when it came, they towed the ship towards their target from astern with triremes. After running the "fire-ship" at full speed upon the mole, they then set the combustible materials on fire with torches. The ship was dashed violently against the mole and the cauldrons scattered the fiery mass in all directions, while the crew of the burning ship swim away to safety.

On hearing that their cities had fallen into Alexander's hands, the kings of Aradus and Byblos, deserted the Persian cause and sailed their fleets to Tyre. When they arrived at the site of the siege with their armed contingents and Sidonian triremes, the offered to join with Alexander. When the kings of Cyprus learned that their enemy Darius has been defeated at Issus by Alexander, they also decided to join him and sailed to Sidon with 120 ships. Additional Triremes arrived from Rhodes, Soli, Mallos, and Lycia along with a fifty-oar ship from Macedon. The chronicler Arrian (2.20.3) records the following: "To all these Alexander let bygones be bygones supposing that it was rather from necessity than choice that they had joined naval forces with the Persians."

While this impressive fleet was being prepared for battle with the Tyrians and his siege engines were being fitted to make the final assault, Alexander took a detachment of archers and heavy cavalry (the "hypasists") and marched into Sidon, where he launched a ground attack which conquered part of the country and caused others to readily surrender. He also managed to seize or collect 120 triremes. When Alexander's fleet hove into view off the coast of the island under siege, the Tyrians refused to fight, permitting the Macedonians to attack the wall without seaward interference.

Realizing Alexander now had his back protected, and the seaward approaches were almost fully in his hands, the Tyrians decided to go on the offensive before Alexander attacked. Their plan was to

---

Indian armies of King Puru (Poros in Greek), but because his troops refused to go further he retreated towards the mouth of the Indus river. He died in Babylon (Iraq), of a fever (possibly of malaria).

[18]   Tyre has been of major importance from ancient times. It was great commercial city on the eastern Mediterranean under the Phoenicians when it came under siege by Nebuchadnezzar in 585 BC during the Babylonian-Phoenician War (585-573 BC). Alexander's siege was the first to successfully take Tyre. David Eggenberger, *An Encyclopedia of Battles*, Dover Publications, Inc., New York, 1985, p. 450.

sink the enemy fleet, including the ships of their sister-cities. This would be difficult to put into effect because the ships from Cyprus blocked the mouth of the Tyrian "Sidonian" port, so-called because it faced north towards Sidon. To conceal their plans and preparations, the Tyrians spread out sails in front of the entrance to the harbor. Waiting until midday when they had determined the Cypriot sailors were not on their guard, the Tyrians set sail with their most effective sea fighting men and attacked the surprised enemy, sinking several ships.

Alexander was infuriated by this setback and ordered his ships to immediately blockade the Tyrian harbor before the raiders escaped. The Tyrian defenders manning the fortresses walls vainly shouted and gestured to the raiders to turn back. Wheeling their ships about, the Tyrians attempted to sail back to the protection of their harbor. Only a few manage to get to safety, but Alexander's naval forces put most of the rest out of action. A handful of the Tyrian crews succeeded in jumping overboard and swimming to land. The result of this abortive naval sally was a victory for Alexander, which allowed him to bring his Macedonian closer to Tyre's city walls.

Shortly after this naval engagement, Alexander had his battering rams brought forward and pressed up against the fortress's north walls. As the war machines drew closer to walls, the attackers discovered the fortifications on the mole were too high for the Macedonians to scale. This forced Alexander to turn south to the "Egyptian" port, so-called because it faced Egypt, while testing the strength of the Tyrian walls along the way. Here he discovered a part of the city's fortifications had broken down. He immediately threw a series of siege bridges over the walls, but the Tyrian defenders repulsed the attack.

Alexander reportedly had a dream that Tyre would fall to him, and as a result, he launched his final assault on the fortress. He ordered his triremes to sail against both the "Sidonian" and "Egyptian" ports simultaneously, with object being to force an entrance. They succeeded in gaining access to both harbors and captured the Tyrian ships. Alexander's ships then closed in on the city from all sides and when they were close enough, siege bridges were thrown over the walls from his vessels. Macedonian soldiers quickly ran across the siege bridges, and advanced through breaches in the walls where they engaged and quickly dispatched or fought off the Tyrian defenders.

During the siege, as the Macedonians attacked the wall, the Tyrians poured hot liquids and sand onto the attackers causing severe burns. Many Tyrians deserted the walls and barricaded themselves in the Shrine of Agenor. The people of Tyre particularly revered this monument for, in legendary tradition, Agenor was their king, the father of Cadmus and Europa. According to the chronicler Arrian (2.24.2), Alexander's bodyguards found and attacked them here killing them all in a bloody massacre. The Macedonians had been infuriated by the Tyrian treatment of their captured companions. When Alexander's men had sailed from Sidon to engage the Tyrians in the earlier sea-battles, the Tyrians had captured a number. These men were dragged up on the fortress walls and executed in full view of Alexander's forces. Their bodies were then flung into the sea. Seeing themselves at last masters of the city, Alexander's bodyguard were determined to avenge the death of their companions and gave no mercy to the Tyrians they held responsible for the murders. It is recorded that a total of 8,000 Tyrians died, with only 400 Macedonians lost in the siege.[19]

The historian Quintus Curtius (4.2.10-12) records that at this time a Carthaginian delegation was in Tyre to celebrate the annual festival of Melkart-Heracles. The king of Tyre, Azemilcus, the chief magistrates and the Carthaginian embassy took refuge in the temple of Heracles. Alexander granted them a full pardon, but he severely punished the people of Tyre. Some 30,000 were sold into slavery. According to Quintus Curtius (4.4.17), 2,000 Tyrians were nailed to crosses along a great stretch of the shore.

Alexander offered a sacrifice to Heracles and held a procession of his armed forces in the city. He also ensured that a naval review was held in the god's honor. The Tyrians had chained a statue of their

---

[19]   Internet: http://oncampus.richmond.edu/academics/as/classics/students/brownie/tyre.htm.

deity Apollo to keep him from deserting them. Alexander therefore solemnly supervised the removal of these golden chains and fetters from Apollo and ordered that henceforth the god be called Apollo "Philalexander." He rewarded those of his men who had distinguished themselves and gave a lavish funeral for his dead. Having completed the successful siege of Tyre, Alexander moved on, and with the fall of Gaza to the south, he headed on to Egypt.[20]

STONE TOWERS, KEEPS AND DONJONS

Although many medieval fortresses consisted of castles rather than of town walls (many of which were built over foundations and stonework dating back to Roman times), there were very few new elements added. Medieval castles were generally centered on massive stone towers, keeps (a type of fortified tower built within castles), or donjons. These were often surrounded by multiple layers of curtain walls (the outer wall of a castle or defensive wall between two bastions), that had covered galleries, buttresses,

---

[20] Following the siege of Tyre, Alexander founded the city of Alexandria at the mouth of the Nile, which was destined to be the new commercial and intellectual center of the Eastern Mediterranean world. In the spring of 331 BC Alexander left the Mediterranean to strike into the heart of the Persian Empire. Near Nineveh he was met by the Persian leader Darius who was accompanied by an army hastily assembled to stop him. In the battle of Arbela which followed, Darius was defeated and fled into Media. Alexander then followed the Tigris River into Babylonia, the central seat of the Persian Empire and its richest region. From here he proceeded on to Susa, and then to the royal city of Persepolis with its enormous treasure. There he destroyed the palace by fire according to the geographer Strabo (15.6), ostensibly in revenge for the burning of Greek temples by Xerxes during the Graeco-Persian wars. Plutarch (38.1-4) gives another version saying that the fire was started during a drunken revelry but was then extinguished by order of Alexander who regretted the deed.

From Ecbatana Alexander pursued Darius to the Caspian Sea. As the Persian Empire crumbled, Darius was deserted by his generals one by one as well as by his troops. His cousin, Bessus, seized this opportunity to rid himself once and for all of the Persian king. At night he and a few followers burst into Darius' tent, tied him up with ropes and carried him to his chariot and on to Bactria. He hoped eventually to offer the Persian king as a hostage in exchange for Alexander's recognition of him as ruler of the eastern satrapies. Alexander followed Darius in hot pursuit. Seeing he could not escape, Bessus suddenly galloped up to the royal chariot, stabbed Darius to death and escaped. When Alexander finally caught up with his rival, he found only Darius' corpse. Alexander looked down on his fallen foe with compassion and covered his body with his purple cloak.

Eventually Bessus was captured and put in chains. Due to the nature of the crime, Alexander had him sentenced by Persian judges, not by himself. Bessus was found guilty of rebellion against his king. The sentence was cruel. Bessus' nose and ears are cut off and he is led to Ecbatana where he was crucified on a tree.

Alexander marched through Bactria and Sogdiana putting down rebellions and founding Greek cities. Then he crossed the Hindu Kush and proceeded on to India. King Porus ruled one of the principalities, situated between the Hydaspes and Ascenines. Alexander crossed the Hydaspes, and encountered Porus, who held the opposite bank with a powerful force and two hundred elephants. During the battle that followed, Porus was wounded and fell into Alexander's hands. Alexander, however, gained the fallen king as a friend.

It is at this time, Plutarch (61.1) records that Bucephalus died, wounded in battle. Others relate that the horse died of fatigue and old age. Alexander was overcome with grief. On the banks of the Hydaspes River he built a city on the tomb of his horse, which he named Bucephalia in his memory. When he reached the Hyphasis River (Beas) the Macedonian army refused to go farther although Alexander believed he had not much more to go to reach the ocean and the eastern limit of the inhabited world. He was obliged to give way and the return began.

In the spring of 323 BC, Alexander returned to Babylon. There he made plans for the construction of a great fleet and the opening of a route by sea from Babylon to Egypt around Arabia. In Babylon, however, he fell ill, consumed by a raging fever that did not leave him. He died towards evening on 13 June 323 BC at the age of thirty-three.

parapets, crenellation, machicolations, flanking towers, sally ports, and protected gates incorporated into their design and construction.

The designs evolved continuously over the lifetime of each fortress or castle, with ditches and moats being added where possible, particularly in Northwestern Europe because of the abundance of water. The primary difference in medieval castles over their primitive predecessors was their function. A castle was used to dominate the countryside it surveyed, which meant many were sited on strategically chosen spurs of hills overlooking all approaches, which gave additional warning and protection. To overcome them, an attacker had to be inventive and utilize increasingly sophisticated methods of siegecraft and siege engines.

(David Perez Photo)

Castle of Arévalo (Castillo de Arévalo), built between the 12th and 16th centuries in the north of the province of Avila in Spain. The ground plan is almost square, round towers at its corners, round sentry boxes on its walls and the large D-shaped keep in one corner. The keep is made of ashlar masonry with later brick additions like the rest of the castle.

(Edal Anton Lefterov Photo)

Château de Vincennes, a massive 14th and 17th century French royal fortress in the town of Vincennes, to the east of Paris. It was constructed for Louis VII about 1150 in a forest that was part of Vincennes. In the 13th century, Philip Augustus and Louis IX erected a more substantial manor. Louis IX is reputed to have departed from Vincennes on the crusade from which he did not return. To strengthen the site, the castle was greatly enlarged replacing the earlier site in the later 14th century. A donjon tower, 52 meters high, the tallest medieval fortified structure of Europe, was added by Philip VI of France, a work that was started about 1337. The grand rectangular circuit of walls was completed by the Valois about two generations later (c1410). The donjon served as a residence for the royal family, and its buildings are known to have once held the library and personal study of Charles V. Henry V of England died in the donjon in 1422 following the siege of Meaux.

At the end of February 1791, a mob of more than a thousand workers marched out to the château, which, rumour had it, was being readied on the part of the Crown for political prisoners, and with crowbars and pickaxes set about demolishing it. The work was interrupted by the Marquis de Lafayette who took several ringleaders prisoners, to the jeers of the Parisian workers. It played no part during the remainder of the Revolution. From 1796, it served as an arsenal. The execution of the duc d'Enghien took place in the moat of the château on 21 March 1804.

General Daumesnil, *"Je rendrai Vincennes quand on me rendra ma jambe"*,
from a painting by Gaston Mélingue.

General Daumesnil who lost a leg at the Battle of Wagram (5–6 July 1809), was assigned to the defence of the château de Vincennes in 1812. Vincennes was then an arsenal containing 52,000 new rifles, more than 100 field guns and many tons of gunpowder, bullets, cannon balls. It was a tempting prize for the Sixth Coalition marching on Paris in 1814 in the aftermath of the Battle of the Nations. However, Daumesnil faced down the allies and replied with the famous words *"Je rendrai Vincennes quand on me rendra ma jambe" ("I shall surrender Vincennes when I get my leg back")*. With only 300 men under his command, he resisted the Coalition until King Louis XVIII ordered him to leave the fortress.

Vincennes also served as the military headquarters of the Chief of General Staff, General Maurice Gamelin, during the unsuccessful defence of France against the invading German army in 1940. It is now the main base of France's Defence Historical Service, which maintains a museum in the *donjon*. On 20 August 1944, during the battle for the Liberation of Paris, 26 policemen and members of the Resistance arrested by soldiers of the Waffen SS were executed in the eastern moat of the fortress, and their bodies thrown in a common grave.

Only traces remain of the earlier castle and the substantial remains date from the 14th century. The castle forms a rectangle whose perimeter is more than a kilometer in length (330 x 175m). It has six towers and three gates, each originally 13 meters high, and is surrounded by a deep stone lined moat. The keep, 52m high, and its enceinte occupy the western side of the fortress and are separated from the rest of the castle by the moat. The keep is one of the first known examples of rebar usage. The towers of the *grande enceinte* now stand only to the height of the walls, having been demolished in the 1800s, save the *Tour du Village* on the north side of the enclosure. The south end consists of two wings facing each other, the *Pavillon du Roi* and the *Pavillon de la Reine*, built by Louis Le Vau. The castle was one of the first buildings in history to use steel to reinforce the walls. (Jean Mesqui, *Châteaux forts et fortifications en France.* Paris: Flammarion, 1997)

Engraving of Echafaud donjon, Coucy, France, a stone tower under construction with scaffolding attached. It rises in a spiral with workers on the top. There are holes for logs in the tower marking the previous position of the scaffolding.

Siege of Holschnitt, Germany, 1502, engraving.

Engraving of the Siege of Magdeburg, Germany 1630-1631.

Siege warfare may have been practiced in Sumer as early as the third millennium BC. Based on ancient reliefs, the Assyrian army that destroyed the Biblical Kingdom of Israel and nearly did the same to Judea, already possessed a considerable array of apparently effective siege engines. They made use of ropes which had been attached to hooks, crowbars, scaling ladders, rams, and siege towers. They constructed mantelets which were basically wagons mounted with armour in front and which could be pushed close to the walls while providing cover for the archers. They also undermined the Hebrew defenses with tunnels and mines.

SIEGE OF DAPUR, C1269 BC

The Siege of Dapur occurred as part of Ramesses II's campaign to suppress Galilee and conquer Syria in 1269 BC. He described his campaign on the wall of his mortuary temple, the Ramesseum in Thebes. The inscriptions say that Dapur was "in the land of Hatti". Although Dapur has often been identified with Tabor in Canaan, it may have been in Syria, to the north of Kadesh. From Egyptian reliefs it appears that Dapur was a heavily fortified city with both inner and outer walls and situated on a rocky hill which was usual for Syrian cities and many other cities in the Bronze Age. Contemporary illustrations of the siege show the use of ladders and chariots with soldiers climbing scale ladders supported by archers. Six of the sons of Ramesses, still wearing their side locks, also appear on those depictions of the siege. (Kitchen, Kenneth A. *Ramesside Inscriptions*, Wiley Blackwell, 1998)

(Nordisk familjebok)
Ramesses II and his Egyptian Army engaged in the siege of Dapur, from a mural in Thebes.

The Egyptians of the New Kingdom which began in 1567 BC engaged in sieges using two new weapon's systems adapted from their temporary conquerors, the Hyksos. The first was a double-convex composite bow made of wood, horn and sinew which was bound or glued together so that when it was unstrung or "at rest," it appeared to be bent in the reverse direction from which it was designed to fire. When it was strung, drawn, and fired, it had a range of 400 yards. Their second development was the single-axle chariot with spoked wheels which provided mobility for their archers and spearmen. When the Egyptians assaulted a fortified city, they hacked at the gates with axes and stormed the walls using scaling ladders. To protect themselves as they did so, they slung their rectangular shields over their backs, which left their hands free for climbing and fighting. Using this method, they successfully stormed and captured the Canaanite city of Megiddo in 1468 BC.[21]

---

[21]   1469 BC: Battle of Megiddo, the first recorded battle of history. Thutmosis led an Egyptian Army of 10,000 men on a rapid and unexpected march into central Palestine. Rebel Chieftains assembled an army at Megiddo, North of Mount Carmel. The King of Kadesh led the rebels, who formed a concave formation to the South. Thutmosis led a Northern "horn" between the rebel flank and the fortress of Megiddo. The victory went to Egypt.

The Egyptian siege of Dapur, Galilee, in the 13th century BC, Bas-relief from the Ramesseum, Thebes.

Ramesses II (The great Sesostris), at the Battle of Khadesh, ca 1274 BC, between the forces of the Egyptian Empire under Ramesses II and the Hittite Empire under Muwatalli II at the city of Kadesh on the Orontes River, just upstream of Lake Homs near the present-day Syrian-Lebanese border.

(I, Luc Viatour Photo)
Reconstruction of Trebuchets at Château de Castelnaud, France.

(Krzysztof Golik Photo)

Château de Castelnaud, a medieval fortress in the commune of Castelnaud-la-Chapelle overlooking the Dordogne River in Périgord, southern France. It was built to face its rival, the Château de Beynac. The oldest documents mentioning it, date to the 13th century, when it figured in the Albigensian Crusade; its Cathar castellan was Bernard de Casnac. Simon de Montfort took the castle and installed a garrison; when it was retaken by Bernard, he hanged them all. During the Hundred Years' War, the castellans of Castelnaud owed their allegiance to the Plantagenets, the sieurs de Beynac across the river, to the king of France. It eventually fell into ruin, but it has been restored and is a private property open to the public, houses a much-visited museum of medieval warfare, featuring reconstructions of siege engines, Mangonneaux and trebuchets.

(I, Luc Viatour Photo)

Château de Beynac, built in the 12th century by the barons of Beynacto to cover the valley. The sheer cliff face being sufficient to discourage any assault from that side, the defences were built up on the plateau. These included double crenellated walls, a double barbican, and double moats, one of which was a deepened natural ravine.

(I, Luc Viatour Photo)

Château de Beynac, castle keep. The oldest part of the castle is a large, square-shaped, Romanesque keep with vertical sides and few openings, held together with attached watch towers, and equipped with a narrow spiral staircase terminating on a crenellated terrace. To one side, a residence of the same period is attached; it was remodelled and enlarged in the 16th and 17th centuries. On the other side is a partly 14th century residence side-by-side with a courtyard and a square plan staircase serving the 17th century apartments. The apartments have kept their woodwork and a painted ceiling from the 17th century.

At the time of the Hundred Years' War, the fortress at Beynac was in French hands. The Dordogne was the border between France and England. Not far away, on the opposite bank of the river, the Château de Castelnaud, was held by the English. The Dordogne region was the theatre of numerous struggles for influence, rivalries and occasionally battles between the English and French supporters. However, the castles fell more often through ruse and intrigue rather than by direct assault because the armies needed to take these castles were extremely costly: only the richest nobles and kings could build and maintain them.

About 1050 AD, both the Christian and Muslim world began to reintroduce siege machines into warfare, and by the time of the Crusades these weapons sometimes numbered in their hundreds. Onagers, mangonels, petriers, arbalasts, stone throwing ballistae and catapults such as trébuchets led to fundamental changes in the nature of siege warfare until the age of gunpowder ushered in the next stage in the level of fire with effect.[22]

---

[22] The manufacture of gunpowder in the 17th century involved extracting and refining the saltpeter from earth found in decomposing organic matter such as the kind found in cattle sheds, sheep pens and dung heaps. It was then

No one side has a monopoly on the employment of useful ideas and weapons for attack and defense, and so it is that the development of enceintes and the siege engines to break them appears to have moved along at the same pace. Outthinking the opposing side became a major problem for the commander. The capture of a well-designed and constructed castle or fortress from the 14th century onwards, for example proved to be an extremely difficult task as will be shown in detail later in these records. Finding a weak spot would prove to be the key, and this was rarely simple. Reconnaissance and good intelligence gathering would prove to be that essential key, permitting the successful commander to find and exploit the weakness in his opponent's position. The result would basically depend on a well-coordinated plan based on a sound assessment of the best method of attack. A good commander who is supported by an excellent staff and the right resources is often in a better position to outthink his opponent, leading him to outfight and defeat him.

This book contains examples of sieges, both successful and unsuccessful, demonstrating that no matter how securely a fortress or defensive position is constructed and defended, eventually a good plan and a determined besieger can overcome it. One way or another, time, willpower and determined effort will be brought together in sufficient quantity and quality to bring a siege or a defence to a successful conclusion. It will be argued through the examples presented in this book that ultimately, "no fortress is impregnable."

SIEGECRAFT

"And it came to pass, when the people heard the sound of the trumpet, and the people shouted with a great shout, that the wall fell down flat, so that the people went up into the city, every man straight before him, and they took the city...and they burnt it."[23]

---

blended with charcoal and brimstone, and then the mixture was milled finely, in a relatively simple but dangerous process. Paul Johnson, *Castles of England, Scotland, and Wales*, Weidenfeld and Nicolson, London,1989, p. 168.

[23] *The Holy Bible*, King James Version, Thomas Nelson Inc., Camden, New Jersey, 1970, *Joshua, Chapter 6, verses 1-20*, p. 166.

(Weapons and Warfare Illustration)
The fall of the walls of Jericho, ca 1400 BC.

The trumpets blew, and in 1400 BC the walls of Jericho that had been built over 9000 years before our present time, came tumbling down. In the intervening years since Joshua besieged Jericho, little has changed in the apparent fact that whenever one group of people sets up a position from which they can defend themselves, another group will soon set to the task of defeating it. Necessity being the mother of invention, as one chieftain, king or pharaoh developed a practicable plan of defense or assault; another would in turn attempt to devise a better one to overcome it.

As the means and methods to wage war developed and became more sophisticated, so too did the ideas and technology that had to be developed for civilizations to survive. The technological battle continues to this day in a constant seesaw of change. This change can perhaps best be described as a form of pendulum that swings on an erratic and often rapid centre-pin of new ideas.

Inventive ideas are something no one has a monopoly on, even though the results of these ideas have come to affect millions of lives touched by them. It has also been observed that no matter how good an idea is, one cannot safely rely on it as a sole means of defense for too long, because a determined enemy willing to pay the price will quickly bring a better idea into play against it. This book will examine the pendulum effect that ultimately renders the newest defensive or offensive idea obsolete in the shortest possible time.

To discuss the issues and events encompassed in this book, the evolution of fortifications and the weapons and methods of sieges used to conquer them will be examined concurrently. Examples of particularly noteworthy sieges both successful and unsuccessful will be discussed to demonstrate the premise that, ultimately, no fortress can be considered impregnable.

Castle under siege, engraving by P. Newark.

EARLY DEFENCES

The first military engineer was probably the cave-dweller who was faced with the problem of defending his lair against both wild beasts and his fellowmen. He may have solved this by improving on an already existing natural obstacle, barricading the entrance, or keeping it just high enough to be able to see over the top and yet still be able to throw missiles through a carefully sighted gap. Other primitive societies would have built their houses in trees, or on piles surrounded by water, all of them either creating an obstacle or improving on a natural one. Early defenders also quickly discovered the advantages of sighting their defensive positions on high ground, finding it easier to throw stones and debris downward upon an attacker, rather than upward. Being in a high place also conferred an advantage of early warning through observation of approaching intruders.[24]

As technology and invention progressed, advances in methods of siege and defence were also made. A simple wall of earth, wood or stone could often adequately provide protection against the primitive weapons in use in ancient times. Basic walls worked well until the invention of practical artillery beginning with catapults and leading into the age of gunpowder. The Greek fortresses of Mycenae and Tiryns were in existence as far back as 1500 BC. Their designs incorporated tortuous approaches and successive turns which forced an attacker to expose his unshielded right side. Both the attacker and the defenders needed large numbers of trained soldiers to ensure a successful outcome, and thus the maintenance of large standing armies became the rule. Over the years however, necessity demanded that the various forms of fixed defence works continue to be expanded and improved upon throughout the world. In time the successful defence of a town, village, city fortification or fortress would often become crucial to the survival of an army or a nation. The construction of walled defenses and fortifications became a science necessary to the preservation of the way of life for many of the earliest civilizations. Fortification can therefore be defined as the deliberate erection of physical structures intended to provide a military advantage to a defender and to impede, or otherwise disadvantage, an attacker.[25]

By the Bronze Age there was unambiguous evidence of fortifications built exclusively for military purposes. The first undisputed example of a fortified city was Urak in Mesopotamia dating from 2700 BC. It enclosed a population of 3,000 to 5,000. The fortress of Buhen built in the Sudan around 2200 BC was 180 yards square, surrounded by a mud-brick wall 15 feet thick and 30 feet high. The wall had firing bastions every 30 feet. A moat surrounded the outer wall and was 26 feet across and 18 feet deep, with yet another steep glacis on the inner slope. The gate complex was 45 feet high and stretched from the inner wall across the moat, allowing archers to control fire along parallel approaches. As impressive as this fortress was, it was dwarfed in size and complexity by fortifications of the Iron Age. The Israelite fortress at Hazor, for example, had walls that ran 3,000 feet by 21,000 feet. The city of Qatna had walls 4 miles long, and the Hittite capital of Boghazkoy had walls that ran for 6 miles. The entire wall of Boghazkoy and its supporting strong points were made of solid rock and brick. So important were fortifications to the ancient armies that the need to secure adequate wood and stone supplies led both Egypt and Assyria to occupy Lebanon for centuries.[26]

Siegecraft is arguably one of the oldest and most successful military tactics in continuous use in warfare, extending back perhaps beyond recorded time. For example, in the period from 400 BC to 200 BC the Greeks made great progress in the use of the principles of tension and torsion, which they applied to the design and implementation of siege artillery. Some of these ancient siege engines had a range of

---

[24] Anthony Kemp, *Castles in Colour*, Blandford Press, Poole, Dorset, 1977, p. 13.
[25] G. J. Ashworth, *War and the City*, Routledge, London, and New York, 1991, p. 12.
[26] Internet: http://www.au.af.mil/au/awc/awcgate/gabrmetz/gabr000d.htm.

more than 500 yards and were extremely well constructed. Archimedes designed a number of them and it has been documented that he took part in the defence of Syracuse in 212 BC.[27]

The Greeks also developed the idea of a "flanking tower," which became an important element in the design of later fortifications. Flanking walls permitted defenders to fire down on their attackers from more than one angle. Sieges therefore began to be drawn out affairs as defensive installations became more difficult to overcome.[28] Whole campaigns came to revolve around some of the most famous sieges, and this in turn caused many of them to be considered more important than battles.[29]

By its very nature, a siege involves an assault on an opposing force attempting to defend itself from behind a position of some strength. For the purposes of this book then, when an attacking force conducts an assault against a place with a view to capturing it or compelling the occupants to surrender, then a state of siege can be said to exist.[30]

The basic methods of attacking a fortification remained essentially the same over the centuries, and include one or a combination of the following: scaling or climbing the obstacle; breaching the obstacle by battering or undermining its gates or walls; setting it on fire; starving out the garrison; making use of treachery, bribery and various methods of deception or trickery.

No fortress could be considered impregnable in view of the available means to defeat them, but from the beginning, fortresses have been designed as places of refuge with the expectation that adequate preparations will be made for defence against a possible siege. An exception to this rule is the Roman villa, which was the castle's predecessor. It was unfortified because it depended entirely on Roman law and the Roman legions for its security and defence.[31]

Not all fortresses are made of walls and stone. In the late 1990's a proposal was made to assemble a so-called protective umbrella of an anti-missile Star Wars system known as SDI. Although it was never implemented, due to the fall of the Soviet Union, Star Wars may be considered an example of modern thinking that still leans towards reliance on an all-encompassing defensive system. At one point there were military and civilian planners who thought Star Wars would be "the last fortress," needed for the defense of North America.[32]

As of 11 September 2001, Osama bin Laden and the terrorists of Al Qaeda have changed that perception by demonstrating that no matter how powerful a state may be, a new or unexpected method may be found to attack it.[33] Technological change is bound to render any existing defensive system obsolete one day, so even Star Wars programs could not have been considered an ultimate safeguard.

---

[27]   212 BC: Siege of Syracuse by Romans. Archimedes designed giant ship lifting cranes and invented a method of training great mirrors onto the Roman ships burning their fleet during the siege. Archimedes died in Syracuse.

[28]   Anthony Kemp, op. cit., p. 14.

[29]   Peter Paret, *Makers of Modern Strategy from Machiavelli to the Nuclear Age*, Princeton University Press, Princeton, New Jersey, 1986, p. 90.

[30]   Charles Connell, *The World's Greatest Sieges*, Odhams Books Limited, Long Acre, London, 1967, p. 9.

[31]   Barbara W. Tuchman, *A Distant Mirror, The Calamitous 14th Century*, Ballantine Books, New York, 1978, p. 5.

[32]   LCol Daniel Gosselin, CFCSC, Toronto, RMC War Studies 500 Program, 14 April 1994.

[33]   At 07:45 Tuesday morning 11 September 2001, American Airlines Flight 11, a Boeing 767, left Boston, Massachusetts bound for Los Angeles, California, with 92 people onboard. At 07:58, United Airlines Flight 175, also a Boeing 767, left Boston for Los Angeles with 65 people onboard. At 08:01 United Airlines Flight 93, a Boeing 757, left Newark, New Jersey bound for San Francisco, California with 45 people onboard. At 08:10, United Airlines Flight 77, also a Boeing 757, left Washington, DC, bound for Los Angeles with 64 people onboard. At 08:45 American Airlines Flight 11 hit the north tower of the World Trade Center in New York. At 09:05, United Airlines Flight 175 hit the south tower of the World Trade Center. At 09:39, American Airlines Flight 77 crashed into the Pentagon outside Washington, DC. At 09:40, the American Federal Aviation Administration halted all flights in the USA> At 09:58 the South tower of the World Trade Center collapsed. At 10:10, United Airlines Flight 93 crashed near Johnstown, Pennsylvania. At 10:25 all overseas flights bound for the USA were diverted to Canada. At 10:28 the World Trade

STRONG WALLS

Sieges are an incredibly old concept and idea but remain a current topic concern. On 5 February 1994 during the 22-month long siege of Sarajevo, a series of mortar rounds were dropped in the city marketplace, killing 69 people and wounding 170 more. I passed by the site of this attack in the fall of 1997, and the shell craters have been filled in, but marked with red paint or wax to leave a continuing reminder of the siege.[34] The attacks by terrorists on the World Trade Center and the Pentagon on 11 September 2001 (now universally known as "9/11") re-ignited Western thinking on how to create a "Fortress America." The concept has gone into high-gear actuality with the inception of United States Northern Command (USNORTHCOM) which officially stood up at Peterson Air Force Base in Colorado Springs, Colorado, on 1 October 2002. USNORTHCOM currently works in close concert with North American Aerospace Defense Command (NORAD) which operates from Cheyenne Mountain Air Force Station (CMAFS), also in Colorado Springs. Cheyenne Mountain itself was once considered an impregnable "fortress," and it may have had its usefulness extended well beyond the nuclear age through the age of counterterrorism. In the end, however it too will one day be overcome by time and technology.

The successful taking of a fortress or systems of defense-works was often due to its defenders being "outthought" long before they were "outfought." As noted, bribery, treachery, deception, and assorted trickery was often brought into play when assaults failed. There were instances of armed men being smuggled into a castle hidden in fodder carts before actual hostilities had begun. Once through the gate, they would leap out and overpower the guard and so let in their comrades. Forgery was also tried. The Krak des Chevaliers, the largest of the Crusader castles, was besieged twelve times without success by the Saracens and continued to hold out when all the other castles had been taken.[35] In 1271 however, the surviving Hospitaller Knights were shown a letter purporting to have come from the Grand Master of his Order, commanding him to surrender, as he could not be relieved. The Castellan accepted this, and surrendered to Sultan Baibar, only to find out later that the letter was a fake.[36]

Center's north tower collapsed. The terrorist group Al Qaeda. led by Osama bin Laden claimed responsibility. *Maclean's,* article, *Special Report After the Terror, 24 September 2001,* p. 14.

[34] *TIME Canada Ltd.,* Toronto, Ontario, 21 February 1994, p. 11.

[35] The castle of Krak des Chevaliers in Syria was captured by the Mameluke Sultan Beibars of Egypt, using a false messenger. It had been the most important possession of the Knights of St John. Beibars had surprised Caesarea in 1265, and stormed Arsouf, a town belonging to the Hospital. Safed, Jaffa, Belfort, and the city of Antioch had fallen in 1266, before Beibars took on the "Castle of Krak." St Jean d'Acre fell 3 years later.

[36] Anthony Kemp, op. cit., p. 167, and Wolfgang F. Schuerl, op. cit., p. 16.

(Bernard Gagnon Photo)
Crusader fortress Krak des Chevaliers, Northwest Syria.

Bribery was also often successful. In 1097, the Crusaders besieged Antioch for six months without success. Bohemond, who was one of their leaders, however, managed to persuade the Muslim commander on one of the towers of the city to admit a troop of his men. They were let in at night, and made themselves masters of the wall, whereby the city capitulated.[37]

In the days following the age of the caveman, defenders often had to rely on natural obstacles such as thorn hedges. Eventually, stronger defenses were required, such as ditches and banks of earth. The first solid obstacle designed to keep invaders out was undoubtedly the "wall." The basic problem faced by besieging forces for all the centuries between ancient civilizations and the Middle Ages and onwards then, was to get over, under or through the protective walls held by a determined defender.[38]

Small numbers of professional soldiers and mercenaries fighting from behind the parapet of a high wall could and often did hold off larger numbers of assailants indefinitely. If both sides in a siege relied upon conventional weapons, the advantage generally lay with the defenders if they had a good wall in front of them. There were many ways for attackers to deal with a wall. They could go over it, using scaling ladders and tall towers; they could go through it using battering rams; or they could go under it by tunneling or mining.[39]

Ditches could be filled with fascines (a bundle of rods, sticks, or plastic pipes bound together, used in construction or military operations for filling in marshy ground or other obstacles and for strengthening the sides of embankments, ditches, or trenches). Fascine bundles were used in military defences for revetting (shoring up) trenches or ramparts, especially around artillery batteries, or filling in ditches from earlier military actions. They were also used as a visual obstruction, providing cover for sappers and engineers. Military fascine bridges were used on a regular basis by the Romans to cross obstacles. Subsequently, the use of fascines by military engineers continued almost wherever armies were deployed.

---

[37] Anthony Kemp, op. cit., p. 167.
[38] Bruce Allen Watson, *Sieges, A Comparative Study*, Praeger Publishers, Westport, Connecticut, 1993, p. 1.
[39] Charles Connell, op. cit., p. 10.

(Alan Wilson Photo)

British First World War Mk. IV (Male) Tank with a fascine. Built in 1917 by William Foster & Co Ltd, this Mk. IV was part of a batch of 101 tanks numbered from 2300 to 2400. It is one of seven survivors from the 1,220 Mk. IV tanks built and is preserved in operational condition, although it is not run to avoid damage from wear and tear. It is currently on display at The Tank Museum, Bovington, Dorset, UK.

In the early stages of a siege against a castle, the attackers would surround and assault the walls with scaling ladders, and the moat could be filled in. Catapults and battering rams would be brought forward and used to open a breach in the wall, which would give the attacker access to the first enclave. All attempts would be made to make a breach sufficiently wide to permit the maximum number of combatants to gain access to the fortress. During a longer siege, trenches and tunnels would undermine the base of the walls and towers, while the defenders would dig counter-saps or attempt to plug the gaps with stockades and abatis of wood. In response, the attackers would fill the tunnels with piles of burning firewood, which in turn weakened the walls causing them to collapse. If all these efforts to reduce the defense systems of the castle failed, then the option of starving the garrison out was employed. Castles could never hold sufficient provisions to keep large numbers of villagers from the surrounding area supplied, and rationing would have been required, leaving the defenders unable to hold out for long periods.[40]

---

[40] Ibid., p. 22.

A 13th century CE illustration showing a medieval siege in France.
From the Maciejowski Bible c1240 CE. (Pierpont Morgan Library)

Starvation as a siege method often required a considerable length of time, something medieval siege armies rarely had available to them. If the Castellan of the besieged castle had done his job well, he would have ensured adequate water and provisions had been stored for all the defenders and livestock present. The attacker in turn had to ensure he had sufficient men to completely cordon off and blockade the defending garrison. He also had to have enough funds to pay his men and sufficient resources to provision them well. If he did not, he could find himself in the position of being forced to raise a siege because of the starvation of his attacking force. In dangerous country, it was difficult to keep an army together, as the larger the force, the farther out foraging parties had to scavenge to gather supplies, which in turn meant there were fewer men to work in the blockading forces. In many instances, the besieging army simply melted away long before the defending forces could be forced to capitulate.[41]

A slow siege that could be sustained by an attacker could force a garrison to surrender to keep its occupants from starving to death. For this reason, castles that were most at risk of being besieged were usually well stocked with food. Food storage was a serious problem, however, as most provisions had only a short shelf-life and had to be frequently renewed. This gave the attacker the incentive to allow sufficient time for the slow process of starvation to compel the surrender of the castle. The besieged, however, could often count on the timely arrival of a relieving force, provided messengers could be sent

---

41   Anthony Kemp, op. cit., pp. 166-167.

to them before the castle was completely cut off by the attacker. For this reason, a set of "rules" was worked out and was generally adhered to. The outcome of a siege under these rules became somewhat of a gamble for both sides, with the "game" being governed by these strict rules. In the siege of Dolforwyn, in England, the garrison "gave eight hostages, the best after the constable, as a guarantee that they will surrender the castle on the Thursday after the close of Easter unless they are relieved by Llewelyn, and if relieved, the hostages are to be returned to them." The choice of date by which the castle should be relieved or surrendered was crucial and represented the gamble in the negotiation. Whenever a castle was yielded the garrison was usually allowed to march away. Only when it was taken by assault do we find evidence of wholesale slaughter.[42]

Early field fortifications were often simple obstacles erected shortly before a battle for temporary use while the battle was being fought. Industrious and frightened defenders eventually began to refine their simple pits or ditches by adding sharpened stakes and complicated gateways. The prehistoric earthworks found in England for example, at such places as Maiden Castle in Sussex, and Old Sarum, near Salisbury dating back to 3600 BC, show ingenious arrangements of obstacles in which an attacker could be trapped and exterminated.[43]

When Rome was captured by the Gauls in 390 BC, a wall was built around it, known as the "Wall of Servius Tullius." Constantine the Great who reigned from 288-337 AD, built the fortress of Deutz 307 AD, and a bridgehead over the Rhine at Cologne. (Constantine is said to have seen the symbol of the cross in the sky just before a battle, and the words, *"In this sign, conquer,"* in 312 AD). In 330 AD Constantine founded the new city of Constantinople, giving it his own name. Constantinople was itself developed on the site of the old Hellenistic town of Byzantium. The fortifications built by the emperor made Constantinople impregnable for many years.

Temporary wooden fortifications were also developed at an early date. When William the Conqueror's Norman soldiers landed in England in 1066, they brought with them prefabricated defense towers which they immediately erected on the beach.[44]

From such early fortifications eventually evolved the concept of constructing long defensive lines consisting of ditches backed by earthen walls. These required great managerial and organizational skills and resources, and the ability to put thousands of men to work in a coordinated fashion. The Chinese, Sumerian, Hellenic and Roman Empires all invested heavily in the erection of continuous barriers. Even the most powerful of these systems, however, were far from impenetrable.[45]

---

[42] N. J. G. Pounds, *The Medieval Castle in England, and Wales.* Cambridge University Press, 1990. Internet: http://www.castlewales.com/siege.html.

[43] Philip Warner, *Sieges of the Middle Ages*, G. Bell & Sons Ltd., London, 1968, p. 5.

[44] William was descended from Vikings who had settled at the mouth of the Seine River in France in 896. This area, known as Normandy, was ceded to Rollo the Viking Chief by Charles the simple in 911. William used Normandy as his base and point of assembly for his invasion fleet in 1066. In the subsequent famous battle, William defeated the Saxon King Harold Godwinson and became the King of Britain. Carlos Paluzie de Lescazes, op cit., p. 84.

[45] Martin van Creveld, *Technology and War, From 2000 BC to the Present*, The Free Press, Collier MacMillan Publishers, London, 1989, p. 25-27.

Sculpture of a Roman watchtower and beacon on the lower Danube frontier, ca 113 AD.

(Ekem Photo)
Roman fortress reconstruction, Saalburg Main Gate (Porta Praetoria), Germany.

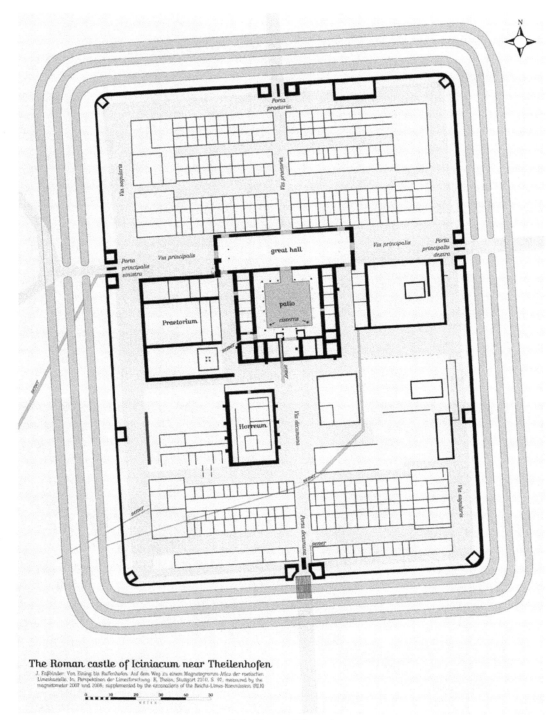

The Roman castle of Iciniacum near Theilenhofen.

J. Faßbinder: Von Eining bis Ruffenhofen. Auf dem Weg zu einem Magnetogramm-Atlas der raetischen Limeskastelle. In: Perspektiven der Limesforschung. K. Theiss, Stuttgart 2010, S. 97, measured by the magnetometer 2007 und 2008; supplemented by the excavations of the Reichs-Limes-Kommission (RLK).

(Mediatus Photo)
Roman castle of Iciniacum near Theilenhofen in Bavaria Germany.

The Romans tried to solve their frontier problems by constructing linear defenses consisting of individual forts connected by continuous stretches of ditch and rampart. The Limes Germanicus for example, ran from the Rhine near Koblenz to the Danube near Regensburg, some 300 miles, and consisted of isolated forts connected by walls, only part of which were stone. The greatest lengths of the Limes, however, consisted of earthen ramparts surmounted by wooden palisades and fronted by a ditch.

Hadrian's Roman Wall in England dates from the earlier period of 120 AD and runs for 73 miles, mostly following high ground that slopes steeply away in front. Sixteen main forts held the Roman garrisons, and every mile there was a smaller work in the form of a rectangular tower. The weakness in this type of defense is that the attacker can choose the time and place of his attack, which means that the whole length of the line must be permanently and equally strongly garrisoned. Once an attack has begun, the threatened sector must be swiftly reinforced with reserves, thereby leaving another area unprotected. The Romans either did not take this factor into account or chose not to build strongpoints behind their lines. Once an invader had broken through, he could easily devastate the countryside behind the wall. This also applied if the attacker was able to outflank the wall, which is what happened in 1940 to France's Maginot Line, when the Germans found a way around it through the Ardennes forest.[46]

(Florival fr Photo)
Musée Mémorial de la Ligne Maginot du Rhin, Maginot Line Casemate, south of Strasbourg, France.

The Great Wall of China, built and expanded on between the 3rd century BC and the 15th century, was primarily put up as a means of protection for the rich interior of China against the attacks of the numerous invaders who sought its riches. It is also an astonishing achievement for human labor, measuring over 6000 km in length and crossing 21 points of longitude.[47]

SIEGE OF SHARUHEN, C1530 BC

Warfare and conflict in the Middle East are vastly ancient in terms of its continued longevity. Following the expulsion of the Hyksos from Egypt in the second half of the 16th century BCE, they fled to Sharuhen and fortified it. Sharuhen was an ancient town in the Negev Desert or perhaps in Gaza. The armies of Pharaoh Ahmose I seized and razed the town after a three-year siege.

The destruction of Sharuhen was merely the first stage of a new policy of pre-emptive warfare waged by the Egyptians. Because the Egyptians of the 17th Dynasty felt deeply humiliated by the 15th and 16th Dynasty rule of the Hyksos (c1650 BCE - c1540 BCE), the Theban dynasty launched an ambitious war, led by Sequenere Tao, against the foreign king, Apepi, to reclaim lost territory. Though his own campaign

46   Anthony Kemp, op. cit., pp. 15-16.
47   Luo Zewen et al, *The Great Wall*, McGraw Hill Book Coy, Maidenhead, England, 1981, p. 67.

to expel the Hyksos from Egypt failed, and he himself was killed in battle, his son, Kamose, launched an attack on the Hyksos capital of Avaris. It was his much younger brother, Ahmose I, however, who finally succeeded in recapturing Avaris, razing it, and expelling the Hyksos rulers from Egypt altogether.

The profound insult of the foreign rule to the honour and integrity of Egypt could be corrected, and its recurrence prevented, only by extending Egypt's hegemony over the Asiatics to the north and east of Egypt. Ahmose I retaliated with a three-year siege of Sharuhen, thereby launching an aggressive policy of pre-emptive warfare. His success was continued by his successor but one, Thutmose I, who extended Egyptian influence as far as the Mitanni kingdom in the north and Mesopotamia in the east, thereby creating what was to become the most extensive empire in the ancient world.

Sharuhen is mentioned in the bible in Joshua 19:6 in the description of the allotment of the Tribe of Simeon. (Donald B. Redford, *The Wars in Syria and Palestine of Thutmose III*, Brill, Laden, Boston, 2003)

SIEGE OF MEGIDDO, C1457 BC

The Battle of Megiddo (15th century BC) was fought between Egyptian forces under the command of Pharaoh Thutmose III and a large rebellious coalition of Canaanite vassal states led by the king of Kadesh. It is the first battle to have been recorded in what is accepted as relatively reliable detail. Megiddo is also the first recorded use of the composite bow and the first body count. All details of the battle come from Egyptian sources, primarily the hieroglyphic writings on the Hall of Annals in the Temple of Amun-Re at Karnak, Thebes (now Luxor), by the military scribe Tjaneni.

The ancient Egyptian account gives the date of the battle as the 21st day of the first month of the third season, of Year 23 of the reign of Thutmose III. It has been claimed that this was 16 April 1457 BC according to the Middle Chronology, although other publications place the battle in 1482 BC or 1479 BC. The Battle of Megiddo was an Egyptian victory and resulted in a rout of the Canaanite forces, which fled to safety in the city of Megiddo. Their action resulted in the subsequent lengthy Siege of Megiddo. By re-establishing Egyptian dominance in the levant, Thutmose III began a reign in which the Egyptian Empire reached its greatest expanse.

(Alma E. Guinness Photo)
Model of the Fortress of Megiddo, 1457 BC.

Pharaoh Thutmose III began a reign in which the Egyptian Empire reached its greatest expanse by reinforcing the long-standing Egyptian presence in the Levant. After waiting impatiently for the end of his regency by the Egyptian Pharaoh Hatshepsut, he immediately responded to a revolt of local rulers near Kadesh in the vicinity of modern-day Syria. As Egyptian buffer provinces in the land of the Amurru along the border with the Hittites attempted to change their vassalage, Thutmose III dealt with the threat personally. The Canaanites are thought to have been allied with the Mitanni and Amurru from the region of the two rivers between the headwaters of the Orontes and the Jordan. The driving and main force behind this revolt was the King of Kadesh. The powerful fortress of Kadesh offered protection to him and the city. The King of Megiddo, with an equally strong fortress, joined the alliance. The importance of Megiddo was its geographical location along the southwestern edge of the Jezreel Valley just beyond the Mount Carmel ridge and the Mediterranean Sea. From this location, Megiddo controlled the Via Maris, the main trade route between Egypt and Mesopotamia.

The Egyptian inscriptions of the campaign on the Temple of Karnak come from a daily journal kept by the scribe Tjaneni during the campaign. In the Egyptian account, Thutmose III gathered an army of chariots and infantry that numbered between ten and twenty thousand men. As the Egyptians mustered their forces, the king of Kadesh gathered many tribal chieftains from Syria, Aram, and Canaan around him, estimated at between ten and fifteen thousand, entered Megiddo and set his forces at the waters of Taanach. He expected that his enemy would come by way of Dothaim - Taanach, the main route from the Mediterranean lowlands into the Valley of Kishon, and from Egypt to Mesopotamia. The army assembled at the border fortress of Tjaru (called Sile in Greek) and arrived ten days later at the loyal city of Gaza. After one day's rest, the army left for the city of Yehem, which was reached after 11 days. Here, Thutmose sent out scouts. To continue north, they had to pass the Mount Carmel ridge. Behind it lay the city and fortress of Megiddo, where the revolting forces had gathered. There were three possible routes from Yehem to Megiddo. Both the northern route, via Zefti and Yokneam, and the southern route, by way of Taanach, gave safe access to the Jezreel Valley. The middle route, via Aruna (modern Wadi Ara), was more direct but risky; it followed a narrow ravine, and the troops could only travel single file. If the enemy waited at the end of the ravine, the Egyptians would risk being cut down piecemeal. The army leaders pleaded with him not to take the difficult road but to take either of the two easier roads. Instead, with information from the scouts, Thutmose III decided to take the direct path to Megiddo. He believed that if his generals advised him to take the easy route, then his enemy would assume he would do so, so he decided to do the unexpected.

The King of Kadesh had left large infantry detachments guarding the two more likely paths, and virtually ignored Aruna, the narrow mountain pass coming in from the south. Ignoring the danger of spreading out his army in the mountains where leading elements might be subject to enemy ambush in narrow mountain passes, and his main force still far behind in Aruna, unable to come to their aid, Thutmose took the direct route through Wadi Ara. To reduce the risk, Thutmose himself led his men through Aruna. With his infantry and the light cavalry of mounted bowmen, known as haibrw or the horsemen going by the side of the mountains, to take out any scouts that might be posted and leaving the road to the main force of chariots, he moved in quickly. With the city lightly guarded by the enemy, Thutmose led a quick assault, scattered the rebels, and entered the valley unopposed. Now, the Egyptian army had a clear path to Megiddo, with large parts of the rebel army far away to the north and south.

Thutmose seized the opportunity. He set up camp at the end of the day, but during the night arrayed his forces close to the enemy; the next morning, they attacked. It cannot be established if the surprised King of Kadesh had managed to fully prepare for battle. Even if he did, it did not do him much good. Though his forces were on high ground adjacent to the fortress, the Egyptian line was arranged in a concave formation, consisting of three wings, that threatened both Caananite flanks. Both the Egyptians and the Caananites are estimated to have had around 1,000 chariots and 10,000 infantry. The Pharaoh led the attack from the center. The combination of position and numbers, superior maneuverability of their left wing along with an early, bold attack, broke the enemy's will; their line immediately collapsed. Those near the city fled into it, closing the gates behind them.

The Egyptian soldiers fell to plundering the enemy camp. During the plunder they captured 924 chariots and 200 suits of armor. Unfortunately for the Egyptians, during this confusion, the scattered Caananite forces, including the kings of Kadesh and Megiddo, were able to rejoin the defenders inside the city. Those inside lowered tied-together clothing to the men and chariots and pulled them up over the walls. Thus, the opportunity of a quick capture of the city following the battle was lost.

The city was besieged for seven months and the King of Kadesh escaped. Tuthmoses built a moat and a wooden palisade, eventually forcing its occupants to surrender. At Karnak it is recorded that the victorious army took home 340 prisoners, 2,041 mares, 191 foals, 6 stallions, 924 chariots, 200 suits of armor, 502 bows, 1,929 cattle, 22,500 sheep, and the royal armour, chariot and tent-poles of the King of Megiddo. The city and citizens were spared. Several other cities in the Jezreel Valley were conquered and Egyptian authority in the area was restored.

Egypt's realm was expanded by this campaign. Thutmose III required from the defeated kings that they each send a son to the Egyptian court. There, they received an Egyptian education. When they returned to their homelands, they governed with Egyptian sympathies. Nevertheless, the victory at Megiddo was only the beginning of the pacification of the Levant. Only after several further campaigns, conducted almost annually, was the unrest cooled. One unanticipated result came in the form of the word Armageddon, which took its root from Megiddo's name. (Cline, Eric H. *The Battles of Armageddon: Megiddo and the Jezreel Valley from the Bronze Age to the Nuclear Age.* University of Michigan Press, May 2002)

JERICHO, 7000 BC

The first town to encircle itself with a complete belt of permanent stone fortifications is thought to have been Jericho, about 7000 BC.[48] The Sumerian cities of Mesopotamia, like Ur and Lagash, whose foundations date back to 3500 BC, were impressive structures with crenellated walls and imposing towered gateways rising high above the irrigated flood plain of the rivers Tigris and Euphrates.[49] A Sumerian wall was built covering some 50 miles between these two rivers about this same time, and enough of it still stood more than 3000 years later, to pose difficulties for Alexander the Great (336-323 BC). The Greek fortresses of Mycenae and Tiryns date back to 1500 BC, but the earliest detailed references about them occur in the period 1300-1200 BC.[50]

The absolute masters of rapid siege assault were the Assyrian armies of the 8th century BC. Their technique was to co-ordinate several different types of assault on the walls at the same time but in different places. Battering rams supported by siege towers were brought into position at several points along the wall. At the same time scaling ladders with lever crews were deployed at other points. Sappers and tunnelers worked to gain entry from beneath by weakening and collapsing a section of the foundation. At the appropriate time, scaling ladders were used to mount attacks over the wall at several points to force the defender to disperse his forces. The idea was to quickly mass more soldiers at the point of entry than the defender could bring to bear. As a rule of thumb, a city could mount about 25 percent

[48]   Martin H. Brice, *Stronghold, A History of Military Architecture*, B.T. Batsford Ltd., London, 1984, p. 33.
[49]   Anthony Kemp, op. cit., p. 14.
[50]   Martin van Creveld, op. cit., p. 28.

of its population to defend against attack. Thus, a city of 30,000 could muster fewer than 8,000 men to defend against an attacking force that typically exceeded 30,000 to 40,000 soldiers. The advantage almost always rested with the besieging army.[51]

A wheeled siege engine is depicted in this 9th century BC bas-relief of an Assyrian attack, found in the palace of Ashurnasirpal II (883-859 BC), at Nimrud.

Strong walls and a good defensive position built high on a rocky hill were in use up through the Middle Ages. Living rock is very hard for an enemy to mine and placing the fortification on high ground gives the defender the gravitational advantage of being able to throw rocks, heavy stones and spears down on the attackers putting them at a severe disadvantage.[52]

As recorded at Jericho however, high walls alone were rarely sufficient to keep out an attacker. Bribery and trickery were often extremely useful tools in a besieger's method-book. Bold men willing to risk all on a slim chance abound in medieval stories and songs. There are many instances of armed men being smuggled into a castle hidden in fodder carts, often well before hostilities began. Once through the gates, they would leap out and overpower the guards, open the doors, and let in their comrades.[53]

The first town to encircle itself with a complete belt of permanent stone fortifications is thought to have been Jericho, about 7000 BC.[54] The Sumerian cities of Mesopotamia, like Ur and Lagash, whose

51   Internet: http://www.au.af.mil/au/awc/awcgate/gabrmetz/gabr000d.htm.
52   Wolfgang F. Schuerl, *Medieval Castles and Cities*, Cassell Ltd., London, 1969, p. 64.
53   Anthony Kemp, op. cit., p. 167.
54   Martin H. Brice, *Stronghold, A History of Military Architecture*, B.T. Batsford Ltd., London, 1984, p. 33.

foundations date back to 3500 BC, were impressive structures with crenellated walls and imposing towered gateways rising high above the irrigated flood plain of the rivers Tigris and Euphrates.[55] A Sumerian wall was built covering some 50 miles between these two rivers about this same time, and enough of it still stood more than 3000 years later, to pose difficulties for Alexander the Great (336-323 BC). The Greek fortresses of Mycenae and Tiryns date back to 1500 BC, but the earliest detailed references about them occur in the period 1300-1200 BC.[56]

The absolute masters of rapid siege assault were the Assyrian armies of the 8th century BC. Their technique was to co-ordinate several different types of assault on the walls at the same time but in different places. Battering rams supported by siege towers were brought into position at several points along the wall. At the same time scaling ladders with lever crews were deployed at other points. Sappers and tunnelers worked to gain entry from beneath by weakening and collapsing a section of the foundation. At the appropriate time, scaling ladders were used to mount attacks over the wall at several points to force the defender to disperse his forces. The idea was to quickly mass more soldiers at the point of entry than the defender could bring to bear. As a rule of thumb, a city could mount about 25 percent of its population to defend against attack. Thus, a city of 30,000 could muster fewer than 8,000 men to defend against an attacking force that typically exceeded 30,000 to 40,000 soldiers. The advantage almost always rested with the besieging army.[57]

Strong walls and a good defensive position built high on a rocky hill were used up through the Middle Ages. Living rock is very hard for an enemy to mine and placing the fortification on high ground gives the defender the gravitational advantage of being able to throw rocks, heavy stones and spears down on the attackers putting them at a severe disadvantage.[58]

As recorded at Jericho however, high walls alone were rarely sufficient to keep out an attacker. Bribery and trickery were often extremely useful tools in a besieger's method-book. Bold men willing to risk all on a slim chance abound in medieval stories and songs. There are many instances of armed men being smuggled into a castle hidden in fodder carts, often well before hostilities began. Once through the gates, they would leap out and overpower the guards, open the doors, and let in their comrades.[59]

It is at the siege of Troy (1194-1184 BC) that the idea of deception is first recorded as having been a successful means of overcoming an impregnable fortress.

THE SIEGE OF TROY, 1194-1184 BC

From the beginning of the Trojan War, the Greek army failed to take into account that the most elementary rules of siegecraft required the use of siege engines and sapping techniques to break into the walled fortress of Troy, sited on a hill in present day Northwest Turkey.[60]

---

[55] Anthony Kemp, op. cit., p. 14.
[56] Martin van Creveld, op. cit., p. 28.
[57] Internet: http://www.au.af.mil/au/awc/awcgate/gabrmetz/gabr000d.htm.
[58] Wolfgang F. Schuerl, *Medieval Castles and Cities*, Cassell Ltd., London, 1969, p. 64.
[59] Anthony Kemp, op. cit., p. 167.
[60] During the Trojan War (1204-1194 BC), a Greek Army, known as the Achaeans, laid siege to the city of Troy in Asia Minor, just south of the Dardanelles. According to Greek mythology, the Greeks were commanded by King Agamemnon of Mycenae, brother of the king of Sparta, Menelaus. The war was reportedly begun when Helen, the wife of Menelaus, was enticed to Troy by Paris, son of the Trojan King, Priam. Four nine years the Greeks failed to penetrate the sturdy walls of the city. In the 10th year Hector, another son of King Priam, was killed in individual combat with the mercurial Greek hero Achilles. Achilles was then killed by Paris. At this point the Greeks made

The battle therefore took on a curious pattern whereby the Trojans, supposedly under siege, staged numerous attacks against the besieger's lines. On one occasion they even reached the Greek ships, setting many of them on fire before successfully withdrawing to their apparently impregnable fortress. According to Homer's Iliad, it took ten years of war for the Greeks to fight their way up to the walls of Troy. The problem remained of how to get inside.

Mykonos vase depicting the Trojan Horse.

A man named Odysseus worked out an ingenious scheme of building a huge wooden horse and equipping it with a small commando force hidden inside. When the horse had been constructed and manned, the main Greek force carried out a successful deception plan by sailing away from Troy. The Trojans believed that their enemies had abandoned the siege and were going back to their own country. The Greeks however, had only sailed just beyond the nearest headland, and were in fact anchored nearby. They had left behind a man named Sinon, who must have been quite an actor, because he was able to convince the Trojans that he was a deserter. More importantly, he also convinced them to tow the wooden horse into Troy.

---

use of their famous wooden horse, as related above, placing 100 warriors inside and pretending to withdraw the rest of their forces to the island of Bozcaada (Tenedos). The ruse worked, the city was subdued, and Helen was returned to her husband. The story is told in the Iliad, Odyssey, and Aeneid. There is considerable historical evidence to support the fact that a war did take place at Troy, although none of the legend of the horse has been confirmed. David Eggenberger, *An Encyclopedia of Battles*, Dover Publications, Inc., New York, 1985, pp. 445-446.

Under the cover of darkness, the task force emerged from the horse and opened a gate in the wall. The rest of the Greek army had meanwhile stealthily returned and had taken up a position just outside the city walls. Achieving complete surprise, the Greeks stormed into Troy and after fierce house-to-house fighting, burning, and looting as they advanced, they forced the Trojans to surrender. The victorious Greeks captured Helen, the woman who started it all by eloping with the Trojan prince, Paris. The Greeks then sacked Troy, killed its king, enslaved its women, and then sailed home with their prisoners.[61]

Triumphant Achilles dragging Hector's body around Troy,
from a panoramic fresco of the Achilleion by Franz Matsch.

Later defensive works would require more direct methods of overcoming a defender's wall than a wooden horse. Philip II of Macedon used siege engines and the services of Greek engineers to great effect in his assaults on the cities of Perinthus and Byzantium, and his son, Alexander the Great was also reputedly a master of siegecraft.[62] He demonstrated his skill in this area at the siege of Tyre.[63]

"MADE IN JERUSALEM ENGINES"

The use of siegecraft and machines to defeat fortresses and defensive positions predates recorded time. They were known to the men of the Old Testament, such as King Uzziah of Judah who "made

---

[61] Archaeologists have determined that the city of Troy was destroyed about the middle of the 13th century BC. It is possible that enemy infiltration brought the long siege to an end, horse, or no horse. The main source for the history is the *Iliad*. Charles Connell, op. cit., p. 21-21.

[62] F.E. Adcock, *The Greek and Macedonian Art of War*, University of California Press, Berkley, 1957, p. 57-62.

[63] Eyewitness accounts of the daring exploits of Alexander unfortunately do not exist. What we know about him comes from secondary sources. Arrian (first century BC) refers to the works of Ptolemy, a general of Alexander, and Aristobolus, whose writings are lost. Diodorus Siculus (first century BC) and Quintus Curtius (first century AD) no doubt had access to earlier histories that have been destroyed.

in Jerusalem engines, invented by cunning men, to be on the towers and upon the bulwarks, to shoot arrows and great stones withal."[64]

Over the years many ingenious siege devices would be invented. Archimedes is known to have designed and manufactured a giant missile-launcher that could throw an 1800-lb boulder for the defense of Syracuse in 215 BC.[65] Other machines were used to fling Greek fire, balls of lead, quick-lime, red-hot sand, boiling water, iron-tipped poles, and huge lumps of baked clay that disintegrated on contact and could not be fired back by the enemy.[66]

GREEK FIRE, C672

Greek fire was an incendiary weapon used by the Eastern Roman (Byzantine) Empire that was first developed c.672. The Byzantines typically used it in naval battles to great effect, as it could continue burning while floating on water. It provided a technological advantage and was responsible for many key Byzantine military victories, most notably the salvation of Constantinople from two Arab sieges, thus securing the Empire's survival.

The impression made by Greek fire on the western European Crusaders was such that the name was applied to any sort of incendiary weapon, including those used by Arabs, the Chinese, and the Mongols. However, these were different mixtures and not the same formula as the Byzantine Greek fire, which was a closely guarded state secret. Byzantines also used pressurized nozzles or *siphons* to project the liquid onto the enemy.

The composition of Greek fire remains a matter of speculation and debate, with various proposals including combinations of pine resin, naphtha, quicklime, calcium phosphide, sulfur, or niter.

---

[64] *The Holy Bible*, King James Version, Thomas Nelson Inc., Camden, New Jersey, 1970, *2 Chronicles*, Chapter 26, Verse 15, p. 341.

[65] Anthony Kemp, op. cit., p. 14.

[66] Greek fire was a name given by the Crusaders to various inflammable mixtures they encountered in their wars against the Muslims. The Byzantines did not call it Greek fire (they regarded themselves as Romans), but Maritime or Sea Fire. The Byzantines reportedly introduced the weapon in 672 at the first Saracenic siege of Constantinople. The exact composition of Greek fire is unknown, but it likely consisted of variations of an oil or petroleum based substance with pitch to make it burn longer, sulphur to make it stick, and quicklime to make it ignite on contact with water. These ingredients were difficult to extinguish, and only sand, vinegar or urine were apparently effective in putting the fire out. The Arab name for the same substance was "Naptha," and they made highly effective use of it against the Crusader's siege engines. The Arabs used small copper, glass or pottery containers filled with naptha and thrown as a form of hand grenade. Hollow arrowheads packed with naptha and sprinkled with powdered black sulphur were turned into arrows which sprang into flame as they traveled through the air. Ordinary flaming arrows with straw and cotton soaked in tar were also used. At sea, naptha was packed into brass-bound wooden tubes and fired by pumping water into the tubes at high pressure. The water ignited the naptha and the combined explosion and water pressure projected the naptha a considerable distance with great effect on wooden ships.

(Harper's engraving)
Engraving of a 13th century catapult throwing Greek fire.

The Catapult, painting by Sir Edward Poynter.

Roman soldiers manning a siege engine for an attack on the walls of Carthage, during the siege which ended in the destruction of Carthage in 146 BC. The image is from a painting by Sir E. Poynter showing a torsion powered arrow shooting catapult crewed by roman soldiers and sheltered under a protective shed. This torsion catapult, powered by a twisted skein of rope, or horsehair, is a cross between Archimedes spring engine and a Roman mangonel or onager. The soldier standing at the top of frame is setting the missile, while the rest of the crew draws down the arm. When released, the arm, complete with fist, strikes the missile and sends it off on a ballistic path toward the enemy. The famous command of Cato the Elder, "Delenda est Carthago" (quoted in Pultarch's "Life of Cato") is carved in the wood of the huge catapult.

Because of their nature and size, solid foundations were needed to support siege engines. The vibration of a torsion device could do as much damage to walls and towers as all the efforts of an attacker combined. Three basic forms of siege artillery came into early use. They were collectively known as "petrarri", or "stone-throwers." The mangonel was an early form of mortar, which used torsion as a source of launching power. Two stout posts were mounted on a firm chassis and joined together with skeins of rope. A beam with a hollowed-out spoon-shaped depression at the throwing end would be placed in-between the two posts. The missile, usually a stone or in some cases a fire pot would be inserted in the scoop; the rope would be twisted by a windlass to create torsion, and the ammunition would be released on command. This would cause the beam to snap forward sharply, propelling its load in a high-arcing trajectory towards the intended target. Dead animals, the heads of prisoners and other items could also be launched. These weapons were not very accurate but could be effective when bombarding the interior structures of a castle, spreading alarm and confusion.[67]

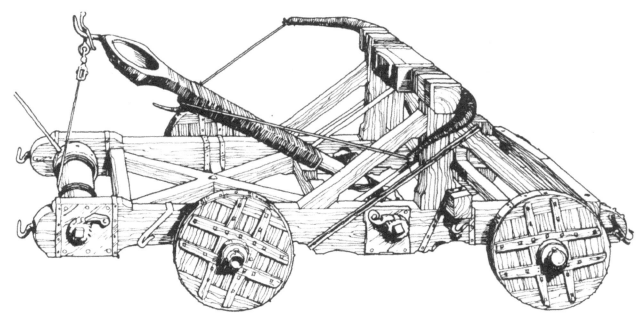

Roman Mangonel

The second type of siege engine used tension as the propelling power for its missiles. These were known as "ballista," and they were similar to a large crossbow, working on the same principle. Like the mangonel, the ballista originated with the Greeks, and it was in use at the siege of Rome in 537 AD. Procopius described them in use as "machines, which have the general shape of a bow, but in the middle

---

[67]   Ibid., pp. 162-163.

is a hollow piece of horn fixed loosely to the bow, and lying over a straight stock.[68] When intending to fire at the enemy, you pull back the short strong cord that joins the arms of the bow, and place in the horn a bolt, four times as thick as the ordinary arrow, but furnished with wooden projections exactly reproducing the shape of the feathers. Men standing on either side of the weapon draw back the cord with winches. When they let it go, the horn rushes forward and discharges the bolt." Procopius later wrote that he saw a mailed Goth impaled against a tree by a bolt from a ballista. In another case a monk named Abbo described a "ballista" in use at the siege of Paris in 885-886 AD.[69] He saw a bolt go through three Danes all at once, leaving them like a "chicken on a spit." Abbot Ebolus, a skilled member of the church militant who had fired the bolt, called down to his comrades and told them they should pick the Danes up and take them to the kitchen. The ballista had a flat trajectory and was reasonably accurate, as it could be aimed by traversing its carriage. Its primary use was as an anti-personnel weapon, although a few versions were used to throw stones.[70]

Roman Ballista.

---

[68] Procopius was a Byzantine historian, born in the latter years of the fifth century at Caesarea in Palestine. He died some time after 562 AD. Little is known of his background except that by a legal and literary training he qualified himself for the civil service. As early as 527 AD, before Justin's death, he became counselor, assessor, and secretary to Belisarius, whose fortunes, and campaigns he followed for the next twelve or fifteen years. He was raised to the dignity of an *illustrius*. He is reckoned the greatest of the later Greek historians. Internet: http://www.newadvent.org/cathen/12450a.htm.

[69] Between 885-886 AD, Viking bands of 100-200 men joined together to form armies. One of these Viking force besieged Paris for 11 months, and it may have involved close to 30,000 men. Vikings also developed their own cavalry units.

[70] Anthony Kemp, op. cit., p. 164.

Roman Ballista. The early Roman *ballistae* were made of wood and held together with iron plates around the frames and iron nails in the stand. The main stand had a slider on the top, into which were loaded the bolts or stone 'shot'. Attached to this, at the back, was a pair of winches and a claw, used to ratchet the bowstring back to the armed firing position. A slider passed through the field frames of the weapon, in which were located the torsion springs (rope made of animal sinew, which were twisted around the bow arms, which in turn were attached to the bowstring. Drawing the bowstring back with the winches twisted the already taut springs, storing the energy to fire the projectiles.

The *ballista* was a highly accurate weapon (there are many accounts right from its early history of single soldiers being picked off by the operators), but some design aspects meant it could compromise its accuracy for range. The lightweight bolts could not gain the high momentum of the stones over the same distance as those thrown by the later onagers, trebuchets, or mangonels; these could be as heavy as 90–135 kg (200-300 pounds). The Romans continued the development of the *ballista*, and it became a highly prized and valued weapon in the army of the Roman Empire. It was used, just before the start of the empire, by Julius Caesar during his conquest of Gaul and on both of his expeditions to Britain.

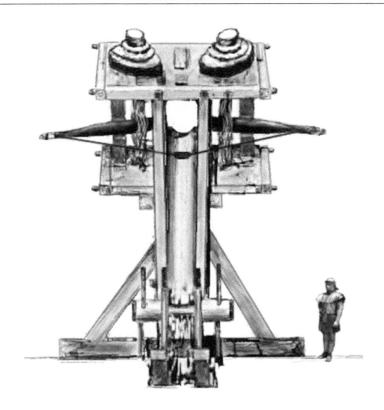

A Roman one talent *ballista* (26 kg weight projectile). The heaviest versions could shoot up to three talents (78 kg), possibly much more.

Medieval Ballista.

The Middle Ages saw the innovation of the third type of siege engine, known as the trébuchet. The trébuchet was a giant sling, which was worked by dropping a counterweight on the end of a throwing beam. It would be classed as a howitzer in present-day artillery terms, but its accuracy was greater than the mangonel, as its range could be adjusted by moving the weight along the arm.[71]

The trebuchet is the only major siege engine that was invented during the Middle Ages. It relied on a counterpoise and was simpler in design and construction than most others. Prince Louis of France is credited with bringing it to England in 1216. Various engines were constructed in the king's North Wales castles of Deganwy and Dyserth, where four "switches" were built for catapults and mangonels. It was usual to drag these machines around the country as need arose.[72]

Siege towers came into use early in the wars, enabling attackers to fight on the same level as their opponents. Many of the larger ones were equipped with one of the missile throwing devices described in the preceding paragraphs, and most of them had drawbridges so that the soldiers manning them would have easy access to the ramparts and battlements. Some of them were mounted on great wheels of solid oak, consisted of several stories, and rose to a height of 150.' The largest siege tower recorded was one Richard I had constructed tall enough to overlook the walls of Acre in 1191.[73]

In 440 BC, Artemon used siege towers in the siege of Samos, but failed to take the city. In 424 BC the Boetians may have used a primitive flame-thrower which consisted of a hollow wooden tube that held a cauldron of burning sulphur, charcoal, and pitch at one end, against the wooden walls of Delium. In 397 BC, Dionysisus successfully used siege towers and rudimentary catapults in the attack on Motya.[74]

Most siege engines were capable of throwing a stone of 300-lbs or more a distance of at least 500'. Stones of this weight have been excavated at Kenilworth Castle, England, where they were probably used in the siege of 1266. Siege engines were heavy and clumsy. The historian Kendall claimed that the seven trébuchets used at Berkhamsted in England, called for fifty-six long-carts for their transport. Generally, it the majority of large siege engines were constructed at the site, as they were when the Welsh attacked the castles of Mold and Dyserth. Wooden towers were sometimes pushed close to the walls, which were then assaulted by foot soldiers gathered on their upper levels. The Justice of Chester was in 1244 ordered to have four good strong wooden towers built in the forest of the Wirral and to have two such towers made as close as possible to the border to carry wherever the king may wish in Wales.[75]

[71]   Ibid., p. 165.
[72]   N. J. G. Pounds, *The Medieval Castle in England, and Wales.* Cambridge University Press, 1990. Internet: http://www.castlewales.com/siege.html.
[73]   Philip Warner, op. cit., p. 29.
[74]   Internet: http://www.au.af.mil/au/awc/awcgate/gabrmetz/gabr000d.htm.
[75]   N. J. G. Pounds, *The Medieval Castle in England, and Wales.* Cambridge University Press, 1990. Internet: http://www.castlewales.com/siege.html.

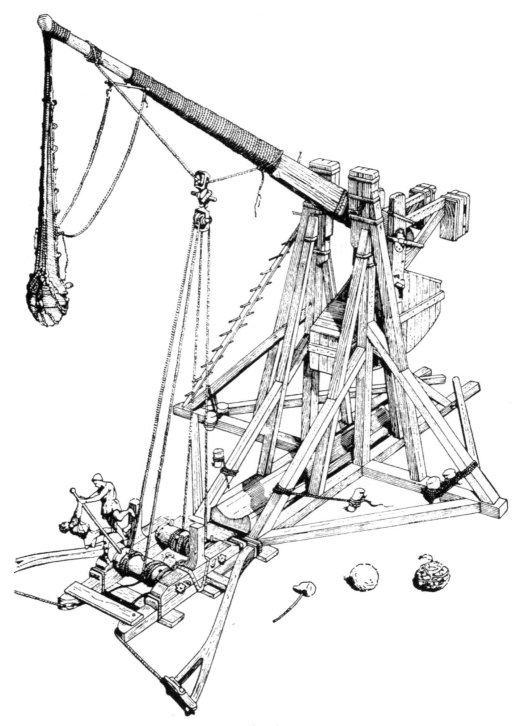

Trébuchet

As assault methods developed in sophistication, it was found that the wall-walk of a fortress or castle could be gained with the use of a device called a "belfry." This was a massive wheeled tower, generally higher than the wall being attacked. The moat or ditch would be filled in with rubble and the belfry would then be pushed across it and pressed up against the curtain wall. The belfries had a wooden framework construction with ladders inside which led up to the fighting level. It could be rigged with a drawbridge or a ramp equipped with hooks, which could be dropped onto the castle's parapet when the assault was ready to be launched. The belfry could have a crenellated roof built above the ramp occupied by archers who kept up a steady covering fire on the defenders to keep them from dislodging the ramp. The whole structure would be covered with wet hides to make it as fireproof as possible. The belfry could also house a battering ram at its base level, which could simultaneously work away at dislodging masonry.

Siege tower (2).

Belfry/Siege Tower

The siege tower was not necessarily used to conduct a direct assault on the walls. In some cased they were built close to the castle under siege as a form of counter-castle. In this case, they were used to guard the attacking force's camp or to sweep a field of fire with the use of crossbows from the roof. Some of these structures were built strong enough to mount stone-throwing engines from the top deck. These counter-castles were sometimes referred to as "malvoisins," meaning "bad neighbours."

Medieval Siege Tower.

Belfries suffered from the disadvantage of weight, and they were vulnerable to fire. They had to be built on site by competent workmen, who also had to ensure that the ditch was filled with adequate materials solid enough to bear the weight of the siege engine as it was rolled forward. There are many reports of the use of belfries. In 1096, Anna Comnena recorded the building of a belfry by Raymond of

Saint-Gilles for the siege of Nicaea, describing it as, "a wooden tower, circular in shape" covered inside and out "with leather hides and filled in the center with intertwined wickerwork.[76]

Bohemond of Taranto mounts the rampart of Antioch, engraving by Gustave Doré.

---

[76]   Anna Comnena (1083-1146), was a Byzantine historian and the eldest daughter of Alexios I Comnenos Emperor of Constantinople (1081-1118), and Irene She received, as was the custom for Byzantine princesses, an excellent education in the Greek classics, history, geography, mythology, and even philosophy. She was married to Nicephorus Bryennius, son of a former pretender to the imperial office, and in 1118 joined in a conspiracy to place her husband on the throne. Failing in her ambition she retired with her mother, the Empress Irene, to a monastery that the latter had founded, where she wrote the *Alexiad*, a 15-volume biography of her father's career from 1069 to his death in 1118. Internet: http://www.newadvent.org/cathen/12450a.htm.

During the siege of Dyrrachium in 1108, Bohemond built a four-sided tower on a wooden base that was high enough to dominate the towers of the city. It was pushed forward on rollers by soldiers who levered it up, in effect making it self-propelled. The many stories of the belfry had coverings with embrasures and openings all around from which volleys of arrows could be fired.[77]

As the towers were being assembled, battering rams were also being constructed and moved into place. Early versions used a hefty tree trunk with a metal head mounted on its end. Variations included a bore, wherein the tree was tipped with a metal spike. To protect the crew operating the battering ram, a covering penthouse or cat was constructed. The cat was essentially a long shed mounted on rollers or wheels and equipped with heavy roof timers from which the ram could be slung on chains. The team of ram-operators could consist of up to 100 men swinging the ram against the targeted wall or gate. The penthouse had a sharply pitched roof designed to deflect projectiles and had to be fireproofed with wet hides or metal plates. It had similar requirements to the belfry, in that the cat had to be used on a firm base such as a well-filled ditch. In some cases, the wheels were removed to give the ram a more solid foundation for the swinging movement.[78]

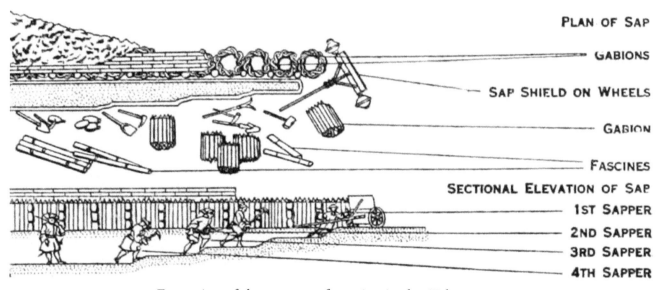

PLAN OF SAP

GABIONS

SAP SHIELD ON WHEELS

GABION

FASCINES

SECTIONAL ELEVATION OF SAP

1ST SAPPER

2ND SAPPER

3RD SAPPER

4TH SAPPER

Engraving of the process of sapping in the 17th century.

Penthouses and cats were also used to shelter miners and sappers. Joinville describes similar structures built by the engineers of St. Louis to shelter troops who were making a causeway across the Nile River in 1249. They were protected at each end by wooden towers, which served as gatehouses. Siege buildings could also be floated into place if the water routes provided adequate access. In 1218, as the warriors in the Fifth Crusade were besieging Damietta at the mouth of the Nile, they were held up by a tower in the middle of the river. A Crusader priest named Oliver Paderborn designed a floating belfry, which was mounted on boats and floated down onto the tower, which it succeeded in overcoming.[79]

---

[77] Anthony Kemp, op. cit., p.161.
[78] Ibid., p. 162.
[79] Ibid., p. 162.

Engraving of a Counter Ram in operation.

Defenders could make use of a counter-ram, a device which was dropped on a battering ram as it was about to hit so as to avoid repetitive impact at the same point. They could retaliate with their own catapults, throwing rocks down on the attackers from their towers and walls. Arrows and fire could also be thrown against the assaulting moving towers and battering rams. When the attackers dug tunnels, the besieged defenders dug counter tunnels through which they tried to penetrate the first tunnel to repel the attacking diggers known as "sappers."[80]

---

[80] Carlos Paluzie de Lescazes, *Castles of Europe*, Crescent Books, Barcelona, 1982, p. 21.

Rams in operation.

ROMAN SIEGE TACTICS

The Romans conducted attacks under the cover of their shields in an assault formation known as a "tortoise." From a woodcut in the 1585 edition of Vegetius' book *"De Re Militari,"* published in Antwerp.

A professional army with regular soldiers is the mainstay of most modern armies. Between 405 and 396 BC, Rome began regular payments to its troops inaugurating the concept of a regular career service. The Roman legion owed much of its success to its effective use of missile throwing machines such as the ballista, mounted on a carriage drawn by mules and served by ten men from the century to which the weapon belonged.[81] They were used not only to defend the entrenchments of camps, but were placed in

---

[81]   Trevor N. Dupuy, *The Evolution of Weapons and Warfare*, Hero Books, Fairfax, Virginia, 1984, p. 30.

the field in the rear of the heavy armed infantry. Each legion had 55 of these engines, as well as 10 onagri, one for each cohort. The onagri were drawn on ready-armed carriages by oxen and were primarily used to defend the camp works by throwing stones with a sling-like device, while the ballista threw darts.[82]

Roman advances in the design, mobility, and firepower of artillery produced the largest, longest-ranged, and most rapid-firing artillery pieces of the ancient world. Roman catapults were much larger than the old Greek models and were powered by torsion devices and springs made of sinew kept supple when stored in special canisters of oil. As Josephus recorded in his account of the siege of Jerusalem, the largest of these artillery pieces, the onager, (called the "wild ass" because of its kick), could hurl a 100-pound stone over 400 yards. Vegetius noted that each legion had 10 onagri, one per cohort, organic to its organization. Smaller versions of these machines, such as the scorpion and ballista were compact enough to be transported by horse or mule. These machines could fire a 7-10-lb stone over 300 yards. Caesar required that each legion carry 30 of these small machines, giving the legion a mobile, organic artillery capability. Smaller machines fired iron-tipped bolts. Designed much like the later crossbow but mounted on small platforms or legs, these machines, which required a two-man crew, could be used as rapid-fire field guns against enemy formations. They fired a 26-inch bolt over a range of almost 300 yards. Larger versions mounted on a wheeled frame were called *carroballistae* and required a 10-man crew. These machines could fire perhaps three to four bolts a minute and they were used to lay down a barrage of fire against enemy troop concentrations. They were the world's first rapid-fire field artillery guns.

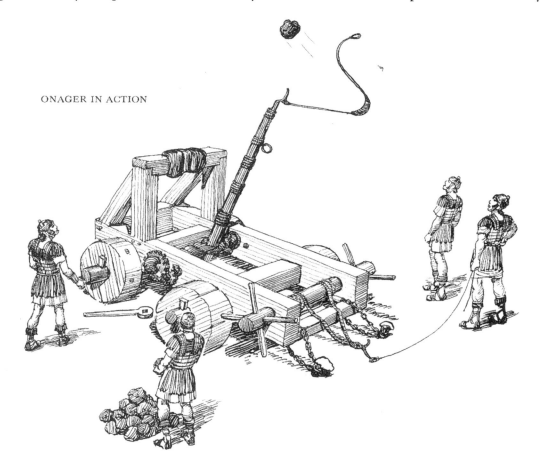

ONAGER IN ACTION

[82] Brigadier-General Thomas R. Phillips, *The Military Institutions of the Romans*, Flavius Vegetius, Stackpole Books, Harrisburg, Pennsylvania, 1965, p. 59-65.

Roman Onager in action. The *onager* was a post-classical Roman siege engine, which derived its name from the kicking action of the machine, similar to that of an onager (wild ass). It is a type of catapult that uses torsional pressure, generally from twisted rope, to store energy for the shot. The onager consisted of a frame placed on the ground to whose front end a vertical frame of solid timber was rigidly fixed; through the vertical frame ran an axle, which had a single stout spoke. On the extremity of the spoke was a sling used to launch a projectile. In action the spoke was forced down, against the tension of twisted ropes or other springs, by a windlass, and then suddenly released. The spoke thus kicked the crosspiece of the vertical frame, and the projectile at its extreme end was shot forward.

The onagers of the Roman Empire were mainly used for besieging forts or settlements. They would often be loaded with large stones or rocks that could be covered with a flammable substance and set alight. In the Middle Ages (recorded from around 1200 A.D.) a less powerful version of the onager was used that employed a fixed bowl rather than a sling, so that many small projectiles could be thrown, as opposed to a single large one. This engine was sometimes called the mangonel although the same name may have been used for a variety of siege engines.

The emergence of siegecraft as a basic requirement of Iron Age armies represented a major innovation in warfare. Without the ability rapidly to reduce cities and fortified strong points, no army on the march in hostile territory could hope to force a strategic decision with any rapidity. The very idea of empire would have been militarily unthinkable in much the same way as it was for the classical Greek armies which had no siegecraft capability. The search for more efficient ways to destroy fortifications produced, perhaps somewhat by accident, the new combat arm of artillery. While Alexander was the first to use it, the Romans gave birth to the idea of using artillery as antipersonnel weapons. Both siege engines and artillery represent the birth of a major new idea in the technology of war, an idea that came to further fruition with introduction of gunpowder a thousand years later.[83]

In 156 BC the Romans had decreed that the inhabitants of the city of Carthage were to move to a site 10 miles from the sea, a condition equivalent to a death sentence. The Carthaginians made their living from the sea, and if they moved inland, they would be left defenceless against attacks from the Numidians. If they abandoned Carthage, they would die either way. The Romans delayed out of a belief that they could capture Carthage at will. This underestimation of one's enemy would prove to be a recurrent theme in most of the battles discussed in this book.

---

[83]   Internet: http://www.au.af.mil/au/awc/awcgate/gabrmetz/gabr000e.htm.

CATAPULT FOR JAVELINS. The legionary is dressed for winter

Roman Javelin catapult.

The Roman delay gave the Carthaginian inhabitants the time they needed to reinforce the city walls and defenses, and to manufacture shields, swords, and javelins in enormous quantities. The ladies of Carthage even cut their hair to be twisted into bowstrings.

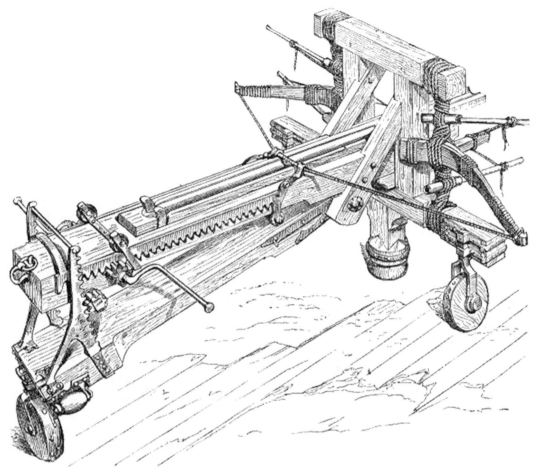

Catapult drawing from the *Dictionary of French Architecture from 11th to 16th Century.*

The Roman siege was long and difficult, and they were only able to make a breach in the Carthaginian walls after suffering heavy losses, and even then, were driven off. Swamp fever added to the attrition of the Roman soldiers. The Carthaginians fought hard, and when the wind was right, they sent fireships into the Roman fleet. To compound the problem, there were 23 miles of fortifications in place. The Romans were therefore unable to guard access to all points, and thus the Carthaginians had no difficulties with resupply.

The arrival of a seasoned Roman commander named Scipio changed the face of the costly siege. He rejuvenated his troops, and then set about building an earthwork barrier to sever the Carthaginian leader Hasdrubal's link with the interior. Scipio then had a massive mole constructed to block the outer mouth of the city harbor, thereby completing the encirclement, and creating a strong blockade of the city. Rather than sustain heavy losses that might jeopardize the assault, Scipio had every building that stood between his army and the citadel burned to the ground. The rubble was then cleared away to allow the free deployment of his forces.

After seven days of fighting, 50,000 Carthaginians surrendered. Their lives were spared, but the remaining 900 fought to the death. In spite of the victory, Scipio saw the pendulum in mid swing, and predicted that what had happened to Carthage would one day happen to Rome.[84]

So, it would come to pass, but when Rome's greatest enemy, the Gothic King Alaric invaded Italy he didn't need a secret weapon to enter the heavily fortified city. The Romans had treated their slaves

---

[84] Charles Connell, op. cit., p. 42-43.

so badly that the slaves themselves opened the gates on the night of 23 August 410 AD, allowing the Barbarians to enter.[85] Treachery could be a remarkably effective siege breaker.

CELTS AND GAULS

The Romans had a long history of battles with the Celts and Gauls. The Celts had their origins in the Danube region of Eastern Europe and gradually migrated towards France, Spain, the British Isles, and Italy. In 387 BC they engaged and defeated a large body of Roman soldiers. Eventually they settled in all the countries of Europe they had overrun, but the greatest concentration of Celtic settlements was in Gaul, which is now modern France. In this same era, the Romans had gradually occupied and imposed their form of government on the Mediterranean coast of Gaul. Between 58 BC and 51 BC, Caesar conquered all of Gaul in a series of battles against the Helveti (58 BC), the Belgii (57 BC), in Brittany and Aquitaine (56 BC). He pursued the Germans and crossed the Rhine and later invaded England (55 BC). In 52 BC he engaged and defeated Vercingetorix, the leader of the Gauls at Alesia in present day France.[86]

Caesar's engineers built "siege terraces" consisting of logs piled in layers enclosing a core of earth and rubble, to defeat the armies of Gaul. Wooden towers several stories high were erected on the terrace, and artillery and snipers placed in them. Unfortunately for Caesar, the Gauls under the leadership of Vercingetorix were ingenious at making the Roman terraces fall in by undermining, as demonstrated at the siege of Avaricum in 52 BC. The Gauls were expert at this because of their extensive experience in mining iron and were thoroughly familiar with the techniques of working underground. The Gauls were also skilled at constructing their own walls complete with towers, furnished with platforms, and protected by hides. Caesar was forced to out build them with his own towers and siege works in order to win the battle of Avaricum.[87]

In order to defeat the Gauls during the battle at Alesia, Caesar's Roman legions had to build a line of fortifications ten miles long around it, with outer walls facing both ways to keep out a relieving army. In effect, to conduct the siege, Caesar had to make a fortress of his own.[88]

After the Romans had captured Gaul, they turned their attention to Germany. Caesar dealt with a great number of opponents who made use of a great variety of tactics. Of all their opponents however, the chroniclers from Tacitus onwards describe the fierce bravery of the Germans and their military effectiveness. The German forces were essentially comprised of men related to one another by ties of blood within a village and organized into a group or tribe known as a "hundred." They did not drill or train as the Roman legions did, but their inner cohesion, based on the certainty of being able to rely on those around them, was superior to that shown by the Romans. When it was defeated, a Roman force usually scattered. A Germanic force in similar straits usually remained intact because it was an organic body.[89]

---

[85]   Charles Connell, op. cit., p. 49-50. The Barbarians crossed the Rhine in 406 AD, and the Visigoth, Alaric, took Rome in 410 AD. Genseric's Vandals took Hippo, St Augustine's city, in 431 AD, then Carthage in 439. They sacked Rome in 455 AD.

[86]   Ibid., p. 84. In 52 BC Julius Caesar defeated and took prisoner Vercingetorix the Celtic leader, at Alesia following its siege and capture. The scarlet cloaked Caesar led 40,000 Legionaries, including some German cavalry, against 100,000 Infantry and 8,000 cavalry under Vercingetorix and Vercassivellaunus. Vercingetorix was taken to Rome in Chains and beheaded.

[87]   Julius Caesar, *The Conquest of Gaul*, translated by S.A. Handford from *The Gallic War* (52 BC), Penguin Books, Harmondsworth, Middlesex, England, 1967, p. 192.

[88]   Julius Caesar, op. cit., p. 223-233.

[89]   H.W. Koch, *Medieval Warfare*, Bison Books Limited, London, 1982, pp. 12-13.

Although the Romans considered the Germanic tribes to be little more than a rabble, their fighting methods were very efficient. Tacitus described the fighting methods used by the Germans as the use of tactical bodies of men which were as deep as they were wide, with the front, rear and both flanks being equally strong, and consisting of 400 men, 20 deep and 20 wide, or 10,000 men, 100 deep and 100 wide. The most exposed positions of such a formation were the warriors at the flanks of the first line, because they would be threatened by their opponent from the front as well as from the side. This square was the basic tactical formation of the Germans as the phalanx was the original tactical formation of the Romans.[90] In the attack, the phalanx had the advantage of bringing more weapons to bear than the square and had greater maneuverability for its wings. The weakness of the Roman Phalanx was the vulnerability of its flanks, particularly when attacked by cavalry, and cavalry was once of the German's strengths. To show equal strength in all directions, the Germans preferred deep formations.[91]

The initial attempts to make inroads into Germany by the Roman Commander Drusus ended in failure and he was forced to withdraw. In his second incursion he used the waterways and built a canal from the Rhine to the Ysel, which gave him access to the North Sea coast via the Zuider Zee. He also used the Lippe River which was navigable in the spring up to its source. He moved along the Lippe upwards into Westphalia, and at the point where the river was no longer navigable, he built a Castle at Aliso. When the Romans attempted to use the castle as a base to establish their supremacy, three of their legions and their auxiliary forces under their commander, Governor P. Quinctilius Varius, were annihilated by the Germans in the Teutoburg Forest in 9 AD.[92]

This came about because Publius Quinctilius Varus had been directed to hold the frontier in Westphalia area. Marching between two rivers (Ems and Weser) which limited maneuver and mobility, his troops were picked off by Germans over several days. By the end, all 20,000 were gone and Varus

---

[90] The Phalanx had proven itself to be effective, but if it was penetrated, the formation tended to fall apart. As an example, the phalanx was used at the Battle of Pydna (near Mount Olympus in Greece) which took place 22 June 168 BC. This was the culminating battle of the Third Macedonian War (172-167 BC). Rome had entered the war on the side of an old ally named Pergamum, when Perseus of Macedonia had tried to murder Eumenes II, ruler of Pergamum. Perseus had defeated three Roman armies in the previous three years. Lucius Aemilius Paulus, son of a Roman consul, arrived with reinforcements. Paulus soon tried an envelopment of the Macedonians, but it failed when Perseus withdrew across the Aeson River. On the afternoon of the 22 June, the battle broke out by accident as both sides were watering their horses. Perseus took the initiative and attacked across the river with his Macedonian phalanx, and the Romans fell back rapidly. But the rolling terrain soon caused gaps in the phalanx, which Paulus saw and was able to take advantage of after rallying his troops. Once penetrated the phalanx collapsed. The Macedonians lost 20,000 killed and 11,000 captured (Perseus escaped but later surrendered). Roman losses were less than 1,000. Macedonia was later partitioned by the Romans into four republics under the protection of Rome.

[91] H.W. Koch, *Medieval Warfare*, Bison Books Limited, London, 1982, p. 13.

[92] The legions under Varus were marching during the autumn with their baggage train to return to their winter quarters on the Rhine or at Aliso. The Roman force consisted of three legions, six cohorts of auxiliaries, and three troops of cavalry, with an estimated strength of between 12,000 to 18,000 combatants and another 12,000 personnel with the baggage train. On hearing the first battle cries of the Germans, the vanguard at the head of the column halted near present day Herford where they quickly fortified a suitable place and surrounded it with a stockade and a moat. As the column arrived it assembled inside the stockade. Varus abandoned his surplus baggage and marched out the next day intending to reach Aliso, but German attacks forced them into a blocked gorge under heavy rains. Roman counter attacks failed to make headway over the muddy ground. Trapped in the Doeren Gorge without any hope of escape, morale disintegrated. Varus and a number of his officers committed suicide and the bearer of the Roman eagle jumped into a swamp to ensure that Rome's insignia would not fall into German hands. The remainder surrendered except for a few, primarily cavalry, who managed to escape and make their way to Aliso where they were besieged. They successfully broke out of the fortress and got back to Roman lines along the Rhine. The Germans, expecting a strong Roman force to return to avenge their comrades, withdrew back into the interior. H.W. Koch, *Medieval Warfare*, Bison Books Limited, London, 1982, p. 14.

committed suicide to avoid capture. News of the massacre prompted Rome to decide the Rhine River could be their eastern border instead of the Elbe River. The Britons continued to put up a spirited defense as well, and in 60 AD, Boudicca burned Roman London. Under the Roman Governor Paulinus, however, the final outcome was more successful for the Roman Legions.[93]

(Paul Walter Photo)
Boudicca statue, Westminster, London.

ICENI QUEEN BOUDICCA, WAR WITH THE ROMANS, C61 AD.

Under Emperor Nero, Roman rule over Britain was benevolent and constructive, except in East Anglia (modern Norfolk and Suffolk). The death of the Iceni king in 61 AD opened the way to plunder and cruelties on the part of the occupying Roman forces. The Iceni took up arms under the leadership of the widowed Queen Boudicca (Boadicea), and attacked the undefended Roman town of Camulodunum (Colchester), slaughtering the Roman settlers and the Britons who collaborated with them. Hurrying

---

[93]   David Eggenberger, *An Encyclopedia of Battles*, Dover Publications, Inc., New York, 1985, pp. 460-464.

from Lindum (Lincoln) to put down the revolt, the Ninth Legion was overcome by sheer numbers and virtually annihilated.

At Gloucester, the Second Legion commander. Poenius Postumus, refused to leave the protection of his encampment. The other two legions in Britain, the Fourteenth and Twentieth, under Governor Suetonius Paulinus, stood in Wales. Before they could intervene, Boudicca's rebels attacked Londinium (London), and burned it to the ground after massacring its inhabitants. Her forces also attacked Verulamium (Saint Albans) killing an estimated 70,000 people in the three rebel onslaughts. Paulinus force-marched his two legions (10,000 men) to the scene from Wales, and, choosing his ground carefully to give maximum advantage to his vastly outnumbered soldiers, directed a coordinated attack on the Briton rebel horde.

The battle was fought without mercy, even for the women and children in Boudicca's wagon train. Roman discipline and tactical skill triumphed in the face of superior numbers. Almost 80,000 Britons were killed at a cost of 400 dead legionaries and a somewhat larger number of wounded. The Iceni queen took poison, while at Gloucester the news of the battle induced Postumus to stab himself to death. The victory of Paulinus gave him rank with Domitius Corbolo, in the East, as the best Roman General of the first century AD.

ISRAELITE EXODUS, C1263 BC

Circa 1263 BC is the approximate date for the Exodus of the Israelites from Egypt under the leadership of Moses. Since that time there have been many conflicts in the region their descendants now occupy in the Middle East, with Jerusalem at the centre of much it.

The destruction of Jerusalem by the Romans, under the command of Titus, AD 70.
Painting by David Roberts.

SIEGE OF JERUSALEM, 70 AD

There have been at least nine separate sieges of Jerusalem, making it one of the most contested and fought over cities in the world.[94] This account concerns the siege that took place in 70 AD, when Rome's General Titus Caesar marched against Jerusalem.[95] Flavius Josephus was a Jew who had gone over to the Romans, and the narrative that follows is an adaptation of chronicle he kept as the siege unfolded. The auxiliaries sent by Rome's allies led the column followed by engineers to ensure clear roadways and to lay out campsites ahead of the marching army. These were followed by the commander's baggage train and then by fully armed soldiers to escort and support them. Titus came next accompanied by a select bodyguard and then ranks of pikemen. The trail was completed with all of the horse that belonged to that particular legion.

The next column included all of the siege engines accompanied by the tribunes and the leaders of the cohorts, with their selected aide-de-camps and retainers.[96] The ensigns and the eagle symbols led by trumpeters followed in succession, and then came the main body of the army in their ranks, every legion being six men deep. The legion's baggage accompanied by the servants belonging to each legion came next, with the mercenaries next to last with the rearguard protecting the trail of the column.

Titus led his army well, and marched through Samaria to Gophan, a city that had been previously captured by his father, and which was at that time garrisoned by Roman soldiers. Here he spent the night and continued his march in the morning up to a valley the Jews had named the Valley of Thorns. Here he pitched his camp close to a village called Gabath-Saul (Hill of Saul) not far from Jerusalem. He selected 600 of his best horsemen and conducted a reconnaissance of the city in order to learn more about the strength of the Jews and to determine if they were prepared to fight or run. He had been provided with limited intelligence information that assessed the Jews were only acting out of fear under the dominion of seditious renegades and robbers, and they actually wanted peace.

---

[94]   The cities of Adrianople (Edirne), Constantinople (Istanbul), and Rome have each been the site of seven separate battles and sieges; Warsaw has borne the brunt of six, Pavia five, and Alexandria, Baghdad, Paris, Prague and Ravenna four each. These cities continue to stand, although the 20th century aerial bombardments of Baghdad may be counted as more recent additions to its score. David Eggenberger, *An Encyclopedia of Battles*, Dover Publications, Inc., New York, 1985, p. iv.

[95]   Jerusalem was besieged and destroyed in 586 BC by Nebuchadnezzar II, King of Babylon, (all its leading personalities were exiled in Mesopotamia, and in turn, Judah ceased to exist as a political entity); Antiochus IV destroyed the wall of Jerusalem between 168-165 BC; the Roman General Pompeii the Great laid siege to Jerusalem in 66 BC, although the city held out for three years. Titus, the son of Titus Flavius Vespasian conducted the 4th siege as related above. The 5th siege took place in 615 AD during the Byzantine-Persian wars, when the Persians stormed the city, reportedly killing 50,000 and taking another 35,000 prisoners back to Persia. The Muslims led by caliph Omar I besieged Jerusalem in 637, taking and holding it until the First Crusade in 1099. Led by Raymond IV of Toulouse, Robert of Normandy, Godfrey de Bouillon, Robert of Flanders and Tancred of Taranto, the Christian army of 1,200 knights and 11,000 foot soldiers began the siege of Jerusalem on 7 June 1099, seizing it by 15 July 1099, and launching a wholesale slaughter of 70,000 of the defenders. The Crusaders were themselves defeated at the Horns of Hattin near Tiberias in 1187, and were therefore unable to come to the aid of Balian of Ibelin when Saladin began his siege of Jerusalem on 20 September 1187. It was over by 2 October with some captives ransomed and the rest sold as slaves. In 1948, the city again came under siege by the Arabs during the first of the modern-era Arab-Israeli wars. The defense of Jerusalem came under the command of Colonel David Shaltiel of the Hagana, and later with Colonel Moshe Dayan on 4 August 1948. When the cease-fire finally came into effect, the city was divided with part of it remaining inside Jordan and remained so until the 1967 six-day war when it came under full Israeli control. Ibid, pp. 211-212.

[96]   The siege of Jerusalem by Titus in AD 70 was conducted with the help of onagers reportedly capable of firing a 20-kilogram stone some 400 meters, although its impact velocity at that range cannot have been high. Anne Gael & Serge Chirol, *Châteaux et Sites de La France Medievale*, Hachette Realites, Paris, 1978, p. 157.

No one appeared from the gates to meet him as he rode along the straight road which led to the wall of the city, but as he veered off the main road that led down towards a tower named Psephinos at the head of his band of horsemen, a great host of Jews combatants suddenly charged at him from a tower gate in the wall known as the Women's Towers, sited near monuments erected for Queen Helena. The Jewish fighting patrol intercepted Titus's horsemen and cut them off from the main body of his reconnaissance party, hemming in threatening Titus and many of his staff. He found it impossible to move forward because the way was obstructed with trenches extending from the main wall that were used to preserve the gardens outside the city. These gardens were full of smaller walls, which ran at oblique angles to the main wall and prevented his escape. The route to his rear presented an equally impossible exit because of the multitude of Jewish combatants that lay between him and his main body of horsemen. Very few of his soldiers were even aware that he had been surrounded, and many withdrew believing Titus was still with them.

Titus could see no other way about but to turn around and charge the Jews, sword in hand, shouting to the crew trapped with him to stay close and to follow him at the gallop into the midst of the sea of soldiers attacking him. Fortune favors the brave, for although Titus was not wearing his helmet and breast plate (he was only conducting an initial reconnaissance and hadn't planned on a battle) and great numbers of darts were thrown at him, he succeeded in breaking through the horde of fighting men without being injured. Any that got close to him were dispatched with deliberate and intensely cutting sword strokes, and others were ridden down under him amidst a great deal of noise. The angry Jews shouted to their companions to stop him and rushed him in great numbers, all of which he cut to pieces or were boldly ridden down. His followers stayed close to him, riding with force and fury, although they were being cut and slashed on all sides. The Roman horsemen were well aware that their only hope of escape lay in assisting Titus in opening a way through the attackers. Two of Titus's companions were surrounded, with one being killed by darts along with his horse, and the second being killed as he jumped off his horse to fight at close quarters. Titus succeeded in escaping with the rest and made it back to his camp in one piece. The Jews for their part revelled in their perceived success and placed a great deal of false hope in their chances of outfighting the Romans in the siege to follow.

The night a second legion marched from Emmaus to join Caesar, and the following day he moved his camp to a place called Scopus. From here he could see the walls of Jerusalem and the great temple, which rose inside it. His camp lay to the north of the city and ran into the plain of Scopus (the prospect) a relatively short distance from the city. He ordered the Roman camp to be fortified for the two legions that were with him. He also directed that another camp be fortified, not far behind the main camp to protect another legion (the 5th) which was marching to join them and which he wanted to be concealed from the Jewish defenders. An additional legion (the 10th), which had marched from Jericho, was also in place at a pass which led into the city. Vespasian had taken this pass to prevent an ambush against his forces at this site. These legions were ordered to make their camps just outside Jerusalem on the Mount of Olives, which was located on the east side of the city separated by the deep valley of Kedron.

Up until this point, several rival factions within the city had fought against each other in a struggle for political supremacy. These combatants had set aside their differences and joined forces to fight the Romans. They observed the Romans constructing three separate fortified camps and realized they would be trapped if they did not act against them. A sortie was prepared and launched against the 10th legion as they were fortifying their camp, catching a number of different work parties unarmed. A great number became casualties in the surprise attack. Many began to withdraw, and the battle would have turned into a Roman slaughter if Titus had not learned of the raid and launched an immediate counterattack which he led himself against the Jewish flank with a select band of troops. His assault on the Jewish raiders pressed them back, with a great number of them being killed or wounded and the remainder being put to flight. Reinforcements arrived for both sides, and the battle continued on into the valley.

Titus brought those who had joined him around to the walls to prevent the Jews from making anymore sallies and ordered the remainder of the legion to return to the upper part of the mountain and to finish fortifying their camp.

The Jews interpreted this disciplined marching withdrawal to be a sign that the Romans were running away. A Jewish watchman therefore gave the defenders inside the walls a signal to send out fresh fighting troops to catch the withdrawing Romans in order to finish them off. A furious screaming mob roared out of the gates and attacked the Roman ranks tearing their formation to pieces and putting many to flight, leaving only Titus and a handful of his staunchest followers in the midst of the Jewish combatants. Titus refused to run, even though his friends and escort earnestly exhorted him to "to give way to these Jews that are desirous of death, and not to run into such dangers before those that ought to stay before him; to consider what his fortune was, and not, when he was master of the war and of the world, to fill the place of a common soldier; nor to withstand so fierce an attack risking everything thereby."

Titus gave them no heed, but drove himself directly into the fighting Jewish mob, hacking and slashing with his gladius and in fact driving them back. He forced them to turn and as a result succeeded in killing a great many. The Jewish reinforcements marching uphill ran into the battered fighters pressing to escape. In spite of their numbers, the mob reared back in admiration of his courage and skill. Even so, the Jews did not run, and continued to drive forward to climb the hill. Titus struck against their flanks and eventually brought them to a fighting standstill before the Roman camp.

The Jews did not withdraw, however, and the Roman workers assembling the fortified camp began to succumb to terror as some of the soldiers began to run from the mob. Much of the legion was dispersed by this time. Even though they believed the Jewish onslaught could not be sustained, it appeared that Titus himself was in flight. They reckoned that if he had been able to keep his position none of the Roman soldiers with him would have taken flight. Surrounded by a fighting mass of swirling combatants panic began to take hold in the Roman lines and a few more began to disperse when suddenly they could see their general slashing his sword into the very center of the mass of fighting men. Several shouted out to their comrades that the general was in danger, causing those who had begun to withdraw to turn and come to his aid. The Romans suddenly rallied and renewed their counterattack, driving the Jewish forces back into the valley behind them.

Having gained the advantage of assaulting from the high ground the Romans forced the Jews to retreat. Titus continued to battle those close to him while again sending the legion again to fortify their camp. He and those in close support kept up the pressure, forcing the Jews to withdraw. He had effectively rescued this legion twice in the space of a few hours and gave them the respite to finish fortifying their camp.

Perceptions and confusion caused some additional surprises for both sides the following night. Titus had given orders for the erection of three towers higher than 50', with one being set on each bank in such a position as to permit his soldiers to drive the Jewish defenders away from their walls. Unfortunately, one of these towers collapsed with a great crash about midnight. The Jewish defenders assumed that the Romans were launching an attack and ran to their battle stations. This in turn set the Roman legions in an uproar because they in turn suspected that the Jews were about to launch another sally from the city gates. Challenges for passwords were given and countered and both sides remained at a high state of confused alert until Titus was informed of what had happened and gave orders that all were to be briefed on the events that had taken place. Once the disturbance had been clarified, the Roman camp settled back to continuing its preparations for the siege of Jerusalem.

The Jews were extremely concerned about the Roman towers because Titus's archers and slingers kept up a steady fire of darts, arrows and large stones against the walls using the heavy Roman siege engines. The Jews couldn't get at them to counter the missiles because of their height, and it was impractical for them to overturn the towers due to their weight. The towers also seemed to be invulnerable to fire because they were covered with iron plates. The Jews therefore withdrew to positions out of the reach of the darts and ceased trying to interfere with the Roman's assault on the lower walls with battering rams. Part of the outer wall began to give way under the continuous Roman battering (the ram was referred to as the "Nico" by the Jews). The Jews had grown weary of maintaining a continuous watch on the Roman battering, and they were also kept away from their inner walls by the constant hail for fire from the Roman siege towers. Because of this, they were not monitoring the progress of the Nico when the Romans succeeded in making a breach in the wall.

Roman soldiers immediately stormed through the gap created by their ramming efforts and the Jews that had been left to guard the wall withdrew to their second of three inner walls. The first line of Romans inside the wall immediately opened the outer gates, which allowed the main body to gain entry to the first level of the walled defenses on the 15th day of the siege. The besiegers quickly demolished a great portion of the wall to prevent it being retaken, along with a great deal of the northern portion of the city.

Titus proceeded to pitch his camp within the city, at a site named the Camp of the Assyrians, having seized upon all the ground that that lay as far back as Cedron, although he was careful to keep his forces out of range of the Jews' darts which they launched from behind their second wall. Titus then launched a co-ordinated set of attacks, which forced the Jews to split their defending forces into several separated sections. The walls were vigorously defended by the Jews from the tower of Antonia, and from the northern cloister of the temple. Separate battles for the walls took place as the Jews under the command of a leader named John fought the Romans in front of the monuments to king Alexander. Other Jewish forces under the command of a leader named Simon occupied a patch of ground sited near John's monument and fortified it as far as the gate which was normally used to bring water into a tower named Hippicus.

The Jews launched a number of violently conducted sallies from their fortified gates engaging the Romans with large bodies of combatants. Quite often, the Jews succeeded in driving the Roman soldiers away from the wall, but when they fought from the wall, the Romans had the superior edge against the Jews with their siege engines. Both sides took heart from their successes, with the Jews believing they could hold out against the Romans while the Romans were certain that the walls would fall to them in due course. There was no let up in the fury of the attacks and counterattacks that took place, and which were kept up against Jerusalem's walls.

The battles continued non-stop through the night with both sides under the constant stress and tension. The Jews worried that the walls would fall unexpectedly, the Romans worried the Jews would catch them unprepared in their large sallies against their camps. Soldiers on both sides slept in their armor when they had a chance to sleep and had themselves ready for battle at first light each day.

Titus stayed at the forefront of each battle, exhorting, and encouraging his troops throughout. He personally viewed his soldiers in action and rewarded those who distinguished themselves. Many chose to seize the opportunity to be recognized in his presence. In the middle of a tremendous exchange of dart fire, Longinus, one of Titus's horsemen leaped into the center of an attacking horde of Jewish soldiers. As the Jews jumped to the side, Longinus killed two of their men using a spear, pulling it out of the face and body of the first and running it through the side of the second as he tried to escape. Longinus then bolted back to his own lines unscathed. Many others also sought to gain recognition for themselves with similar actions

For their part, many of the Jews sought to take down as many Romans as possible in what seemed to be suicidal attacks. Titus insisted that this not be emulated in his own troops, telling them that "inconsiderate violence was madness," and that they were to pan and prepare their attacks with a great deal of forethought to ensure the maximum damage was inflicted on the Jewish defenders with the least amount of losses being incurred. His view would appear to have coincided with the theme of this book, in that the opposing force must be outthought before it is outfought.

Titus brought one of his siege engines to the middle tower on the north part of the Jewish wall, which was being defended by an intelligent Jew named Castor. Castor was hiding in the tower with ten other combatants hoping to ambush the Romans as they came forward with their battering rams. As the tower began to shake and vibrate from the battering, Castor rose up and petitioned Caesar for mercy. Titus gave Castor the benefit of the doubt and called for the ramming to cease to hear him out. Castor's aim was to delay the attack, and he managed to convince the Romans that some his men wanted to surrender, although others would not. This discussion went on for some time until a Roman dart injured Castor. Titus reproved the one who had shot the dart and directed his aide Josephus to stand with Castor as a sign of good faith. Josephus was certain Castor was up to no good and declined to go. A deserter named Aeneas went in his place, at which point Castor threw a great stone down on him. Then missile missed but injured another Roman soldier, and Titus now understood Castor had been using delusion to divert him from the siege. Titus gave orders for the ramming team to drive full out and to complete the breaching of the wall as quickly as possible. Castor and his companions set their tower on fire, and jumped through the flames as it collapsed, making their way into a hidden vault, and thereby escaping. To the Romans, it appeared as if they had died in the fire.

Caesar took this wall there on the fifth day after he had taken the first. As the Jews fled from him, he entered the fortifications with a thousand armed men. Among these were some of his best troops, who quickly found themselves in the sector of the city occupied by wool merchants, braziers, and the cloth marker, all sited on streets which ran obliquely back to the wall. Rather than demolish this area, which might have proven militarily useful, Titus chose to leave it intact with the idea that the Jews might appreciate his willingness to do the minimum damage necessary and to leave the city able to restore its ability to function economically after the battle.

He did not widen the breach to leave himself a safe retreat if it proved necessary later. He gave his soldiers orders do not kill any of those they captured, nor were the Jews homes to be burned. He directed that non-combatants be left alone and promised the people that their personal effects would be restored to them, with the object of preserving the city for his own use and keeping the temple intact for the sake of the city. The people reacted favorably to his instructions, but the Jewish fighting contingents saw them as a sign of Titus's weakness and came to believe that Titus might not be able to take the rest of the city. As a result, they threatened death to any who went along with the Roman's proposals or talked of surrender. The few who did have their throats cut. The Jewish soldiers then attacked the Romans that had already entered inside the city walls.

Battles were fought in the narrow streets, and some of the Romans were attacked from the houses that lined them. At the same time the Jews made a sudden sally out at the upper gates and assaulted the Romans that were beyond the wall. In some cases, a few of the soldiers guarding the wall jumped down from their siege towers and withdrew back to their camps. The Roman soldiers under attack inside the walls raised a great hue and cry, calling for reinforcements to join them. The Jews had a considerable advantage over the Romans, knowing the lay of the streets and alleys and using them to great effect to wound, delay and ambush the Romans at all turns, until the invaders had been driven out of the city.

Not all of the Romans were able to escape via the original breach they had made, since it hadn't been widened sufficiently as was their normal practice. Many more would have been cut to pieces if Titus hadn't sent in reinforcements. He also ordered archers to stand at the upper ends of the narrow lanes, and he positioned himself where he could overlook the greatest number of the Jewish defenders. The archers and their darts put a stop to the. A valiant soldier named Domitius Sabinus stood with him, as Caesar continued to direct the dart fire at the Jews, driving them off his soldiers and enabling those remaining to complete their withdrawal from the city.

The Jews believed that their success in driving the Romans out of the second wall was a sign that the Romans would cease their attack and give up trying to gain access to the city. They were of the opinion that if all stuck together, the siege could be successfully weathered, blind to the greater size of the attacking Roman force. The Jews were also seemingly unaware that their food supplies were about to give out. The Romans renewed their assault and began to open a number of breaches in the walls. In desperation, the Jewish defenders began to plug the gaps and openings with a wall of their own bodies whenever a fresh portion was knocked down. The Jews kept up this desperate defense for another three days, but on the fourth day they were overwhelmed by Titus siege engines and forced to withdraw. This time Titus demolished the northern part of the city completely, and then placed a garrison inside the towers that overlooked the southern parts of the city. With his forces in place, he planned and prepared for his assault on the third wall.[97]

As Titus surveyed the remaining defenses, the Jews continued to hold out on the strong heights of Sion, the citadel of the Antonia, and within the fortified Temple. Titus hoped to preserve the remainder of the city intact, and withheld from attacking for a few days, with the aim of letting hunger and the hopelessness of the defender's situation sink in. He placed his soldiers on parade and conducted a review of his army in full armor gave them their pay in view of the city, the battlements being thronged by spectators who watched in dismay.

The famine inside the walls forced the defenders into desperate acts for survival. A few ventured outside the walls at night to try and find food in the ravines. They were caught, scourged, tortured, and crucified in full view of the defenders in order to terrify them. This practice went on until, in Josephus words, "there was not wood enough for crosses."

Terrible crimes were committed in the city. The aged high-priest, Matthias, was accused of communicating with the enemy, and as a penalty, three of his sons were killed in his presence. He was then executed in sight of the Romans, together with sixteen other members of the Sanhedrin. Eventually the famine took such a grim toll that the defenders were reduced to appalling choices. It is reported that one woman devoured the body of her own child. At length, after fierce fighting, the Antonia was scaled, and Titus ordered its demolition.

Titus now promised the city leaders that the Temple should be spared if the defenders would come out and fight in another location. The Jewish leader John and the Zealots, however, refused to surrender it. Titus then proceeded to attack the outer cloisters and outer court with rams for several days, but the immense and compact stones resisted the ram's blows. Many of his soldiers were killed as they attempted to storm the cloisters, and thus Titus ordered the gates to be set on fire. Through that night and the next day, the flames raged through the cloisters. Then, in order to save the Temple itself, Titus ordered the fire to be quenched. On the 10th of August, the same day of the year on which Nebuchadnezzar had destroyed the Temple built by Solomon, a cry rang through the remaining population that the Temple was on fire. The Jews took up their swords and rushed to take revenge on their enemies or die trying.[98]

The slaughter continued while the fire raged. Soon no part of the Temple remained was left but a small portion of the outer cloisters, where 6,000 people had taken refuge. These people had been led by a false prophet who had there promised that God would deliver His people in His Temple. The soldiers set the building on fire and all perished. Titus next spent eighteen days in preparations for the attack on the upper city, which was then speedily captured. By this time, the Romans were no longer in the mood to display any mercy and killed as many as possible until nightfall put an end to the carnage. Josephus concludes his commentary by noting that during the whole of the siege of Jerusalem, 1,100,000 were slain, and the prisoners numbered 97,000.

---

[97] Extrapolated from *The Works of Flavius Josephus*. (London: 1906). http://www.hillsdale.edu/academics/history/War/Classical/Rome/70-Jerusalem-Josephus.htm.

[98] The temple was burnt 10 August AD 70, on the exact same day and month on which it had been burnt by the king of Babylon: Josephus, Ant. b. xx. c. 11. s. 8.

27 SIEGES OF JERUSALEM

Additional records suggest Jerusalem has been besieged at least 27 times in recorded history, with the first attack carried out by the tribe of Judah against the Jebusites, about 1443 B.C. This was some 700 years before Rome was founded. The siege appears to have been only partially successful, as in the reign of King David the Jebusites occupied the citadel (the future Zion). According to the Biblical record, David made war against the Jebusites (2Sam. 5:6-10; 1Chron. 11:4-7), about 960 B.C. Shishak, King of Egypt fought against Rehoboam (1Kings 14:25, 26. 2Chron. 12:2-12), about 875 B.C. He succeeded in capturing Jerusalem and the Temple was plundered. About 794 C.C. the Philistines, Arabians, and Ethiopians launched a coordinated assault against Jehoram (2Chron. 21:16, 17. In this siege the royal palace was sacked, and the Temple was again plundered. About 739 B.C. Jehoash King of Israel, fought against Amaziah King of Judah (2Kings 14:13, 14). The wall was partially broken down, and the city and Temple were pillaged. A long succession of sieges followed with attacks launched by Rezin king of Syria, and Pekah king of Israel, against Ahaz (2Chron. 28), about 630 B.C. The city held out, but Ahaz sought the aid of Tiglath-Pileser king of Assyria, for whom he stripped the Temple. By Sennacherib king of Assyria, against Hezekiah (2Kings 24:10-16), about 603 B.C. In this case the siege was reported to have been raised by a Divine interposition, as foretold by Isaiah the prophet. By Nebuchadnezzar king of Babylon, against Jehoiakim (2Chron. 36:6-7), about 496 B.C., when the Temple was partly pillaged. By Nebuchadnezzar again, against Jehoiachin (2Chron. 36:10), about 489 B.C., when the pillage of the Temple was carried further, and 10,000 people carried away. By Nebuchadnezzar, against Zedekiah (2Chron. 36:17-20), 478-477 B.C. In this case the Temple was burned. The city and the Temple lay desolate for fifty years. By Ptolemy Soter king of Egypt, against the Jews, 320 B.C. More than 100,000 captives were taken to Egypt. By Antiochus, the Great, about 203 B.C. By Scopus, a general of Alexander, about 199 B.C., who left a garrison. By Antiochus IV, surnamed Epiphanes, 168 B.C. This was the worst sieges to date. The whole city was pillaged; 10,000 captives taken; the walls destroyed; the altar defiled; ancient manuscripts perished; the finest buildings were burned; and the Jews were forbidden to worship there. By Antiochus V, surnamed Eupator, against Judas Maccabaeus, about 162 B.C. This time honorable terms were made, and certain privileges were secured. By Antiochus VII, surnamed Sidetes King of Syria, against John Hyrcanus, about 135 B.C. By Hyrcanus (son of Alex. Jannaeus) and the priest Aristobulus. The siege was raised by Scaurus, one of Pompey's lieutenants, about 65 B.C. By Pompey against Aristobulus, about 63 B.C. The siege engines and war machines were moved on the Sabbath when the Jews made no resistance. 12,000 Jews were slain. (Antigonus, son of Aristobulus, with a Parthian army, took the city in 40 B.C.; but there was no siege, the city was taken by surprise.) Herod with a Roman army besieged the city in 39 B.C. for five months. By Titus, A.D. 69. The second Temple (Herod's) was burned, and for fifty years the city disappeared from history. In A.D. 135, the Romans besieged the city again against the false Messiah, Bar-Cochebas, who had acquired possession of the ruins. The city was obliterated, and renamed AElia Capitolina, and a temple was erected to Jupiter. For 200 years the city passed out of history, no Jews being permitted to approach it. Over the next 400 years of Roman colonization, thousands were massacred, and the Church of the Holy Sepulchre was destroyed. The Emperor Heraclius defeated the inhabitants and restored the city and the church. In A.D. 636-637 the Caliph Omar besieged the city against Heralius. It was followed by capitulation on favorable terms, and the city passed into the hands of the Turks, in whose hands it remained until 1917. Afdal, the Vizier of the Caliph of Egypt, besieged the two rival factions of Moslems, and pillaged the city in 1098. In 1099 it was besieged by the army of the first Crusade. In 1187 it was besieged by Saladin for seven weeks. In 1244 the wild Kharezmian Tartar hordes captured and plundered the city, slaughtering the monks and priests. The Arab-Israeli wars led to significant changes in the present-day governance of Jerusalem.[99]

---

[99] Internet: http://www.angelfire.com/nv/TheOliveBranch/append53.html.

MASADA, 72-73 AD

The Romans engaged in sieges over a wide portion of the known world. Perhaps one of the best known is the siege of Masada (72-73 AD). This massive, fortified rock rising over the Dead Sea was the site of a Jewish last stand in a 7-year war against Rome. Rather than surrender when the Roman siege ramp being prepared to take the fortress neared completion, 960 Jews set fire to their belongings and then committed mass suicide.

The Romans raised the art of circumvallation and contravallation to new heights at Masada, where they built a stone wall around the entire mountain. Manned at regular intervals with soldiers, the purpose of the wall was to prevent anyone from escaping the besieged fortress. When there was a threat of an attack from a relieving army, circumvallation was supplemented by contravallation, in which yet another wall was built so that troops could defend against an attack from a relieving force. These techniques often took a great deal of time. In the case of Masada, the Romans laid siege to the mountaintop fortress for 3 years. In the process they built a 3-mile-long sloping earthen ramp to the top, along which they moved siege machinery and troops for the final assault.[100]

The siege took place along these lines. Flavius Silva was the Roman procurator in Judea in AD 72 during the suppression of a Jewish revolt. Most of the country had been subdued in the revolt except for a single major stronghold, the fortress of Masada, defended by a group known as the Sicarii under the command of a man named Eleazar. The Roman general gathered his soldiers and had them construct garrisons and a strong wall completely surrounded the entire fortress to ensure none could escape. This wall also ensured the defenders would be unable to bring in food, water, and other supplies, since the site was barren. When the wall was complete, Silva ordered the siege to begin.

The fortress was constructed on a tall rock formation surrounded by steep sides and deep valleys with extremely limited access to the top. One difficult route led up from lake Asphaltitis, which faced Eastwards, the other had an easier ascent but was also well defended. The fortress had been constructed under the direction of King Herod and consisted of white stone 8' thick and 12' high. Built into the walls were 38 towers, each of them 50' high, which led into smaller defense works built on the inside and running the complete length of the inner wall. There was a small area of arable land for growing food for the garrison. On the western portion of the fortress Herod had a palace built on the inside but with its main portion facing the north side. The palace walls were very thick and towers 60' high were constructed in each of its four corners. There were many other structures within this complex, including cloisters, baths and large buildings supported on pillars of single stones on every side. The walls and floors of the palace were decorated with multi-colored stones. Herod also had a number of large pits cut into the floor, which served as reservoirs for water. The road constructed up to the palace was protected by a large fortified tower at its narrowest point some 1000' from the top of the hill. The combination of natural rock and man-made defenses made Masada a formidable fortress.

---

[100]   Internet: http://www.au.af.mil/au/awc/awcgate/gabrmetz/gabr000d.htm.

(Godot13 Photo)
Aerial view of the fortress of Masada, Israel.

The fortress had been well-stocked with fine furniture, corn and food-stocks including considerable quantities of wine and oil, pulse, and dates, all of which were seized by Eleazar and his Sicarii when they took possession of the fortress. A considerable quantity of weapons was stored in Masada, sufficient to equip 10,000 men. Herod had ensured that stores of cast iron, brass, and tin were kept on hand for any emergency or occasion in which such supplies would be required. He had originally assembled this material in case the Jews tried to depose him, or he was attacked by Queen Cleopatra of Egypt. He was well aware of her intentions, having been informed that she had spoken to Mark Antony, and with the request that he cut off Herod, and bestow the kingdom of Judea upon her. (It was, in fact, a surprise that he didn't do this, as it is well documented that Antony was "miserably enslaved in his passion for her.")

Silva found only one place that he could launch his assault against the fortress, and this was a large outcrop of rock sited behind the great tower which secured the road leading up to the palace. It was positioned some 300' beneath the highest part of Masada, and was called the White Promontory. Silva directed his engineers to build a large and embankment of earth some 200' high. To the surface of this he added another 50' high and wide level of stones on which he mounted his siege engines.

The siege engines consisted of similar types which had been devised by the Roman general Vespasian, and afterwards by Titus. Silva also made use of a 60; high siege tower covered with iron. From behind this tower, Roman slingers fired stones and darts, which eventually forced many of the defenders to withdraw from the walls or to keep their heads down while the Romans brought a battering ram forward.

The Romans succeeded in damaging the walls with the ram, but the Sicarii quickly constructed another wall inside the first, made of softer materials which absorbed the shock of the ram. They did this by laying together great wooden beams cut lengthways and piled in two rows parallel to one another out from the first wall and filled with earth. As the ram pounded the outer walls, the earth on the inner walls was compacted together more tightly, make the walls even more resistant to the ramming. Silva observed this and ordered this wall to be set on fire with soldiers flinging burning torches at it. Unfortunately, a strong north wind blew the great flames back on the Romans and threatened to destroy their siege engines. Eventually the wind changed direction and carried the flames to the fortress walls leaving the Romans convinced they could take the garrison by storm the following morning.

Silva saw the Romans would eventually succeed in overcoming Masada's defenses and understood there could be no escape. He gave a great speech to the remaining defenders, and proposed that while they had the choice, they should destroy their treasures and goods, and slay themselves rather than be taken prisoner and made slaves of the Romans. He ordered that the provisions be left intact as a testimonial to prove that they had chosen suicide, not because of want, but because they preferred death to submission and slavery.

Although the decision was debated at length, following Eleazar's speech the defenders eventually chose to destroy themselves by their own hands. Men killed their own families, then ten were chosen by lot to kill the rest. When this had been done, lots were cast again for one who killed the remaining nine, and then ran his sword through himself. Only one old woman and five children who had hidden themselves in the underground cisterns survived to tell the story of the 960 who died in the mass suicide in the fortress.

The Romans had been preparing for a difficult battle in the morning, and accordingly donned their armor, lad bridges of planks across the siege banks and proceeded carry out their final assault. They met by nothing but fires and silence inside. They could not understand what had happened, until the old woman and the five children emerged from their hiding place and informed the Romans of what had taken place. It is said that the Romans took no pleasure in discovering what had been done to their enemies within the walls of the fortress at Masada, and nor could they do other than wonder at the courage of their resolution, and the immovable contempt of death which so great a number of them had shown by taking such an action.[101]

---

[101] *The Works of Flavius Josephus.* (London: 1906). Internet: http://www.hillsdale.edu/academics/history/War/ Classical/Rome/72-Masada-Josephus.htm.

The Goths at the Battle of Mons Lactarius during the Gothic War, 535-553.
Painting by Alexander Zick.

HUNS, OSTROGOTHS AND VISIGOTHS

The period between 232 and 552 AD marked the transition from Roman to Medieval forms of war. As the struggle between the Germanic tribes and the Roman Empire drew to a close, so did the era of the Roman Empire. Cavalry had taken supremacy over infantry. As an example, at the Battle of Adrianople which took place 9 August 378 AD, near Constantinople (modern Istanbul), Valens, Roman emperor of the East led an expedition to punish the Visigoths for actions they had taken in Thrace. Finding the main Visigoth force near Adrianople without its cavalry, Valens attacked without waiting for reinforcements already on their way from Italy. Unfortunately, the cavalry then came back and was key in the killing of some 20,000 of the 30,000 Romans, including Valens. The victory convinced most strategists that cavalry was better than infantry.

Raiding Huns attack a Roman Villa. Roche Grosse.

One of the causes of Rome's final collapse was the sudden invasion of eastern Europe by the Huns, a new race of formidable and highly mobile horsemen, in great numbers and well-armed masters in the use of bow and arrow. The Huns encountered the Goths, a Nordic Germanic tribe which had left Sweden early in the 3rd century, spreading from Pomerania to the Carpathian Mountain region and from there to the Black Sea. This movement was part of the Great Migrations during which Franks, Allemani and Burgundians moved into the lands between the Harz mountains and the Danube River. When the Allemani began to move further westwards, they posed an impressive threat to Gaul. In August 357 AD they were met and defeated in a battle near Strasbourg by the Emperor Julian.[102]

---

[102] H.W. Koch, *Medieval Warfare*, Bison Books Limited, London, 1982, p. 16.

Engraving of Ostrogoths entering Rome.

The Goths (Ostrogoths and Visigoths) were the first to be affected by the Huns who inflicted a terrible defeat on them at the Dnieper River in 374 AD. Forced to seek refuge south of the Danube, the Goths raided the eastern and southeastern borders of the Roman Empire. Eventually the threat of the Huns forced the Goths to join forces with their former enemies, and for a brief period the Ostrogoths, the Romans and the Germans became allies against the Huns. Together in 450 AD they faced the Huns on the plain of Châlon, winning a victory over the Huns primarily through the use of heavy horsemen who rode them down.[103]

Fury of the Goths, depicting the Battle of the Sabis, 57 BC, painting by Paul Ivanovitz.

CHARLEMAGNE

Gaul was invaded by a great number of attackers following the fall of the Roman Empire. These invaders included the Burgundians, Visigoths and Franks in the 4th and 5th centuries, although the Franks ultimately outlasted the other competing tribes and rose to power, founding the ruling dynasty of the Merovingians and later the Carolingians. In 732, Charles Martel halted the Muslim advances into Gaul at Poitiers. Pepin III (Pepin the Short, 751-768 AD) deposed the last Merovingian king and became the first Carolingian king of France, starting the Carolingian Dynasty. In 755 AD and again in 756 AD, Pepin intervened against invading Lombards on behalf of the Pope, cementing his rule.

Between 768 and 814, Charlemagne founded his great empire centered on France and much of present-day Germany. He empire eventually grew to encompass Germany, Austria, Friesland, Saxony,

---

[103] Ibid, p, 16.

Bavaria, Italy, the frontier Marches of Spain, Brittany, and Carinthia. Unfortunately, these great land holdings were divided equally into three kingdoms on Charlemagne's death, and his successors were unable to successfully govern this far-flung empire.[104]

Charlemagne's Frankish vanguard fought many battles against the Saxons between 778 and 792. In spite of his successes, he was soon forced to revive the use of field fortification, learning the hard way that a conquered region could not be allowed an opportunity to begin fresh uprisings when the conquering forces moved on to other territories.[105] Charlemagne would select a strong natural position and built a "burg" on it, with a palisade and ditch around it. These early fortifications served as a headquarters for a permanent garrison, and were linked together with roads.[106] In 762 Charlemagne fortified Fronsac in Saxony, installed a garrison in Sigiburg, and later built a castle in Hohbeck in 789.[107] There were also several larger and more famous imperial palaces built by Charlemagne called palatinates, such as those at Ingelheim, Nimwegen and Aachen.[108]

Towards the end of his reign, Charlemagne's forces fought and annihilated the Avars, an Asiatic people who had terrorized Eastern Europe for two centuries. The Avars had settled along the Danube in "rings," or great enclosures defended by earthworks, the largest of which has been described as 38 miles in circumference. The Franks succeeded in capturing their chief ring and eventually destroyed all that was left of the Avars.[109]

---

[104]   Carlos Paluzie de Lescazes, *Castles of Europe*, Crescent Books, Barcelona, 1982, p. 84.

[105]   742-814 AD: Charlemagne (born 2 Apr 742, died 28 Jan 814) fought 40 campaigns in a 43-year reign, while carrying his sword Joyeuse. Offa King of Mercia (757-796 AD) was the only monarch he treated as an equal. (Offa constructed Offa's Dyke separating England from Wales.) He stimulated and encouraged revivals of learning, art, and literature. After Charlemagne came the emergence of feudal society, based on the mounted knight and the fortified castle. The strong protected the weak, and the weak paid a price. Freemen of some wealth and property became vassals of the neighbouring lord, and in return for his promise of protection, pledged themselves (and retainers, if any) to serve him as cavalry or soldiers under certain clearly defined conditions i.e.: Viking or Magyar raids. Charlemagne established a logistical organization including supply trains with food and equipment sufficient to maintain his troops for several weeks in the field. Replenishment of supplies was done on an orderly basis, both by systematic foraging and by convoying additional supply trains to the armies in the field. This permitted Charlemagne to carry war a thousand miles from the heart of France and to maintain armies in the field on campaign or in sieges, throughout the winter, something unknown in Western Europe since the time of the Romans.

[106]   Lynn Montross, *War through the Ages*, Harper & Brothers Publishers, New York & London, 1946, p. 97.

[107]   Carlos Paluzie de Lescazes, *Castles of Europe*, Crescent Books, Barcelona, 1982, p. 11.

[108]   Wolfgang F. Schuerl, op. cit., p. 74.

[109]   Lynn Montross, op. cit., p. 97-98.

Statue of Charlemagne (742-814), from the 9th century, in the Louvre, Paris, France.

Imperial Coronation of Charlemagne, painting by Friedrich Kaulbach, 1861.

BYZANTINE ARMIES

The centuries of invasion, civil war, and general decay took their fatal toll on the Roman empire of the West. From the 4th century onward the legacy of Rome was gradually transferred to its eastern capital, Constantinople, where Roman emperors attempted to stem the tide of barbarism and preserve the essence of Roman culture. By 650 AD the empire of the east was resigned to the loss of the western provinces, and found itself confronted with numerous military threats, especially from Islam, closer to home. These threats occupied the empire's attention for the next 800 years, and it is a testimony to Byzantine greatness and skill that the empire survived and prospered for more than a millennium after the collapse of Rome until suffering its final defeat at the hand of Ottoman armies in 1453. The Western Roman Empire had lasted for 500 years. The Eastern empire (395-1453) endured for over a thousand.

The imposition of Roman administrative machinery upon the Byzantine population in the early years kept the traditions of Roman military science and law intact, and preserved Roman culture and achievement for more than a thousand years until, as Allbutt noted, "Western Europe was once again fit to take care of them." Byzantium suffered no period of general degradation and decay like the Middle Ages in Europe and, for the most part, remained the most refined and developed culture in the world until the very end.

Vital to Byzantine survival was the maintenance of its military capability which, as Oman notes, "was, in its day, the most efficient military body in the world." Despite many evolutionary changes in details, the Byzantine military machine remained Roman in both its organization and values, and it continued to produce excellent soldiers and commanders long after the Roman legions had disappeared in the West. The basic administrative and tactical unit of the Byzantine army, for both cavalry and infantry, was the *numerus* comprised of 300-400 men, the equivalent of the old Roman cohort. Each *numerus* was commanded by the equivalent of a colonel. A division or *turma* was comprised of five to eight battalions commanded by a general. Two or three *turmae* could be combined into a corps commanded by a senior general called a *strategos*. The empire was geographically organized into provinces or *themes*, each of which had a military commander responsible for security with deliberately unclear lines between civil and military administration so as to give priority to military defense. For more than four centuries the Byzantine army numbered approximately 150,000 men almost evenly split between infantry and heavy cavalry forces.

Military manpower was obtained through universal conscription, but in practice recruiting and stationing military forces within each *theme* allowed commanders to recruit the best manpower from within each province. The army attracted the best families for its soldiers, thereby avoiding the fatal mistake of the Western empire which relied heavily upon barbarian soldiers while the best Roman citizens served not at all. Whereas Rome had relied heavily upon infantry until too late, the Byzantines adjusted to the new forms of highly mobile mounted warfare by relying primarily upon an excellent heavy cavalry of their own. Byzantine military commanders were quick to adopt a number of weapons and tactics of their enemies, so that as the infantry legion had symbolized the might of Rome, the mounted heavily armored horseman, the *cataphracti*, came to symbolize the military might of Byzantium.

The organizational infrastructure of the army of Byzantium was every bit as well-organized and efficient as it had been under the old Roman legions. The army had organic supply and logistics trains comprised of carts and pack animals to speed mobility, excellent siegecraft capabilities to include the full range of Roman artillery and siegecraft specialists, a fully articulated staff organization professionally trained in military academies, and a powerful navy to support ground operations. The genius of the Romans for military organization was preserved intact in almost all its earlier aspects.[110]

CASTLES AND FORTIFICATION

In the 8th to 12th centuries, the science of fortification in Europe was forced to grow out of the necessity to defend against the increasingly predatory raids of the Norse invaders.[111] The Vikings themselves appear to have understood the necessity for defensive structures. About the year 808, King Godfred of Denmark may have begun building or strengthened an already existing timber and earth rampart built to defend Denmark's southern frontier. Known as the Dannevirke, this defensive system became a complex series of earthworks that continued to be used right up to the time of the Second World War, when it served as a mount for anti-aircraft guns.[112]

When the Danish King Svein Forkbeard, c985-1014, mounted massive raids on England from the 980's, he had four major fortifications built in Denmark to serve as a staging base and barracks during his reign.[113] These include one in the shape of a ringfort at Trelleborg in West Zealand, with 16 great wooden halls, two others at Nonnebakken on Funen and at Fyrkat, and a larger site at Aggersborg on the Lim Fjord with 48 houses.[114] Their first permanent fortress built in the west however, was in Dublin. In the Netherlands they made Asseult, Louvain, Ghent, and Courtrai into fortified sites, which proved extremely hard to take. They also built permanent fortifications in the east to guard their trade routes and their great cities of Kiev and Novgorod.[115]

---

[110]   Internet: http://www.au.af.mil/au/awc/awcgate/gabrmetz/gabr0015.htm.
[111]   Lynn Montross, op. cit., p. 99.
[112]   James Graham-Campbell and Dafydd Kidd, *The Vikings*, British Museum Publications, London, 1980, p. 122.
[113]   William Anderson, *Castles of Europe, From Charlemagne to the Renaissance*, Ferndale Editions, London, 1980, p. 41.
[114]   Ian Heath, *The Vikings*, Osprey Publishing, London, 1985, p. 61.
[115]   William Anderson, op. cit., p. 39. The first date in Russian history according to Byzantine sources is 860 AD, when the Kiev Vikings (Rus) now known as Russians made their first attack and siege on Constantinople. The Patriarch Photius attempted to convert them to Christianity between 864-867 AD.

The Storming of Ipswich by the Danes, painting by Lorentz Ipplich. After the invasion of 869 Ipswich fell under Viking rule. The earth ramparts circling the town centre were probably raised by Vikings in Ipswich around 900 to prevent its recapture by the English. They were unsuccessful.

The necessity for defense against invading forces from every direction resulted in the construction of great numbers of fortified manors, castles and strongholds and caused the rise of feudalism. Feudalism was a social and political system which came into vogue with the death of Charlemagne and disintegration of the Carolingian Empire in the 9th and 10th centuries in Europe, eventually branching out from France and Germany and spreading to Italy, England and Northern Spain. The origins of feudalism lay in the Low Roman Empire, which led to the proliferation of large estates (called latifundia), and a new class of powerful landowners who became defacto rulers of their fiefs. Fiefs have their origins in the combination of two institutions, the first being the right to the use of land, and the second vassalage. The right to land represented the privilege of using it during the lifetime of the individual to whom the right was granted, while vassalage meant the swearing of allegiance and the rendering of services by one man to another in exchange for protection by the overlord. This agreement of service had a direct bearing on how strong a fortification could be in a crisis. Those serving the overlord were expected to offer armed service in defense of the overlord's castle, although this service was limited to forty days a year. If there was an attack, the people in the surrounding area (known as serfs), took refuge in the castle.[116]

Earth and wood had been the chief construction materials for early castles, but stone fortifications began to appear at the end of the tenth century. Fulk Nerra the Black built a stone keep in 994, the ruins of which still stand in the park of the Château of Langeais, Indre-et-Loire. It is the oldest surviving

---

[116]   Carlos Paluzie de Lescazes, *Castles of Europe*, Crescent Books, Barcelona, 1982, pp. 5-6.

rectangular stone built keep in France.[117] The earliest known "castle" site is found in Doue-la-Fontain, at Maine-et-Loire also in France, dating from about 950.[118] These early stone structures were the start of a new evolution in fortification and siege warfare. From that time onward there was a virtual explosion of castle building, with some 1590 castles sites in England and Wales constructed in the 11th and 12th centuries.[119]

(John5199 Photo)

Cahir Castle (*Caisleán na Cathrach*), one of the largest castles in Ireland, is sited on an island in the river Suir. It was built from 1142 by Conor O'Brien, Prince of Thomond. The castle was sited on and near an earlier native fortification known as a cathair (stone fort), which gave its name to the place. The core structure of the castle dates to construction in the 13th century. The castle was built in two parts. Granted to the powerful Butler family in late 14th century, the castle was enlarged and remodelled between the 15th and 17th centuries. It fell into ruin in the late 18th century and was partially restored in the 1840s. The Great Hall was partly rebuilt in 1840.

Unlike their Anglican kinsmen, this branch of the Butler dynasty sided with the Roman Catholic Irish in the Elizabethan wars. In 1599 the castle was captured after a three-day siege by the army of the Earl of Essex. During the Irish Confederate Wars the castle was besieged twice. In 1647, George Mathew, the guardian of the young Lord Cahir, surrendered to Murrough O'Brien following his victory at the Battle of Knocknanauss. In 1650 he surrendered again to Oliver Cromwell, during his conquest of Ireland without a shot being fired. In 1961 the last Lord Cahir died, and the castle reverted to the Irish state.

---

[117] Wolfgang F. Schuerl, op. cit., p. 80., and William Anderson, op. cit., p. 45.
[118] R. Allen Brown et al, *Castles, A History and Guide*, Blandford Press, Poole, Dorset, 1980, p. 19.
[119] R. Allen Brown et al, op. cit., p. 18.

(p.schmelzle Photo)

Steinsburg Castle, Sinzheim, Germany, present day. The castle was first mentioned in the year 1109. In the 13th century the owners of the castle were the Counts of Oettingen. Later the castle became home to the Counts palatine of the Rhein. In 1517 the castle was purchased by the Lords of Venningen. Shortly after this purchase the castle was burnt down during the Peasants' revolt. The rebellious peasants had to pay 5000 Gulden for the rebuilding of the castle. After heavy damage in 1777 by a lightening strike, the castle was left in disrepair. Since 1973 the castle has been owned by the Sinsheim council, who had large parts of the castle restored. The keep, the moat and the towers may still be viewed today.

When Hildebrand became Pope Gregory VII (1073-1085), he excommunicated the Holy Roman Emperor Henry IV (1076), whose enemies begin to build castles in Germany at a frenzied pace. Some 10,000 castles were built in Germany in the Middle Ages, while in France the number is estimated at over 20,000 and in Spain some 2,500 castles still survive. Even the small countries have a substantial number of medieval fortifications, with Belgium for instance, boasting more than 900.[120]

Construction of a castle was tightly governed and controlled, with only those nobles who pledged allegiance to the key overlord being permitted to erect them. This same overlord was also entitled to destroy any castle erected without his consent. Unfortunately, this happened more often than not, and in many cases, the ensuing conflict often led to open warfare and insurrection against the overlords. In time, the largest of the landholders established a sovereign central power and imposed its authority with an army. Siegecraft played an important role in this imposition of authority, and therefore the construction of defense works became increasingly sophisticated.

The Vikings in Normandy, (who eventually became the Normans), began to build small stone castles with great attention to detail in their construction in the 10th century. They used the same basic ground layout as earlier defense-works which consisted of a wall of stakes surrounded by a wide moat, with a multi-storied fortified tower often made of stone and encompassed by a second moat. Often there was only a single entrance to this tower sighted well above ground level, and accessible only by a ladder or a

---

120   Wolfgang F. Schuerl, op. cit., p. 7.

bridge across the moat. In 915, for example, the lords of the Luxembourg-Tréveris region covered their mountains with castles, which ranged in location from Esch-sur-Sure to Luxembourg itself.

Fortresses were large buildings of fortified enclosures, which tended to house a permanent garrison and were established to defend a particular site and its surroundings. Kings or highborn princes generally controlled them. Castles were specifically designated strong buildings, which were strategically sited and easily defended by a small garrison of often exclusively military forces. Castles were often the residences for the feudal overlords. A castle would generally have a chapel, barracks for soldiers and officer's quarters, granaries, a mill, and an oven arranged in the center of a walled or enclosed space. Open grounds could be used for stables or fence works for sheep, cattle and horses, and additional shelters could be included for the use of the overlord's serfs who were entitled to claim protection.[121]

Fortress of Luxembourg, painting by Christoph Wilhelm Selig, 1814.

The Fortress of Luxembourg refers to the former fortifications of Luxembourg City, the capital of the Grand Duchy of Luxembourg, which were mostly dismantled in 1867. The fortress was of great strategic importance for the control of the Left Bank of the Rhine, the Low Countries, and the border area between France and Germany.

---

[121]   Carlos Paluzie de Lescazes, *Castles of Europe*, Crescent Books, Barcelona, 1982, p. 9.

The fortifications were built gradually over nine centuries, from soon after the city's foundation in the tenth century until 1867. By the end of the Renaissance, Luxembourg was already one of Europe's strongest fortresses, but it was the period of great construction in the 17th and 18th centuries that gave it its fearsome reputation. Due to its strategic location, it became caught up in Europe-wide conflicts between the major powers such as the Habsburg-Valois Wars, the War of the Reunions or the French Revolutionary Wars, and underwent changes in ownership, sieges, and major alterations, as each new occupier, the Burgundians, French, Austrian and Spanish Habsburgs, and Prussians, their own improvements and additions.

Luxembourg took pride in the flattering historical epithet of the "Gibraltar of the North" as a result of its alleged impregnability. By 1443 it had only been taken by surprise by Phillip the Good. In 1795, the city, expecting imminent defeat and for fear of the following pillages and massacres, surrendered after a 7-month blockade and siege by the French, with most of its walls still unbreeched. On this occasion, advocating to extend the revolutionary wars across the French borders, the French politician and engineer Lazare Carnot explained to the French House of Representatives, that in taking Luxembourg, France had deprived its enemies of "….the best fortress in Europe after Gibraltar, and the most dangerous for France", which had put any French movement across the border at a risk. Thus, the surrender of Luxembourg made it possible for France to take control of the southern parts of the Low Countries and to annex them to her territory.

The city's great significance for the frontier between the Second French Empire and the German Confederation led to the 1866 Luxembourg Crisis, almost resulting in a war between France and Prussia over possession of the German Confederation's main western fortress. The 1867 Treaty of London required Luxembourg's fortress to be torn down and for Luxembourg to be placed in perpetual neutrality, signalling the end of the city's use as a military site. Since then, the remains of the fortifications have become a major tourist attraction for the city.

Château du Haut-Kœnigsbourg is a medieval castle located in the commune of Orschwiller in the Bas-Rhin department of France, in the Vosges mountains west of Sélestat.[122] It is situated in a strategic location on a rocky spur overlooking the Upper Rhine Plain, and as a result, it was used by successive powers from the Middle Ages until the Thirty Years' War when it was abandoned. From 1900 to 1908 it was rebuilt at the behest of the German emperor Wilhelm II. Today it is a major tourist site, attracting more than 500,000 visitors a year.

It is not known when the first castle was built on the site, but a *Burg Staufen (Castrum Estufin)* is documented in 1147. By 1192 the castle was called *Kinzburg (Königsburg*, "King's Castle"). In the early thirteenth century, the fortification passed from the Hohenstaufen family to the dukes of Lorraine, who entrusted it to the local Rathsamhausen knightly family and the Lords of Hohenstein, who held the castle until the fifteenth century. As the Hohensteins allowed robber barons to use the castle as a hideout, and their behaviour began to exasperate the neighbouring rulers, in 1454 it was occupied by Elector Palatine Frederick I. In 1462 the castle was set on fire by the unified forces of the cities of Colmar, Strasbourg, and Basel.

---

[122]   The Haut-Koenigsbourg was constructed in the 12th century and suffered numerous sieges and assaults until it was taken and destroyed by the Swedes during the 30 Years War in the 17th century. It was restored at the turn of the 20th century. Anne Gael & Serge Chirol, *Châteaux et Sites de La France Medievale*, Hachette Realites, Paris, 1978, p. 236.

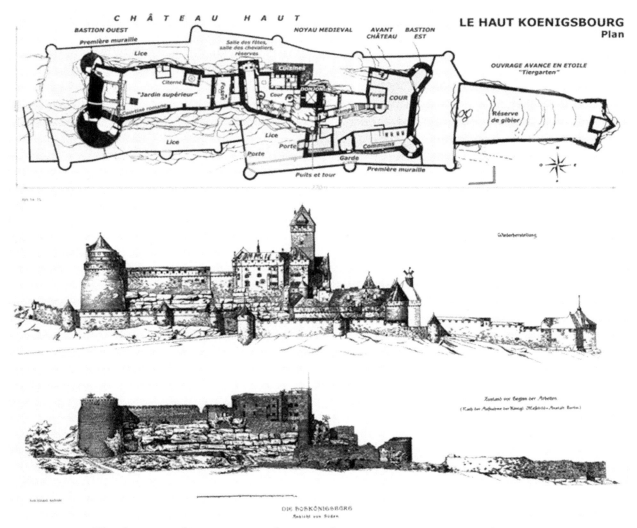

The fortress of Haut Koenigsbourg, Alsace, Lorraine, France, plan view,
and profile views before and after restoration, 1900-1908.

In 1479, the Habsburg emperor Frederick III granted the castle ruins in fief to the Counts of Thierstein, who rebuilt them with a defensive system suited to the new artillery of the time. In 1517 the last Thierstein died and the castle reverted back to a fief. It again came into the possession of the Habsburg emperor of the day, Maximilian I. In 1633, during the Thirty Years' War in which Catholics forces fought Protestants, the Imperial castle was besieged by Protestant Swedish forces. After a 52-day siege, the castle was burned and looted by the Swedish troops. For several hundred years it was left unused, and the ruins became overgrown by the forest.

The ruins were purchased by the township of Sélestat in 1865. After the Franco-Prussian War of 1870 to 1871 the region was incorporated into the German Imperial Territory of Alsace-Lorraine, and in 1899 the citizens granted what was left of the castle to the German emperor Wilhelm II. Wilhelm wished to create a castle lauding the qualities of Alsace in the Middle Ages and more generally of German civilization stretching from *Hohkönigsburg* in the west to Marienburg Castle (also restored) in the east. The management of the restoration of the fortifications was entrusted to the architect Bodo Ebhardt, a proven expert on the reconstruction of medieval castles. Work proceeded from 1900 to 1908. Ebhart's aim was to rebuild it, as near as possible, as it was on the eve of the Thirty Years' War. He relied heavily on historical accounts but, occasionally lacking information, he had to improvise some parts of the stronghold. (For example, the Keep tower is now reckoned to be about 14 metres too tall). Bodo Ebhardt restored the castle following a close study of the remaining walls, archives and other fortified castles built at the same period. On 13 May 1908, the restored *Hohkönigsburg* was inaugurated in the presence of the Emperor.

(Rolf Kranz Photo)
Château du Haut-Kœnigsbourg, view from the battlements, Alsace, Lorraine, France.[123]

Around each fortress would be a constellation of castles, generally sighted within 15 miles, but often within 6 to 9 miles of each other. Eventually the strength of these positions began to evolve as the feudal overlords attempted to expand their holdings and to assert greater control and authority over their fiefdoms. By the 14th and 15th centuries, the kings and overlords had seized or established almost complete control of military construction which in turn led to the development of more advanced types of fortification. Emphasis moved away from the castle as a defensive structure and shifted towards the development of the fortified house and manor. Communities of citizens began to fortify their villages and towns, which in turn led to the development of more advanced techniques to overcome them.[124]

---

[123] The Haut-Koenigsbourg was constructed in the 12th century and suffered numerous sieges and assaults until it was taken and destroyed by the Swedes during the 30 Years War in the 17th century. It was restored at the turn of the 20th century. Anne Gael & Serge Chirol, *Châteaux et Sites de La France Medievale*, Hachette Realites, Paris, 1978, p. 236.
[124] Carlos Paluzie de Lescazes, *Castles of Europe*, Crescent Books, Barcelona, 1982, p. 12.

Top: Bombard, Mons Meg, Edinburgh Castle, Scotland. (Kim Traynor Photo).
Bottom: Dulle Griet (Crazy Griet), a medieval supergun from the first half of the 15th century from Ghent, Belgium. (Karelj Photo)

As fortifications became increasingly more sophisticated and difficult to overcome, more planning and preparation was required to enable a capture. An assault, therefore, would often begin with an attempt to ambush or surprise and overpower the guards. If that failed, bribery or trickery would be tried, with every effort made to subvert a garrison before resorting to the formal siege or blockade.

The defenders also had their work cut out for them. When a siege threatened to be brought upon a castle, the Castellan or Constable had a great deal of responsibility in the form of preparations to be carried out before hostilities began. All able-bodied men in the district had to be recruited, specifically those men with feudal obligations to defend their overlord's castle. Provisions had to be gathered in, and the surrounding countryside as far as possible had to be stripped of anything that could be used by the attackers to subsist. The scorched earth policy used by the Russians to aid in the defeat of Napoleon's forces in the early 19th was born in the much earlier era of medieval tactics. Nearby trees had to be felled and stored inside the castle to deny their use to the enemy for shelter, and to be kept readily available for making running repairs. Non-combatants would have been expelled unless sufficient provisions could be stored to feed them.

(Person Scott Foresman Archives)

Illustration showing an object being dropped from a machicolation that is supported by stone corbels.

Weaknesses in a castles walls and battlements which had been neglected in peacetime would have to be rapidly repaired or shored up. Armourers would have to sharpen weapons and service defense equipment to ensure they were in working order. Scouting parties would be sent out to gather intelligence or to burn standing crops in all directions. Other workers would be carrying stocks of missiles up to the wall-walk and into the towers, stacking arrows, preparing buckets of pitch and sand to heat or boil. Water had to be readily available for firefighting and to keep the defenders well supplied. Non-combatants could also be press-ganged into clearing the defensive ditch of brushwood, or to dig entrenchments, throw up earth mounds and build additional obstacles. Once the final warning came and the attackers were sighted, all moved quickly inside, the drawbridge was raised, and the portcullis was lowered. The garrisoned would man the battlements on the walls and prepare to receive their adversary. From then on, the siege took its course.[125]

---

[125] Anthony Kemp, op. Cit., pp. 168-169.

SIEGE OF ACRE, 1799

The Siege of Acre of 1799 was an unsuccessful French siege of the Ottoman-defended, walled city of Acre (now Akko in modern Israel) and was the turning point of Napoleon's invasion of Egypt and Syria. It was Napoleon's first strategic defeat as three years previously he had been tactically defeated at the Second Battle of Bassano.

SIEGE OF BADAJOZ, 1812

In the Siege of Badajoz (16 March – 6 April 1812), also called the Third Siege of Badajoz, an Anglo-Portuguese Army, under General Arthur Wellesley (later the Duke of Wellington), besieged Badajoz, Spain, and forced the surrender of the French garrison.

The siege was one of the bloodiest in the Napoleonic Wars and was considered a costly victory by the British, with some 4,800 Allied soldiers killed in a few short hours of intense fighting during the storming of the breaches as the siege drew to an end. Enraged at the huge number of casualties they suffered in seizing the city, the troops broke into houses and stores consuming vast quantities of alcohol with many of them then going on a rampage. Threatening their officers and ignoring their commands to desist, and even killing several, the troops massacred about 4,000 Spanish civilians. It took three days before the men were brought back into order.

After capturing the frontier towns of Almeida and Ciudad Rodrigo in earlier sieges, the Duke of Wellington's army moved south to Badajoz to capture this frontier town and secure the lines of communication back to Lisbon, the primary base of operations for the allied army. Badajoz was garrisoned by some 5,000 French soldiers under General Philippon, the town commander, and possessed much stronger fortifications than either Almeida or Ciudad Rodrigo. With a strong curtain wall covered by numerous strongpoints and bastions, Badajoz had already faced two unsuccessful sieges and was well prepared for a third attempt, with the walls strengthened and some areas around the curtain wall flooded or mined with explosives.

The allied army, some 27,000 strong, outnumbered the French garrison by around five to one and after encircling the town on 17 March 1812, began to lay siege by preparing trenches, parallels and earthworks to protect the heavy siege artillery, work made difficult by a week of prolonged and torrential rainfalls, which also swept away bridging works that were needed to bring the heavy cannon and supplies forward. On 19 March, the French made a strong sally with 1,500 men and 40 cavalry which surprised the working parties and caused losses of 150 officers and men before being repulsed. By 25 March batteries were firing on the outwork, Fort Picurina, which that night was stormed by 500 men and seized by redcoats from General Thomas Picton's 3rd Division. Casualties were high with 50 killed and 250 wounded, but the fort was captured. The French made several raids to try to destroy the lines advancing toward the curtain wall but were repeatedly fended off by the famed British 95th Rifles while simultaneously being counter-attacked by line infantry.

The capture of the bastion allowed more extensive siege earthworks to be dug and with the arrival of heavy 18 lb (8.2 kg) and 24 lb (11 kg) howitzers, breaching batteries were established. On 31 March, the allies began an intense bombardment of the town's defences. Soon a maze of trenches was creeping up to the high stone walls as the cannons continued to blast away at the stonework. On 2 April, an attempt was made to destroy a barrier that had been erected amongst the arches of the bridge to cause flooding that was hampering the siege. The explosion of 450lbs of powder was only partly successful.

By April 5 two breaches had been made in the curtain wall and the soldiers readied themselves to storm Badajoz. The order to attack was delayed for 24 hours to allow another breach to be made in the wall. News began to filter to the allies that Marshal Soult was marching to relieve the town and an order was given to launch the attack at 22:00 on April 6.

The French garrison were well aware of what was to come and mined the large breaches in the walls in preparation for the imminent assault.

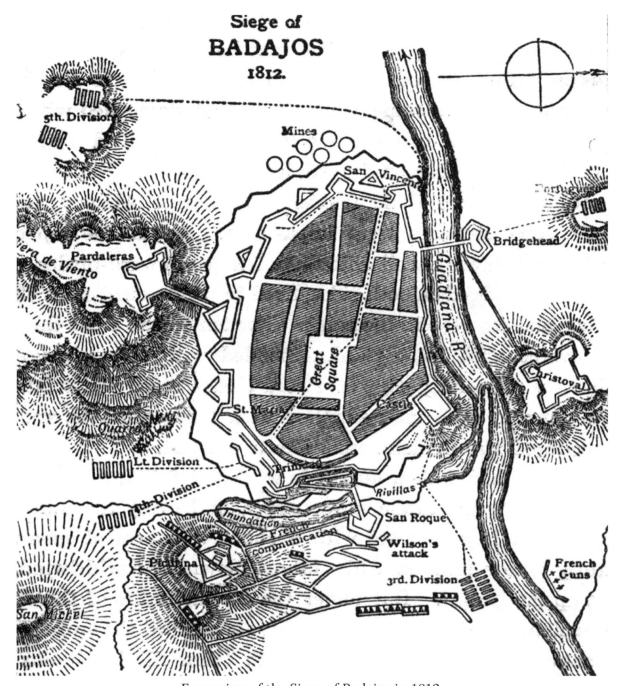

Engraving of the Siege of Badajos in 1812.
(Archibald Wilberforce, editor - The great battles of all nations)

With three large gaps in the curtain wall and with Marshal Soult marching to the town's aid, Wellington ordered his regiments to storm the town so at 22:00 on the 6th and the troops made their way forward with scaling ladders and various tools. Three attacks would be mounted. The first men to assault the breaches were the men of the Forlorn Hope, who would lead the main attack by the 4th Division on two of the breaches. The third breach would be assaulted by Craufurd's Light Division while diversionary attacks were to be made to the north and the east by Portuguese, and British soldiers of the 5th Division and Picton's 3rd Division would assault the Castle from across the river.

Just as the main Forlorn Hope were beginning their attack, a French sentry was alerted and raised the alarm. Within seconds the ramparts were filled with French soldiers, who poured a lethal hail of musket fire into the troops at the base of the breach. The British and Portuguese surged forward *en masse* and raced up to the wall, facing a murderous barrage of musket fire, complemented by grenades, stones, barrels of gunpowder with crude fuses and bales of burning hay to provide light.

The furious barrage devastated the British soldiers at the wall and the breach soon began to fill with dead and wounded, over whom the storming troops had to struggle. The carnage, rubble and loss of guiding Engineering officers led the Craufurd's Light Division to become confused; assaulting an outlying ravelin that led nowhere, the troops got mixed up with those of the 4th Division. Despite the carnage the redcoats continued to surge forward in great numbers, only to be mown down by endless volleys and shrapnel from grenades and bombs. The French could see they were holding the assault and the British were becoming stupefied and incapable of more exertion. In just under two hours, some 2,000 men had been killed or gravely wounded at the main breach, while countless more men of the 3rd Division were shot down as they made their diversionary assault.

"The Devil's Own" 88th Regiment at the Siege of Badajoz.
Watercolour en grisaille by Richard Caton Woodville Jr.

Picton's 3rd Division managed to reach the top of the castle wall, without General Picton, who was wounded as he climbed a ladder to try to reach the top of the wall, and found themselves secure within the castle, but as all doors into the town were blocked up, could not immediately come to the assistance of the other divisions.

Everywhere they attacked, the allied soldiers were being halted and the carnage was so immense that Wellington was just about to call a halt to the assault when he heard that the soldiers had gained a foothold in the castle. He ordered the castle gates to be blown and that the 3rd Division should support the assaults on the breaches with a flank attack.

The 5th Division, which had been delayed because their ladder party had become lost, now attacked the San Vicente bastion; losing 600 men, they eventually made it to the top of the curtain wall. Fitzroy Somerset, Wellington's military secretary (and the future Lord Raglan), was the first to mount the breach, and afterwards secured one of the gates for British reinforcements before the French could organise a fresh defence.

The town's fate was sealed with the link up with men of the 3rd and 5th Divisions, who were also making their way into the town. Once they had a foothold, the British and Portuguese soldiers were at an advantage. Seeing that he could no longer hold out, General Philippon withdrew from Badajoz to the neighbouring outwork of San Cristobal; however, he surrendered shortly after the town had fallen.

When dawn finally came on 7 April, it revealed the horror of the slaughter all around the curtain wall. Bodies were piled high and blood flowed like rivers in the ditches and trenches. Surveying the destruction and slaughter Wellington wept openly at the sight of British dead piled upon each other in the breaches and bitterly cursed the British Parliament for granting him so few resources and soldiers. The assault and the earlier skirmishes had left the allies with some 4,800 casualties. Estimates of the numbers vary between 4,924 and 4,760. The elite Light Division had suffered badly, losing some 40 percent of their fighting strength.

With success came mass looting and disorder as the redcoats turned to drink and reprisals. The wanton sacking of Badajoz has been noted by many historians as a particularly atrocious conduct committed by the British Army: many homes were broken into, property vandalized or stolen, Spanish civilians of all ages and backgrounds killed or raped, and many officers were also shot by the men they were trying to bring to order.

After fifteen to eighteen hours Wellington finally issued an order that the sack of Badajoz should cease and ordered detachments to restore order beginning at 5 a.m. the next day. It was some 72 hours before order was completely restored, however. Many British soldiers were flogged as punishment and a gallows was erected, but no one was hanged.

From an engineering viewpoint, the requirement to undertake the assault in a hasty manner, relying upon the British bayonet, rather than scientific methods of approach, undoubtedly resulted in heavier casualties, as did the lack of a corps of trained sappers. The siege was to lead, within 2 weeks, to the formation of the Royal School of Military Engineering. (Fletcher, Ian. *In Hell before Daylight: The Siege and Storming of the Castle of Badajoz, March–April 1812*, Spellmount Ltd.); and (Jac Weller. *Wellington in the Peninsula 1808–1814*, London. 1962)

SIEGE OF BURGOS, 1812

Siege of Burgos, Spain, 1812, painting by Francois Joseph Heim.

The Siege of Burgos took place from 19 September to 21 October 1812, during the Peninsular War, part of the Napoleonic Wars. The initial siege was carried out by an Anglo-Portuguese Army led by General Arthur Wellesley, Marquess of Wellington, in an attempt to capture the castle of Burgos from its French garrison under the command of General of Brigade Jean-Louis Dubreton. The French repulsed every attempt to seize the fortress, resulting in one of Wellington's rare withdrawals, as he went on to defeat the army sent to flank him at the Lines of Torres Vedras. He pursued the French, and then returned to complete the siege of Burgos and capture the city . Burgos is located about 210 kilometres (130 mi) north of Madrid.

British engineers quickly began digging in batteries on the horn work hill, the first battery (protective position for the guns) was finished on 22 September but hoping to get lucky again, Wellington ordered an attack on the night of 22/23 September before his guns had fired a shot. Men of the 1st and 6th Divisions rushed forward against the palisades with axes, followed by men with just five ladders to scale the 24 foot wall, they failed to receive the support of other troops and were easily repelled with 150 of the 400 men killed and wounded. The engineers then began digging a mine 60 feet to get under the fort's west wall. When this was detonated in the early hours of the 29 September, part of the wall collapsed, the advanced party of British dashed forward but were not supported and were soon driven back from the defences. It turned out that the mine was run under an ancient buried wall that was in front of the modern wall. Consequently, the main French defenses were unscathed by the explosion.

A frustrated Wellington ordered his engineers to dig a new mine. Meanwhile, he had his soldiers work overnight to erect a breaching battery close to the walls. At daybreak on 1 October, the French discovered this position and immediately zeroed in their defending artillery. They rapidly destroyed two of the three cannons and inflicted heavy losses on the gun crews. The following night the British re-established the battery only to see it destroyed again in the morning. On 2 October, Wellington asked Popham to send two 24-pound cannons to replace his lost artillery. As it happened, these guns would not arrive in time. When the new mine was finally ready on 4 October, it was fired, blowing a 100-foot gap in the northwest wall, and killing most of the defenders in that area. The subsequent attack managed to secure a foothold in the outer defenses after heavy fighting and 220 casualties.

After the Allies began digging a new trench against the inner defenses, Dubreton launched a sortie without warning on 5 October. The attackers killed and wounded almost 150 Allies and carried off or spoiled much of their equipment. No sooner had Wellington resumed siege operations than Dubreton struck again. At 2am on the 8th, with perfect timing, the French swarmed out of the fort and inflicted 184 casualties while suffering small losses. Rain began to fall in sheets, flooding the siege trenches. The British guns on the horn work ran so low on ammunition that French cannonballs were retrieved and reused. Wellington wrote, "This is altogether the most difficult job I ever had in hand with such trifling means. God send that they may give me a little more time."

A third mine was dug and on 18 October, at 4.30pm the mine was detonated under the Chapel of San Roman near the south wall. Assaults were mounted against the west and north walls, but support for the assaults was weak and as before, these attacks withered in the face of intense fire and 170 more casualties were added to the butcher's bill. With a French army threatening his position and with the problems arising from the shortage of artillery and ammunition, Wellington prepared to retreat on 21 October. However, he was unable to withdraw all his siege guns. The engineers tried to demolish the captured horn work, but their charges failed to explode. British losses in the siege amounted to 550 killed, 1,550 wounded, and three guns . The French lost 304 killed and 323 wounded, plus the 60 captured. (Glover, Michael. *The Peninsular War 1807-1814*. London: Penguin, 2001, p. 213)

The Spaniards built a great many castles to counter the Muslim threat, but the Muslim armies were superior in the field. When Alfonso VI, the Valiant of Castile and León seized Toledo in 1085, the alarmed Muslims called for aid from Yusuf ibn-Tashfin, chief of the Almoravids, the Berber sect that had conquered northwestern Africa. Ibn-Tashfin landed at Algeciras, west of Gibraltar in 1086 and marched north through Seville and Badajoz. At Zalaca, he met the army of Christian knights and infantry under Alfonso on 23 October. The swift Berber horsemen utterly routed the Spanish, who had a marked superiority in numbers but lacked maneuverability and discipline. King Alfonso barely escaped with his life.

EL CID

During the next 20 years, ibn-Tashfin ruled with a firm hand all of Spain south of Toledo. The temporary exception was Valencia, which became an independent Moorish kingdom in 1094 under the Spanish soldier of fortune Rodrigo (Ruy) Díaz de Bivar, the (El) Cid. The city reverted to Muslim control when the great folk hero was killed by the Almoravids five years later.[126]

---

[126] David Eggenberger, *An Encyclopedia of Battles*, Dover Publications, Inc., New York, 1985, p. 487.

Santa Gadea Oath, an 1864 painting by Marcos Giráldez de Acosta depicting Alfonso VI (at the centre with a red cape) swearing with his right hand on the Bible that he did not take part in the murder of his brother Sancho II, while El Cid stands as a witness in front of him.

Rodrigo Díaz de Vivar, known to his men as El Cid (meaning "The Lord"), was a Spanish nobleman and military leader of the medieval kingdom of Castile. Raised in the court of King Ferdinand the Great, he rose to become the commander and standard-bearer of Castile's military, and served under Ferdinand's son, Sancho II. Rodrigo led several successful campaigns against Sancho's brothers, and the local Muslim nations. Sancho was later assassinated, and the throne passed to his brother Alfonso, who gave the order to have Rodrigo exiled.

Rodrigo went on to command the armies of the Muslim state of Zaragoza. He led Zaragoza's army to victory over their enemies several times, and even defeated the large Christian army of the Kingdom of Aragon. His newfound reputation led Alfonso to put aside his personal grudges and invite him back to the court of Castile.

Rodrigo refused Alfonso's request for aid, instead deciding to focus on his own ambitions. With his army, he marched his army towards the coastal city of Valencia, intending to create his own kingdom there. Along the way, he defeated the army of Barcelona and conquered many towns and cities. He laid siege to Valencia, and by the time the siege was broken, Valencia had been made into Rodrigo's own principality that he ruled independently. The city was made up of both Christians and Muslims, who lived in peace.

Rodrigo (Ruy) Díaz de Bivar, El Cid, Burgos, Spain.

In 1111, Louis VI conducted an attack on the castle of Le Puiset. According to an account written by Archbishop Suger, after the defenders had been driven inside the castle, an attempt was made to storm the gatehouse of the bailey, and then to set it on fire. Carts full of wood soaked in fat were pushed up to the walls under a storm of missiles thrown by the garrison. The defenders managed to extinguish the burning cars, and then repelled an assault across the castle's ditch and up the rampart. Eventually, the attackers succeeded in making a breach in the castle's palisade, thereby forcing the garrison to retreat into the tower on the motte. Shortly afterwards, the garrison surrendered. The siege was brief and characterized by hand-to-hand combat. Both sides used spears, bows, swords, and axes.[127]

---

[127] Anthony Kemp, op. cit., p. 96.

Medieval crossbowmen. (Payne-Gallwey)

Early medieval bowmen were equipped with either a short-stringed bow or a crossbow, although crossbows are known to have been in use by the Romans. William the Conqueror's army may have used them at the battle of Hastings in 1066, and they were clearly in use by the Crusaders who arrived at Constantinople on the First Crusade in 1096. The crossbow of this era was described by Anna Comnena as "a weapon of war which had to be stretched lying almost on one's back. The feet were pressed against the bow while the string was tugged back towards the body. In the middle of the string was a groove into which a short, thick, iron-tipped arrow was fitted. On discharge, such arrows could transfix a shield, cut through a heavy iron breastplate and resume their flight on the other side." Anna's account may be slightly exaggerated, but the crossbow clearly demonstrated it had heavy hitting power. Improvements were made in later versions wherein the string could be tensioned by levers or ratchets, which permitted them to be armed and used by even the weakest bowman. Crossbows were considered to be so deadly that at the Lateran Council in 1139,they were banned as inhuman weapons. The ban had no effect on the users. The crossbows limitations were its slow rate of fire and the cost of the bolts that it fired.[128]

The defence was assisted from the later years of the 12th century by the introduction of the crossbow. The traditional English bow was the short-bow, with a range of no more than 600'. The medieval crossbow derived from the classic *ballista*. It was a more accurate weapon, with a longer range, and the quarrel which it fired was in all respects more deadly than a simple arrow. It had been condemned by the Papacy in 1139, but never ceased to be used. It was adopted in England in the later years of the 12th century. Richard I favored it, and from the time of King John small bands of *balistarii*, or crossbowmen, were stationed in the more important castles. The crossbow gave the defence a considerable advantage during the 13th century. But it's rate of fire was slow, and the archer needed protection while drawing his bow. Loops facilitated sighting the bow, and the wide internal splay gave the bowman room to handle his weapon. The crossbow was a remarkably accurate weapon, capable of picking off defenders on the walls and even of shooting a quarrel through a loop and hitting the defender. Its accuracy and range led to the construction of wooden shutters and bretaches over the tops of castle walls.[129]

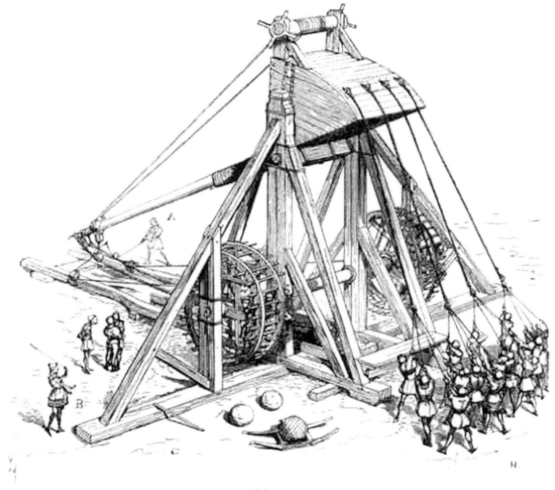

Mangoneau.

---

[128] Ibid, p. 96.

[129] N. J. G. Pounds, *The Medieval Castle in England, and Wales.* Cambridge University Press, 1990. Internet: http://www.castlewales.com/siege.html.

The 12th century development of the trebuchet proved to be an effective counter to stone walls although the trebuchet appears to have been a better "mortar" than catapult.[130] Other weapons were developed, including a form of land mine called a caltrop. It was constructed from four iron spikes joined to form a tetrahedron so that when thrown on the ground one spike was always face up. Numerous devices of this kind were strewn on the ground forward of a fortification and posed a serious threat to horses, often disabling them and forcing a rider to dismount.

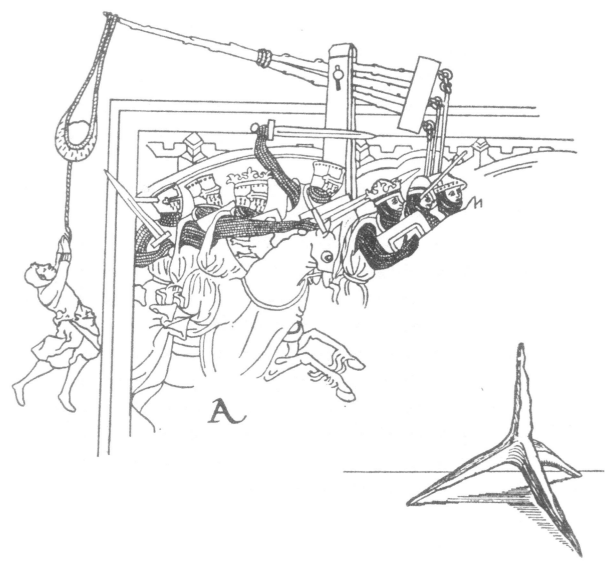

Trebuchet and caltrop.

Logistics were another important consideration. When an army had eaten a district bare, it was often forced to move on, even though a siege or battle task was only half complete. Neither friend nor foe was spared the ravages of a hungry army, and as a result, everyone within the sound of an alarm would

---

[130]   Hannibal von Luttichau-Barenstein, *Alte Burgen-schone Schlosser, Eine romantische Deutschlandreise, (Old Fortresses and beautiful Castles, a romantic German tour)*, Verlag Das Beste GmbH, Stuttgart, 1980, p. 273.

race to get behind the protective walls of the nearest castle on the appearance of one. Such conditions speeded up the development of fortification, which in turn shut off the remaining sources of supply.[131]

Catapult used by the Crusaders during the First Crusade, ca 1097, engraving by Gustave Doré.

Large armies would be forced to come to terms with all these advances in siege engines during the Crusades. They would also learn to develop an adequate logistic train. The First Crusade launched in 1095 led to the successful siege of Antioch in 1098, and the capture of Jerusalem after a six-week siege on 15 July 1099. The Crusaders then erected strong fortresses at vulnerable points along the frontier, and made important advances in the art of castle building.[132] The Muslims were not long in uniting against them, and on 4 July 1187 the Kurdish leader Saladin decisively defeated the armies of the Second Crusade at the battle of Hattin. He then went on to recapture Jerusalem on 2 Oct 1187.

---

[131] Lynn Montross, op. cit., p. 161-165.
[132] Carlton J.H. Hayes et al, *History of Western Civilization*, The MacMillan Company, New York, 1964, p. 179.

12th century Crusaders. Mary Evans Picture Library.

The fall of Jerusalem led Richard I of England, Philip Augustus II of France, and the Emperor Frederick Barbarossa of Germany to prepare for a vast expedition to the Holy land. During these preparations, Guy of Lusignan had attempted and failed to capture Jerusalem due to his lack of siege engines.

Frederick's German force may have been the largest single army ever seen up to that time, and it moved very slowly overland towards the Holy Land. Unfortunately for the Crusaders, Frederick drowned in Cilicia en route to the war in 1190, and the German army subsequently melted away.[133]

---

[133] G. Braun, *Stauferburgen am Oberrhein (Staufer Castles on the Upper Rheinland)*, GmbH, Karlsruhe, 1977, p. 24.

Crusaders ambushed by the Turks, engraving by Gustave Doré.

Although Philip II was the first to arrive at Acre, it was Richard I who made it his business to assume command in 1191. Philip's gunners along with those of the Templars and Hospitallers, had been bombarding Acre by hurling stones from great siege engines, but when Richard arrived, he doubled the barrage, using the trebuchet, a counter-weight operated war engine and ranks of mangonels and catapults, petriers and arbalasts.[134] His superior siege machines could fling bigger missiles to a greater

---

[134] 1113-1118 Knights Templar founded by Baudoin I (crowned 18 July 1100). When the Crusaders took the city of Jerusalem on 15 Jul 1099, there was in existence a small hospital for Christian pilgrims dedicated to St John the Baptist and under the rule of a certain Brother Gerard. Brother Gerard had taken care of many wounded Christian soldiers and had his hospital had so impressed Duke Godfrey of Bouillon that he endowed it with the manor of Montboise, in Brabant. Other Crusaders also gave grants. They decided to formalize the hospital with a regular constitution. The Knights of the Order of the Hospital of St John of Jerusalem (Hospitallers of St John

distance than those already in use. Even the strongest masonry cracked under such an irresistible pounding. Most of the renewed attacks on the walls were ineffective, as the defenders discouraged their foes with showers of arrows, stones and burning pitch, and thousands died in the battle.

When Richard fell sick Philip carried on the attack using a massive siege engine called the "Bad Neighbor" to send hammer-blows against the wall of the largest part of Acre's bastions known as the "Cursed Tower." The defenders countered with a similar contraption mounted on the tower, called the "Evil Kinsman" and destroyed the French weapon. Philip replied with another piece of technology, a new type of scaling ladder equipped with a protective mantlet, but when this failed, he ordered another general assault against the walls.

Although the defenders offered to surrender on certain conditions, the attackers continued the siege. A breach was made in the wall not far from the Cursed Tower, but an assault led by Aubrey Clement, Marshal of France failed to force its way through the gap. He and all his men were cut down. Richard by now recovered from his illness, took charge of the final assault in spite of another attempt by the defenders to surrender with conditions. On 11 July 1191, the Cursed Tower fell. The English and their Pisan allies hacked their way into the wide breach, only to be driven back by a concentrated downpour of Greek fire.

At this point, Philip negotiated a surrender, although Richard refused to ratify the agreement. The garrison was allowed to march out provided three conditions were met, which included the return of

---

of Jerusalem) were confirmed by the 1113 order of Pope Pascal II as a military order to protect pilgrims and also to defend the Latin states in the East. They adopted the Augustinian rule, and took as their habit the black robe, with a white cross of eight points on the left side near the heart. It originally consisted mostly of French Knights (1119-1120), but nine women as nursing sisters were also original members of the Hospitallers at Jerusalem. About 50 women were generally part of the establishment for the next 150 years. When Brother Gerard died in 1120, the Hospitallers elected Raymond du Puy, the second founder of the Order, whose destinies he guided for the next 40 years to 1160. He was the first to take the title of Master. Pope Clement V suppressed the Order 22 Mar 1312, and two years later burnt the last Grand Master Jacques de Molay, the ancestor of the Rosicruscians & Freemasons.

Knights dubbed at the tomb of Christ were known as Knights of the Holy Sepulchre. When Acre fell in 1291, they lost their last stronghold in the Holyland. The Order of the Hospital of St John of Jerusalem (Hospitalers) later retreated to Cyprus, then Rhodes, where it ruled for 200 years. The Sealords of Sultan Suleiman besieged Rhodes in 1522 and forced them out after six months. Seven years later the Knights were offered Malta by the HRE Charles V (with Tripoli included), for the payment in rent of one falcon. The Knights arrived in Malta in 1530. The Order of the Temple of Solomon (Templars) was followed by the Order of St Lazarus, all at the end of the 11th Century. The orders were comprised of a Grandmaster, Pillars of Lands (provincial masters), Grand Priors, Commanders, and Knights.

In Spain, several orders were established in Castille between 1156-1171, including The Orders of: Calatrava; Alcantara; and Santiago (St James). In Portugal, the Orders of Avis; Montesa (Aragon); and the Order of Christ. The Teutonic Order-Great Order of German Knights. There are awards still presented for the Orders of: The Garter; the Golden Fleece; of St Michael; the Most Ancient Order of the Thistle; the Most Honourable Order of the Bath; the British Empire; the Chrysanthemum; and the Companions of Honour.

The Knights of Malta still exist and continue to function to this day. Their Order was divided into langues, or tongues: Auvergne, Provence, France, Aragon, Castille, England, Germany, and Italy. The Turks attacked Malta in 1547 and 1551 unsuccessfully, although the Knights were driven out of Tripoli in 1551. On 18 May 1565, the Ottoman Turks and their allies totaling 48,000 troops attacked the 8000 men (540 Knights, 4000 Maltese, and Spanish and Italian Mercenaries) in Malta. The Grand Master, La Valette defeated the Turks. Six years later the Turks are also defeated at Sea- the Battle of Lepanto. Napoleon captured Malta in Jun 1798, but it was retaken by the British in Oct the same Year. In 1802 the Treaty of Amiens ended the war between England and France, and Malta was returned to the Order of St John. In 1814, under the Treaty of Paris, Malta became a UK possession.

the true cross, the release of 1500 prisoners and 200 nobles, and the payment of a ransom of 200,000 bezants to Philip and Richard. Until these conditions were met, the garrison of Acre was held hostage.[135]

Saladin failed to meet the terms of surrender, even though Richard extended the time limit to three months. Richard subsequently gave orders to "Keep those of rank for ransom. Keep the strong for sale into slavery. Kill the rest." 2,700 were executed, leading Saladin to reply with equally harsh countermeasures.[136] Terrorism would be a key weapon in future sieges and add its morally devastating effect to the list of standard practices in siegecraft. We see its effects even now in the atrocities being perpetrated in Bosnia, Cambodia, Rwanda, Haiti, and of course by the Osama bin Laden minions of Al Qaeda.

It has been said that the Crusaders brought back to Europe techniques, which had wide effects on castle building in the 12th century.[137] T.E. Lawrence disputed this however, after he had examined the castles of Syria and Palestine in 1909. He had attempted to determine the influence of the Crusades on European military architecture to the end of the 12th century, and came to doubt the traditional view that the Crusaders drew their excellence in castle building from the East. He stated that "there is no evidence that Richard borrowed anything great or small, from any fortress he saw in the Holy Land, and that it was not likely that he would do so, since he would find better examples of everything in the South of France, which he knew so well."[138] He summed up his observations by saying that "the Crusading architects were for many years copyists of the Western builders." Lawrence did acknowledge however, the possibility of mutual influence and the transfer of trifling detail, because of the constant interchange among the East-West upper classes.[139]

When Lawrence produced his thesis on *"The Crusading Castles of Syria"* in 1910, he wrote, "the aim in the mind of every architect…was to find such a site for his buildings that the waste and weakness of equal accessibility on all sides might be avoided; then he could multiply defenses on the one weak face alone."[140]

This meant the attacking commander had his work cut out for him once he decided to conduct an attack or siege. His first duty was to ensure that he had enough troops to adequately surround the fortification he intended to assault, in order to prevent supplies and reinforcements from gaining access to the garrison inside. If a relieving forces was likely to arrive on the scene, he would have to fortify his own camp by digging lines of trenches, ditches, ramparts and possibly his own fortresses much as Caesar did in his battle with the Gauls at Alesia. In effect, it might have been necessary to build a fortress in order to besiege a fortress. On one side, these defense-works would face the castle under siege with the primary intent being to counter sallies by the defending garrison, while the rear of the system being erected would face the open country to protect the attacker against a relieving field army. If the relieving force did arrive before the siege was complete, the roles could be reversed, with the besieger finding his forces besieged in his own entrenched camp. Completing an assault with all possible speed became extremely important where relieving forces could be called upon to alter the circumstances of the attack.[141]

Of the methods of attack available, escalade was the quickest and simplest, but carried with it the greatest risks in terms of potential troop losses. Numerous scaling ladders would be thrown up simultaneously, often with well-armed troops already perched on the top, while archers kept up covering

---

[135]   Charles Connell, op. cit., p. 56.

[136]   Charles Connell, op. cit., p. 57.

[137]   William Anderson, *Castles of Europe, from Charlemagne to the Renaissance*, Ferndale Editions, London, 1980, p. 46.

[138]   A.W. Lawrence, *T.E. Lawrence by His Friends*, Jonathan Cape, London, 1954, p. 53.

[139]   John E. Mack, *A Prince of Our Disorder, The Life of T.E. Lawrence*, Mack, London, 1976, p. 52-54.

[140]   Desmond Stewart, *T. E. Lawrence*, Paladin, Granada Publishing, London, 1979, p. 61-62.

[141]   Anthony Kemp, op cit., p.96 & p. 161.

fire over the top of the climbing troops to keep some of the defender's heads down. The intrepid climbers would be subjected to a wide variety of deadly devices designed to repel them. Quicklime and boiling liquids such as oil or lead would be poured on them, along with red-hot sand or various heavy objects such as iron bars, bricks, or rocks. Red-hot sand was particularly effective against attackers wearing armor or chainmail, as it got inside the joints and incapacitated or at least made the victim extremely uncomfortable. If the scaler fell or was thrown from the ladder into the ditch, his ordeal could get worse. At least one unfortunate knight who found himself in this position had brushwood dropped onto him, which was then set on fire, roasting him alive in his armor. Ladder and scaling assaults were most effective when conducted as part of a surprise night attack, or against a lightly held part of the defenses in conjunction with a diversionary assault.[142]

Siege of the Castle of Schwanau in Alsace, 1333, painting by Émile Schweitzer.

Trebuchets were used to destroy countless numbers of castles in medieval Germany until few remained that had not been destroyed and rebuilt numerous times, with the possible exception of the Marksburg Castle on the north bank of the Rhine River overlooking the town of Braubach. The Marksburg was first mentioned in 1231, and was the only Rhine castle to escape capture in the Thirty Years War.[143] It also achieved the remarkable success of being the only fortress of over 500 in the

---

[142] Ibid., p.161.

[143] Defenestration of Prague took place on 23 May 1618, leading to the start of the Thirty Years War. Most of the battles took place in Germany. The war ended on 20 August 1648 with the signing of the Treaty of Westphalia

Rhineland-Pfalz area of present-day Germany to withstand all sieges against it between the 14th and 18th centuries.[144]

(Tobi 87 Photo)
Marksburg Castle on the Rhine River, Germany.

The French emperor Napoleon seized then abolished the Holy Roman Empire in 1806. He gave the Marksburg to his ally the Duke of Nassau for his service. He used the castle as a prison and as a home for disabled soldiers. After the Austro-Prussian War of 1866 the Duchy of Nassau became a territory of Prussia, which took ownership of the Marksburg. It was sold in 1900 for a symbolic price of 1,000 Goldmarks to the German Castle Association, which had been founded a year earlier as a private initiative to preserve castles in Germany. The Marksburg has been the head office of this organisation since 1931. In March 1945, the castle was severely damaged by American artillery fired from the other side of the Rhine.

The French forces of the north that carried out the Albigensian Crusade in the south of France were very well equipped with siege catapults and used them to effectively reduce the Cathar fortresses high in the Pyrenees.[145]

---

which recognized the independence of the Netherlands.

[144] Werner Bornheim et al, *Burgen un Schlosser, Kunst und Kultur in Rheinland-Pfalz, (Fortresses and Castles, Art and Culture in the Rhineland-Pfalz Region)*, Ahrtal-Verlag, Bad Neuenahr-Ahrweiler, 1981, p. 31. H. von Luttichau-Barenstein, *Alte Burgen-schone Schlosser*, Verlag Das Beste, Stuttgart, 1980, p. 137.

[145]

ADVANCES IN SIEGE ENGINES

(Oren Rozen Photo)
Replica of Roman Ballista in the Hecht Museum, Haifa, Israel.

Catapults and ballistae were eventually replaced with cannon. Artillery was used at Rouen in 1338, and at Florence in 1326. In 1356 the Black Prince of England used artillery at the siege of Romorantin to set the town on fire and forced it to capitulate. As will be shown, the capture of Constantinople by the Turks in 1453 was a direct result of the decisive use of gunfire.[146]

---

[146]   Steven Runicman, *The Fall of Constantinople, 1453,* Cambridge at the University Press, 1965, p. 77-78, 95-97.

Medieval bombard.

Weather and the forces of nature have a major role to play in any battle, as any intelligence officer will attest to. The massive eight-and-a-half-mile long stone walls of the city of Nineveh fell in 612 BC, because of the incessant rains that caused Tigris River to overflow and batter them down.[147]

ALBIGENSIAN CRUSADE, 1209-1229

The Albigensian Crusade or the Cathar Crusade (1209–1229, was a 20-year military campaign initiated by Pope Innocent III to eliminate Catharism in Languedoc, in southern France. The Crusade was prosecuted primarily by the French crown and promptly took on a political flavour, resulting in not only a significant reduction in the number of practising Cathars, but also a realignment of the County

---

[147]   Trevor N. Dupuy, *The Evolution of Weapons and Warfare*, Hero Books, Fairfax, Virginia, 1984, p. 27.

of Toulouse in Languedoc, bringing it into the sphere of the French crown and diminishing the distinct regional culture and high level of influence of the Counts of Barcelona.

The Cathars originated from an anti-materialist reform movement within the Bogomil churches of Dalmatia and Bulgaria calling for a return to the Christian message of perfection, poverty and preaching, combined with a rejection of the physical to the point of starvation. The reforms were a reaction against the often scandalous and dissolute lifestyles of the Catholic clergy in southern France. Their theology, neo-Gnostic in many ways, was basically dualist. Several of their practices, especially their belief in the inherent evil of the physical world, conflicted with the doctrines of the Incarnation of Christ and sacraments, initiated accusations of Gnosticism and brought them the ire of the Catholic establishment. They became known as the Albigensians, because there were many adherents in the city of Albi and the surrounding area in the 12th and 13th centuries.

Between 1022 and 1163, the Cathars were condemned by eight local church councils, the last of which, held at Tours, declared that all Albigenses should be put into prison and have their property confiscated. The Third Lateran Council of 1179 repeated the condemnation. Innocent III's diplomatic attempts to roll back Catharism were met with little success. After the murder of his legate, Pierre de Castelnau in 1208, Innocent III declared a crusade against the Cathars. He offered the lands of the Cathar heretics to any French nobleman willing to take up arms.

From 1209 to 1215, the Crusaders experienced grand success, capturing Cathar lands and perpetrating acts of extreme violence, often against civilians. From 1215 to 1225, a series of revolts caused many of the lands to be lost. A renewed crusade resulted in the recapturing of the territory and effectively drove Catharism underground by 1244. The Albigensian Crusade also had a role in the creation and institutionalization of both the Dominican Order and the Medieval Inquisition. The Dominicans promulgated the message of the Church to combat alleged heresies by preaching the Church's teachings in towns and villages, while the Inquisition investigated heresies. Because of these efforts, by the middle of the 14th century, any discernible traces of the Cathar movement had been eradicated.

SIEGE OF BÉZIERS, 1209

By mid-1209, around 10,000 crusaders had gathered in Lyon before marching south. Many Crusaders stayed on for no more than 40 days before being replaced. A large number came from Northern France, while some had volunteered from England. The crusaders turned towards Montpellier, and the lands of Raymond Roger Trencavel, aiming for the Cathar communities around Albi and Carcassonne. Raymond Roger, Raymond's nephew, and Count of Foix, was a supporter of the Cathar movement. He initially promised to defend the city of Béziers, but after hearing of the coming of the Crusader army, he abandoned that city and raced back to Carcassonne to prepare his defences.

The Crusaders captured the small village of Servian and then headed for Béziers, arriving on 21 July 1209. Under the command of the papal legate, Arnaud Amalric they began to besiege the city, calling on the Catholics within to come out, and demanding that the Cathars surrender. Neither group did as commanded. The city fell the following day when an abortive sortie was pursued back through the open gates. The entire population was killed, and the city burned to the ground. It was reported that Amalric, when asked how to distinguish Cathars from Catholics, responded, "Kill them all! God will know his own." Whether this was actually said is sometimes considered doubtful, but, according to historian Joseph Strayer, it captures the "spirit" of the Crusaders, who killed nearly every man, woman, and child in the town.

Amalric and Milo, a fellow legate, in a letter to the Pope, claim that the crusaders "put to the sword almost 20,000 people." Strayer insists that this estimate is too high, but noted that in his letter "the legate expressed no regret about the massacre, not even a word of condolence for the clergy of the cathedral who were killed in front of their own altar." News of the disaster quickly spread and afterwards many settlements surrendered without a fight.

SIEGE OF CARCASSONNE, 1209

After the Massacre at Béziers, the next major target was Carcassonne a city with many well known Cathars. Carcassonne was well fortified, but vulnerable, and overflowing with refugees. The Crusaders traversed the 45 miles between Béziers and Carcassonne in six days, arriving in the city on 1 August 1209. The siege did not last long. By 7 August they had cut the city's water supply. Raymond Roger sought negotiations but was taken prisoner while under truce, and Carcassonne surrendered on 15 August. The people were not killed but were forced to leave the town. They were naked according to Peter of Vaux-de-Cernay, a monk and eyewitness to many events of the crusade, but "in their shifts and breeches," according to Guillaume de Puylaurens, a contemporary.

Simon de Montfort, a prominent French nobleman, was then appointed leader of the Crusader army, and was granted control of the area encompassing Carcassonne, Albi, and Béziers. After the fall of Carcassonne, other towns surrendered without a fight. Albi, Castelnaudary, Castres, Fanjeaux, Limoux, Lombers and Montréal all fell quickly during the autumn.

The next battle centred around Lastours and the adjacent castle of Cabaret. Attacked in December 1209, Pierre Roger de Cabaret repulsed the assault. Fighting largely halted over the winter, but fresh Crusaders arrived. In March 1210, Bram was captured after a short siege. In June, the well-fortified city of Minerve was besieged. The city was not of major strategic importance. Simon's decision to attack it was probably influenced by the large number of perfects who had gathered there. Unable to take the town by storm because of the surrounding geography, Simon launched a heavy bombardment against the town, and in late June the main well was destroyed and on 22 July, the city, short on water, surrendered. Simon wished to treat the occupants leniently but was pressured by Arnaud Amalric to punish the Cathars. The Crusaders allowed the soldiers defending the town as well as the Catholics inside of it to go free, along with the non-*perfect* Cathars. The Cathar "perfects" were given the opportunity to return to Catholicism. Only three women did. The 140 who refused were burned at the stake. Some entered the flames voluntarily, not awaiting their executioners.

In August, the Crusade proceeded to the stronghold of Termes. Despite sallies from Pierre-Roger de Cabaret, the siege was solid. The occupants of Termes suffered from a shortage of water, and Raymond agreed to a temporary truce. However, the Cathars were briefly relieved by an intense rainstorm, and so Raymond refused to surrender. Ultimately, the defenders were not able to break the siege, and on 22 November 22 the Cathars managed to abandon the city and escape.

By the time operations resumed in 1211, the actions of Arnaud-Amaury and Simon de Montfort had alienated several important lords, including Raymond de Toulouse, who had been excommunicated again. The crusaders returned in force to Lastours in March and Pierre-Roger de Cabaret soon agreed to surrender. In May, the castle of Aimery de Montréal was retaken; he and his senior knights were hanged, and several hundred Cathars were burned. Casses fell easily in early June. Afterwards, Simon marched towards Montferrand, where Raymond had placed his brother, Baldwin, in command. After a short siege, Baldwin signed an agreement to abandon the fort in return for swearing an oath to go free and to not fight again against the Crusaders. Baldwin briefly returned to Raymond, but afterward defected to the Crusaders and remained loyal to them thereafter. After taking Montferrand, the Crusaders headed for Toulouse. The town was besieged, but for once the attackers were short of supplies and men, and Simon de Montfort withdrew before the end of the month. Emboldened, Raymond de Toulouse led a force to attack Montfort at Castelnaudary in September. Montfort broke free from the siege but Castelnaudary fell that December to Raymond's troops and Raymond's forces went on to liberate over thirty towns before the counter-attack ground to a halt at Lastours in the autumn.

The Cathars now faced a difficult situation. To repel the Crusaders, they turned to Peter II of Aragon for assistance. A favourite of the Catholic Church, Peter II had been crowned king by Innocent III in 1204. He fought the Moors in Spain and served in the Battle of Las navas de Tolosa. However, his sister, Eleanor, had married Raymond VI, securing an alliance. His victories in the south against the Spanish, along with the persuasion of a delegation sent to Rome, had led Innocent III to order a halt to the crusade. On 15 January 1213, he wrote the legate Arnaud Amaury and to Simon, ordering Simon to restore the lands that he had taken. Concerned also that Simon had grown too powerful, Peter decided to come to the aid of Toulouse. The Crown of Aragon, under Peter II, allied with the County of Toulouse and various other entities. These actions alarmed Innocent, who after hearing from Simon's delegation denounced Peter and ordered a renewal of the crusade.

On 21 May, he sent Peter a letter severely castigating him for allegedly providing false information and warning him not to oppose the Crusaders. However, Peter's coalition force engaged Simon's troops on 12 September 1213 in the Battle of Muret. The Crusaders were heavily outnumbered. Peter and Simon both organized their troops into three lines. The first of the Crusader lines was beaten back, but Simon managed to outflank the coalition cavalry. Peter II was struck down and killed. The coalition forces, hearing of his death, retreated in confusion. This allowed Simon's troops to occupy the northern part of Toulouse.

It was a serious blow for the resistance, and in 1214 the situation became worse. As the Crusaders continued their advance, Raymond and his son were forced to flee to England, and his lands were given by the Pope to the victorious Philip II, a stratagem which finally succeeded in interesting the king in the conflict. In November, Simon de Montfort entered Périgord and easily captured the castles of Dommel and Montfort; he also occupied Castlenaud and destroyed the fortifications of Beynac. In 1215, Castelnaud was recaptured by Montfort, and the Crusaders entered Toulouse. The town paid an indemnity of 30,000 marks. Toulouse was gifted to Montfort. The Fourth Council of the Lateran in 1215 solidified Crusader control over the area by officially proclaiming Simon the Count of Toulouse. (Stayer, Joseph R. The Albigensian Crusades. The Dial Press, New York, NY, 1971)

SIEGE OF CARCASSONNE, 1240

The walled city of Carcassonne above the Aude River, aerial view (Chensiyuan Photo), and oblique view (Jean-Paul Grandmont Photo). This city in the southeast of France came under siege in the autumn of 1240.[148] One account exists of this siege:

---

[148] Carcassonne, situated in the middle of the Languedoc on the Aude River in southern France, with portions which date from the 6th century, although its current castle was constructed in the first half of the 12th century. The original town was built on a bluff sloping down steeply on all sides. It is an amalgam of mainly Romanesque and Gothic buildings which were restored by Viollet-le-Duc in the 19th century. Wolfgang F. Schuerl, op. cit., p. 143.

"The attackers began a mine against the barbican gate of Narbonne. And forthwith, we, having heard the noise of their work underground, made a counter-mine, and constructed a great and strong wall of stones laid without mortars in the inside of the barbican, so that we thereby retained full half of the barbican. When they set fire to the hole in such wise that the wood having burned out, a portion of the barbican fell down! The outer defense line, the barbican of Carcassonne, was then still constructed of wood.

They then began to mine against another turret of the lices; we counter-mined and got possession of the hole which they had excavated. They therefore began to tunnel a mine between us and a certain wall and destroyed two embrasures of the lices. But we set up there a good and strong palisade between us and them.

They also started a mine at the angle of the town wall, near the bishop's palace, and by dint of digging from a great way off arrived at a certain Saracen wall, by the wall of the lices; but at once, when he detected it, we made a good and strong palisade between us and them, higher up the lices, and counter-mined. Thereupon they fired their mine and flung down some ten fathoms of our embrassured front. But we made hastily another good palisade with a brattice upon it and loopholes; so, none among them dared to come near us in that quarter.

They also began a mine against the barbican of the Rodez Gate, and kept below ground, wishing to arrive at our walls, making a marvelous great tunnel. But when we perceived it, we forthwith made a palisade on one side and the other of it. We counter-mined also, and, having fallen in with them, carried the chamber of their mine."[149]

Both sides in a siege could make use of fire. Many parts of a castle were made of wood, particularly in the inner courtyard or "bailey." These wooden buildings often housed provisions and other stores, and their destruction could greatly reduce a defender's long-term ability to resist. Wooden hoardings were also vulnerable, unless they were protected by hides. The defenders, on the other hand, would try to ignite the besieger's equipment, either by throwing burning material on them or by sallying out on horseback with torches in hand.[150]

Mining played a major role in the methods used to gain entry to a castle. It was time-consuming and required skill and perseverance. The technique involved the excavation of a cavity under a part of the wall, generally at the angle of a tower. Timber props would be used to shore up the tunnel created, and the space was then filled with combustible material (fat pigs were used to undermine the castle at Rochester, England in 1216). The props and material would be consumed in the fire, causing the masonry above to collapse, and hopefully creating a breach sufficient for the attacker to assault through. According to Herodotus, such mining techniques were in use at the siege of Barca in 510 BC. Mining became more difficult with the introduction of round towers and plinths. If mining activities against a castle under siege were detected, the defending garrison could countermine by digging their own tunnel to break in on the enemy excavators. Once they had opened a breach in the attackers mine, hand-to-hand combat with shovels and picks would follow. Alternatively, the defenders could flood the tunnel with water, or smoke them out with fire, provided the wind was right.[151]

The technology required to wage war often led to the development of innovative "secret" weapons. Some time prior to the 5th century BC, the defenses of Delium for example, fell to fire propelled through a kind of gigantic blowpipe. The secret of Greek fire was as jealously guarded by the Byzantines as are our technological weapons are today. To this day the exact composition of this terror weapon remains a mystery. It was a liquid, could be blown from a tube, would burn on water, and even stone and iron

---

149 H.W. Koch, *Medieval Warfare*, Bison Books Limited, London, 1982, p. 85.
150 Ibid., p. 166.
151 Anthony Kemp, op. Cit., p. 166.

could not resist it. It could be extinguished only by sand, vinegar, or urine. The ancient Greeks used mixtures of pitch, resin and sulphur, and the Romans used quicklime and sulphur (which ignited on contact with water).

Even biological warfare is not new. Hannibal, when in command of a Hellenic fleet, sent his sailors on shore to collect poisonous snakes alive. These he enclosed in fragile jars and propelled them into the enemy ships.[152] Beehives and dead horses would also be launched into a fortification.[153]

The invention of the torsion catapult and its variants added to an army's capability for assaulting a city. With this technological advance in weaponry, it became possible to provide a longer-range, more intensive barrage, which would keep down the heads of the besieged at the moment of assault, and break down the parapets, which sheltered them. The various projectile-throwing weapons, operating by springs, thongs, counterpoised weights, and twisted ropes, remained in use up to and during the 15th century. They reached the peak of their technological development however as early as 200 BC, when mathematical formulae were devised to relate power to size. Their use then entered a period of stagnation until about 1050, when both the Christian and Muslim world reintroduced the machines into warfare, sometimes on a massive scale running into hundreds of units.[154]

Because of their complexity and the skill required to operate the various siege engines, engineers and the gunners used to man them had begun to take up an increasing percentage of an attacker's force. Mercenaries were usually hired for this work. The mercenaries equipped themselves, which was an important factor when a "contractor" had to calculate the expense of construction and the operation of costly items of siege equipment.[155]

Counter-siegecraft had to be developed for the purposes of self-preservation. Defenders hurled down siege ladders along with the attackers climbing up on them, or poured boiling oil, lead or pitch on their heads (as graphically depicted in the *"Lord of the Rings"* book and film trilogy). Sometimes grappling irons would be lowered from the top of the wall to hook the men from the ladders before dropping them into the ditch. Alternatively, if the attacking soldiers approached on the tops of siege towers, showers of arrows and flaming torches discouraged them.[156]

It was Philip II of Macedon who first organized a special group of artillery engineers within his army to design and build catapults. Philip's use of siegecraft allowed Greek science and engineering an opportunity to contribute to the art of war, and by the time of Demetrios I (305 BC), known more commonly by his nickname "Poliocretes" (the Besieger), Greek inventiveness in military engineering was probably the best in the ancient world. Alexander's engineers contributed a number of new ideas. In honor of the Greek contributions, to this day the military art of siege warfare is called "poliocretics."

The most important contribution of Greek military engineering of this period was the invention of artillery, the earliest of which took the form of catapults and torsion-fired missiles. The earliest examples date from the 4th century BC and were called *gastraphetes*, literally, "belly shooter." It was a form of primitive crossbow that fired a wooden bolt on a flat trajectory along a slot in the aiming rod. Later, weapons fired by torsion bars powered by horsehair and ox tendon (the Greeks called this material *neuron*) springs could fire arrows, stones, and pots of burning pitch along a parabolic arc. Some of these machines were quite large and mounted on wheels to improve tactical mobility and deployment. One of these machines, the *palintonon*, could fire an 8-lb stone over 300 yards, a range greater than that of a Napoleonic cannon. These weapons were all used by Philip as weapons of siege warfare, but it was

---

[152] Philip Warner, op. cit., p. 30.
[153] Wolfgang F. Schuerl, op. cit., p. 68.
[154] Martin van Creveld, op. cit., p. 33.
[155] H.W. Koch, *Medieval Warfare*, Bison Books Limited, London, 1982, p. 128.
[156] Charles Connell, op. cit., p. 11.

Alexander who used them in a completely different way, as covering artillery. Alexander's army carried prefabricated catapults that weighed only 85 pounds. Larger machines were dismantled and carried along in wagons.[157]

SIEGE OF LISBON, 1147

A painting by Roque Gameiro of the siege of Lisbon in 1147.

The **Siege of Lisbon**, from 1 July to 25 October 1147, brought the city of Lisbon under definitive Portuguese control and expelled its Moorish overlords. The Siege of Lisbon was one of the few Christian victories of the Second Crusade. It was "the only success of the universal operation undertaken by the pilgrim army", i.e., the Second Crusade, according to the near contemporary historian Helmold, although others have questioned whether it was really part of that crusade. It is seen as a pivotal battle of the wider Reconquista.

The Fall of Edessa in 1144 led to a call for a new crusade by Pope Eugene III in 1145 and 1146. In the spring of 1147, the Pope authorized the crusade in the Iberian peninsula. He also authorized Alfonso VII of León and Castile to equate his campaigns against the Moors with the rest of the Second Crusade. In May 1147, a contingent of crusaders left from Dartmouth in England. They had intended to sail directly to the Holy Land, but weather forced the ships to stop on the Portuguese coast, at the northern city of Porto on 16 June 1147. There they were convinced to meet with King Alfonso I of Portugal.

---

[157]   Internet: http://www.au.af.mil/au/awc/awcgate/gabrmetz/gabr000e.htm.

The crusaders agreed to help the King attack Lisbon, with a solemn agreement that offered to the crusaders the pillage of the city's goods and the ransom money for expected prisoners. The siege began on 1 July 1147. The city of Lisbon at the time of arrival consisted of sixty thousand families, including the refugees who had fled Christian onslaught from neighbouring cities of Santarémand others. Also reported by the De expugnatione Lyxbonensi is that the citadel was holding 154,000 men, not counting women and children; after 17 weeks of siege the inhabitants were despoiled, and the city cleansed.

After four months, the Moorish rulers agreed to surrender on 24 October, primarily because of hunger within the city. Most of the crusaders settled in the newly captured city, but some of the crusaders set sail and continued to the Holy Land. Lisbon eventually became the capital city of the Kingdom of Portugal, in 1255.[158]

SIEGE OF CHÂTEAU GAILLARD, 1203-1204

(Sylvain Verlaine Photo)
Aerial view of Château Gaillard.

---

[158] Runciman, Steven. *A History of the Crusades, vol. II: The Kingdom of Jerusalem and the Frankish East, 1100–1187.* (Cambridge University Press, New York, 1952).

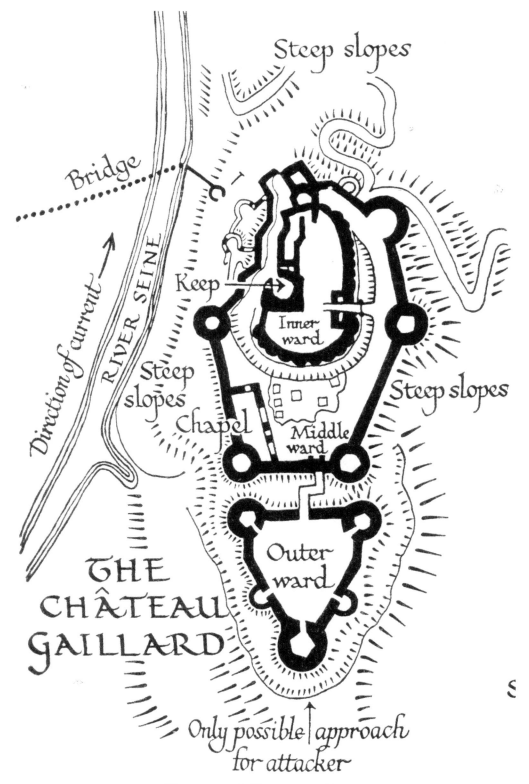

Plan view of Château Gaillard.

CHÂTEAU GAILLARD

Richard Coeur de Lion's career dramatizes the military trends and siege methods of his day. When he returned from the Crusades he began to apply the principles he had learned to castles he built in France. It has also been said that Syrian workmen were imported to build his most famous castle, the Château Gaillard.[159]

Château Gaillard, one of Europe's earliest examples of rounded keeps and concentric fortifications and sighted to dominate Rouen in Normandy, was besieged in 1203-4 by Philip II. The siege of this famous Château come about as a result of the long struggle between the Angevin and Capetian kings in the 12th century. The rivalry was brought to a head when Richard built Château Gaillard in order to compensate for the loss of Gisors, which had been ceded to Philip by the Treaty of Issoudun in 1195.[160]

(Nitot Photo)
Chateau de Gisors.

---

[159]   John E. Mack, op. cit., p. 52-53.

[160]   In 1152, Eleanor of Aquitaine, divorced wife of Louis VII of France, married the Count of Anjou, who became Henry II of England in 1154. Her dowry was half of France. For the next 300 years, France and England would be at war over these territories. In 1214, Philip II Augustus of France defeated the English ally Emperor Otto IV of Germany. Louis IX (Saint Louis) crushed a rebellion of nobles supported by England. This resulted in England being forced to give up all of her French territories except for Aquitaine by the Treaty of Paris in 1259. The dispute continued long after the treaty was signed, with England's Edward II launching the "Hundred Years War" in 1339. In spite of his victory at Crécy, his campaign was brought to a halt by lack of money. Carlos Paluzie de Lescazes, *Castles of Europe*, Crescent Books, Barcelona, 1982, p. 84.

When Richard built the stronghold in 1197, he introduced the design of outer wards and fore works beyond the main walls. The castle had a strong keep and occupied a well-chosen strategic position on a steep height defending Rouen, the capital of Normandy, from every direction. The outer defenses included a bridgehead covering the Seine.

Although Richard believed his fortress was impregnable, he never had the chance to prove it, as he was mortally wounded by a crossbow shot in 1199 during a minor siege at Chalus. The defense of the Château therefore fell to Richard's brother John, who was no match for Philip.[161]

An engraving by Eugène Viollet-le-Duc, a 19th-century architect experienced in renovating castles, of how the Siege of Château Gaillard would have looked.

---

[161] John Lackland (1199-1216) was defeated by the Capetian Philip Augustus in 1214 at Roche-au-Moine, and his allies, Otto IV of Brunswick and the Counts of Flanders and Boulogne, had also been defeated at the Battle of Bouvines. His barons took advantage of this to force him to accept the conditions of Magna Carta in 1215.

In August 1203 Philip brought a great army with him, to lay siege to Château Gaillard as the first stage in his conquest of Normandy. Philip gained an almost immediate success in destroying Richard's elaborate system of defenses across the Seine. Strong swimmers broke up a palisade built across the river, and a fort on the island was taken. Another swimmer who had carried a sealed pot of coals managed to burn down a wooden stockade around the township of Les Andelys. The unfortunate citizens fled into the castle. The only offensive by John's forces was a night attack, which failed miserably. In September, Philip built double lines of circumvallation and sat down to wait.

The garrison of Château Gaillard was capably commanded by constable Roger de Lacy, with 40 knights, 200-foot sergeants, and about 60 engineers and crossbowmen. Hundreds of refugees however, had fled to the shelter of the castle on the approach of the French forces. To save his supplies, de Lacy expelled many who were allowed to pass through the French lines. A second wave of about 400 were not, however, allowed to pass through by the French, who hoped de Lacy would take them back. De Lacy refused to do so, and these unfortunate people had to spend the winter outside the castle, in between the warring factions and in danger of missiles from both sides. When Philip finally relented and let them through, it was too late for most of them, as they died of the effects of starvation and exposure. The blockade went on for six months.

By February 1204, the French towers and siege-engines were ready, and the assault began. Ground was leveled and materials were brought up to fill in the castles protective ditch. Catapults and siege towers were constructed on site and hurried into action. Both sides employed picked marksmen. The first success, however, went to the miners. While working under the cover of mantelets for protection, they picked holes in the foundation of the curtain wall of the outer bailie, and set fire to wooden props, which caused the wall to collapse. The defenders burned everything behind them and retreated to the next obstacle. This was a 30' deep ditch forward of the inner bailie, whose walls rose flush from the ditch and gave no purchase for the miners.

The siege would have dragged on for some time, but a small group of Philip's soldiers suddenly noticed that a latrine shaft was open on the west side of the castle just below an unbarred window of the castle chapel. One man managed to crawl up the drain of the privy, entered the chapel, and reached the window through which he pulled up other soldiers. There they raised an uproar, which made the defenders believe a great many of them had gained entrance. In the ensuing confusion they managed to get to the drawbridge and let it down. The defenders failed in an attempt to smoke them out, panicked, and fled to the safety of the inner bailie. The paradox is that it was John who had added the chapel and had thus introduced a weakness into Richard's design.[162]

Siege engines made no impression on the walls of the inner bailie, which had an odd scalloped design that made it particularly difficult for the miners to attack. There was however, one place under a stone bridge, which afforded them some protection. Philip brought in a great catapult named Cabalus to reinforce their efforts. The defenders made a brave attempt at countermining, but their efforts only weakened the wall further without driving off the attackers. There was a huge fall of masonry and the defenders, not even bothering to retreat to the keep, tried to flee by a postern gate where they were met and forced to surrender.

The unusual strength of Philip's army, and the length of the winter siege were the important factors in the castles fall, rather than the design of the fortress. It would not have fallen if adequate steps had been taken for its relief.[163] The seizure of Normandy rapidly followed the fall of Château Gaillard, and Philip Augustus eventually gained the Angevin Empire.[164]

---

[162] Anthony Kemp, op. cit., p. 170.
[163] Anthony Kemp, op. cit., p. 171.
[164] William Anderson, op. Cit., p. 118-124.

(Bill Taroli Photo)
Mural of siege warfare, Genghis Khan Exhibit, Tech Museum, San Jose.

In the 13th century, the Mongols invaded Europe.[165] They had developed a cold and efficient method of siegecraft based on their extensive battlefield experience.[166] Their system made use of secret agents who took advantage of cowardice or treachery. If they failed, the next step was a blockade and bombardment by their war engines, whose essential parts were carried on packhorses. Finally, if a city could not be betrayed, battered, or starved into submission, a continuous day and night attack was carried on by troops serving in relays.[167]

---

[165] c1162-1227 Genghis Khan, son of Mongol chieftain Yesugai, born in the south east of the Baikal. His son Tuli took over after his death. The Mongols withdrew undefeated in 1242. Khan Toktamish and Tamerlane lead both the White Horde and the Golden Horde, uniting them 1243-1400.

[166] Genghis learned from Chinese engineers the use of siege engines, mangonels, and catapults. Trevor N. Dupuy, *The Evolution of Weapons and Warfare*, Hero Books, Fairfax, Virginia, 1984, p. 71.

[167] In the first decades of the 13th Century the Mongol horsemen, united by Genghis Khan in 1206, conquered the empire of the Chin Tartars to the South of their homelands, and advanced west through Muslim Asia as far as the Caucasus, thus creating the nucleus of an empire that would become, under Kublai Khan, larger than any the world had seen.

The term horde, denoting a Mongol tribe or a field army, did not necessarily mean large numbers of men. Genghis Khan and his successors accomplished feats that would be hard, if not impossible, for modern armies to duplicate, principally because they had one of the best-organized, best trained, and most thoroughly disciplined armies ever created. The Mongol army was usually smaller than those of its principal opponents. The largest force Genghis Khan ever assembled was 240,000 men, with which he conquered Persia. The Mongol armies that later conquered Russia and all of eastern and central Europe never exceeded 150,000 men.

Mongols besieging a city in the Middle East, 1 January 1307.

The Mongols themselves had no illusions as to their own invincibility, and their primary interest was in plunder. The wooden castles and log palisades of Russia, Poland and Hungary offered few difficulties for them, but the remainder of Europe was principally a terrain of forests and mountains, of miserable roads and massive stone fortifications. The invaders, it appears, prudently took note of these obstacles, and decided not to venture outside their own tactical element.[168]

---

[168] Trevor N. Dupuy, *The Evolution of Weapons and Warfare*, Hero Books, Fairfax, Virginia, 1984, p. 72.

Polish soldiers armed with early firearms, 1674-1696.

Simple handguns first began to appear in the second quarter of the 14th century, in the form of short tubes of brass or iron closed at one end. Near the closed end, the breech was pierced by a small hole through which the charge could be fired with a piece of burning slow-match or tinder. This barrel could be fixed to the end of a wooden staff and aimed rather roughly, by tucking it under the arm, or by supporting it on a rest. In either case, the rear end of the staff could be stuck into the ground to take the recoil.[169]

Handguns were reportedly in use at the Battle of Crécy in 1346, and again at Agincourt in 1415, but without noticeable effect or influence on the outcome of either battle.[170] In 1521 France's Francis I went to war with the Holy Roman Emperor Charles V, making use of guns with six-foot long barrels and one-inch bores. The French infantry used these long-barreled firearms to rake the parapets of Charles' castles, forcing the defenders to take cover.

---

[169]   A.V.B. Norman and G.M. Wilson, *Treasures from the Tower of London*, Lund Humphries, Bradford, 1982, p. 29. Werner Meyer and Erich Lessing, *Deutsche Ritter, Deutsche Burgen*, Orbis Verlag, 1990, p. 211.

[170]   Under Charles V of France, Bertran Du Guesclin began the reconquest of the French territories captured by England in the Hundred Years War at that time. The balance of power returned to the English forces again when Henry V of England landed in France in 1415 and won the battle of Agincourt. Carlos Paluzie de Lescazes, op. cit., p. 85.

Early handgunner team.

The manufacture of firearms and cannon was an expensive business. In most cases, only kings or powerful overlords with considerable financial resources at hand could afford to have them made in numbers substantial enough to make a difference in a major siege or battle. Once they did have them, however, the effects could be devastating. In 1494, France's Charles VIII invaded Italy, bringing with him a siege train that included 40 bronze cannon with barrels eight feet long. These guns were easily elevated or depressed because they moved on two prongs or trunions placed just forward of the barrel's balancing point. Except for the heaviest, these cannon were easily moved by lifting the trail of the gun mount and shifting it to one side or the other. They fired iron balls at ranges equal to those of earlier cannon that were three times their caliber. Charles guns were transported on carriages that increased their ease of mobility. His cannon struck the Italian fortresses with an effect that resembled German Blitzkrieg warfare of World War II. The Italian fortress of San Giovanni had once been besieged for seven years. The French gunners destroyed it in eight hours and then slaughtered the defending garrison. The era of the long siege was closing but would never be completely eliminated.

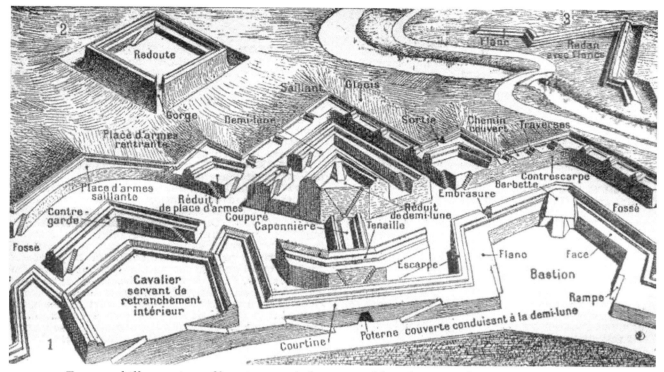

Engraved illustration of bastions and elements of fortifications from the Vauban era.

To counter the increase in firepower, new designs in fortification were developed. Squared castle designs gave way to the lower silhouette of the square fort with corner bastions which were constructed to support a pro-active defense. The post-gunpowder era fortresses had to have walls thick enough to absorb cannon fire and sloped enough to counter scaling. The bastions had to be sited to ensure there was no dead ground where an attacker go undermine the wall or otherwise get close to it unobserved. Inventive minds did not necessarily restrict themselves to designing fortresses using only increased stonework. Vauban and other fortress designers incorporated log and earthwork components into their outer walls to absorb cannon fire. When the Spanish attacked the fortress at Santhia in 1555, its multi-layered and reinforced earth walls reportedly absorbed some 6,300 artillery rounds over three days with suffering major damage. This put the onus back on the designer of siege weapons to develop new tactics, or to increase the capability of his cannon and firearms.

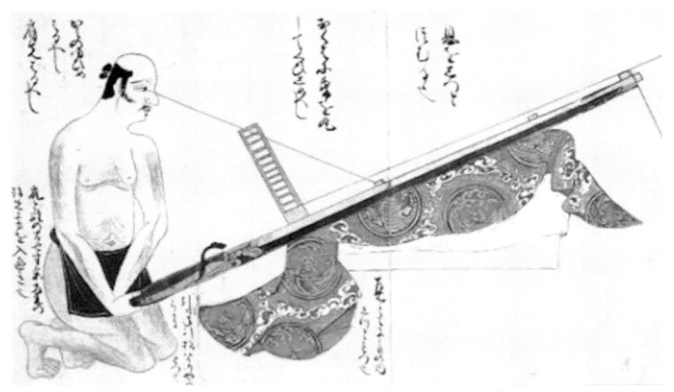

Japanese matchlock sighting instructions for indirect fire.

The increase in the availability of technologically advanced weapons played a major role in this change, and as will be shown in the following chapter, at the siege of Orleans, gunpowder took a leading part.

SIEGE OF ORLEANS, 1428

Orléans in September 1428, the time of the Siege.

The ancient city of Orleans on the Loire had withstood many assaults since the days of the Romans, including an attempt by Attila's Huns in 451.[171] It came under siege during the Hundred Years War (1339-1453) when the French were trying to drive out the English forces. Orleans was protected by walls six feet thick, which rose from 13 to 33 feet above the moat, while five gates and 34 towers completed a system of outer defenses topped by stone battlements and parapets. In addition to war engines of all sorts, the city had provided itself with 70 mortars, bombards, and culverins. This may have been one of the most impressive concentrations of artillery ever seen in the Middle Ages since many of the pieces were borrowed from other towns.

(Greenshed Photo)
English bombards abandonded by Thomas Scalles at Mont Saint-Michel on 17 June 1434.
Calibre 380 – 420-cm.

---

[171] Attila the Hun reached Metz in June 451 AD, but he was defeated in the Battle of Chalons-sur-Marne. He went on to invade northern Italy in 452 AD. He died in 453 AD.

Joan of Arc at the Siege of Orléans, painting by Jules Lenepveu.

A strong garrison manned the city when an English army of about 4,000 appeared in October 1428, with a siege train of mortars and bombards drawn by oxen. The first act of the assailants was to conscript the labor of the district to build two huge stone and wood bulwarks. These would be used later to storm the walls of the city.

During the siege, the town's normal population of 15,000 swelled to 40,000 people, most of them men-at-arms or refugees from outlying regions. Tempers were worn thin by overcrowding, and constant friction occurred between the townsmen and soldiers. Despite a gross lack of sanitary precautions, Orleans managed to escape the usual epidemic. The English blockade could not prevent merchants from entering the gates with grain, cattle, and gunpowder. This in fact put the besiegers in a worse position than the defenders since they did not have adequate food and supplies.

The women and children were tasked with the manufacture of the thousands of darts and crossbow bolts that were shot from the battlements. Twelve master gunners, with many apprentices and laborers to do their bidding, served the myriad instruments of destruction employed by the city. For their part, the English managed several times to launch large stone balls weighing 150 pounds into the city, causing considerable destruction.

Despite such exceptions, the artillery of 1429, while potent against smaller strongholds, had not yet become a threat to walled cities of any strength. Attrition was the only result of the seven-month gunnery duel at Orleans. From the beginning of the battle, the material advantage had been on the side of the defenders, who were superior in numbers, guns, and supplies. Orleans might still have fallen due to low morale, were it not for the appearance of Joan of Arc.[172] Her very innocence of military affairs proved an incentive to burghers who distrusted their own men-at-arms. They rallied behind her and stormed by sheer weight of numbers the two English bulwarks commanding the walls. After severe losses, the invaders lifted the siege in May 1429, and retreated in the conviction that they had been overcome by sorcery.[173] Joan was eventually captured by Burgundians and sold to the English.[174] She was put on trial and burnt at the stake in Rouen.[175]

Although the siege of Orleans was not successful, the use of gunpowder was to set the tone for most of the sieges that followed. The Wars of the Roses (1455-1485) saw many sieges involving firearms.[176] During the Hussite Wars (1419-1436) the Hussites adopted a distinguishing feature of battle in their

---

[172] During the reign of Charles VII, King of France (1422-1461), the country was divided into three large areas: The English occupied Normandy, Poitou, and Aquitaine; Burgundy was an independent state and the remainder consisted of Anjou and the south of France under the French crown. Joan of Arc was aided and, in many ways, manipulated by a number of ruling powerbrokers, serving as a powerful and near-mystical symbol in the battles which helped to turn the tide in favor of France. Normandy was ultimately recovered by France in 1450, and Aquitaine in 1461. Carlos Paluzie de Lescazes, op. cit., p.85.

[173] Lynn Montross, *War through the Ages*, Harper & Brothers Publishers, New York, and London, 1946, p. 183.

[174] During the reign of Louis XI (1461-1483), Burgundy was annexed after the death of its ruler, Charles the Bold, at which time Maine and Provence fell to the French on the death of King René. France lost Flanders in 1482 as it formed part of the dowry of Marie of Burgundy when she married Maximillian of Austria. When the Burgundian inheritance was divided by the Treaty of Senlis in 1493, the groundwork was laid for the future rivalry between France and the Hapsburgs. Carlos Paluzie de Lescazes, op.cit., p. 85.

[175] There is nothing to show that Joan had military ability, as the French men-at-arms often averted a disaster by declining to attack when the tactical circumstances were unwinable. Joan would eventually be taken prisoner, tried, and convicted on charges of heresy, and burnt at the stake in Rouen by the English. After her martyrdom, it took 15 years of anarchy and civil strife before another woman helped to transform warfare as it was then known. Agnes Sorel, one of the first of the royal mistresses to mold French history, urged Charles to create a formal military establishment. As a result, the first standing army of the Middle Ages came into being. It consisted of 9,000 permanent troops, paid, and equipped by the king, and which could be used to crush his enemies. The raising of this small force set a precedent for other monarchs and is one of the landmarks of military history. With these forces at his disposal, Charles conducted a series of swift campaigns which cleared France of the invaders, leaving the English only Calais as the prize of a century's conquests.

[176] The Wars of the Roses took place 1450-1485 in England between the houses of York (White Rose) under Richard Plantagenet, and Lancaster (Red Rose) under Henry VI. A scion of the latter house founded a new dynasty in 1485, when the Tudor, Henry VII, became king of England.

employment of the wagon-fort as the unit of tactics. These wagon-forts could more accurately be described as an armored car pierced with loopholes for crossbows and handguns. Twenty warriors were attached to each unit, half of them pikemen who manned the gaps between vehicles to guard against cavalry assault. In line of battle, a ditch protected the front of wagon-forts linked by chains, though both drivers and horses were also trained for offensive maneuver. Contemporaries have left a legend of complex movements executed at a gallop, but the results indicate that mobility was not sacrificed with the use of the heavy iron cover on the cars.

(PHGCOM Photos)

Hand bombard, 1390–1400, Musee de l'Armee, Paris, and a 200 kg, 82-cm long wrought iron bombard, circa 1450, Metz, France. It was built by forging iron bars together, held in place by iron rings. It fired 6 kg stone balls.

The handgun was most effective, and the Bohemian leader Ján Zizka armed one third of his infantry with this weapon. Here, the mobility of the wagon-fort had its tactical effect, since the rolling fortresses permitted cool and deliberate aim by sheltered men firing from a rest. Ziska was also the first to maneuver with artillery in the field, using heavy bombards of medium caliber. All of his cannon were mounted on four-wheeled carts which could be brought up into the gaps between wagon-forts for a concentration of fire upon any part of the enemy's line. Stone balls weighing upwards of 100 pounds were thus sent with deadly effect into massed squadrons of feudal cavalry. In 14 years, Ziska's tactics had won at least 50 battles, while accounting for the sack of 500 walled towns or monasteries, all without suffering a single noteworthy defeat.[177]

---

[177] Lynn Montross, op. cit., p. 189-190.

The armies of France were not slow to perceive the possibilities of artillery firepower, and the gun founders of the country soon led in creative experiment. In 1494, Charles VIII of France invaded Italy with a siege train that included 40 bronze cannon with barrels eight feet long, mounted on carriages to increase their mobility. These guns were used to destroy the fortress of San Giovanni, once besieged for seven years, in only eight hours.[178] The first significant effect of firearms then, was not to increase firepower on the battlefields, but to destroy the immunity of fortresses.[179]

Gunpowder may have originated in China where it was used in the production of fireworks, but the Europeans appear to have been the first to make use of it in firearms, as this is where the Chinese imported them from during the 1400s. The English Franciscan monk Roger Bacon described a formula for gunpowder in the early 14th century, which consisted of "seven parts saltpeter, five of young Hazelwood (charcoal), and five of sulphur." It proved to be effective, for when this compound of traditional black powder is ignited, it expands to 4000 times its volume in a very short period of time. Small arms (firearms used by a single soldier) possibly came into use by 1284. By 1326, the city of Florence was paying for the construction of cannon and the manufacture of gunpowder. In 1331, cannons were used at the siege of Cividale in Italy, and by 1339, the first cast guns were being made. These guns were initially cast using the same techniques used to cast church bells. Artillery weapons were cast with bronze, a material with a low melting point and considerable toughness.[180]

Advances in the technique and use of the weight, power and destructive capability of artillery quickly led to the development of stronger and more effective fortifications. Most of the early works were Italian. Artists such as the Sangallo family working out of Rome, Leonardo da Vinci, and Michelangelo brought their fertile imaginations to fortress design. In Germany, the painter and printmaker Albrecht Durer contributed new designs. These designs in turn pointed the way towards the development of the military engineer as a specialist in his own right.[181] Engineering however, would not save the city of Constantinople in 1453 as we shall see in the next chapter.

CONSTANTINOPLE, 1203

Constantinople had been heavily fortified since the sixth century with a strong system of triple walls, augmented with a moat 60 feet wide and 20 feet deep. The moat could be filled with water, which was piped from distant hills, although it was generally used as a dry ditch. Behind the scarp, a battlemented wall six feet high was constructed to provide cover for archers. Sixty feet behind this obstacle rose another wall 27 feet high, which was studded with 96 towers, which projected over the wall in such a manner that they were able to permit flanking fire. These towers were spaced 180 feet apart and varied in height from 30 to 35 feet above the wall.

The third great wall was connected to the second by a covered way. This allowed the safe passage of troops, was 30 feet high and nearly as thick, and had a rear drop of 40 feet to the level of the city. Protruding from this barrier was another system of 96 towers, which in turn were twice the height of the second wall and laid out in a checkerboard fashion along the wall.[182]

---

[178] Bruce Allen Watson, op. cit., p. 2.

[179] General Sir John Hackett, *The Profession of Arms*, Sidgwick & Jackson Ltd., Great Britain, 1983, p. 57.

[180] Hans Halberstadt, *The World's Great Artillery, from the Middle Ages to the Present Day*, Barnes & Noble Books, New York, 2002, p. 11.

[181] Bruce Allen Watson, op. cit., p. 2.

[182] Lynn Montross, op. cit., p. 111-112.

In spite of their strength, the walls fell to the armies of the Fourth Crusade. The defending garrison beat off wave after wave of attackers, but the Crusaders made good use of the torch. Advancing behind the flames, they had barely secured a foothold, when the Varangian Guards, the best troops of the city, chose this moment to demand arrears in pay.[183] With mutiny added to the fire, the morale of the defenders collapsed and Constantinople fell on 7 April 1203.[184]

CONSTANTINOPLE, 1453

The Ottoman Turks transport their fleet overland into the Golden Horn,
painting by Kusatma Zonaro.

The defenses of Constantinople survived, but in 1453 there was only a small garrison of troops to defend the city when a Turkish army arrived to take it. Constantinople was defended by 7000 troops under (Giovanni) Giustiiniani. The Turks dragged 70 light ships one mile overland to bypass a heavy iron chain across the Golden Horn, completely blockading the city. On 18 Apr 1453 Turkish Sultan Mohammed II

---

183   The conquest of Constantinople took place from 11-13 April 1204. The Varangian (English/Danish) Guard fought well but were destroyed by the Crusaders and Venetians.
184   Martin H. Brice, op. cit., p. 95.

(Mehmet II) began to use 70 cannon and 80,000 troops to besiege and capture the city of Constantinople, which he succeeded in doing after a series of attacks on 7,12,and 21 May 1453. The Major assault came on 29 May when 12,000 Jannisary Infantry stormed the gates. A key role was played by the artillery.

Sultan Mehmed II and the Ottoman Army approaching Constantinople with a giant bombard, painting by Fausto Zonaro.

(The Land Photo)

The Dardanelles Gun, a very heavy 15th-C bronze muzzle-loading cannon of type used by Turks in the siege of Constantinople in 1453, showing ornate decoration. It is currently on display at Fort Nelson, Hampshire, UK.

The siege resolved itself into a contest between the new weapons of gunpowder and Europe's mightiest system of fortifications. Even in their decline, the walls were more formidable than any masonry yet conquered by cannon, although the Turks brought a siege train of 70 pieces which also merited comment. One of their enormous weapons was a bombard named Basilica. Drawn by 60 oxen, it fired a stone ball weighing 800 pounds. This monster cracked after a few days, but eleven other bombards continued to send projectiles crashing into the outer works. At first the Turkish artillery made the mistake of firing at random, hoping to make a few lucky hits. It initially appeared that the defenses might resist this hammering, but the repeated battering by the weighty stone balls eventually shook the defenses and even breached them in places. As they gained experience, the besiegers learned how to direct their fire more efficiently, and to concentrate their cannon fire against a previously selected section of the wall.[185]

After 40 days four towers were leveled and so many breaches had been opened that a general land and sea assault succeeded in a few hours. The fall of Constantinople proved that the mightiest walls were no longer safe against gunpowder.[186] (Constantinople was renamed Istanbul in 1930).

The evolution forced military architects to design defenses that were dug in for protection instead of building upward to create targets.[187] Defences had to be made strong enough to withstand not only the battering of an enemy's cannon, but allow adequate support for the mounting of bigger and better forms of artillery on the battlements of the defender.

SHABETZ, 1521

The Turkish Sultan Suleiman the magnificent appeared with a large army before Shabetz in 1521 and carried the walls by storm. Marching 40 miles east, where Belgrade commanded the junction of the rivers Danube and Save, the Muslims bridged the latter and cut the great fortress off from supplies or reinforcements. Belgrade, like Shabetz, was woefully undermanned, and the Turkish sappers created breaches by means of gunpowder mines. The inevitable surrender, after a resistance of a few weeks, found only 400 able-bodied defenders in the citadel.

---

[185] Charles Connell, op. cit., p. 59.
[186] Lynn Montross, op. cit., p. 195.
[187] Lynn Montross, op. cit., p. 223.

Sultan Mehmed II's entry into Constantinople, painting by Fausto Zonaro.

For the next few years, Suleiman turned to developing a Muslim navy, with the intention of seizing control of the Mediterranean Sea. His next expedition was against Rhodes, the last great outpost of Christendom in the Aegean, and reputedly the world's strongest fortress.

RECONQUISTA, 1492

The *Reconquista* (reconquest) is a Spanish and Portuguese term used to describe the period in the history of the Iberian Peninsula of about 780 years between the Umayyad conquest of Hispania in 711 and the fall of the Nasrid Kingdom of Granada to the expanding Christian kingdoms in 1492. The completed *Reconquista* was the context of the Spanish voyages of discovery and conquest (Colón got royal support in Granada in 1492, months after its conquest), and the Americas, then known as the "New World", ushering in the era of the Spanish and Portuguese colonial empires.

Western historians have marked the beginning of the *Reconquista* with the Battle of Covadonga (718 or 722), one of the first victories by Christian military forces since the 711 Islamic conquest of Iberia by the Umayyad Caliphate. In that small battle, a group led by the nobleman Pelagius defeated a caliphate's army in the mountains of northern Iberia and re-established the independent Christian Kingdom of Asturias. The Spanish reconquest reached a climax with the fall of Seville in 1248 and the submission of the Moorish kingdom of Granada as a Castilian vassal state.

During the Reconquista, the Spanish captured and enslaved the Moors (North African Muslims) as new territories were liberated by advancing forces. The practice that developed during this extensive campaign against the Muslims, granting privileges (encomienda rights) to certain Christian warriors (adelantados) who re-established Spanish control, was the same system that was later modified and employed to subjugate indigenous populations in the Americas.

Crusader privileges were given to those aiding the Templars, the Hospitallers, and the Iberian orders that merged with the orders of Calatrava and Santiago. The Christian kingdoms pushed the Muslim Moors and Almohads back in frequent Papal-endorsed Iberian Crusades from 1212 to 1265. By 1491, the city of Granada itself lay under siege. On 25 Nov 1491, the Treaty of Granada was signed, setting out the conditions for surrender. On 2 Jan 1492, the last Muslim leader, Muhammad XII, known as *Boabdil* to the Spanish, gave up complete control of Granada, to Ferdinand and Isabella, the Catholic Monarchs, at which point the Muslims and Jews were finally expelled from the peninsula.

The surrender of Granada, 1492, painting by Pradilla.

The Christian ousting of Muslim rule on the Iberian Peninsula with the conquest of Granada did not extinguish the spirit of the *Reconquista*. Isabella urged Christians to pursue a conquest of Africa. About 200,000 Muslims are thought to have emigrated to North Africa after the fall of Granada. Initially, under the conditions of surrender, the Muslims who remained were guaranteed their property, laws, customs, and religion. This, however, was not the case, causing the Muslims to rebel against their Christian rulers, culminating with an uprising in 1500. The rebellion was seen as a chance to formally end the Treaty of Granada, and the rights of Muslims and Jews were withdrawn. Muslims in the area were given the choice of expulsion or conversion. In 1568–1571, the descendants of the converted Muslims revolted again, leading to their expulsion from the former Emirate to North Africa and Anatolia. For Jews as well, a period of mixed religious tolerance and persecution under Muslim rule in Spain came to an end with their expulsion by the Christian monarchy in 1492.[188]

SIEGE OF RHODES, 1522

Siege of Rhodes, 1522, engraving by Guillaume Caoursin.

In 1522 the Sultan Suleiman the Magnificent prepared an expedition against Rhodes, the last great outpost of Christendom in the Aegean, and reputedly the world's strongest fortress.[189] The Knights

---

[188]   Barton, Simon. *A History of Spain*. Palgrave Macmillan, 2004.
[189]   In 1444, a great Egyptian armada, too powerful for the galleys of "the Religion," had landed a force of 18,000 Mamelukes on the island of Rhodes. The island of Rhodes was ravaged from end to end, and the siege of the city

Hospitallers, as masters of Rhodes, had incorporated all of the leading improvements in defense-works into their fortress, at an enormous expenditure in time and money. Suleiman, however, crossed from the Asiatic shore with a great artillery train and an army of 150,000, which included a host of sappers from the mines of the Balkans. The siege of Rhodes was conducted throughout the summer and autumn of 1522 and proceeded to clearly prove the superiority of the new fortifications over the most powerful offensive of its time. Although the invaders brought huge mortars firing stone cannon balls, the bastion stood firm and returned a cannonade, which caused frightful losses among the assailants. The Turks excavated 54 gunpowder mines without gaining a permanent lodgment, being frustrated in most instances by countermines. In desperation, Suleiman made several attempts to carry Rhodes by storm, but few of his troops were able to penetrate beyond the shot-swept glacis and ditch.

(Norbert Nagle Photo)
Gate of Saint Athanasiou, Rhodes.

lasted 40 days. The Egyptians had concentrated their fire on the outlying fort covering the entrance to the Harbor of the Galleys, where the Castle of St Nicholas was later built, and on the curtain, wall linking the harbor to St Peter's Tower. By mid August, the curtain wall began to show a serious breech, and John de Lastic decided to take the offensive and to make a sortie in force with all the troops at his disposal. On 24 August 1444, in the darkness of the early morning the garrison silently filed out of the fortress and formed up in front of the ditch, light troops in front, supported by a stand of pikes and the archers on the flanks. As soon as daylight began to appear, the drums and trumpets sounded the charge, and the Egyptian camp was successfully rushed. A great number of Mamelukes were killed, and the remainder, taken completely by surprise, fled in panic to their galleys and hastily embarked, abandoning guns, stores, and baggage to the garrison.

(PHGCOM Photo)
Bombard-Mortar of the Knights of Saint John of Jerusalem, Rhodes, 1480-1500.

The fortress might have held out indefinitely except for a dire shortage of gunpowder, which in the end caused the Knights to accept the remarkably easy terms of victors whose losses were estimated as high as 60,000 slain. Ottoman sea power rather than siegecraft deserved the credit however, since neither Venice nor any other Christian state chose to risk a naval encounter with the blockading galleys.[190]

(Norbert Nagel Photo)

---

[190] Lynn Montross, op. cit., p. 225.

The English Post, the scene of heaviest fighting; the tenaille is on the left and the main wall is further behind it, visible in the background; on the right of the wide dry ditch is the counterscarp that the attackers had to climb down before storming the city wall. The ditch is enfiladed by the Tower of St. John, its bulwark and lower wall providing vertically stacked fields of overlapping fire. The stone cannonballs seen in the ditch are from the fighting.

The Tower of Italy had a round bulwark built around by Grand Master Fabrizio del Carretto in 1515–17, and provided with gun ports at lowest level covering the ditch in every direction, for a total of three stacked tiers of cannon fire (two from the bulwark, one from the tower).

The tower of St. John at the East end of the English sector was built under Grand Master Antonio Fluvian (1421–37), and it had a gate. Later a barbican was built around it under Grand Master Piero Raimundo Zacosta (1461–67). Finally, the large pentagonal bulwark was built in front of it c1487, and the gate was removed.

Although the Knights had lost the Fortress of Rhodes, when Suleiman decided to attack them again in their new stronghold on Malta in 1565, they were better prepared.[191]

The island of Malta had command of the East-West trade routes and its strategic position could not be ignored. Once it was in Turkish hands, Suleiman could use the island as a base from which he could conquer Sicily and Southern Italy. A seaborne invasion was launched in the spring of 1565.[192]

The island had little to offer except for a good harbor, and much construction would be needed to build up its defenses. Although the capital, Medina, was initially poorly protected, the Fort St Angelo at the tip of the Birgu peninsula was strengthened as were the fortifications at Birgu where the order had its headquarters. Fort St Michael was built at the neck of the Senglea Peninsula, and on the sea point of Mount Sciberras construction was started on the star-shaped Fort St Elmo.[193]

KOLOSSI CASTLE, CYPRUS

Kolossi Castle is a former Crusader stronghold on the south-west edge of Kolossi village 14 kilometres (9 mi) west of the city of Limossol on the island of Cyprus. It held great strategic importance in the Middle Ages and contained large facilities for the production of sugar from the local sugarcane, one of Cyprus's main exports in the period. The original castle was possibly built in 1210 by the Frankish military, when the land of Kolossi was given by King Hugh I to the Knights of the Order of St John of Jerusalem (Hospitallers)

---

[191] Craig Philip, *Last Stands, Famous Battles Against the Odds*, Bison Books Ltd., Kimbolton House, London, 1994, Introduction.

[192] William Seymour, *Great Sieges of History*. Brassey's (UK), Oxford, 1991, p. 46.

[193] William Seymour, op. cit., p. 47.

(Michael Photo)

Kolossi Castle in its present-day form, was built in 1454 by the Hospitallers under the Commander of Kolossi, Louis de Magnac, whose arms can be seen carved into the castle's walls. Owing to rivalry among the factions in the Crusader Kingdom of Cyprus, the castle was taken by the Knights Templar in 1306 but returned to the Hospitallers in 1313 following the abolition of the Templars. The castle today consists of a single three-storey keep with an attached rectangular enclosure or bailey about 30 by 40 metres (98 by 131 ft).

As well as its sugar. the area is also known for its sweet wine, Commandaria. At the wedding banquet after King Richard the Lionheart's marriage to Berengaria of Navarre at nearby Limassol, he allegedly declared it to be the "wine of kings and the king of wines." It has been produced in the region for millennia and is thought to be the oldest continually-produced and named wine in the world, known for centuries as "Commandaria" after the Templars' Grand Commandery there.

SIEGE OF MALTA, 1565

The Great Siege of Malta took place in 1565 when the Ottoman Empire tried to invade the island of Malta, then held by the Knight's Hospitaller. The Knights, with approximately 2,000 foot soldiers and 400 Maltese men, women, and children, withstood the siege and repelled the invaders. This victory became one of the most celebrated events in sixteenth-century Europe. The siege was the climax of an escalating contest between a Christian alliance and the Islamic Ottoman Empire for control of the Mediterranean, a contest that included the Turkish attack on Malta in 1551, the Ottoman destruction of an allied Christian fleet at the Battle of Djerba in 1560, and the decisive Battle of Lepanto in 1571.

The island of Malta had command of the East-West trade routes and its strategic position could not be ignored. Once it was in Turkish hands, Suleiman could use the island as a base from which he could conquer Sicily and Southern Italy. A seaborne invasion was launched in the spring of 1565.[194]

(5afd4770411ca76c Photo)
Fort Saint Angelo de la Valette on the Birgu peninsula.

The island had little to offer except for a good harbour, and much construction would be needed to build up its defenses. Although the capital, Medina, was initially poorly protected, the Fort Saint Angelo at the tip of the Birgu peninsula was strengthened as were the fortifications at Birgu where the order had its headquarters. Fort St Michael was built at the neck of the Senglea Peninsula, and on the sea point of Mount Sciberras construction was started on the star-shaped Fort St Elmo.[195]

The Grand Master of the Order, Jean Parisot de la Valette had made it his business to improve the island's defenses and developed it into a powerful fortress. La Valette had fought at Rhodes and learned much from his many experiences in battle. He made good use of natural and artificial obstacles, repaired old watchtowers, enlarged ramparts, strengthened walls, and deepened ditches. La Valette realized that he could count on little in the way of aid and set up his command to be as self-sufficient as possible. He

---

[194]   William Seymour, *Great Sieges of History*. Brassey's (UK), Oxford, 1991, p. 46.
[195]   William Seymour, op. cit., p. 47.

was left to defend the island with a force of about 600 Knights and some 8,500 soldiers including 3,000 Maltese regulars who fought well.

Detailed Map of the Siege of Malta, a fresco by Egnazio Dante.

Preparing for the forthcoming siege, foodstuffs were stored away, weapons and firebombs were made, and training was stepped up. La Valette prepared his plans and eliminated any weaknesses in the island's defenses, for he knew full well that if Malta fell, the Order was finished. The steel-clad Knights carried a heavy two-handed sword and had an assortment of weapons that included pikes, spears, harquebuses, muskets, and a variety of fireworks that included a combustible pot used like a grenade/flame-thrower. They used a refined form of Greek fire in a device called a trump, as well as specially prepared flaming hoops. These were particularly deadly, for they could encircle three or four Janissaries at a time and set alight their voluminous robes with unquenchable flame. In the matter of cannon however, the Turks had the advantage in numbers and weight.[196]

The Turks assembled a huge armada of 181 vessels to transport the invasion army to Malta, and set off with troops well furnished with personal weapons, equipment and rations, and had been well briefed that they would find neither houses for shelter, nor earth, nor wood and would not be living off the land. Both sides appear to have had good intelligence on the ground and the coming battle.

Lookouts spotted the Turkish fleet and fired cannon shots to warn the Knights. Over 30,000 Turkish troops landed, including 6,300 Janissaries and 6,000 Spahis (who were expert bowmen), far too many

---

[196] William Seymour, op. cit., p. 49.

for La Valette to counterattack with his force of 9000. He instead withdrew to the strongpoints and fortifications he had already prepared.

The command of the Turkish force was split, with the army commanded by Mustapha Pasha who had also fought at Rhodes, and the fleet commanded by Piali. They had a vast quantity of stores with them in a transport fleet, including food, powder, shot, tents, and clothing, as well as a number of horses to drag the heavy guns. It was a well-executed logistic undertaking.[197]

The initial Turkish attacks against the strongpoints were thrown back with significant losses to the Turks. Two fortified islands at the entrance to the harbor, St Elmo, and St Angelo, were now targeted for assault. 50 Knights and 500 men garrisoned St Angelo. St Elmo was a well-defended old-fashioned star fortress on a rocky headland, defended by some 53 knights and 800 soldiers. On 31 May the Turks had 24 guns aligned against the front of St Elmo, and shelled the fort for days, but suffered heavy losses while pressing home the attack. Pounded by a hail of stone, marble and iron cannonballs, the walls of St Elmo began to crack. In desperation the garrison sortied out and inflicted huge casualties on the panic-stricken Turks. The Janissaries of Mustapha Pasha checked their retreat and the attack was renewed.

More Turkish ships arrived with another 1,500 soldiers under the command of Dragut, the Governor of Tripoli. He redirected the efforts against the walls of St Elmo and effected breaches in several places. Exhausted as the defenders were, however, they still managed to beat off a scaling party, driving the Turks back with musket shots, stone blocks, boiling pitch, and Greek fire. Wave after wave of Janissaries were cut down by the defenders. After losing nearly 2,000 men, Mustapha called off the first attack. A second attack was put in at night, leaving another 1500 Turks dead or dying just outside the fort, for the loss of only 60 defenders. Six days later the Turks tried again, after a prolonged bombardment. Fighting back with firebombs and incendiaries, the invaders were again thrown back with tremendous casualties, to the loss of 10 Knights and 73 soldiers for the defenders.

Dragut was killed on 18 June, but the fortress of St Elmo finally fell on 23 June. Although the crescent flag of Islam finally flew over the fort, the victory gave them little joy. For every one of the 1,500 Christian casualties, the Turks lost seven. The only survivors of St Elmo were nine Knights taken as hostages and a handful of Maltese who swam across the harbor to safety. All the others were decapitated, and their heads fixed on stakes turned towards the other fort of St Angelo. In retaliation, La Valette gave orders that all the Turkish prisoners were to lose their heads, which were then fired like cannonballs into the captured St Elmo fort.

Mustapha's next move was against the two peninsulas on Senglea and Birgu on the main island. The Grand Master strengthened the defenses of both and ensured that adequate food stocks were in place. A bridge of boats connecting the two peninsulas was maintained so that men on one could go to the help of the other if attacked. The Turks managed to bring some 80 ships overland and into the Grand Harbor, clearly indicating that the next attack would be against St Michael's fort and the Senglea peninsula. The chain and the guns of St Angelo would keep these ships from the Birgu peninsula. This was confirmed when a Greek officer serving in the Turkish army defected and disclosed Mustapha's intentions.

As a result, when Senglea was attacked simultaneously by land and sea on 15 July, the Knights and their Maltese supporters were able to counter both threats. Even the local inhabitants joined in, women and children flinging down missiles and pouring boiling water on the unlucky Turks who tried to scale the walls. This attack cost the Turkish forces another 3,000 casualties. The Hospitallers had lost 250, but these included the commander of the spur.

The Turkish commander then attacked both garrisons simultaneously, so that one could not reinforce the other. Mustapha led the attack personally, but it again failed. In spite of the fact that he had lost over 10,000 men since his landing in Malta, he chose to continue the siege. La Valette confirmed that he

---

[197] William Seymour, op. cit., p. 50.

had adequate supplies but was unlikely to receive outside help. If the Turks were victorious however, he concluded that no one would be spared. He only course, therefore, was to continue to resist.

The Turks now resorted to mining. They also brought up a special siege engine; a tall tower complete with drawbridge for use against the wall after their mines had exploded. They again preceded the grand assault with a massive bombardment. 26 guns rained shot on the Castile bastion, while St Angelo was under fire from two batteries, and those on Coradin took care of Senglea. The damage was considerable, but not nearly as great as Mustapha had hoped. Although they managed to blast a hole in the wall of one of the bastions, the attackers who pushed through the gap were beaten back on 2 August, in one of the bloodiest encounters of the siege. Although the offensive was resumed under cover of darkness, the Turks were forced to withdraw at dawn. The battle dragged on, and on 18 Aug Mustapha had a large mine detonated under the main wall of the Castile bastion but owing to the personal intervention of the Grand Master this attack also failed. Mustapha then ordered a large siege tower laden with troops brought forward to the wall, but La Valette was ready for it. His workmen punched a hole in the wall opposite the base of the machine, trained a cannon on the lower part of the structure and shattered its foundations with chain shot. The whole affair collapsed, and the men inside were thrown to the ground.

It was not a good day for the Turks. They prepared a second invention, a kind of homemade shrapnel bomb. It came in the form of a large cylinder filled with shot, stones and nails timed to explode when it had been maneuvered and dropped over the wall, but it had a faulty fuse and failed to explode. Profiting by the delay, the Knights hauled it to the top of the wall and dropped it in the ditch among the attacking party. It blew up almost at once with horrendous effect, scattering the Turks as they ran for their lives.

The Turks had fired some 70,000 cannonballs in the siege, and they were running short of powder. They needed a success, and the attacks continued to the end of August, but without noticeable change in either position except the wearing down of the forces of both sides.

Lifting of the Siege of Malta, painting by Charles Philippe Lariviere.

Although Mustapha maintained his efforts, a new problem confronted him. The Viceroy of Sicily, an ally of the Knights, sailed to Malta on 25 August with a relief force of nearly 10,000 men. Misinformed by a slave who had been deliberately permitted to escape by la Valette, Mustapha was led to believe that the Viceroy had brought 16,000 troops. This led Mustapha to make up his mind to evacuate Malta. He discovered that he had been misled during the embarkation and immediately halted the evacuation, landed about 9000 men, and unhesitatingly gave battle. La Valette's Knights, led by Ascanio de la Corna, made a spectacular charge, and utterly routed the Turks. Mustapha was only saved from capture by a devoted group of Janissaries. A Turkish rearguard of arquebusiers was formed and these men did their work well until forced to retire when confronted by the full weight of de la Corna's force. The Turks lost another 1,000 men, and on the evening of 8 September 1565 the Turkish fleet finally sailed from Malta.

The cost to the island had been severe, as out of the original 9000 only 600 were strong enough to bear arms. Of the Knights, close to 250 had died, along with 7,000 Maltese, Spaniards, and other nationals. The Turkish forces had suffered over 30,000 casualties, and it is thought that no more than 10,000 of the force of nearly 40,000 reached Constantinople, and many of those were wounded or sick. This unsuccessful siege marked the end of the Turkish dreams of conquest and domination, and as a result, the whole of Europe had good reason to be grateful to the island that refused to surrender.[198]

TENOCHTITLAN, 1521

The ideas of the old world were not long in coming to the new one. Conquest and the Spanish Inquisition soon followed.[199] Between May and August 1521, the Spanish conquistador Hernán Cortés and his forces attacked Tenochtitlan, the capital of Mexico's Aztec empire in an assault that left more than 100,000 dead.[200] The Aztecs fought hard; in one gruesome, defiant act, they first humiliated their Spanish prisoners by making them dance and wear feathers, then ripped out their hearts and threw the bodies down a temple pyramid's steps. After 80 days of onslaught, the Aztec king, with his people ill and starving, surrendered to Cortés, and the Aztec empire vanished.[201]

---

[198] Charles Connell, op. cit., p. 75-84.

[199] The Inquisition began in 1478, instituted by Isabel in Castile, Spain. The Spanish Inquisition was formally established by a union of the Inquisitions of Aragon and Castile in 1483. Torquemada was appointed Grand Inquisitor 1493. The Inquisition lasted until the 19th Century and is estimated to have been inflicted on 3 million people.

[200] Having set out from Cuba, Hernan Cortes (1485-1547), landed near the site of modern Veracruz with 500 men on 22 April 1519. He then marched on Mexico, arriving in August, and entered Tlaxacallan on 23 September. He destroyed Cholula on 18 October and entered Mexico City on 8 November where he took power. He conquered the Aztec empire of Montezuma in two years.

[201] *TIME* magazine, 21 February 1994, p. 11.

(Infrogmation Photo)
The Last Days of Tenochtitlan, Conquest of Mexico by Cortez",
a 19th-century painting by William de Leftwich Dodge.

Mexico fell to Cortés on 13 August 1521. The Aztec Empire then became New Spain under the authority of Cortes, who was named Captain General. In effect Cortés, with the aid of 600 soldiers, sixteen horses, ten cannons and thirteen harquebuses conquered a country that in 1519 had 20 million subjects under the reign of Motecuhzoma II. The valley of Mexico, which alone may have had as many as five million inhabitants, was at that time the greatest urban concentration in the world.

SIEGE OF NAGSHINO, 1575

The Battle of Nagashino (*Nagashino no Tatakai*) took place in 1575 near Nagashino Castle on the plain of Shitarabara in the Mikawa Province of Japan. Takeda Katsuyori attacked the castle when Okudaira Sadamasa rejoined the Tokugawa, and when his original plot with Oga Yashiro for taking Okazaki Castle, the capital of Mikawa, was discovered.

Takeda Katsuyori attacked the castle on 16 June, using Takeda gold miners to tunnel under the walls, rafts to ferry samurai across the rivers, and siege towers. On 22 June, the siege became a blockade, complete with palisades and cables strewn across the river. The defenders then sent Torii Suneemon to get help. He reached Okazaki, where Ieyasu and Nobunaga promised help. Conveying that message back to the castle, Torii was captured and hung on a cross before the castle walls. However, he was still able to shout out that relief was on the way before he was killed.

Both Tokugawa Ieyasu and Oda Nobunaga sent troops to assist Sadamasa and break the siege, and their combined forces defeated Katsuyori. Nobunaga's skillful use of firearms to defeat Takeda's cavalry tactics is often cited as a turning point in Japanese warfare; many cite it as the first "modern" Japanese battle. In fact, the cavalry charge had been introduced only a generation earlier by Katsuyori's father, Takeda Shingen. Furthermore, firearms had already been used in other battles. Nobunaga's innovation was the wooden stockades and rotating volleys of fire, which led to a decisive victory at Nagashino.

Nobunaga and Ieyasu brought a total of 38,000 men to relieve the siege on the castle by Katsuyori. Of Takeda's original 15,000 besiegers, only 12,000 faced the Oda–Tokugawa army in this battle. The remaining 3000 continued the siege to prevent the garrison in the castle from sallying forth and joining the battle. Oda and Tokugawa positioned their men across the plain from the castle, behind the Rengogawa, a small stream whose steep banks would slow down the cavalry charges for which the Takeda clan was known.

Seeking to protect his arquebusiers, which he would later become famous for, Nobunaga built a number of wooden palisades in a zig-zag pattern, setting up his gunners to attack the Takeda cavalry in volleys. The stockades served to blunt the force of charging cavalry.

Of Oda's forces, an estimated 10,000 Ashigaru arquebusiers, 3,000 of the best shots were placed in three ranks under the command of Sassa Narimasa, Maeda Toshiie and Honda Tadakatsu. Okubo Tadayo was stationed outside the palisade, as was Sakuma Nobumori, who feigned a retreat. Shibata Katsuie and Toyotomi Hideyoshi protected the left flank. Takeda Katsuyori arranged his forces in five groups of 3,000, with Baba Nobuharu on his right, Naito Kiyonaga in the center, Yamagata Masakage on the left, Katsuyori in reserve and the final group continuing the siege. A night attack on the eve of the battle by Sakai Tadatsugu killed Takeda Nobuzane, a younger brother of Shingen.

The Takeda army emerged from the forest and found themselves 200–400 meters from the Oda–Tokugawa stockades. The short distance, the great power of the Takeda cavalry charge and the heavy rain, which Katsuyori assumed would render the matchlock guns useless, encouraged Takeda to order the charge. His cavalry was feared by both the Oda and Tokugawa forces, who had suffered a defeat at the Mikatagahara.

The horses slowed to cross the stream and were fired upon as they crested the stream bed within 50 meters of the enemy. This was considered the optimum distance to penetrate the armor of the cavalry. In typical military strategy, the success of a cavalry charge depends on the infantry breaking ranks so that the cavalry can mow them down. If the infantry does *not* break, however, cavalry charges will often fail, with even trained warhorses refusing to advance into the solid ranks of opponents.

Between the continuous fire of the arquebusiers' volleys and the rigid control of the *horo-shu*, the Oda forces stood their ground and were able to repel every charge. Ashigaru spearmen stabbed through or over the stockades at horses that made it past the initial volleys and *samurai*, with swords and shorter spears, engaged in single combat with Takeda warriors. Strong defenses on the ends of the lines prevented Takeda forces from flanking the stockades. By mid-day, the Takeda broke and fled, and the Oda forces vigorously pursued the routed army. Takeda suffered a loss of 10,000 men, two-thirds of his original besieging force. Several of the 24 Generals of Takeda Shingen were killed in this battle.[202]

THE SCIENCE OF FORTIFICATION

The Spanish built one of the earliest fortified settlements in North America along the Florida coast at St Augustine in 1565. It included eight artillery bastions and a star citadel. Quebec City, founded in 1608 on the St Lawrence was sited on a defendable position and equipped with artillery emplacements covering both the land and river approaches from its walled citadel.[203]

The citadel of Antwerp was built in 1567 in the wake of religious wars in the Netherlands. It was commissioned by the Duke of Alva sent by Philip II of Spain to quell any resistance in Antwerp. It served both as a defensive structure as well as a base of operations for Spanish, Austrian, French, Dutch and Belgian forces. The citadel features a five-pointed star with bastions and was constructed close to the Scheldt river.

---

202 Turnbull, Stephen. *Battles of the Samurai*. London: Arms and Armour Press, 1987.
203 G. J. Ashworth, *War and the City*, Routledge, London, and New York, 1991, p. 31.

In 1572 the citadel was completed, and a garrison moved in. It became notorious for the Spanish Fury in 1576 where the city was plundered, and many citizens lost their lives. In a response to the atrocities committed during the Spanish Fury notables of Antwerp ordered the wall facing the city to be demolished in 1577. When hostilities resumed, it became a citadel once again. The five bastions were named Toledo, Pacietto, Alva, Duc, and Hernando. The citadel featured many buildings including powder magazines and a chapel and has been updated several times. The French refitted the citadel when Antwerp became the Arsenal for a Maritime assault force that was planned for an invasion force for England. The lunets named of Kiel and Saint Laurels were added at that time. During the Belgian occupation of the fort an extra battery on the terreplein was also added. 1832 it became the theater of Dutch resistance during the Belgian war of independence as a French army besieged this fortress under the command of Marshal Gérard. In 1870 King Leopold II of Belgium ordered the sale and leveling of the citadel, and thus, no visible traces exist.

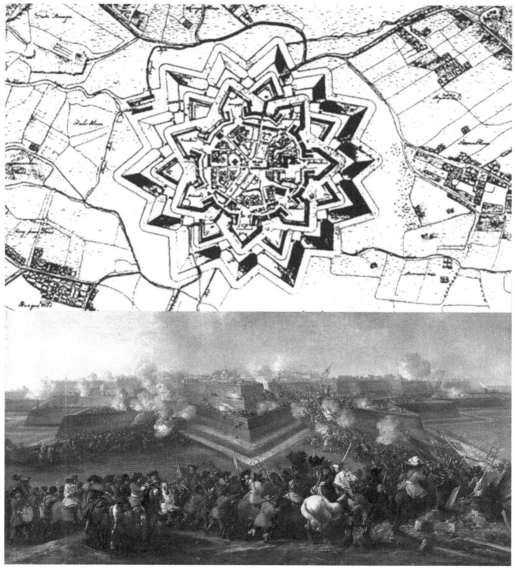

(Rijkmuseum Photo)

Coevorden citadel diagram, Netherlands, and a painting of the re-capture of Coevorden by Dutch troops commanded by Carl von Rabenhauptin December 1672, as part of the Franco-Dutch War.

The idea of using bastions in fort design was expanded and soon multi-pointed star forts were being developed towards the end of the 16th century. Maurice of Nassau for example, rebuilt Coevorden, Holland by adding bastions resulting in the formation of a 14-point star. Palmanova, Italy, was planned as an 18-point star.[204]

The city of Coevorden was captured from the Spanish in 1592 by a Dutch and English force under the command of Maurice, Prince of Orange. The following year it was besieged by a Spanish force, but the city held out until its relief in May 1594. Coevorden was then reconstructed in the early seventeenth century to an *ideal city* design, similar to Palmanova. The streets were laid out in a radial pattern within polygonal fortifications and extensive outer earthworks.

The city of Coevorden may have indirectly given its name to the city of Vancouver, which is named after the 18th-century British explorer George Vancouver. The explorer's ancestors (and family name) may have originally come to England "from Coevorden" (van Coevorden > Vancoevorden > Vancouver).

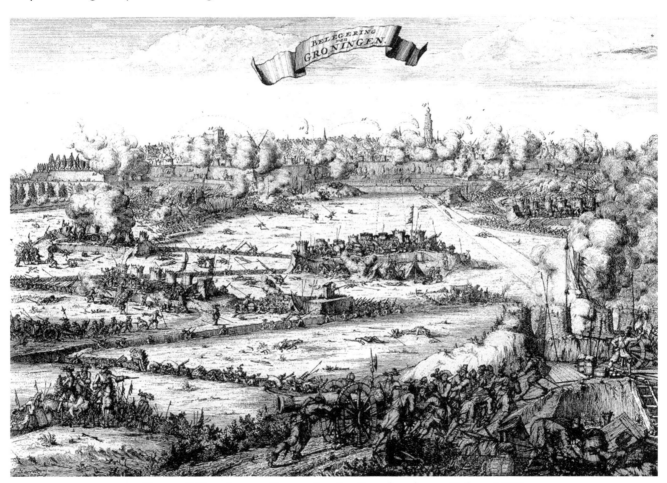

Siege of Groningen. Engraving by Bernhard von Galen, 1672.

---

[204] Bruce Allen Watson, op. cit., p. 3.

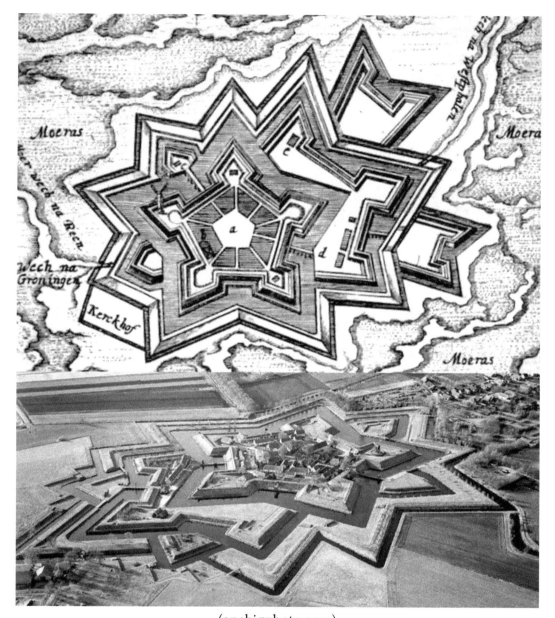

(onebigphoto.com)
Fort Bourtange, diagram and aerial view of a star fort located in the
village of Bourtange, Groningen, Netherlands.

Fort Bourtange was built in 1593 under the orders of William the I of Orange, its original purpose was to control the only road between Germany and the city of
Groningen controlled by the Spaniards during the time of the Eighty Years' War. After experiencing its final battle in 1672, the Fort continued to serve in the defensive network on the German border until it was finally given up in 1851 and converted into a village. Fort Bourtange currently serves as a historical museum.

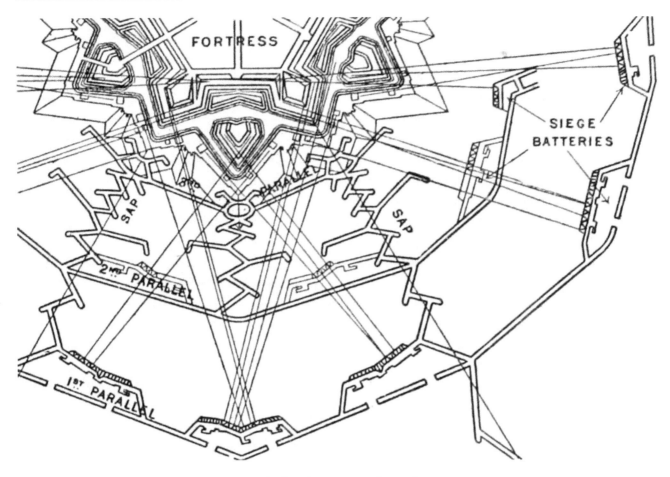

Vauban's system of attack.

European engineers such as Marchi and Busca in Italy, and de Ville and Pagan in France, helped to develop the science of fortification. The two most prolific designers in Northern Europe were Sebastien le Prestre de Vauban (1633-1707), and Menno de Coehorn (1641-1704). Vauban devised a method of conducting sieges that involved a geometric advancement of trenchworks and approaches that moved from parallel to parallel against enemy fortifications that was highly successful.[205] He used these parallels in the attack on Maastricht in 1673, capturing the "impregnable" fortress after an assault of only 13 days.[206] Vauban applied the use of common sense rather than untried theory to achieve these successes.[207] Be that as it may, his ideas were to be put into use for the next 200 years.[208]

Coehorn is renowned not only for the small, mobile mortar that bears his name, but for his skill in strengthening fortifications at such places as Coevorden, Bergen-op-Zoom and Namur, and for his treatise on fortifications. He designed his systems with certain specific principles in mind: to provide powerful flank defense; to deprive an attacker of the means of making lodgments; to give ample facilities

---

[205] Russell F. Weigley, *The Age of Battles: the Quest for Decisive Warfare from Breitenfeld to Waterloo.* Indiana University Press, 1991, p. 55.

[206] Reginald Bloomfield, *Sebastien le Prestre de Vauban, 1633-1707,* Methuen & Company Ltd., London, 1938, p. 61.

[207] Harold A. Skaarup, *Vauban: His Fortifications and Methods of Siege,* RMC War Studies 500 Paper, 14 January 1994, p. 3.

[208] Bruce W, Fry, *"An Appearance of strength" The Fortifications of Louisbourg,* Volume One and Volume Two. Canadian Government Publishing Centre, Supply and Services Canada, Hull, Quebec, 1984, p. 45.

for sorties; and to avoid unnecessary expense. Whenever possible, he relied on water as a means of defense. While generally keeping to the usual bastioned polygon of his era, he adopted earthwork counterguards which he made too narrow for an attacker to use as gun platforms. He developed the fausse braye into a narrow embankment alongside the ditch protecting it by means of a counterscarp gallery (a loopholed passage behind the counterscarp wall), a wide promenade which was virtually the same as that of the water in the ditch and which was carefully flanked by artillery casemates and musketry galleries. Its level was deliberate; if an attacker attempted to cut a trench across, they would immediately strike water. Similarly, the covered way was close to the water level so as to deter any attempts to sap or trench across it.[209]

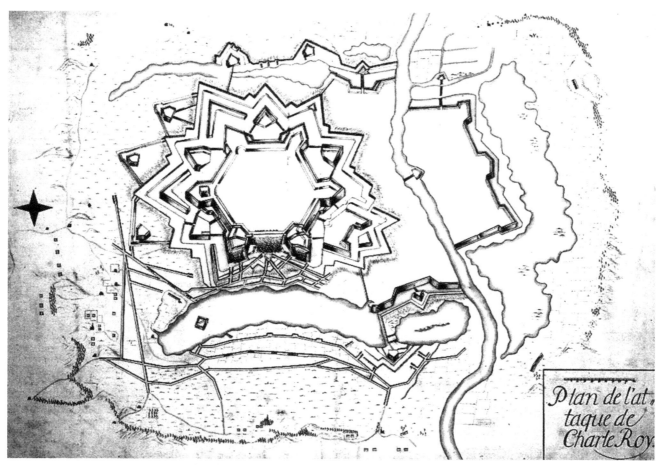

Fortress Charle Roy, France, diagram of the plan of attack, 1693.

---

209   Ian Hogg, op. Cit., p. 129-130.

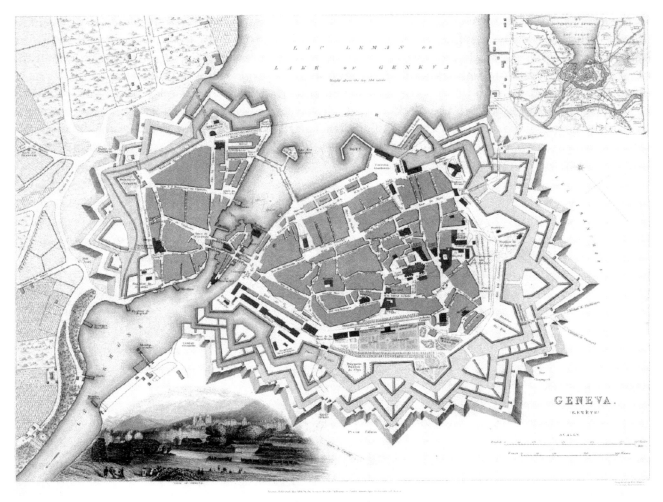

(B.R. Davies)

Plan of Geneva, Switzerland, and environs, showing the massive fortifications in 1841, which were demolished in 1850.

In 1777, the Marquis de Montalembert designed a fortress known as a caponiere. It was a heavily walled structure three stories high and at a right angle to the main wall. Each story was a great gun platform, effectively placing large numbers of guns and therefore concentrated firepower on any attacking force. These forts were primarily sited in the defense of harbors and have been built all over Europe at sites from Sebastopol in the Crimea, to Toulon in southern France, to Portsmouth, England and then across the Atlantic to Fort Sumter in South Carolina, and Fort Point in San Francisco Bay, California.[210] Eventually, fortified places could not be properly defended without large field armies supporting them. Even then, once the field army was defeated, it was almost inevitable that the fortresses would fall. Often armies would just bypass them altogether.[211]

Explosive technology also progressed. Although rockets may have been used as early as the 13th century in Asia, the British army noted what seems to have been the first modern use of a war-rocket by the Sultan

---

[210]   Bruce Allen Watson, op. cit., p. 7.

[211]   Bernard L. Montgomery, *A History of Warfare*, Collins, London, 1968, p. 295

Tipu at the siege of Seringapatam in 1799. Rockets were used in 1806 at the siege of Boulogne to set the town on fire, and at Walcheren and Copenhagen in 1807, at the battles of Leipzig and Waterloo and at New Orleans in 1815.[212] Hitler and his V2 rockets launched during the Second World War against allied cities in 1944, was followed a generation later by Iraq's Saddam Hussein firing on the cities of Iran and Israel in 1991.

Good intelligence often had a decisive role to play in the outcome of a siege. Because every major siege of the 17th and 18th centuries involved major problems of logistics operations, preparations were extremely hard to conceal. Vauban stated that the foremost fault committed in siegecraft came from insufficient attention to basic security and secrecy. He also stated that no fortress, however well defended, could hold out indefinitely.[213]

ENGLISH CIVIL WAR, 1642-1651

The English Civil War was a series of armed conflicts and political machinations between Parliamentarians ("Roundheads") and Royalists ("Caviliers") over, principally, the manner of England's government. The first war (1642–1646) and second war (1648–1649) pitted the supporters of King Charles I against the supporters of the Long Parliament, while the third war (1649–1651) saw fighting between supporters of King Charles II and supporters of the Rump Parliament. The war ended with the Parliamentarian victory at the Battle of Worcester on 3 Sep 1651.

(Tate Collection)
Oliver Cromwell at Dunbar, painting by Andrew Carrick Gow.

---

[212] J.F.C. Fuller, Major General, *The Conduct of War, 1789-1961*, Lyre and Spottiswoode, London, 1962, p. 90-91.
[213] Marguerita Z. Herman, *Ramparts, Fortifications From the Renaissance to West Point*, Avery Publishing Group Inc., Garden City park, New York, 1992, p. 46-47.

The overall outcome of the war was threefold: the trial and execution of Charles I (1649); the exile of his son, Charles II (1651); and the replacement of the English monarchy with, at first, the Commonwealth of England (1649–1653) and then the Protectorate under the personal rule of Oliver Cromwell (1653–1658) and subsequently his son Richard (1658–1659). The monopoly of the Church of England on Christian worship in England ended with the victors consolidating the established Protestant Ascendancy in Ireland. Constitutionally, the wars established the precedent that an English monarch cannot govern without Parliament's consent, although the idea of Parliament as the ruling power of England was only legally established as part of the Glorious Revolution in 1688.

The English Civil War of the 1640s saw the development of surprisingly defendable town walls, in spite of the already extensive use of cannon to degrade stone fortifications. Complicated lines of circumvallation and earth work bulwarks and bastions laid out in scientifically calculated patterns by Dutch designers gave the defender a fighting chance against a determined attacker. Bernard de Gomme of the Netherlands was one of the most celebrated engineers of his time for his designs of effective fortification systems. Gomme set up a new and very strong system at Newark, the strongest royal city after Oxford which was defended by the "royalists," and attacked by the "parliamentarians."

This city was sited on the Trent River and had been regarded as a strategic location since ancient times. There were Roman defense works in two places, which were later superseded by "New Work" in 900, (from which the town received its name) to protect the site against the Danes. Early in the 12th century, the town and manor came under the control of the bishops of Lincoln, who built a finely ornamented stone castle on a commanding position overlooking the river, a bridge and the road leading to it. Throughout the Middle Ages the fortress at Newark was strengthened and added to, and even in the 17th century is was still one of the most powerful river castles in England.

At the end of 1642, King Charles generals decided to fortify and to heavily garrison Newark. It became in fact, the center of a large fortified area and was used as a rallying point for the King's army, as well as a supply center. Newark had to be held because it overlooked the Great North Road which bridged the Trent River and bisected the main road linking Lincoln to Nottingham and Leicester. It protected the lines of communication between the King's headquarters in Oxford and his strongholds in Yorkshire and Newcastle, where his supplies of arms that were brought in by sea from the Netherlands were usually landed. By holding Newark, it was also possible for the King make effective use of his "army of the north" under the command of the Earl of Newcastle to launch a thrust into the territory of the Eastern Association. This was the main source of parliamentary military power.

SIEGE OF NEWARK, 1645-1646

Map of the siege of Newark (6 March 1645 – 8 May 1646) showing a sap that allows Roundhead siege artillery to be placed closer to the fortifications of Newark than the circumvallation. Notice that the lines of advance of the zigzag are at such an angle and position that the defenders were unable to bring enfilade fire to bear.

The castle at Newark and its defensive system was linked to other royalist castles in the area, including Belvoir, all of which were heavily garrisoned. From this defensive zone a large area was scoured for supplies and manpower. It also served as a base from which to mount cavalry raids into the neighboring parliamentary territory.

The Parliamentarians made three major attempts to take the city. Major General Thomas Ballard launched an attack in February 1643 with 6,000 men and ten guns, most of which were small six-pounders. He fired 80 shots into the town. But a fierce counterattack cost him three of his guns and 60 prisoners and broke the siege.

The second parliamentary attack came which came a year later in February 1644, was even less successful. Sir John Meldrum surrounded the defensive zone with 2,000 horsemen, 5,000 foot-soldiers, eleven cannon and two mortars. The cannon included one famous monster which had been named "Sweet Lips" (after a notorious Hull whore of that time). Sweet Lips was described as a "great basilisk" from Hull, four yards long and probably cast in the 16th century. The gun fired a 30-lb ball to a distance of 400 yards at point blank range and possibly as far as 2,400 yards at ten degrees of elevation.

Meldrum built a pontoon bridge of boats over the Trent River to help his forces conduct an investment of the royalist lines. In the process, however, he was surprised and surrounded by Prince Rupert and was forced to surrender in what could be assessed as the single worst parliamentary disaster of the war. He was allowed to march wary, but lost all of his guns, his small arms, and his ammunition train.

The third siege began in November 1645,when the main Scots army joined General Poyntz and his English force. This was the first time the Newark defenders commanded by Lord John Belasyse faced determined professional soldiers. The Scots constructed a great battering-fort they named "Edinburgh", a siege device which was the 17th century equivalent of a malvoisin. General Poyntz also had a giant bastion brought into play which was named "Colonel Grey's Sconce." The Scots set up two boat bridges and brought up an armed pinnace which also mounted two guns manned by 40 musketeers. These were used to penetrate the Trent River defenses to within half a mile of the castle itself. General Poyntz also dammed the Smite River and the arm of the Trent which ran directly under the castle, putting the town mills out of action.

By the end of March 1646, some 7,000 Scots and 9,000 English had dug themselves into the town roughly to within the range of cannon shot. By April, General Poyntz had diverted both rivers away from Newark and had dug saps up to the main outwork of Newark, which had been named the "Queen's Sconce." He had also built a battery within musket shot of one of the town gates. The Scots by this time had the castle itself within range of their guns. The defenders surrendered in May.

Lord John Belasyse had done his best to provision the town the previous winter, but the defenders were now reduced to eating their horses. Plague broke out, and because they had been deprived of water for cleaning and washing, everyone in the town suffered.[214] Even so, Belasyse had to be ordered to surrender. He didn't want to, as his men were still in good heart, and in the end, he marched out with a company of about 1,500. General Poyntz was awarded a £200 sword by the Commons, and lands worth £300 a year. Newark was the last major action of the First Civil War; Oxford would surrender in the following month.

The royalists had demonstrated in two out of three sieges, that if a fortification were properly garrisoned and provisioned, they could withstand a considerable amount of punishment. Even primitive

---

[214] The first wave of the Black Death swept through Europe between 1347-1350. The Black Death originated in the steppes of Central Asia and traveled the trade routes opened up by the Mongols, reaching Constantinople in 1347. By the end of the following year it had spread through Italy, France, Spain, and Portugal, and had appeared in southern England. The infection was then carried north, through Scotland and Germany, reaching the Baltic in 1350. A few sparsely populated areas were spared, but overall, perhaps a third of the population of Europe perished in the first epidemic of 1347-1350. Outbreaks continued for many years afterwards.

earthworks could keep a besieger's cannon from firing point-blank at the walls and towers and could enable them to hold out long enough for a relieving force to arrive. The castle at Donningham, for example, was fortified in September 1643 and defended by Colonel John Boys, who built a complete set of star-shaped earthworks around it. In July 1644, the Earl of Essex sent General Middleton to take it with 3,000 dragoons and light cavalry. Middleton had no "big" guns and lost 300 men in a hopeless attempt to attack the fortifications with scaling ladders. In September, Colonel Horton took over with a siege train. He shot at it for 12 days and "beat down three towers and a part of a wall," but could not compel the defenders to surrender. In October, the Earl of Manchester wanted to try to take it by storm again, but apparently his men declined to carry it out. They had fired over 1,000 rounds of "great shot" in 19 days against the defender's walls without causing any further damage to the garrison except wrecking some more of its defenses.

Eventually, Donningham was besieged again at the end of 1645 when Cromwell ordered Colonel Dalbier to take it. Colonel Boys delayed the end by building a large satellite bastion on the castle hill, from which he launched a number of sorties. Unfortunately, he couldn't match a giant mortar which Colonel Dalbier had acquired. This mortar fired 17 large rounds against the staircase tower of the fortification's gatehouse, pounding a large hole in it. After a parley in March 1646, Colonel Boys surrendered with 200 men, 20 barrels of gunpowder and six guns. His men marched out with colors flying, muskets loaded and every man packing as much ammunition as he could carry, under the honorable terms and conditions agreed to at the parley.[215]

SIEGE OF VIENNA, 1529

In 1526 Suleiman the sultan invaded Europe marching from Constantinople to the Danube and gaining considerable success against the army of King Louis of Hungary. Much of his success was due to his massed use of artillery. Suleiman annexed the kingdom, and in view of this success embarked on a second invasion in 1529 with an army estimated at 120,000 troops and 20,000 baggage camels. Realizing that the medieval walls of Vienna targeted by the sultan were not impregnable, Ferdinand, the archduke of Austria, was determined to rely on his troops rather than masonry. His force was augmented by Spanish infantry sent by Charles from his army in Italy, a veteran German infantry regiments making up the remainder of his garrison of about 20,000.

215 Paul Johnson, *Castles of England, Scotland, and Wales,* Weinfeld and Nicolson, London, 1989, pp. 168-173.

Siege of Vienna, contemporary 1529 engraving of clashes between the Austrians and Ottomans outside Vienna by Bartel Behmam.

The Turks spread out on both sides of the Danube, but before they could move their 300 guns into position a sortie of 2,500 defenders inflicted a sharp defeat on advance posts. This blow was followed only three days later by a surprise attack of Spanish units which added to the casualties of the besieging forces. From this point onwards, the defenders continued to take away the initiative from their attackers at every opportunity.

Ferdinand's engineers proved so successful at countermining that many of the enemy's mine-heads were detected and blown up before they could do any harm. Whenever a breach was opened, the garrison threw up new works while beating off the sultan's storming parties. Finally, a great Christian sortie of 8,000 men fell upon the invaders at dawn one morning with enormous destruction of Turkish troops and material. The adage that "the best defence is a vigorous attack", has seldom been put to better effect.

As a last resort, Suleiman ordered a general storm of Vienna. His men, by now dispirited by the numerous past reverses, were unable to make any headway against the Spanish and German harquebuses. The assault failed with heavy losses, and that night the Ottoman host began a retreat which became one of the great catastrophes of military history. Snow fell in October, weeks earlier than expected in the Danube country. Horses and camels floundered to their deaths in roads resembling morasses, while Austrian horsemen hung on the flanks of the beaten army to cut off stragglers. The sultan's entire transport had to be burned, and most of his artillery was destroyed or captured before the shrunken remnant reached Constantinople in December.

The outstanding defence of Vienna in 1529 may be considered the first great turning point in the struggle between Muslims and the Christian world. It did not deter Suleiman from conducting a third invasion in 1532, but this time he discretely avoided Vienna.

Ottoman Siege of Vienna, 1683.

Well-placed and utilized artillery could often offset seemingly overwhelming numerical forces set against an opposing side. The lack of it could also change the tide in a siege where relief could arrive at any time. At the siege of Vienna in 1683, a coalition of Polish, German, and Austrian forces faced a much larger Turkish army of about 15,000 Tatars. The Turkish forces were led by a relatively unspectacular general, the Grand Vizier Kara Mustafa.

From the month of March, the Turks prepared to launch an attack on the Hapsburg capital of Vienna and had gathered their forces together to conduct the advance fairly efficiently. By June, the Turks had invaded Austria, and on 14 July 1683, they reached Vienna, where they began to lay siege to the great city. The Turks were inadequately equipped with artillery, which caused the siege to drag out. Although the defenders resisted effectively, their food supply and ammunition stocks became depleted. As the siege wore on, the Turks managed to affect a number of breaches in Vienna's walls, but the barricades erected by the defenders hindered their efforts.

In an early version of the NATO and Warsaw Pact treaties that were formed during the Cold War, Austrian King Jan III Sobieski (1674-1696) had signed the Treaty of Warsaw with the Holy Roman Emperor Leopold earlier that year on 31 March 1683. In the terms of the treaty, each of the co-signers agreed to come to the other's aid if the Turks attacked either Krakow or Vienna. With the Turkish attack clearly underway, Sobieski proceeded to march to Vienna with an army of about 30,000 men, where he joined his forces with the Austrians and Germans. Sobieski launched a mounted attack against the weakest point in the Turkish lines, using his "husaria," (Polish Hussars) on 13 September, completely surprising Kara Mustafa and causing heavy losses. It is claimed that this victory prevented Europe from being dominated by the Ottoman Turks and halted further invasions from their domain. It also secured Christianity as the main religion in Europe.[216]

SIEGE OF CHITTORGARH, 1567-1568

The City of Chittorgarh located in the State of Rajasthan in Western India, on the banks of river Gambhiri and Berach. Chittorgarh is home to the Chittor Fort, the largest fort in India and Asia. It was the site of three major sieges (1303, 1535 and 1567-1568) by Muslim invaders against its Hindu rulers who fought fiercely to maintain their independence. On more than one occasion, when faced with a certain defeat, the men fought to death while the women committed suicide by jauhar (mass self-immolation).

---

[216]   Wimmer, Jan, *The 1683 Siege of Vienna* (Warsaw; Interpress, 1983); Internet:

http://campus.northpark.edu/history/WebChron/EastEurope/ViennaSiege.html.

(Ssjoshi111 Photo)

Chittorgarh Fort. Originally called Chitrakuta, the Chittor Fort is said to have been built by Chitranga, a king of the local Maurya dynasty. The Guhila (Gahlot) ruler Bappa Rawal is said to have captured the fort in either 728 CE or 734 CE. In 1303, the Delhi Sultanate ruler Alauddin Khalji defeated the Guhila king Ratnasimha and captured the fort. The fort was later captured by Hammir Singh, a king of the Sisodia branch of the Guhilas. Chittor gained prominence during the period of his successors, which included Rana Kumbha and Rana Sanga. In 1535, Bahadur Shah of Gujarat besieged and conquerd the fort. After he was driven away by the Mughal emperor Humayun, the Sisodias regained control of the fort. In 1567-68, the Mughal emperor Akbar besieged and captured the fort.[217]

SIEGE OF BIJAPUR, 1686

On the 12th of September 1686, the Mughals under the command of Aurangzeb Alamgir conquered the great fort of Bijapur, thus ending the rule of the Adil Shahi dynasty.

---

[217] Paul E. Schellinger; Robert M. Salkin, eds. *International Dictionary of Historic Places: Asia and Oceania*, Routledge/ Taylor & Francis, 1994.

(Yuvraj Chauhan Photo)

The legendary "Malik-i-Maidan" Gun is reported to be the largest piece of cast bronze ordnance in the world. The following inscription is engraved on the famous Malik-i-Maidan cannon: "There is one God, and no one besides him. In the 30th regnal year, equivalent to the year 1097 of the Hijra era, Shah Alamgir, the Ghazi, the Padshah who is the asylum of religion. He who administered justice and took the realm of kings".

The Siege of Bijapur began in March 1685 and ended in September 1686 with a Mughal victory. The siege began when the Aurangzeb dispatched his son Muhammad Azam Shah with a force of nearly 50,000 men to capture Bijapur Fort and defeat Sikander Adil Shah, the then ruler of Bijapur who refused to be a vassal of the Mughal Empire. The Siege of Bijapur was among the longest military engagements by the Mughals, lasting more than 15 months until Aurangzeb personally arrived to organize a victory.

In 1637, the young Prince Aurangzeb was the Subedar of Deccan, under the reign of his father the Mughal Emperor Shah Jahan. He led a 25,000 strong Mughal Army to besiege Bijapur Fort and its ruler, Mohammed Adil Shah. The siege, however, was unsuccessful because the Adil Shahi dynasty sought peace with Shah Jahan, mainly through the cooperation of Dara Shikoh.

Ali Adil Shah II inherited a troubled kingdom. He had to face the onslaught of the Maratha led by Shivaji, who had fought and killed Afzal Khan, the most capable commander in the Bijapur Sultanate. The leaderless troops of Nijapur were consequently routed by Shivaji's rebels. As a result, the Adil Shahi dynasty was greatly weakened mainly due to the rebellious Maratha, led by Shivaji and his son Sambhaji.

Sikandar Adil Shah was chosen to lead the Adil Shahi dynasty. He allied himself with Abdul Hasan Qutb Shah, and refused to become a vassal of the Mughal Empire. Angered by his refusal to submit to Mughal authority, Aurangzeb and the Mughal Empire declared war.

In 1685, Aurangzeb dispatched his son Muhammad Azam Shah alongside Ruhullah Khan the *Mir Bakshi* (organizer) with a force of nearly 50,000 men to capture Bijapur Fort. The Mughal Army arrived at Bijapur in March 1685. Elite Mughal Sowars, led by Dilir Khan and Qasim Khan, surrounded and captured crucial positions around Bijapur Fort. After the encirclement was complete Prince Muhammad Azam Shah initiated siege operations by positioning guns around Bijapur Fort.

Bijapur Fort, however, was well-defended by 30,000 men led by Sikandar Adil Shah and his commander Sarza Khan. Attacks by Mughal gun batteries were repulsed by the large and heavy Bijapur guns such as the famous *"Malik-i-Maidan"*, which fired cannonballs 69-cm in diameter. Instead of capturing territories on open ground, the Mughals dug long trenches and carefully placed their artillery but made no further advancements.

The Mughals could not cross through the 10-foot deep moat surrounding Bijapur Fort. Moreover, the 50-ft high 25-ft wide fine granite and lime mortar walls were almost impossible to breach. The situation for the Mughals worsened when Maratha forces led by Melgiri Pandit, under Maratha Emperor Sambhaji, blockaded food, gunpowder and weapon supplies arriving from the Mughal garrison at Solapur. The Mughals began to struggle on two fronts and became overburdened by the ongoing siege against Adil Shahi and the roving Maratha forces. Things worsened when a Bijapuri cannonball struck a Mughal gunpowder position causing a massive explosion into the trenches that killed 500 infantrymen.

In response to their hardships, Aurangzeb sent his son Shah Alam and his celebrated commander Abdullah Khan Bahadur Firuz Jang. Not wanting to permit the collapse of the Mughal Army outside Bijapur Fort, the Mughal commander Ghazi ud-Din Khan Feroze Jung I led a massive expeditionary reinforcement force to alleviate the hard-pressed Mughal Army, and drove out the Maratha forces. Abdullah Khan Bahadur Firuz Jang, a highly experienced Mughal commander positioned at the outpost of Rasulpur, routed a 6,000-strong infantry contingent led by Pam Naik, which had intended to carry supplies to Bijapur Fort during a night attack.

The Mughals regained control of the supply routes leading to Solapur, but no successful advancement was made into Bijapur Fort. The lengthy siege turned into a stalemate. Aurangzeb therefore personally gathered a massive army in July 1686 and marched slowly towards Bijapur Fort. On his arrival outside Bijapur Fort, he established encampments beside Abdullah Khan Bahadur Firuz Jang on 4 September 1686. Aurangzeb personally rode out inspiring his army of almost a 100,000 men to begin a full-scale assault. After eight days of intense fighting, the Mughals had successfully damaged the five gates of Bijapur Fort and collapsed substantial portions of the fortified walls, thus enabling them to breach the moat and conquer the city. They captured Sikandar Adil Shah and bound him in silver chains before presenting him to Aurangzeb.

Sikandar Adil Shah had suffered many wounds and ultimately died on 12 September 1686, resulting in the end of the Adil Shahi dynasty. Aurangzeb then appointed Syed Mian (father of the Sayyid brothers) as the first Mughal Subedar of Bijapur.

The Mughals had annexed and conquered a weakened Bijapur, but their control of the region began to weaken after the death of Bahadur Shah I in 1712. The Nawabs in the region declared their independence after a few decades. Eventually, after 1753, the Marathas occupied much of Bijapur.[218]

---

[218] Hugh Chisholm, Editor, *Bijapur.* Encyclopaedia Britannica (11th ed.), Cambridge University Press, 1911.

SIEGE OF LONDONDERRY, 1688

In December 1688, the town of Londonderry declared its gates closed to James II, then fighting to regain the throne of England that he had lost in the 'Glorious Revolution', a bloodless coup d'etat in which William of Orange had been invited to become king.

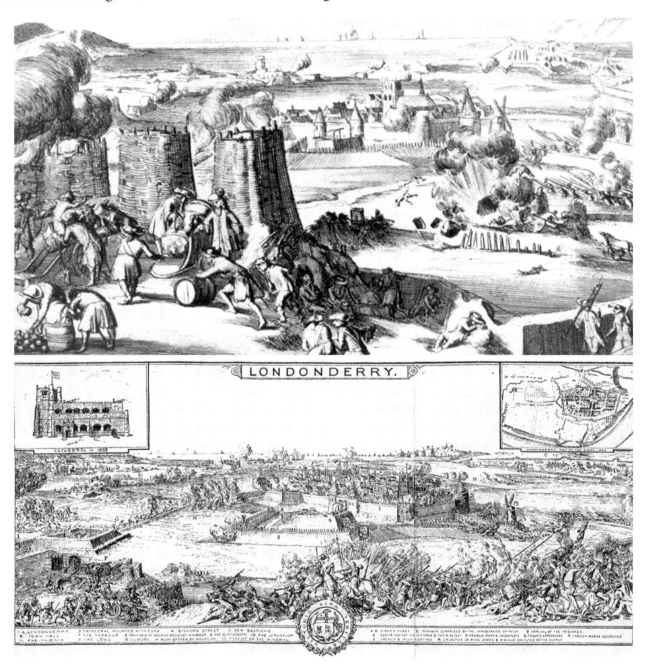

On 13 April 1689 James came to the gates of Londonderry and called on the city to surrender. But thirteen apprentice boys ran to the city gates and shut them in the face of his army.

A siege began which lasted until 28 July, a total of 105 days. It was a brutal affair, fully in keeping with the standards of seventeenth century warfare. Thousands died as James's army rained down cannon balls and mortars on the town. Disease and famine also took a terrible toll, among the attacking soldiers as well as the townsfolk. Eventually, an English ship called the Mountjoy managed to break through a boom which had been set up across the river Foyle by the besieging army and relieved the town.

The armed merchant ships *Mountjoy* and *Phoenix*
break through the defensive boom to relieve the Siege of Derry. (James Grant)

SÉBASTIEN LE PRESTRE DE VAUBAN, SEIGNEUR DE VAUBAN AND LATER MARQUIS DE VAUBAN (1 MAY 1633 – 30 MARCH 1707)

Sébastien Le Prestre de Vauban, Seigneur de Vauban and later Marquis de Vauban
(1 May 1633 – 30 March 1707)

Sébastien Le Prestre de Vauban, a Marshal in the army of Louis XIV, was a member of the French bourgeoisie who made important contributions to the field of engineering and in the application of science to warfare. Vauban devised a method of siege that involved a geometric advancement of trenchworks and approaches that moved from parallel to parallel against enemy fortifications that was phenomenally successful. The widespread adoption of his practical solutions to the problems of siege warfare resulted in a remarkable order by Louis XIV to commanders of all French fortifications. The king ruled that should a fortress commander come under attack by an enemy using Vauban's methods of siege, the commander might honorably surrender once an initial breach had been made in his citadel and he had repulsed one assault.[219] In effect, Vauban's methods of siegecraft virtually guaranteed the successful completion of an assault on the defense-works and fortifications in existence at that time, and indeed for many years to follow after his death.[220]

The sciences of artillery ballistics and the design of fortifications that could withstand artillery projectiles had both been making rapid advances. Artillery had long since negated the existing defenses

---

[219] Russell F. Weigley, *The Age of Battles: the Quest for Decisive Warfare from Breitenfeld to Waterloo*. Indiana University Press, 1991, p. 55

[220] Reginald Bloomfield, *Sebastien le Prestre de Vauban*, 1633-1707, Methuen & Company Ltd., London, 1938, p. 61.

of the old high-walled medieval castles that had been designed to withstand early siege methods. Fortress design had become highly standardized. Low-silhouette gun platforms would be laid out to conform to the conventional pattern of a polygonal bastion. The bastions would in turn be adapted to the contours of the terrain and the dimensions of the site to be defended. Heavy inner ramparts were designed into fortifications, with a parapet for the mounting of additional guns. A broad ditch would be dug outside the walls, followed by the construction of an outer rampart called a "glacis." This would consist of a wall with an open, gentle slope up which an attacking force would have to advance while being continuously exposed to the defender's fire. The key element in the layout of these fortifications, consisted in the positioning of outlying bastions. These were designed so that they placed every potential axis of attack not only under direct fire, but also under mutually supporting crossfire. The design of the bastions had therefore come to be a matter of applying standard geometric rules, formulated largely by Blaise, Comte de Pagan, who was a mathematical theorist rather than a practicing engineer.[221]

Blaise François, Comte de Pagan, engraving.
(Charles Perrault, *Les Hommes illustres qui ont paru en France pendant ce siècle*, Paris, 1696)

---

[221] Russell F. Weigley, op. cit., p. 53-54.

Although Vauban studied and made use of Pagan's idea's, he proceeded to develop several specific and separate ideas of his own in his designs of fortifications. One of these was to build ramparts of earth rather than of stone. He had sound reasons for this, based on his personal observation of cannon-fire. Stone ramparts shattered stone cannonballs, causing them to break-up and shoot off dangerous fragments. Earth walls, which could absorb the impact of incoming rounds, were therefore safer, and had the added advantages of being cheaper and more easily built. Secondly, he designed angled rather than rounded bastions, therefore making it possible for all parts of defended walls to be covered by enfilade fire against attackers. These ideas had already been applied to some extent in the wars since the mid-sixteenth century, but no one thus far had thought them out and applied them to their fullest extent. Vauban's methods transformed this branch of warfare into a geometric exercise, with the result that his defenses eventually became too formidable to allow frontal assaults by irreplaceable soldiers. In a logical extension of his methods, he always made the best use of the ground to assist and expand the depth of his defensive network.[222]

Vauban adhered to simple basic principles in his fortifications, but followed no set design.[223] He retained the traditional ground plan for a fortress, which consisted of an inner enclosure, a rampart, a moat and an outer rampart. Existing fortresses could last intact only until the main body of their fortifications had been breached, and the result of a siege was thus in large part a question of which side could hold out the longest. To counter this problem, Vauban endeavored to extend the fortification of his outworks as far as possible. He thus compelled the enemy to begin his siege operations at a distance and multiplied the obstacles in his way so that the difficulties in gaining ground never ceased. If the outworks should fall to the enemy, they were still commanded by fire from the main central works.[224]

Vauban's geometrical skill and practical eye for ground enabled him to design fortifications in such a way that every wall facing outwards was flanked and supported by additional works behind and beside it. The basic element in these designs, multiplied and varied in scale, was a large outward-pointing triangle with its inner side missing.[225] The outward point made a difficult target for the enemy to breach and thus forced him to concentrate his forces vulnerably. Each outward-facing wall of the triangle was so angled as to cover the area of wall between it and the face of the next salient. This was the principle of the great bastions on every angle of the main polygon. The large bastions were interspersed with smaller ones along the curtain wall, close enough together for each to be able to cover the next with small-arms fire. Other triangles, widely varying in size, called "ravelins," or "demi-lunes" (half-moons), if they were actually crescent shaped, stood in a dry moat. The demi-lunes projected farther forward in such a manner that they covered each other, as well as being covered from behind. Repeated complexes of fortifications of this type often extended 300 yards from the central rampart and made powerful obstacles to a siege.[226]

The forts designed by Vauban for Louis XIV have come to be divided by historians into three stages of development. An examination of specific details found in several key fortresses of his design follows, including Lille, Arras, Besançon, Belfort, Landau, Neuf Brisach and Louisbourg.

---

[222]   Field-Marshal Viscount Bernard L. Montgomery of Alamein, *A History of Warfare*, (Collins, London, 1968), p. 293.
[223]   Reginald Bloomfield, op. cit., p. 56.
[224]   Bernard L. Montgomery, op. cit., p. 293.
[225]   A list of definitions, terms and illustrations used to describe the fortifications is included in the appendix.
[226]   Bernard L. Montgomery, op. cit., p. 295.

(Photo du comité régional du tourisme de Franche Comté)
Citadel of Besançon, fortifications designed by Vauban, aerial view.

This 17th-century fortress stands in Franche-Comté, France. It is one of the finest masterpieces of military architecture designed by Vauban. The Citadel occupies 11 hectares (27 acres) on Mount Saint-Etienne, one of the seven hills that protect Besançon, the capital of Franche-Comté. Mount Saint-Etienne occupies the neck of an oxbow formed by the river Doubs, giving the site a strategic importance, that Julius Caesar recognised as early as 58 BC. The Citadel overlooks the old quarter of the city, which is located within the oxbow, and has views of the city and its surroundings.

Vauban's first system was essentially the same as that devised by Blaise Françoise, Comte de Pagan (1604-1665), who was another practical soldier with an equally remarkable career. In spite of having been blinded in battle, Pagan achieved the rank of Maréchal-de-Camp, as well as having written a book advocating a new order in which works should be constructed. In Pagan's opinion the bastions were the most important features against which the main force of an attack would fall, and therefore the integrity of this work depended on its being sited correctly. Once the works had been sited, they could then be connected by ramparts in such a way as to give whatever space was necessary inside the walls, and not inside the bastion salients. Pagan strengthened his works by fortifying outwards. He later proposed a second method in which he converted the ravelins and counterguards into a continuous protective envelope around the work, echoing the bastioned shape and furnished with three-tier batteries at every flanking angle. A second wet ditch was placed in front of this envelope, protected by more ravelins and then the usual covered way and glacis. The only fortress in existence today attributable to Pagan is that of Blaye, on the Gironde. Construction of Blaye according to Pagan's designs began in 1652 and was completed in 1685 by Vauban, thus forming an interesting link between two successive masters.[227] The

---

[227] Ian Hogg, *The History of Fortification*, Orbis Publishing Ltd., New York, 1981, p. 120-121.

major modifications that were to make Vauban the most renowned of military engineers came late in his career, after he had already constructed most of his fortresses.

(Eremeev Photo)
Ravelin Peter (1708) and access bridge, Petersberg Citadel, Erfurt, Germany.

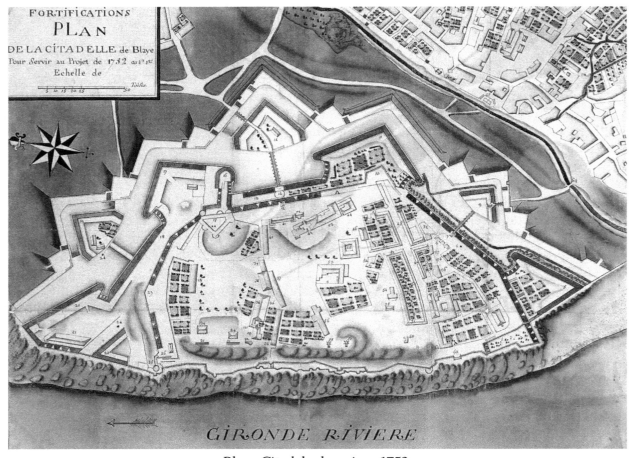

Blaye Citadel, plan view, 1752.

When French forces seized Flanders in 1667, the situation created the necessity to strengthen fortifications or add citadels at strategic places in, or adjacent to, the disputed territory. The citadels at Arras and Lille were thus the first major projects undertaken by Vauban, along with the strengthening of other town fortifications.[228] The resulting construction produced specific and identifiable elements that were to characterize most of his later fortifications.[229] Lille, however, was highly regarded as one of the engineer's finest works, a classic example of a "bastioned" defence.[230]

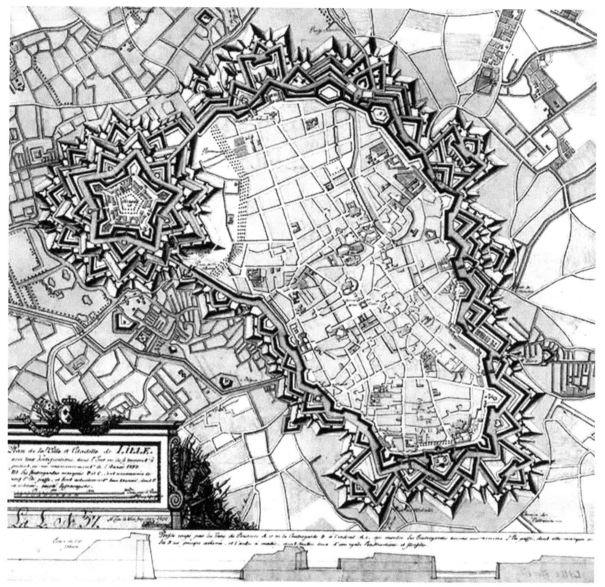

The fortification of Lille, France, designed by Vauban in 1709.

---

[228] The large citadel Vauban built at Arras still stands today. Peter and Helen Titchmarsh, *Exploring France*, Warwick, 1990, p. 191.

[229] Bruce W. Fry, *"An appearance of strength" The Fortifications of Louisbourg, Volume One*, (Parks Canada, 1984), p. 38.

[230] Ibid. p. 38.

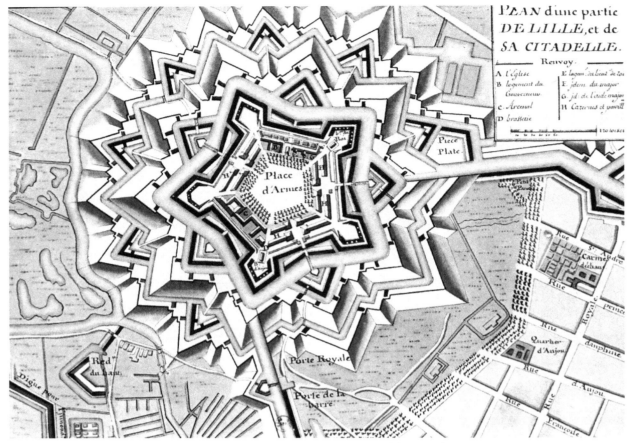

The Citadel of Lille, detailed view, designed by Vauban in 1709.

As an example of Vauban's "first" system, the citadel of Lille was laid out on a perfect pentagon, each front (measured from one flanked angle to the next), being 300 metres long and the curtains between bastions being half that length. The bastions are large and spacious, with straight flanks set at an obtuse angle (106 degrees) to the curtains in accordance with Pagan's concepts. There are no right angles to be seen in the fortification.[231] The outworks Vauban placed in the ditch before the curtains were an innovation of his. Instead of the "fausse-braye" so widely favored at the time, he introduced a variant he called a "tenaille."

Vauban's tenaille was a low, parapetted work built along the prolongation of the lines of defence works from the faces of the adjacent bastions and which formed a re-entrant angle where the lines intersected midway along the curtain. The resulting defence works thus presented an obstacle in the form of a shallow V in front of the curtain, so that an enemy gaining the "covered way" of the glacis would find an additional area behind which the defence could continue a spirited resistance with small arms. In addition, the work masked the base of the curtain and adjacent flanks from enemy batteries. The function of the tenaille was essentially the same as that of the fausse-braie, but Vauban had detached these works from the base of the rampart and advanced them into the ditch, aligning them along the line of defence. He thereby achieved more efficient flanking fire, as defenders would be augmenting the fire from the faces of the adjacent bastions instead of simply firing straight out from the curtain. At the same time, he lessened the likelihood of debris from the parapets on the main "enceinte" collapsing

---

[231] Loc. cit., p. 38.

onto the heads of the defenders below after an artillery strike. Vauban was convinced of the utility of additional defence in this location and situated tenailles of one form or another in all of his fortresses whenever possible.[232]

Vauban's use of defence in depth was well advanced even in his earliest fortifications, when he endeavored to present to the enemy a series of obstacles, each of which had to be overcome in turn before reaching the main body of the place under attack. At Lille for example, the "practitioner" initially placed a "demi-lune" on each front before the tenaille and the curtain. For greater resistance, each demi-lune contained in its gorge a redoubt, separated from the larger work by a small branch of the ditch. In addition, beyond the 40-metre wide flooded ditch and the glacis, he added another wet ditch. In the re-entrants of this advanced ditch on all fronts except the two covered by the town itself, were placed seven small demi-lunes or lunettes in total. Finally, an additional covered way and glacis encircled the entire site.[233]

Vauban surveyed the site not only from the point of view of an engineer, but from his observations as a soldier of what might work and what did not. For the main enceinte for example, he calculated that an escarp inclined to a "batter" of one in five would retain the 12-metre high earthen rampart if counterforts spaced at 18 pieds (5.8 metres) were used and the top of the escarp was 4 1/2 pieds (1.4 metres) thick. The base of the wall, the angles and the cordon were all in dressed stone, as were the gateways. The revetments were all in brick. In the interior, the buildings were similarly furnished with dressed stone surrounds and brick walls. From the parapets, the defence commanded the tenailles, demi-lunes, covered ways, and glacis. From the tenailles, the ditch, covered way and the rear of the demi-lunes could be swept. From the demi-lunes, fire could be directed into the advanced works. In reverse, however, each successive work masked the next, so that only the parapet of the main enceinte was visible. Lille therefore exemplifies Vauban's concerns with the practical aspects of construction of his fortifications.[234]

The citadel of Lille was built on a site never previously used for fortifications, in an area of perfectly flat, open ground, permitting a "textbook symmetry" rarely found in Vauban's works. Regular fortifications were held to be preferable, as they were equally strong all around. Engineers, however, would more often than not be confronted with an existing enceinte to be strengthened or unfavorable terrain to be fortified. Simple geometry was not enough in situations that were by definition, exceptions to the rules. This problem was not new to Vauban, and he knew that his predecessor Pagan also had to deal extensively with designs for irregular fortifications.[235]

Vauban's methods were not only developed from Pagan's principles but expanded upon whenever the opportunity presented itself. For example, in designing the new defenses for the town of Ath, similar dispositions of "fronts" to those of Lille were employed, using six sides of an irregular heptagon. On the seventh side, however, he imposed a modification on the existing town and walls. The straight curtain in which the medieval castle was set was too long to be treated as a single front, so Vauban constructed a flat bastion around the castle midway along the curtain wall. An outer ditch was added to the front of this wall, and a horn-work was added to cover a potential weak point where the River Dendre entered the town.[236]

During this same period, Vauban built the citadel at Arras and improved the town's defenses. The most striking difference between Lille and Arras is that, in Arras, he designed his bastions with orillons and retired flanks.[237]

---

[232] Bruce W. Fry, op. cit., p. 39.
[233] Ibid. p. 39.
[234] Loc. cit.
[235] Loc. cit.
[236] Loc. cit.
[237] Loc. cit.

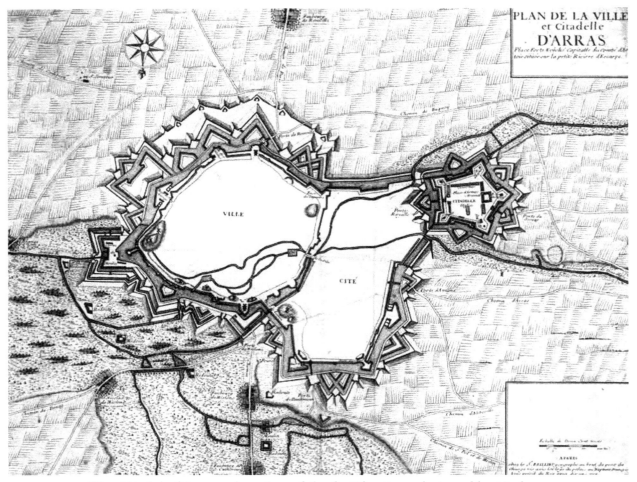

The Citadel of Arras, plan view of the fortifications designed by Vauban.

Vauban made liberal use of orillons throughout his fortifications for the next 20 years following the design of Lille and Arras, but only rarely used casemates, and then only under exceptional circumstances. He instead designed solid retired flanks that permitted artillery fire from the parapet level only. Such flanks were built on a graceful arc that permitted the defenders more room to maneuver. In order to gain additional room, Vauban modified his design of the curtain wall without leaving a continuous straight line to directly join the flank. Instead, a short distance before the junction, he angled the curtain slightly back. This break or "brisure" kept the entire curve of the flank unobstructed. It has been said (by Muller) that this was Vauban's only original design element. Vauban may have been influenced in this by Pagan, since he later completed Pagan's citadel of Blaye where curved flanks are in evidence. Whatever the inspiration, Vauban rapidly introduced this design (in the true style of a sound practitioner), on all the frontier strongholds of France, and it is therefore the one most readily identified with the great engineer.[238] There are still several well-preserved partial fronts designed by Vauban in existence.[239] Many of Vauban's fortresses still stand, and are a visible reminder of the lasting qualities that helped to make his fortresses as nearly impregnable as the engineering of the age would allow.[240]

---

[238] Loc. cit.
[239] Some of which are visible in the fortifications at Longwy, Mauberge and Verdun, where one can see the characteristic designs of Vauban in the curved flanks protected by orillons. Loc. cit.
[240] Peter and Helen Titchmarsh, op. cit., Index.

It is difficult to get an exact figure for the number of fortresses connected with Vauban's name, as the figures vary from author to author. Dupuy, for example, has stated that Vauban built 33 new fortresses, and remodeled 300 others. Goetz and Hogg have both indicated that he worked on 160, and Koch states that Vauban built 90 fortresses.[241] All those that are presently associated with this remarkable engineer however, have been constructed on the basis of precise mathematical calculations and usually contain a practical layout of depots, arsenals and storage of supplies which would in turn provide a very secure base for offensive operations.[242]

The second of Vauban's systems began to appear in 1682 and was used for the first time at Belfort and then later at Besançon. Being a practical engineer, Vauban took note of deficiencies in his first system and improved on it. The second system was therefore devised in a logical and practical extension of the first. He retained the use of a basic polygon structure, but the curtain walls in the regions between the bastions were lengthened. The bastions themselves were replaced at both sites by a small work or tower at the angles, these in turn being covered by so-called detached bastions constructed in the ditch.[243]

Before the innovation of Vauban's second system, the outlying bastions all remained attachments of the main enclosure, or the "main enceinte." If any of them fell, the citadel itself was immediately threatened. Vauban's replacement of the bastions at the angles of the polygon with these small works or towers that were themselves covered by detached bastions, forced an assailant to work his way through them. Even then, an attacker would still not be in a position to threaten the principal defensive works.[244]

Another fortress most commonly classified as belonging to Vauban's second system is that of Landau, which is comparable in size and scope to Belfort. The most striking characteristic of both of these fortresses is the fragmentation of the design of the enceinte. Small masonry gun towers or "tours bastionnes" project from the curtain walls, while expansive faces and flanks that typify Vauban's bastions have been detached from the enceinte and placed before the towers. This design is somewhat like the face-covers or counterguards Pagan had originally proposed. The size of these works, together with the fact that they were designed with true flanks, resulted in their being referred to as "bastions detacheés," or "bastions a contregarde," rather than face-covers.

The problem of commanding heights is of fundamental concern to all military engineers and throughout his career, Vauban made masterly use of heights when attacking a place. Vauban fortified places in mountainous districts such as Mont Louis in the Pyrenees, Briançon, and Mont Dauphin and Château Queyras on the Savoy frontier.[245] He also made every attempt to minimize the danger when fortifying places where he had no choice in the selection of the terrain.[246] Concerning hill fortifications, Vauban commented for example, that "the frontier of the Savoy was so extremely hilly that I was obliged to invent a new system of fortifications so to take advantage of it." He also mentioned Colmar, Entrevaux and Guillames as being "situated in hilly country and commanded from far and near by surrounding high ground, (and therefore) only the method of fortifying with tower bastions should be followed." He used "tours bastionneés" in the Alpine region, for example, but developed a completely different arrangement in the Pyrenees.

In the valley of the Tet, on the route from Roussillon to the pass into Spain, lies the formerly Spanish town of Ville-franche-de-Conflènt, fortified since medieval times and improved by Vauban after his inspection in 1669. Describing the place, he wrote that it was "tightly hemmed in by surrounding high mountains with steep slopes so close that even the most distant was within sling-shot", but because of

---

[241] Colonel T.N. Dupuy, *The Evolution of Weapons and Warfare*, Indianapolis, 1980, p. 110. Ian Hogg, *The History of Fortification*, St. Martin's Press Inc, New York, 1981, p. 122.

[242] H.W. Koch, *History of Warfare*, Bison Books Ltd., London, 1987, p. 193.

[243] Peter Paret, op. cit., p. 81.

[244] Russell F. Weigley, op. cit., p. 56.

[245] Reginald Bloomfield, op cit., p. 59.

[246] Bruce W. Fry, op. cit., p. 41.

the sharp inclines and extreme height of the mountains, no artillery could be brought to bear. However, outcrops afforded "positions for musketry, from which anyone showing his nose in the streets could be picked off like a sitting duck."

(A1AA1A Photo)
Ville-franche-de-Conflènt fortifications, overlooked by Fort Liberia.

The original town dates from 1098 and was fortified because of its strategic position in lands that changed hands between French and Spanish occupation. In 1374, Villefranche resisted the siege of Jaume III the son of last King of Majorca. In July 1654, the French captured the city after eight days, and the troops of Louis XIV took Puigcerda from the Spaniards. The town was part of the program of construction and improvement of outlying French defences through 1707 by Marshal Vauban.

To afford adequate protection for the defenders of fortifications in hilly terrain, Vauban ensured that normally exposed parapets were roofed over in the most vulnerable sectors, so that bastions and curtains assumed the appearance of a medieval "chemin de ronde," or covered street. At the Northeast angle of the town of Ville-franche-de-Conflènt for example, the parapets of the Bastion du Roi were extremely high in relation to the terreplein they covered. This gave the gunners manning the embrasures maximum protection. Masonry traverses bisecting the bastions were included to reduce the risk of enfilading fire sweeping across one flank and taking defenders of the other flank in the rear. This worked well in this fortress, but Vauban did not repeat the idea in any others.[247]

---

[247] Ibid. p. 42.

Vauban continued to make further revolutionary improvements to his method of defence in depth. In all previous cases, adaptation of fortifications to mountainous terrain had been through projecting crown works or horn works, and when this was done, the main line was directly affected. Vauban gained flexibility by adapting his designs to the terrain without imperiling the main line of defence.[248]

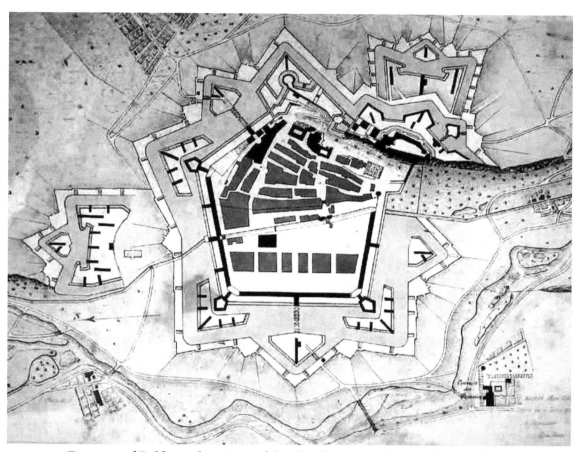

Fortress of Belfort, plan view of the fortifications designed by Vauban.

The fortresses of Belfort and Landau both used towers and detached bastions to replace the conventional bastions. Tower bastions were actually first introduced when they were added to the existing enceinte at Besançon, years earlier. There, and at Villefranche, Vauban's task was to improve the existing defenses of a town. Its medieval walls were built on the river's edge and were within range of commanding heights. On the limited ground available on two fronts, squat, compact artillery towers were built.

One of the criticisms of Vauban's tower bastions was that they were too vulnerable to artillery fire. The towers at Besançon were commanded by heights that Vauban was careful to fortify, but if these had fallen into enemy hands, the towers could have been bombarded with ease. It is therefore unlikely that Vauban the practitioner considered his towers as offering improved defence against artillery, and thus the local constraints at Besançon may have been the immediate reason behind his new approach. Although the situation at Villefranche was better since artillery could not readily be brought into action except in the pass, Vauban would likely have employed tower and detached bastions had he considered them effective alternatives to standard bastions at the time.[249]

---

[248]   Peter Paret, op. cit., p. 82.
[249]   Bruce W. Fry, op. cit., p. 42.

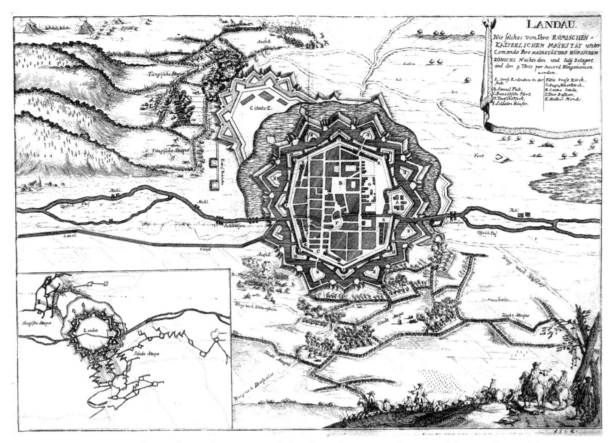

Fortress of Landau, plan view of the fortifications designed by Vauban. T
his fortress came under siege in 1702.

After the construction at Besançon, Vauban favored further experimentation along the same lines. At Belfort, the limitations on design are less apparent, and could have been resolved by a series of strong outworks such as he had already used at Arras or Bayonne. The change in approach is even more marked in the defenses of Landau, where clear details of Vauban's second system can be seen in the plan of the fortress, such as his use of tower bastions on the main enceinte protected by detached bastions or counter-guards. The intervening tenailles cover the curtains, which rise from a wet ditch. Demi-lunes are located in advance of the tenailles on all fronts, and a wet outer ditch surrounds the place at the foot of the glacis. Two large horn-works in the conventional manner with fronts comprised of two half-bastions with orillons and retired, curving flanks are located south of the town. An additional outer perimeter of detached redoubts was placed beyond the glacis, as discovered by attacking forces during four sieges made on the site during the War of Spanish Succession. These works, shaped like demi-lunes and open at the rear so that they would be exposed to defensive fire if taken by the enemy, demonstrate Vauban's increased preoccupation with defence in depth. Here again, he deliberately placed as many obstacles in series in the way of an attacker, well before the main body of the fort could be reached. It has also been suggested by the engineer Lazard, that Vauban developed his second system as a means of countering the effects of ricochet fire.[250]

Vauban's unconventional designs were not entirely impregnable, in spite of the strengths of the bastioned system of fortification. Landau for example, changed hands often during the War of the

---

[250] Bruce W. Fry, op. cit., p. 43.

Spanish Succession, being taken by the Allies in 1702, recaptured by the French in 1703, taken again by the Allies in 1704, and finally recaptured by the French in 1703. These battles demonstrated that no fortress or system could be considered impregnable, and Vauban's successors did not attempt to emulate his second or third systems. He had, however, spent a lifetime providing the country with a formidable barrier of fortresses along every frontier and exposed coastline, a barrier that, in spite of all the wars, had held. It was thanks to the holding power of Vauban's fortifications (and to the generalship of Villars), that France secured very reasonable terms at the final Treaty of Utrecht in 1713.[251] When peace came, the French frontiers were still secure.[252]

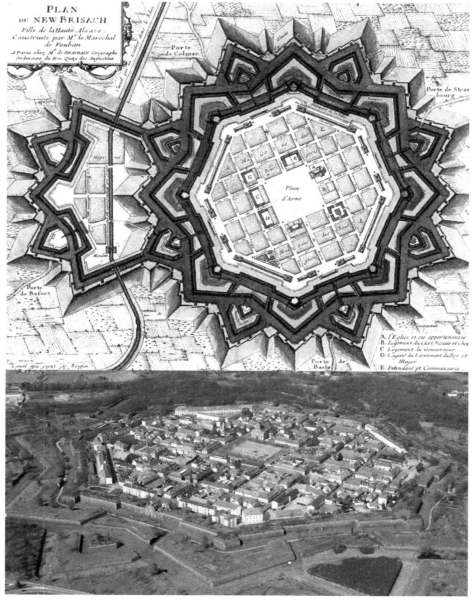

(Luftfahrer Photo)
Neuf Brisach, France, plan view and aerial view of the fortifications designed by Vauban.

---

251   Field Marshal Viscount Bernard L. Montgomery of Alamein, op. cit., p. 313.
252   Bruce W. Fry, op. cit., p. 44-45.

Neuf Brisach was intended to guard the border between France and the Holy Roman Empire, subsequently the German states. It was built after the Treaty of Ryswick, in 1697, that resulted in France losing the town of Brisach, on the opposite bank of the Rhine. The town's name means *New Breisach*.

Vauban's third system consists in fact, of a single fortress, that of Neuf-Breisach in Alsace. It was designed in 1697, and not completed until 1708, a year after Vauban's death. It was the last major work he designed, and although he used the same basic principles introduced at Belfort and Landau, the practitioner side of him led him to the increase the scale of almost all elements of this major new fortress. Everything was made larger than in his previous designs, including the towers, or "tours bastionées" at the angles of the fortress, covered by detached bastions.[253]

In this scheme the curtain is modified in shape to permit an increased use of cannon in defence, and the towers, the detached bastions, and demi-lunes are all increased in size.[254] The differences are in detail only, an additional flank being provided on the curtains by adding re-entrant angles. In plan, the enceinte gives the appearance of a series of shallow bastions with the towers located at the flanked angles. Casemates were provided in the small flanks thus created. The demi-lunes were made stronger by the inclusion of a detached redoubt in each gorge. In profile, the counterguards or detached bastions are seen to be demi-riveted. The masonry escarp is only as high as the level of the covered way. The rampart above is of sloped earth with a line of pickets and a quickset hedge at the foot of the slope. Detached works beyond the glacis are absent and none were needed.[255]

Neuf Breisach was an entirely new place, built on the flat, open land that was the old floodplain of the Rhine River. Vauban selected the site at some distance from the river in order to keep the fort out of range of guns on the higher ground of Alt-Brisach. Vauban had submitted three schemes to the King, who after close study approved the third one. This design provided an octagon fort with bastioned towers in the angles, detached bastions, tenailles, demi-lunes, and with a moat filled from the Rhine. (The estimated cost was 4,048,875 livres, and it was not completed until 1708).[256] No earlier defenses had to be considered, nor were any constraints imposed by the lie of the land. All of the experience and expertise at Vauban's disposal were given free reign in the layout and design of his third system. Defence in depth and the formidable array of barriers at Neuf Breisach were the culminating result.[257]

In essence, the third system was only a modification of the second. Although it was used for only a single work, Neuf-Breisach is considered the great masterpiece of Vauban.[258] This should be considered from the point of view that during a half century of ceaseless effort, Vauban conducted nearly fifty sieges and drew the plans for well over a hundred fortresses and harbor installations. For example, during the interval between the cessation of French hostilities with Spain in 1659 and Louis XIV's first "War of Conquest" in 1667, Vauban worked to repair and improve numerous fortifications of the kingdom under the direction of Clerville.

---

[253] Ibid. p. 43.
[254] Peter Paret, op. cit., p. 81.
[255] Bruce W. Fry, op. cit., p. 43.
[256] Reginald Bloomfield, op. cit., pp. 141-142.
[257] Bruce W. Fry, op. cit., p. 43.
[258] Peter Paret, op. cit., p. 81.

The War of Devolution (1667–68) saw the French armies of Louis XIV overrun the Habsburg-controlled Spanish Netherlands and the Free County of Burgundy, only to be pressured to give most of it back by a Triple Alliance of England, Sweden and the Dutch Republic, in the Treaty of Aix-la-Chapelle. The painting by Charles Le Brun shows Louis XIV visiting a trench during the war.

In 1667 Louis XIV attacked the Low Countries. It was during this brief "War of Devolution", that Vauban so distinguished himself as a "master of siegecraft" and the other branches of his trade that Louvois noticed his distinct superiority to Clerville and made him virtual director, as commissaire general, of all the engineering work in his department. The acquisitions of the War of Devolution launched Vauban on his great building program. Important towns in Hainaut and Flanders were acquired, including Bergues, Furnes, Tournai, and Lille. These and many other important positions were then fortified according to one of the three systems developed by Vauban.[259]

Vauban's systems of fortification evolved from his experience on the battlefield, and from the exercise of considerable common sense. The systems attributed to Vauban were categorized on the basis of regular fortifications, although the majority of Vauban's works, adapted as they were to the terrain, were highly irregular.[260] He did not reinvent the wheel if it wasn't necessary, and as noted, his first system was primarily based on a trace originally designed by Pagan, almost without modification. The outlines of these early fortification designs were, whenever possible, regular polygons, i.e.: octagonal, quadrangular, and even roughly triangular, as at Kenoque.

Bastions were still the key to the defensive system, though they tended to be smaller than those of Vauban's predecessors. Except for the improvements of detail and the greater use of detached exterior defenses, little had altered since the days of Pagan.[261] All works with recognizable bastions, whether

---

259 Peter Paret, op. cit., p. 75
260 Bruce W. Fry, op. cit., p. 41.
261 Peter Paret, op. cit., p. 81.

having straight flanks or curved one with orillons, were classed in the first system. Within this system, considerable variances in the lengths of fronts, curtains, faces, and flanks occur according to the dictates of the terrain. Vauban did not decree specific dimensions. The same holds true for the plans in profile, as the low, earth-topped, tree lined ramparts as seen in the fortress at Bergues, are adapted to the flat, inundated meadowlands of the Low Countries and bear no resemblance to the multi-tiered effect created by the defenses of the citadel at Besançon, in the foothills of the Jura.[262]

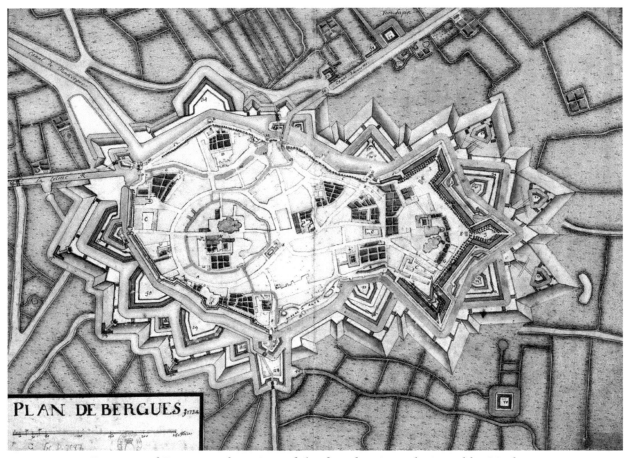

Fortress of Bergues, plan view of the fortifications designed by Vauban.

Vauban received and evaluated considerable information concerning the colonies of France including Canada, from some of the administrators and officers that he knew there, and from engineers that were sent there following his recommendation.[263] Vauban also examined all plans of fortifications for New France, corrected them and sometimes executed changes to the drawings sent to him for review.[264] His correspondence with people in New France covered a great variety of subjects ranging from fortification to recommendations for town planning. For example, the work on the redoubt at Cape Diamond, Quebec, was carried out by Gedeon de Catalogne, under the direction of Marshal Vauban.[265] This

[262] Bruce W. Fry, op. cit., p. 41.
[263] Louise Déchene, *la correspondance de Vauban relative au Canada.* Ministere des affaires culturelles, (Paris, 1968), p. 3, 3rd para, and André Charbonneau, *Québec*, p. 35 & 99.
[264] Ibid. p. 4, 3rd para, free translation.
[265] Leslie F. Hannon, *Forts of Canada, The Conflicts, Sieges, and Battles that Forged a Great Nation.* McClelland and Stewart Ltd., 1969, p. 62.

fortification held dozens of guns and was built with solid earthworks faced with stone, which girdled the city from the Cape to St. Charles. Quebec as a fortress was considered impregnable, partly because it had been modeled on Vauban's pattern of fortifications.[266] The star-shaped stronghold of Louisbourg sited in Cape Breton, Nova Scotia, is in many respects the final memorial to the Marquis de Vauban.[267] Two of Vauban's pupils, Verville and Verrier, made extensive use of Vauban's ideas and designs to make the fortress of Louisbourg one of the greatest strongholds of New France.

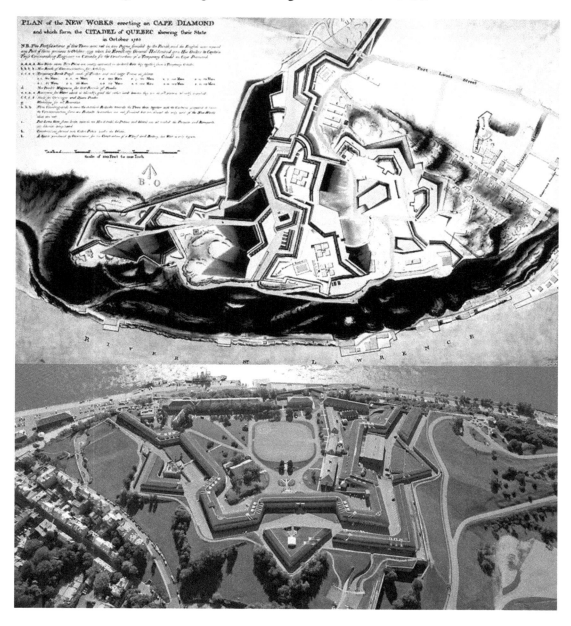

Cape Diamond, Quebec, plan view of the fortifications, 1783. (Library and Archives Canada Photo, MIKAN No. 4128628); and aerial view of la Citadelle de Québec. (Caporal David Robert, Musée Royal 22e Régiment Photo)

---

266 H. W. Koch, *History of Warfare*, p. 276.
267 Leslie F. Hannon, op. cit., p. 30.

The star-shaped stronghold of Louisbourg sited in Cape Breton, Nova Scotia, is in many respects the final memorial to the Marquis de Vauban.[268] Two of Vauban's pupils, Verville and Verrier, made extensive use of Vauban's ideas and designs to make the fortress of Louisbourg one of the greatest strongholds of New France.

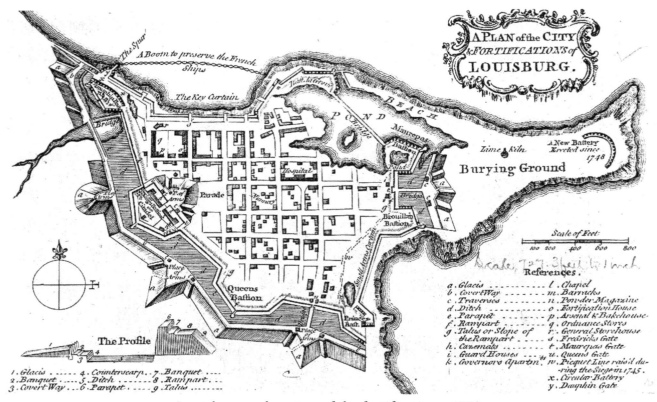

Louisbourg, plan view of the fortifications, 1758.

The fortress of Louisbourg is built on a narrow headland, with water on three sides. The sea itself provides a moat, and on nine days out of ten the surf pounds hard on the rock-strewn shore. There is a string of shoals and islands that reduces the harbor entrance to a mere 400 yards, and which offers positions for gun emplacements that command the roadstead and the only channel into the harbor. The landward side was very marshy in its day and would have severely impeded the movement of any heavy artillery that an enemy might try to drag onto the low hillocks that rise up over half a mile away. Built using Vauban's principles, the walls were ten feet thick and faced with fitted masonry that rose thirty feet behind a steep ditch. This in turn was fronted by a wide glacis, with an unobstructed sloping field of fire that could be raked at point-blank range with cannon and musket shot. In places where the often-violent seashore itself was the first line of defence, additional earthworks and sometimes ponds and palisades were deemed to be sufficient. Enough gun emplacements for 148 cannon, including 24 and 42-pounder's, jutted from the walls, enabling all-round fire, or massive concentrations at danger points. Covered ways gave shelter to the defenders against bomb splinters.[269]

In the end, following two sieges, Louisbourg was considered such a threat by the English that it had to be destroyed.[270] The characteristic outlines of the plan of this fortress, which was strongly influenced by the

---

268 Leslie F. Hannon, op. cit., p. 30.
269 Leslie F. Hannon, op. cit., p. 30.
270 The English captured Louisbourg in 1745, during King George's War (1744-1748). This was the third French-English conflict in North America, which ended with the Peace of Aix-la-Chapelle.

concepts of Vauban, have become more discernible during the continuing restoration of this remarkable fortress in present day Nova Scotia. The sieges that overcame it are discussed in the following chapter.

LOUISBOURG, 1745 AND 1758

Serendipity sometimes has a role to play in the successful outcome of a siege. During the first siege of Louisbourg on 28 May 1745, the combined forces of William Pepperell and Admiral Warren lacked the heavy cannon needed to reduce the fortifications of the Gabarus island battery blocking access to the harbor defenses. This was due to poor and hasty planning and should have caused the siege to end in failure. During a reconnaissance by a landing party however, a sharp-eyed man looking down into the clear water saw what incredibly appeared to be a whole battery of guns half hidden in the sand below. This is exactly what it was, ten bronze cannon which had slid from the deck of a French Man-o'-War years earlier and had been left in the water by the profligate Governor. The men swiftly raised the guns, scoured them off, hoisted them onto the headland and were soon blasting shot across the half-mile gap onto the French battery. When one shot finally hit the island's powder magazine, the French commander d'Aillebout had to surrender. With this vital position in hand the siege was then brought to a successful conclusion, having lasted 46 days.

(F. Stephen)
English landing on Cape Breton Island to attack the fortress of Louisbourg in 1745.

After Louisbourg's surrender and occupation, Admiral Warren put the French flag back up. Thus, French ships kept sailing into Louisbourg's harbor, including one carrying a cargo of gold and silver bars. 850 guineas were given to every sailor as prize money.[271]

Engraving made after a painting by Richard Paton. Burning of the French ship Prudent 74 guns and capture of Bienfaisant 64 guns during the siege of Louisbourg in 1758.

The second siege of Louisbourg was more orthodox in example and was fought 1-26 July 1758. The French forces of Governor Augustin de Droucourt defended the fortress with 3,080 men and 219 cannon against the combined forces of Major General Amherst and Admiral Boscawen. With 25,000 men and 1,842 guns afloat, some 200 ships left England in February 1758 with orders to take Canada. James Wolfe was one of the three brigade commanders onboard. The force conducted amphibious training in Halifax before sailing to Louisbourg where a 49-day siege was successfully carried out. The fortress was bombarded in a well-planned and concerted manner, to the point where the defenders were left with only three cannon able to fire, at which point Governor Augustin surrendered. Shortly afterwards, the task force set off to take Quebec, which fell to Wolfe on 13 September 1759.[272]

[271]   Leslie F. Hannon, *Forts of Canada, The Conflicts, Sieges, and Battles that Forged a Great Nation.* McClelland and Stewart Ltd., 1969, p. 30.
[272]   Leslie F. Hannon, op. cit., p. 30.

Surrender of Louisbourg, 1758.

SIEGE OF YORKTOWN, 1781

The Siege of Yorktown began on 29 Sep and ended on 19 Oct 1781 at Yorktown, Virginia. It was a decisive victory by a combined force of American Continental Army troops led by General George Washington and French Army troops led by the Comte de Rochambeau over a British Army commanded by British peer and Lieutenant-General Charles Cornwallis. As the culmination of the Yorktown campaign, the siege proved to be the last major land battle of the American Revolutionary War in the North American theatre, as the surrender by Cornwallis, and the capture of both him and his army, prompted the British government to negotiate an end to the conflict. The battle boosted faltering American morale and revived French enthusiasm for the war, as well as undermining popular support for the conflict in Great Britain.

In 1780, approximately 5,500 French soldiers landed in Rhode Island to assist their American allies in operations against British-controlled New York City. Following the arrival of dispatches from France that included the possibility of support from the French West Indies fleet of the Comte de Grasse, Washington and Rochambeau decided to ask de Grasse for assistance either in besieging New York, or in military operations against a British army operating in Virginia. On the advice of Rochambeau, de Grasse informed them of his intent to sail to the Chesapeake Bay, where Cornwallis had taken command of the army. Cornwallis, at first given confusing orders by his superior officer, Henry Clinto, was eventually ordered to build a defensible deep-water port, which he began to do in Yorktown, Virginia. Cornwallis' movements in Virginia were shadowed by a Continental Army force led by the Marquis de Lafayette.

The French and American armies united north of New York City during the summer of 1781. When word of de Grasse's decision arrived, both armies began moving south toward Virginia, engaging in tactics of deception to lead the British to believe a siege of New York was planned. De Grasse sailed from the West Indies and arrived at the Chesapeake Bay at the end of August, bringing additional troops and creating a naval blockade of Yorktown. He was transporting 500,000 silver pesos collected from the citizens of Havana, Cuba, to fund supplies for the siege and payroll for the Continental Army. While in Santo Domingo, de Grasse met with Francisco Saavedra Sangronis, an agent of Carlos III of Spain. De Grasse had planned to leave several of his warships in Santo Domingo. Saavedra promised the assistance of the Spanish navy to protect the French merchant fleet, enabling de Grasse to sail north with all of his warships. In the beginning of September, he defeated a British fleet led by Sir Thomas Graves that came to relieve Cornwallis at the Battle of the Chesapeake. As a result of this victory, de Grasse blocked any escape by sea for Cornwallis. By late September Washington and Rochambeau arrived, and the army and naval forces completely surrounded Cornwallis.

After initial preparations, the Americans and French built their first parallel and began the bombardment. With the British defense weakened, on 14 Oct1781 Washington sent two columns to attack the last major remaining British outer defenses. A French column under Wilhelm of the Palatinate-Zweibrücken took Redoubt No. 9 and an American column under Alexander Hamilton took Redoubt No. 10. With these defenses taken, the allies were able to finish their second parallel. With the American artillery closer and its bombardment more intense than ever, the British position began to deteriorate rapidly, and Cornwallis asked for capitulation terms on 17 Oct. After two days of negotiation, the surrender ceremony occurred on 19 Oct; Lord Cornwallis was absent from the ceremony. With the capture of more than 7,000 British soldiers, negotiations between the United States and Great Britain began, resulting in the Treaty of Paris of 1783.[273]

Yorktown surrender of British forces, 178. This painting by painting by John Trumbull depicts the forces of British Major General Charles Cornwallis, 1st Marquess Cornwallis (1738-1805) (who was

[273] Alden, John. *A History of the American Revolution*. New York: Da Capo Press, 1969.

not himself present at the surrender), surrendering to French and American forces after the Siege of Yorktown (September 28 – October 19, 1781) during the American Revolutionary War. The central figures depicted are Generals Charles O'Hara and Benjamin Lincoln.

GIBRALTAR, 1782

The siege of Gibraltar by the Spanish in July 1782, demonstrated that old artillery tactics from the 15th century could be successfully adapted to more modern times. The British garrison in Gibraltar had successfully held out for three full years, when the Spanish tried a new siege method. They built ten ships armored six feet thick with green timbers reinforced by iron, cork, and raw hides. Mounting heavy siege artillery on these gunboats, they anchored near the British works and began a harsh pounding of Gibraltar's defenses. Ordinary round shot buried themselves harmlessly in the wooden armor, but the garrison had been experimenting with cannon balls heated in furnaces. The shore guns changed to red-hot shot, and after 8,300 rounds the grand assault failed with every Spanish ship blown up or burnt down to the water line. Although the siege lasted seven more months, "the Rock" was never again in serious danger.[274]

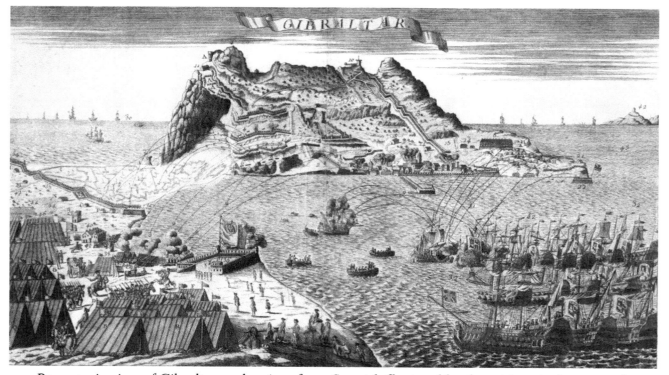

Panoramic view of Gibraltar under siege from Spanish fleet and land positions in foreground, created in 1778.

---

274   Lynn Montross, op. cit., p. 442.

THE ALAMO, 1836

The siege of the Alamo took place during what is known as the Texan War of Independence. Texas had been a state of Mexico until American settlers north of the Rio Grande began agitating for independence. After losing San Antonio to the Texans during the Siege of the Bexar, Mexican General Antonio de Santa Anna was determined to retake this key location and at the same time impress upon the Texans the futility of further resistance to Mexican rule. With these goals in mind, Santa Anna marched into Texas with some 6,000 troops under his command. The vanguard of his army arrived in San Antonio about 23 February 1836. Some 145 Texans in the area took refuge in the fortified grounds of an old Spanish Franciscan mission that had been converted into a fort. It was known as Alamo, and at the time of the siege was under the joint command of the Commandant, William B. Travis (for the regular army), and James Bowie (for the volunteers). Famous American frontiersmen Davy Crockett and James Bonham were also participants in the battle.

(Robert Jenkins Onderdonk)

The Fall of the Alamo, Davy Crockett is wielding his rifle as a club against Mexican troops who have breached the walls of the mission.

Over the following two weeks, the Mexican forces continually strengthened to over 2000 troops. During the same period, a few reinforcements for the Texans answered Travis' famous appeal for aid and managed to penetrate enemy lines and enter the Alamo grounds, bringing the total strength of the defenders to about 189 men.

After periodic bombardment, the siege ended on the morning of 6 March 1836, when the Mexicans stormed the Alamo fortress. During the battle, no quarter was given, and all of the Texan defenders were killed. Several non-combatants were spared, including Susanna Dickenson, the wife of one of the defenders, Susanna's baby, and a servant of Travis. Partly to reinforce his goal of terrorizing colonists in Texas, Santa Anna released this small party to inform Texans of the fate of the defenders.

Losses in the battle have been placed at 189 Texans against about 1,600 for the Mexicans. This was only the first of eight battles that Santa Anna would fight against American troops. He continued his march eastward, destroying American settlements that lay in his path, until he reached Galveston Bay five weeks later. In a convention at Washington on 2 March 1866, Texas had proclaimed its independence from Mexico. Sam Houston was named commander of the Army. On 21 April, Houston met Santa Anna's 1,200 Mexicans along the western bank of the San Jacinto River near its mouth. In spite of being outnumbered, the Texans routed the Mexicans, and captured Santa Anna. He agreed to recognize the independence of Texas (although this agreement was later repudiated by the Mexican Congress). Texas would later be admitted to the United States on 29 December 1845.[275]

(Author Photo)
The Alamo as it appears today.

---

[275] David Eggenberger, *An Encyclopedia of Battles*, Dover Publications, Inc., New York, 1985, p. 382.

SIEGE OF LUCKNOW, 1857

The Siege of Lucknow was the prolonged defence of the British Residency (a group of several buildings in a common precinct in the city of Lucknow). It served as the residence for the British Resident General who was a representative in the court of the Nawab. Construction took place between 1780 and 1800 AD. Between 1 July 1857 and 17 November 1857, the Residency was subject to the siege during the Indian Rebellion of 1857. After two successive relief attempts had reached the city, the defenders and civilians were evacuated from the Residency, which was then abandoned.

The state of Oudh/Awadh had been annexed by the British East India Company and the Nawab Wajid Ali Shah was exiled to Calcutta the year before the rebellion broke out. This high-handed action by the East India Company was greatly resented within the state and elsewhere in India. The first British Commissioner (in effect the governor) appointed to the newly acquired territory was Coverley Jackson. He behaved tactlessly, and Sir Henry Lawrence, a very experienced administrator, took up the appointment only six weeks before the rebellion broke out.

The sepoys (Indian soldiers) of the East India Company's Bengal Presidency Army had become increasingly troubled over the preceding years, feeling that their religion and customs were under threat from the evangelising activities of the Company. Lawrence was well aware of the rebellious mood of the Indian troops under his command (which included several units of Oudh Irregulars, recruited from the former army of the state of Oudh). On 18 April, he warned the Governor General, Lord Canning, of some of the manifestations of discontent, and asked permission to transfer certain rebellious corps to another province.

The flashpoint of the rebellion was the introduction of the Enfield rifle; the cartridges for this weapon were believed to be greased with a mixture of beef and pork fat, which was felt would defile both Hindu and Muslim Indian soldiers. On 1 May, the 7th Oudh Irregular Infantry refused to bite the cartridge, and on 3 May they were disarmed by other regiments.

On 10 May, the Indian soldiers at Meerut broke into open rebellion, and marched on Delhi. When news of this reached Lucknow, Lawrence recognised the gravity of the crisis and summoned from their homes two sets of pensioners, one of sepoys and one of artillerymen, to whose loyalty, and to that of the Sikh and some Hindu sepoys, the successful defence of the Residency was largely due.

On 23 May, Lawrence began fortifying the Residency and laying in supplies for a siege; large numbers of British civilians made their way there from outlying districts. On 30 May (the Muslim festival of Eid ul-Fitr), most of the Oudh and Bengal troops at Lucknow broke into open rebellion. In addition to his locally recruited pensioners, Lawrence also had the bulk of the British 32nd Regiment of Foot available, and they were able to drive the rebels away from the city.

On 4 June, there was a rebellion at Sitapur, a large and important station 51 miles (82 km) from Lucknow. This was followed by another at Faizabad, one of the most important cities in the province, and outbreaks at Daryabad, Sultanpur and Salon. Thus, in the course of ten days, British authority in Oudh practically vanished.

On 30 June, Lawrence learned that the rebels were gathering north of Lucknow and ordered a reconnaissance in force, despite the available intelligence being of poor quality. Although he had comparatively little military experience, Lawrence led the expedition himself. The expedition was not very well organised. The troops were forced to march without food or adequate water during the hottest part of the day at the height of summer, and at the Chinhat they met a well-organised rebel force, led by Barkat Ahmad with cavalry and dug-in artillery . Whilst they were under attack, some of Lawrence's sepoys and Indian artillerymen defected to the rebels, overturning their guns, and cutting the traes. His exhausted British soldiers retreated in disorder. Some died of heatstroke within sight of the Residency.

Lieutenant William George Cubitt, 13th Native Infantry, was awarded the Victoria Cross several years later, for his act of saving the lives of three men of the 32nd Regiment of Foot during the retreat. His was not a unique action; sepoys loyal to the British, especially those of the 13th Native Infantry, saved many British soldiers, even at the cost of abandoning their own wounded men, who were hacked to pieces by rebel sepoys.

As a result of the defeat, the detached turreted building, Machchhi Bhawan (Muchee Bowan), which contained 200 barrels (~27 t) of gunpowder and a large supply of ball cartridges, was blown up and the detachment withdrew to the Residency.

Lawrence retreated into the Residency, where the siege now began, with the Residency as the centre of the defences. The actual defended line was based on six detached smaller buildings and four entrenched batteries. The position covered some 60 acres (240,000 m^2) of ground, and the garrison (855 British officers and soldiers, 712 Indians, 153 civilian volunteers, with 1,280 non-combatants, including hundreds of women and children) was too small to defend it effectively against a properly prepared and supported attack. Also, the Residency lay in the midst of several palaces, mosques, and administrative buildings, as Lucknow had been the royal capital of Oudh for many years. Lawrence initially refused permission for these to be demolished, urging his engineers to "spare the holy places". During the siege, they provided good vantage points and cover for rebel sharpshooters and artillery.

One of the first bombardments following the beginning of the siege, on 30 June, caused a civilian to be trapped by a falling roof. Corporal William Oxenham of the 32nd Foot saved him while under intense musket and cannon fire and was later awarded the Victoria Cross. The first attack was repulsed on 1 July. The next day, Lawrence was fatally wounded by a shell, dying on 4 July. Colonel John Inglis of the 32nd Regiment took military command of the garrison. Major John Banks was appointed the acting Civil Commissioner by Lawrence. When Banks was killed by a sniper a short time later, Inglis assumed overall command.

About 8,000 sepoys who had joined the rebellion and several hundred retainers of local landowners surrounded the Residency. They had some modern guns and also some older pieces which fired all sorts of improvised missiles. There were several determined attempts to storm the defences during the first weeks of the siege, but the rebels lacked a unified command able to coordinate all the besieging forces.

The defenders, their number constantly reduced by military action as well as disease, were able to repulse all attempts to overwhelm them. On 5 August, an enemy mine was foiled; counter mining and offensive mining against two buildings brought successful results. Several sorties were mounted, attempting to reduce the effectiveness of the most dangerous rebel positions and to silence some of their guns. The Victoria Cross was awarded to several participants in these sorties: Captain Samuel Hill Lawrence and Private William Dowling of the 32nd Foot and Captain Robert Hope Moncrieff Aitken of the 13th Native Infantry. Also, William Hall (Quartermaster) was awarded a Victoria Cross, because he bravely stayed his ground and shot the wall (under heavy cannon and musket fire) down when only him and an officer were still alive.

Captain of the Foretop, Quartermaster William Hall, VC.

"On the west of Lucknow stood a huge mosque, the Shah Najaf, from which issued a deadly hail of musket balls and grenades. The British had to take the mosque, but without scaling ladders and with a 6-metre wall to surmount, they had to breech the walls. They dragged the guns to within 350 metres of the wall, banging shell after shell at it, making little impact. The guns had to move closer."

"The sailors dragged the guns up, sustaining heavy casualties in the process. The mosque walls were loopholed in such a way that the naval gunners were safe from fire at a certain point. But every shot from the big guns caused them to recoil back into the fire zone. Soon only Hall and one officer, Lt Thomas Young, who was wounded, were still standing to man their 24-pounder gun. Hall, now Number One on the gun, kept loading and firing, dragging it back after every recoil, over and over. Finally, the wall was breached sufficiently to allow a number of Highlanders to scramble through and open the gate to admit the rest of the force. For his heroic actions that 16 November 1857, Hall was awarded the Victoria Cross. He served in the Royal Navy until 1876, then retired in Horton Bluff, Nova Scotia, where he lived until his death."

The joint citation in the Gazette reads:

Lieutenant (now Commander) Young, late Gunnery Officer of Her Majesty's ship " Shannon," and William Hall, "Captain of the Foretop," of that Vessel, were recommended by the late Captain Peel for the Victoria Cross, for their gallant conduct at a 24-Pounder Gun, brought up to the angle of the Shah Nujjiff, at Lucknow, on 16 November 1857.

(In February 2010 Canada Post issued a commemorative stamp honouring Hall's VC. On 26 June 2015 it was announced that the fourth ship in the Royal Canadian Navy's *Harry DeWolf* class would be named for William Hall. The ship will be constructed at the Halifax Shipyards in Halifax.)

On 16 July, a force under Major General Henry Havelock recaptured Cawnpore, 48 miles (77 km) from Lucknow. On 20 July, he decided to attempt to relieve Lucknow, but it took six days to ferry his force of 1500 men across the Ganges River. On 29 July, Havelock won a battle at Unao, but casualties, disease and heatstroke reduced his force to 850 effectives, and he fell back.

Havelock managed to get a spy through to the Residency, telling them that 2 rockets would be fired at a certain time on the night when the relief force was ready to attack. There followed a sharp exchange of letters between Havelock and the insolent Brigadier James Neill who was left in charge at Cawnpore. Havelock eventually received 257 reinforcements and some more guns and tried again to advance. He won another victory near Unao on 4 August but was once again too weak to continue the advance and retired.

Havelock intended to remain on the north bank of the Ganges, inside Oudh, and thereby prevent the large force of rebels which had been facing him from joining the siege of the Residency, but on 11 August, Neill reported that Cawnpore was threatened . To allow himself to retreat without being attacked from behind, Havelock marched again to Unao and won a third victory there. He then fell back across the Ganges and destroyed the newly completed bridge. On 16 August, he defeated a rebel force at Bithur, disposing of the threat to Cawnpore.

Havelock's retreat was tactically necessary but caused the rebellion in Oudh to become a national revolt, as previously uncommitted landowners joined the rebels.

Havelock had been superseded in command by Major General Sir James Outram. Before Outram arrived at Cawnpore, Havelock prepared for another relief attempt. He had earlier sent a letter to Inglis in the Residency, suggesting he cut his way out and make for Cawnpore. Inglis replied that he had too few effective troops and too many sick, wounded and non-combatants to make such an attempt. He also pleaded for urgent assistance. The rebels meanwhile continued to shell the garrison in the Residency, and also dug mines beneath the defences, which destroyed several posts. Although the garrison kept the rebels at a distance with sorties and counterattacks, they were becoming weaker and food was running short.

Outram arrived at Cawnpore with reinforcements on 15 September. He allowed Havelock to command the relief force, accompanying it nominally as a volunteer until Lucknow was reached. The force numbered 3,179 and was composed of six British and one Sikh infantry battalions, with three artillery batteries, but only 168 volunteer cavalry. They were divided into two brigades, under Neill and Colonel Hamilton of the 78th Highlanders.

The advance resumed on 18 September. This time, the rebels did not make any serious stand in the open country, even failing to destroy some vital bridges. On 23 September, Havelock's force drove the rebels from the Alambagh, a walled park four miles south of the Residency. Leaving the baggage with a small force in the Alambagh, he began the final advance on 25 September. Because of the monsoon rains, much of the open ground around the city was flooded or waterlogged, preventing the British making any outflanking moves and forcing them to make a direct advance through part of the city.

The force met heavy resistance trying to cross the Charbagh Canal but succeeded after nine out of ten men of a Forlorn Hope were killed storming a bridge. They then turned to their right, following the west bank of the canal. The 78th Highlanders took a wrong turning but were able to capture a rebel battery near the Qaisarbagh palace, before finding their way back to the main force. After further heavy fighting, by nightfall the force had reached the Machchhi Bhawan. Outram proposed to halt and contact the defenders of the Residency by tunnelling and mining through the intervening buildings, but Havelock insisted on an immediate advance. (He feared that the defenders of the Residency were so weakened that they might still be overwhelmed by a last-minute rebel attack.) The advance was made through heavily defended narrow lanes. Neill was one of those killed by rebel musket fire. In all, the relief force lost 535 men out of 2000, incurred mainly in this last rush.

By the time of the relief, the defenders of the Residency had endured a siege of 87 days and were reduced to 982 fighting personnel. Originally, Outram had intended to evacuate the Residency, but the heavy casualties incurred during the final advance made it impossible to remove all the sick and wounded and non-combatants. Another factor which influenced Outram's decision to remain in Lucknow was the discovery of a large stock of supplies beneath the Residency, sufficient to maintain the garrison for two months. Lawrence had laid in the stores but died before he had informed any of his subordinates. (Inglis had feared that starvation was imminent.)

Instead, the defended area was enlarged. Under Outram's overall command, Inglis took charge of the original Residency area, and Havelock occupied and defended the palaces (the Farhat Baksh and Chuttur Munzil) and other buildings east of it. Outram had hoped that the relief would also demoralise the rebels but was disappointed. For the next six weeks, the rebels continued to subject the defenders to musket and artillery fire and dug a series of mines beneath them. The defenders replied with sorties, as before, and dug countermines. Twenty-one shafts were sunk, and 3,291 feet of gallery were constructed by the defenders. The enemy dug 20 mines: three caused loss of life, two did no injury, seven were blown in, and seven were tunnelled into and their galleries taken over.

The defenders were able to send messengers to and from the Alambagh, from where in turn messengers could reach Cawnpore. (Later, a semaphore system made the risky business of sending messengers between the Residency and the Alambagh unnecessary.) A volunteer civil servant, Thomas Henry Kavanagh, the son of a British soldier, disguised himself as a sepoy and ventured from the Residency aided by a local man named Kananji Lal. He and his scout crossed the entrenchments east of the city and reached the Alambagh to act as a guide to the next relief attempt. For this action, Kavanagh was awarded the Victoria Cross and was the first civilian in British history to be honoured with such an award for action during a military conflict.

The rebellion had involved a very wide stretch of territory in northern India. Large numbers of rebels had flocked to Delhi, where they proclaimed the restoration of the Mughal Empire under Bahadur Shah II. A British army besieged the city from the first week in June. On 10 September, they launched a storming attempt, and by 21 September they had captured the city. On 24 September, a column of 2,790 British, Sikh, and Punjabi troops under Colonel Greathed of the 8th (The King's) Regiment of Foot marched through the Lahore Gate to restore British rule from Delhi to Cawnpore. On 9 October, Greathed received urgent calls for help from a British garrison in the Red Fort at Agra. He diverted his force to Agra, to find the rebels had apparently retreated. While his force rested, they were surprised and attacked by the rebel force, which had been close by. Nevertheless, they rallied, defeated, and dispersed the rebel force. This Battle of Agra cleared all organised rebel forces from the area between Delhi and Cawnpore, although guerrilla bands remained.

Shortly afterwards, Greathed received reinforcements from Delhi, and was superseded in command by Major-General James Hope Grant. Grant reached Cawnpore late in October, where he received orders from the new commander-in-chief in India, Sir Colin Campbell, to proceed to the Alambagh, and transport the sick and wounded to Cawnpore. He was also strictly enjoined not to commit himself to any relief of Lucknow until Campbell himself arrived.

Campbell was 64 years old when he left England in July 1857 to assume command of the Bengal Army. By mid-August, he was in Calcutta preparing his departure upcountry. It was late October before all preparations were completed. Fighting his way up the Grand Trunk Road, Campbell arrived in Cawnpore on 3 November. The rebels held effective control of large parts of the countryside. Campbell considered, but rejected, securing the countryside before launching his relief of Lucknow. The massacre of British women and children following the capitulation of Cawnpore was still in recent memory. In British eyes, Lucknow had become a symbol of their resolve. Accordingly, Campbell left 1,100 troops in Cawnpore for its defence, leading 600 cavalry, 3,500 infantry and 42 guns to the Alambagh, in what Samuel Smiles described as an example of the "women and children first" protocol being applied.

British warships were dispatched from Hong Kong to Calcutta. The marines and sailors of HMS *Shannon*, HMS *Pearl*, and HMS *Sanspareil* formed a Naval Brigade with the ships' guns (8-inch guns and 24-pounder howitzers) and fought their way from Calcutta until they met up with Campbell's force.

The strength of the rebels investing Lucknow has been widely estimated from 30,000 to 60,000. They were amply equipped, the sepoy regiments among them were well trained, and they had improved their defences in response to Havelock's and Outram's first relief of the Residency. The Charbagh Bridge used by Havelock and Outram just north of the Alambagh had been fortified. The Charbagh Canal from the Dilkusha Bridge to the Charbagh Bridge was dammed and flooded to prevent troops or heavy guns fording it. Cannon emplaced in entrenchments north of the Gumti River not only daily bombarded the besieged Residency but also enfiladed the only viable relief path. However, the lack of a unified command structure among the sepoys diminished the value of their superior numbers and strategic positions.

At daybreak on 14 November, Campbell commenced his relief of Lucknow. He had made his plans on the basis of Kavanagh's information and the heavy loss of life experienced by the first Lucknow relief column. Rather than crossing the Charbagh Bridge and fighting through the tortuous, narrow streets of Lucknow, Campbell opted to make a flanking march to the east and proceed to Dilkusha Park. He would then advance to La Martiniere (a school for British and Anglo-Indian boys) and cross the canal as close to the River Gumti as possible. As he advanced, he would secure each position to protect his communications and supply train back to the Alambagh. He would then secure a walled enclosure known as the Secundrabagh and link up with the Residency, whose outer perimeter had been extended by Havelock and Outram to the Chuttur Munzil.

For 3 miles (4.8 km) as the column moved to the east of the Alambagh, no opposition was encountered. When the relief column reached the Dilkusha park wall, the quiet ended with an outburst of musket fire. British cavalry and artillery quickly pushed past the park wall, driving the sepoys from the Dilkusha park. The column then advanced to La Martiniere. By noon, the Dilkusha and La Martiniere were in British hands. The defending sepoys vigorously attacked the British left flank from the Bank's House, but the British counter-attacked and drove them back into Lucknow.

The rapid advance of Campbell's column placed it far ahead of its supply caravan. The advance paused until the required stores of food, ammunition and medical equipment were brought forward. The request for additional ammunition from the Alambagh further delayed the relief column's march. On the evening of 15 November, the Residency was signalled by semaphore, "Advance tomorrow."

The next day, the relief column advanced from La Martiniere to the northern point where the canal meets the Gumti River. The damming of the canal to flood the area beneath the Dilkuska Bridge had left the canal dry at the crossing point. The column and guns advanced forward and then turned sharp left to Secundra Bagh.

The Secundra Bagh is a high walled garden approximately 120 square yards (100 m²), with parapets at each corner and a main entry gate arch on the southern wall. Campbell's column approached along a road that ran parallel to the eastern wall of the garden. The advancing column of infantry, cavalry and artillery had difficulty manoeuvering in the cramped village streets. They were afforded some protection from the intense fire raining down on them by a high road embankment that faced the garden. Musket fire came from loopholes in the Secundra Bagh and nearby fortified cottages, and cannon shot from the distant Kaisarbagh (the former King of Oudh's palace). Campbell positioned artillery to suppress this incoming fire. Heavy 18-pounder artillery was also hauled by rope and hand over the steep road embankment and placed within 60 yards (55 m) of the enclosure. Although significant British casualties were sustained in these manoeuvres, the cannon fire breached the southeastern wall.

Elements of the Scottish 93rd Highlanders and the 4th Punjab Infantry Regiment rushed forward. Finding the breach too small to accommodate the mass of troops, the Punjab Infantry moved to the left and overran the defences at the main garden gateway. Once inside, the Punjabis, many of whom were Sikhs, emptied their muskets and resorted to the bayonet. Sepoys responded with counterattacks. Highlanders pouring in by the breach shouted, "Remember Cawnpore!" Gradually the din of battle waned. The dwindling force of defenders moved northward until retreat was no longer possible. The British numbered the sepoy dead at nearly 2000.

By late noon, a detachment of the relief column led by Adrian Hope disengaged from the Secundra Bagh and moved towards the Shah Najaf. The Shah Najaf, a walled mosque, is the mausoleum of Ghazi-ud-Din Halder, the first king of Oudh in 1814. The defenders had heavily fortified this multistory position. When the full force of the British column was brought to bear on the Shah Najaf, the sepoys responded with unrelenting musketry, cannon grape shot and supporting cannon fire from the Kaisarbagh, as well as oblique cannon fire from secured batteries north of the Gumti River. From heavily exposed positions, for three hours the British directed strong cannon fire on the stout walls of the Shah Najaf. The walls remained unscathed, the sepoy fire was unrelenting and British losses mounted. Additional British assaults failed, with heavy losses.

However, retiring from their exposed positions was deemed equally dangerous by the British command. Fifty Highlanders were dispatched to seek an alternate access route to the Shah Najaf. Discovering a breach in the wall on the opposite side of the fighting, sappers were brought forward to widen the breach. The small advance party pushed through the opening, crossed the courtyard, and opened the main gates. Seeing the long-sought opening, their comrades rushed forth into the Shah Najaf. Campbell made his headquarters in the Shah Najaf by nightfall.

Within the besieged Residency, Havelock and Outram completed their preparations to link up with Campbell's column. Positioned in the Chuttur Munzil, they executed their plan to blow open the outer walls of the garden once they could see that the Secundra Bagh was in Campbell's hands.

The Moti Mahal, the last major position that separated the two British forces, was cleared by charges from Campbell's column. Only an open space of 450 yards (410 m) now separated the two forces. Outram, Havelock and some other officers ran across the space to confer with Campbell, before returning. Stubborn resistance continued as the sepoys defended their remaining positions, but repeated efforts by the British cleared these last pockets of resistance. The second relief column had reached the Residency.

The Relief of Lucknow, 1857, painting by Thomas Jones Barker.

Although Outram and Havelock both recommended storming the Kaisarbagh palace to secure the British position, Campbell knew that other rebel forces were threatening Cawnpore and other cities held by the British, and he ordered Lucknow to be abandoned. The evacuation began on 19 November. While Campbell's artillery bombarded the Kaisarbagh to deceive the rebels that an assault on it was imminent, canvas screens were erected to shield the open space from the rebels' view. The women, children and sick and wounded made their way to the Dilkusha Park under cover of these screens, some in a variety of carriages or on litters, others on foot. Over the next two days, Outram spiked his guns and withdrew after them.

At the Dilkusha Park, Havelock died (of a sudden attack of dysentery) on 24 November. The entire army and convoy now moved to the Alambagh. Campbell left Outram with 4,000 men to defend the Alambagh, while he himself moved with 3,000 men and most of the civilians to Cawnpore on 27 November. The first siege had lasted 87 days, the second siege a further 61.

The rebels were left in control of Lucknow over the following winter but were prevented from undertaking any other operations by their own lack of unity and by Outram's hold on the easily defended Alambagh. Campbell returned to retake Lucknow, with the attack starting on 6 March. By 21 March 1858, all fighting had ceased.

During the siege, the Union Jack had flown day and night (against the usual practice, which is to strike national flags at dusk), as it was nailed to the flagpole. After the British re-took control of Lucknow, by special dispensation (unique within the British Empire), the Union Jack was flown 24 hours a day on the Residency's flagpole, for the rest of the time the British held India. The day before India became independent, the flag was lowered, the flagpole cut down, and the base removed and cemented over, to prevent any other flag from ever being flown there.

The largest number of Victoria Crosses awarded in a single day was the 24 earned on 16 November, during the second relief, the bulk of these being for the assault on the Secundrabagh.

The Indian Mutiny Medal had three clasps relating to Lucknow: Defence of Lucknow, awarded to the original defenders for service from 29 June to 22 November 1857; Relief of Lucknow, awarded to the relief force in November 1857; and Lucknow, awarded to troops in the final capture of Lucknow in November 1857. (Chisholm, Hugh, ed. "Indian Mutiny, The". Encyclopaedia Britannica (11th ed.). Cambridge University Press, 1911)

The Residency has been maintained as it was at the time of the final relief, and the shattered walls are still scarred by cannon shot. Even since Indian Independence, little has changed. The ruined building is surrounded by lawns and flowerbeds and is a tourist attraction nowadays. The cemetery at the nearby ruined church has the graves of 2000 men, women, and children, who died during the siege.

SIEGE OF FORT PULASKI, 1862

Rifled artillery could have a devastating effect against what had previously been termed "impregnable" masonry. This was amply demonstrated during the siege and reduction of Fort Pulaski in the American Civil War.[276] The fortification was built with 25 million bricks, from 1829 to 1847 on Cockspur Island at the mouth of the Savannah River and named after Count Casimir Pulaski, who died defending the town of Savannah during the Revolutionary War. The walls of the massive five-sided fort were seven feet thick.

---

[276] The American Civil War was fought between April 1861 and 1 April 1865. The issue of slavery, particularly in the new states being formed from western territories, drove an ever-larger wedge between the free states of the North and the slave holding states to the South. When the Republican candidate for President of the United States, Abraham Lincoln, won election on 6 November 1860, the situation reached a crisis. South Carolina seceded from the Union on 20 December 1860, declaring that its sovereignty now stood in jeopardy. Six other states followed suit from 9 January to 1 February 1861: Mississippi, Florida, Alabama, Georgia, Louisiana, and Texas.

On 4 February representatives from these states formed the Confederate States of America, with Jefferson Davis elected President. Federal forts and arsenals were seized throughout the South. Confederate shore batteries forced the surrender of Fort Sumter outside Charleston, South Carolina on 13 April. President Lincoln then called for 75,000 volunteers to put down the "insurrection" against the United States. From 17 April to 20 May, four more states left the Union: Virginia, Arkansas, Tennessee, and North Carolina. The Confederate government established its capitol at Richmond, Virginia, and mobilized for war. Its chief aim was to force the North to recognize its independence. The 23 states of the North and West, under the leadership of Lincoln, sought originally only to restore the Union. However, after the President's Emancipation Proclamation of 1 January 1863, freeing the slaves became an almost equally important objective.

For four years the United States was torn by bitter civil war. The major theater of operations was east of the Appalachians, especially in northern Virginia between the two hostile capitals of Washington, DC, and Richmond. From the Appalachians westward to the Mississippi River an important secondary theater developed. The last two Confederate armies in the field surrendered on 9 April and 18 April 1865. In the costliest war in United States history (in the proportion of casualties to participants), the Confederate government was decisively abolished. In all, the North mobilized 1,557,000 men, the South 1,082,000. Federal losses were 359,528 dead (of these 110,070 were killed or mortally wounded in battle), 275,175 wounded. Confederate casualties were 258,000 dead (including 94,000 battle deaths) and more than 100,000 reported wounded.

(Edibobb Photo)

Fort Pulaski. Rifled artillery could have a devastating effect against what had previously been termed "impregnable" masonry. This was amply demonstrated during the siege and reduction of Fort Pulaski in the American Civil War.[277] The fortification was built with 25 million bricks, from 1829 to 1847 on

[277] The American Civil War was fought between April 1861 and 1 April 1865. The issue of slavery, particularly in the new states being formed from western territories, drove an ever-larger wedge between the free states of the North and the slave holding states to the South. When the Republican candidate for President of the United States, Abraham Lincoln, won election on 6 November 1860, the situation reached a crisis. South Carolina seceded from the Union on 20 December 1860, declaring that its sovereignty now stood in jeopardy. Six other states followed suit from 9 January to 1 February 1861: Mississippi, Florida, Alabama, Georgia, Louisiana, and Texas.

On 4 February representatives from these states formed the Confederate States of America, with Jefferson Davis elected President. Federal forts and arsenals were seized throughout the South. Confederate shore batteries forced the surrender of Fort Sumter outside Charleston, South Carolina on 13 April. President Lincoln then called for 75,000 volunteers to put down the "insurrection" against the United States. From 17 April to 20 May, four more states left the Union: Virginia, Arkansas, Tennessee, and North Carolina. The Confederate government established its capitol at Richmond, Virginia, and mobilized for war. Its chief aim was to force the North to recognize its independence. The 23 states of the North and West, under the leadership of Lincoln, sought originally only to restore the Union. However, after the President's Emancipation Proclamation of 1 January 1863, freeing the slaves became an almost equally important objective.

For four years the United States was torn by bitter civil war. The major theater of operations was east of the Appalachians, especially in northern Virginia between the two hostile capitals of Washington, DC, and Richmond. From the Appalachians westward to the Mississippi River an important secondary theater developed. The last two Confederate armies in the field surrendered on 9 April and 18 April 1865. In the costliest war in United States history (in the proportion of casualties to participants), the Confederate government was decisively abolished. In all, the North mobilized 1,557,000 men, the South 1,082,000. Federal losses were 359,528 dead (of these 110,070 were killed or mortally wounded in battle), 275,175 wounded. Confederate casualties were 258,000 dead (including 94,000 battle deaths) and more than 100,000 reported wounded.

Cockspur Island at the mouth of the Savannah River and named after Count Casimir Pulaski, who died defending the town of Savannah during the Revolutionary War. The walls of the massive five-sided fort were seven feet thick.

Georgia state troops occupied Fort Pulaski in January 1861. During the fall of that year Union troops seized Port Royal and Hilton Head Island, South Carolina, and threatened the Georgia coast. Confederate authorities immediately concentrated troops around Savannah and increased the garrison at Fort Pulaski to some 360 soldiers. Soon after Federal forces occupied Tybee Island, a short distance by water from the Confederate fort, the expedition's engineering officer, Capt. Quincy A. Gillmore (soon breveted brigadier general), announced that the walls of the fort could be knocked down with new heavy-caliber rifled weapons firing grooved James projectiles. Despite opinions by the best officers, (both North and South), that the fort could not be reduced by artillery, Gillmore ordered heavy weapons brought to Tybee at night. Sailors rowed vessels bearing guns, whose barrels alone weighed 17,000 pounds, close to shore and dumped them at high tide; these were recovered after the tide ran out and were then hauled hundreds of yards on planks laid across mud and sand and placed in batteries supported by sand bags. Two hundred and fifty soldiers were needed to move mortars weighing over eight tons. Parapets of sand and mud were constructed to hide the weapons.

Fort Pulaski under fire. (Leslie's Weekly Magazine, 1 May 1862); and a cast iron 8-inch smoothbore muzzleloading (SBML) Confederate Columbiad cannon, M1861, damaged, inside Fort Pulaski. (Author Photo)

By 10 April 1862, there were eleven batteries or thirty-six weapons in place on Tybee Island; five rifled artillery pieces were aimed at Fort Pulaski, about 1,650 yards distant. That same day Gen. David Hunter, commanding officer of the Federal troops, demanded the surrender of Col. Charles H. Olmstead, commander of Fort Pulaski. When Olmstead refused, Hunter gave the order to fire. Over the following two days more than 5,300 shells were hurled at Fort Pulaski, blasting away bricks and dismantling Confederate guns. The rifled guns firing James projectiles were especially effective. When shells passing through the breached walls of the fort threatened to detonate the magazine, Olmstead surrendered. As cheers rang from battery to battery, Lieutenant Horace Porter shouted, "Sumter is avenged!" Afterwards, General Hunter summarized the significance of the fall of the Confederate strongpoint, "No works of stone or brick can resist the impact of rifled artillery of heavy caliber."

(Library of Congress Prints and Photographs Division Washington, D.C.)

Union battery of two 30-pounder Parrot Rifles and ammunition, Morris Island, South Carolina, 31 Dec 1864. Five Parrotts were used to conduct massed fire of percussion shells on the fort.

This successful attack led to more remarkable engineering feats directed by General Gillmore who had brought his big guns to bear on the fort, all of which was a practice run for him. In just over a year Gillmore would position heavy artillery in the mud and sand of James and Morris Islands for the bombardment of Charleston.[278]

SIEGE OF VICKSBURG, 1863

The Siege of Vicksburg (18 May – 4 July 1863) was the final major military action in the Vicksburg Campaign of the American Civil War. In a series of maneuvers, Union Major-General Ulysses S. Grant and his Army of the Tennessee crossed the Mississippi River and drove the Confederate Army

---

[278] Herbert M. Schiller *Sumter Is Avenged! The Siege and Reduction of Fort Pulaski*. White Mane Publishing Co., Shippenburg, Pennsylvania, 1996. Commentary by Walter J. Jr., Fraser.

of Mississippi, led by Lieutenant-General John C. Pemberton, into the defensive lines surrounding the fortress city of Vicksburg, Mississippi.

As the Confederate forces approached Vicksburg, Pemberton could put only 18,500 troops in his lines. Grant had over 35,000, with more on the way. However, Pemberton had the advantage of terrain and fortifications that made his defense nearly impregnable. The defensive line around Vicksburg ran approximately 6.5 miles, based on terrain of varying elevations that included hills and knobs with steep angles for an attacker to ascend under fire. The perimeter included many gun pits, forts, trenches, redoubts, and lunettes. The major fortifications of the line included Fort Hill, on a high bluff north of the city; the Stockade Redan, dominating the approach to the city on Graveyard Road from the northeast; the 3rd Louisiana Redan; the Great Redoubt; the Railroad Redoubt, protecting the gap for the railroad line entering the city; the Square Fort (Fort Garrott); a salient along the Hall's Ferry Road; and the South Fort.

Grant wanted to overwhelm the Confederates before they could fully organize their defenses and ordered an immediate assault against Stockade Redan for 19 May. Troops from Sherman's corps had a difficult time approaching the position under rifle and artillery fire from the 36th Mississippi Infantry, Brigadier-General Louis Hebert's brigade, they had to negotiate a steep ravine protected by abatis and cross a 6-foot-deep (1.8 m), 8-foot-wide (2.4 m) ditch before attacking the 17-foot-high (5.2 m) walls of the redan. This first attempt was easily repulsed. Grant ordered an artillery bombardment to soften the defenses and at about 2 p.m., Sherman's division under Major-General Francis P. Blair tried again, but only a small number of men were able to advance even as far as the ditch below the redan. The assault collapsed in a melee of rifle fire and hand grenades lobbing back and forth.

The failed Federal assaults of 19 May 19 damaged Union morale, deflating the confidence the soldiers felt after their string of victories across Mississippi. They were also costly, with casualties of 157 killed, 777 wounded, and 8 missing, versus Confederate casualties of 8 killed and 62 wounded. The Confederates, assumed to be demoralized, had regained their fighting edge.

Vicksburg, Battery Sherman, 1863. (*The Photographic History of the Civil War in Ten Volumes.*
The Review of Reviews Co., New York. 1911)

Grant planned another assault for May 22, but this time with greater care; they would first reconnoiter thoroughly and soften up the defenses with artillery and naval gunfire. Union forces bombarded the city all night, from 220 artillery pieces and naval gunfire from Rear-Admiral David D. Porter's fleet in the river, and while causing little property damage, they damaged Confederate civilian morale. On the morning of May 22, the defenders were bombarded again for four hours before the Union attacked once more along a three-mile front at 10 a.m. The lead units were supplied with ladders to ascend the fortification walls. Grant did not want a long siege, and this attack was to be by the entire army across a wide front. The attacks were repulsed with heavy losses on the Union side, and by 11 a.m., it was clear that a breakthrough was not forthcoming and the advances by Sherman and McPherson were failures.

Sherman ordered two more assaults. At 2:15 p.m., Giles Smith and Ransom moved out and were repulsed immediately. At 3 p.m., Tuttle's division suffered so many casualties in their aborted advance that Sherman told Tuttle, "This is murder; order those troops back." By this time, Steele's division had finally maneuvered into position on Sherman's right, and at 4 p.m., Steele gave the order to charge against the 26th Louisiana Redoubt. They had no more success than any of Sherman's other assaults. Logan's division made another thrust down the Jackson Road at about 2 p.m. but met with heavy losses and the attack was called off. McClernand attacked again, reinforced by Quinby's division, but with no success. Union casualties were 502 killed, 2,550 wounded, and 147 missing, about evenly divided across the three corps. Confederate casualties were not reported directly but are estimated to be under 500.

Grant reluctantly settled into a siege. On 25 May, Lieutenant-Colonel John A. Rawlins issued Special Orders No. 140 for Grant: "Corps Commanders will immediately commence the work of reducing the enemy by regular approaches. It is desirable that no more loss of life shall be sustained in the reduction of Vicksburg, and the capture of the Garrison. Every advantage will be taken of the natural inequalities of the ground to gain positions from which to start mines, trenches, or advance batteries. ..." Grant wrote in his memoirs, "I now determined upon a regular siege, to 'out-camp the enemy,' as it were, and to incur no more losses."

Federal troops began to dig in, constructing elaborate entrenchments (the soldiers of the time referred to them as "ditches") that surrounded the city and moved closer and closer to the Confederate fortifications. With their backs against the Mississippi and Union gunboats firing from the river, Confederate soldiers and citizens alike were trapped. Pemberton was determined to hold his few miles of the Mississippi as long as possible, hoping for relief from Johnston or elsewhere.

A new problem confronted the Confederates. The dead and wounded of Grant's army lay in the heat of Mississippi summer, the odor of the deceased men and horses fouling the air, the wounded crying for medical help and water. Grant first refused a request of truce, thinking it a show of weakness. Finally, he relented, and the Confederates held their fire while the Union recovered the wounded and dead, soldiers from both sides mingling and trading as if no hostilities existed for the moment.

After this truce, Grant's army began to fill the 12-mile ring around Vicksburg. In short time it became clear that even 50,000 Union soldiers would not be able to carry out a complete encirclement of the Confederate defenses. Pemberton's outlook on escape was pessimistic, but there were still roads leading south out of Vicksburg unguarded by Federal troops. Reinforcements were brought in, and with their arrival, Grant had 77,000 men around Vicksburg.

During the siege, Union gunboats lobbed over 22,000 shells into the town and army artillery fire was even heavier. As the barrages continued, suitable housing in Vicksburg was reduced to a minimum. A ridge, located between the main town and the rebel defense line, provided a diverse citizenry with lodging for the duration. Over 500 caves, known locally as "bombproofs," were dug into the yellow clay hills of Vicksburg. Whether houses were structurally sound or not, it was deemed safer to occupy these dugouts. People did their best to make them comfortable, with rugs, furniture, and pictures. They tried to time their movements and foraging with the rhythm of the cannonade, sometimes unsuccessfully. Because of the citizens' burrowing, the Union soldiers gave the town the nickname of "Prairie Dog Village." Despite the ferocity of the Union fire against the town, fewer than a dozen civilians were known to have been killed during the entire siege.

Late in the siege, Union troops tunneled under the 3rd Louisiana Redan and packed the mine with 2,200 pounds of gunpowder. The explosion blew apart the Confederate lines on 25 June, while an infantry attack made by troops from Logan's XVII Corps division, followed the blast. The 45th Illinois Regiment (known as the "Lead Mine Regiment"), under Colonel Jasper A. Maltby, charged into the 40-foot (12 m) diameter, 12-foot (3.7 m) deep crater with ease, but were stopped by recovering Confederate infantry. The Union soldiers became pinned down while the defenders also rolled artillery shells with short fuses into the pit with deadly results. Union engineers worked to set up a casemate in the crater in order to extricate the infantry, and soon the soldiers fell back to a new defensive line. From the crater left by the explosion on 25 June, Union miners worked to dig a new mine to the south. On 1 July, this mine was detonated but no infantry attack followed. Pioneers worked throughout 2 and 3 July to widen the initial crater large enough for an infantry column of four to pass through for future anticipated assaults. However, events the following day negated the need for any further assaults.

On 3 July, Pemberton sent a note to Grant regarding the possibility of negotiations for peace. Grant, as he had done at Fort Donelson, first demanded unconditional surrender, but he reconsidered, not wanting to feed 30,000 hungry Confederates in Union prison camps, and offered to parole all prisoners. Considering their destitute state, dejected and starving, he never expected them to fight again; he hoped they would carry home the stigma of defeat to the rest of the Confederacy. In any event, it would have occupied his army and taken months to ship that many prisoners north. Pemberton officially surrendered his army on 4 July. Most of the men who were paroled on 6 July were exchanged and received back into the Confederate Army on 4 August 1863, at Mobile Harbor, Alabama.

Union casualties for the battle and siege of Vicksburg were 4,835; Confederate were 32,697 (29,495 surrendered). The full campaign, since 29 March, claimed 10,142 Union and 9,091 Confederate killed and wounded. In addition to his surrendered men, Pemberton turned over to Grant 172 cannons and 50,000 rifles.

Vicksburg was the last major Confederate stronghold on the Mississippi River; therefore, capturing it completed the second part of the Northern strategy, the Anaconda Pla. When two major assaults (19 May and 22 May 1863) against the Confederate fortifications were repulsed with heavy casualties, Grant decided to besiege the city beginning on 25 May. After holding out for more than forty days, with their reinforcement and supplies nearly gone, the garrison finally surrendered on 4 July.

The successful ending of the Vicksburg Campaign significantly degraded the ability of the Confederacy to maintain its war effort. The Confederate surrender on 4 July 1863, is sometimes considered, when combined with General Robert E. Lee's defeat at Gettysburg by Major-General George Meade and retreat beginning the same day, the turning point of the war. It cut off the states of Arkansas, Louisiana, and Texas from the rest of the Confederate States, effectively splitting the Confederacy in two for the duration of the war.[279]

"Whistling Dick" was the name given to this specific Confederate 18-pounder Model 1839 smoothbore muzzle-loading gun that was later rifled, because of the peculiar noise made by its projectiles. The cast iron rifled gun had reinforced bands on the back to prevent the tube from exploding when fired. It had been built at Tredegar Ironworks in Richmond and was part of the defensive batteries facing the Mississippi River at Vicksburg. On 28 May 1863, its fire sank the USS *Cincinnati*.

---

[279] Ballard, Michael B. *Vicksburg, The Campaign that Opened the Mississippi.* Chapel Hill: University of North Carolina Press, 2004.

SIEGE OF PARIS, 1870-1871

The Siege of Paris, lasting from 19 September 1870 to 28 January 1871, and the consequent capture of the city by Prussian forces, led to French defeat in the Franco-Prussian War and the establishment of the German Empire as well as the Paris Commune.

The Siege of Paris, 1870-1871, painting by Jean-Louis-Ernest Meissonier.

As early as August 1870, the Prussian 3rd Army led by Crown Prince Frederick of Prussia (the future Emperor Frederick III), had been marching towards Paris. The army was recalled to counter the French forces accompanied by Napoleon III. These forces were crushed at the Battle of Sedan, and the road to Paris was left open. King William I of Prussia, personally led the Prussian forces, along with his chief of staff Helmuth von Moltke, took the 3rd Army and the new Prussian Army of the Meuse under Crown Prince Albert of Saxony, and marched on Paris virtually unopposed. In Paris, the Governor and commander-in-chief of the city's defenses, General Louis Jules Trochu, assembled a force of 60,000 regular soldiers who had managed to escape from Sedan under Joseph Vinoy or who were gathered from depot troops. Together with 90,000 *Mobiles* (Territorials), a brigade of 13,000 naval seamen and 350,000 National Guards, the potential defenders of Paris totalled around 513,000 personnel. The compulsorily enrolled National Guards were, however, untrained.

The Prussian armies quickly reached Paris, and on 15 September Moltke issued orders for the investment of the city. Crown Prince Albert's army closed in on Paris from the north unopposed, while Crown Prince Frederick moved in from the south. On 17 September, a force under Vinoy attacked Frederick's army near Villeneuve-Saint-Georges in an effort to save a supply depot there, but it was eventually driven back by artillery fire. The railroad to Orleans was cut, and on the 18th Versailles was taken, and then served as the 3rd Army's and eventually Wilhelm's headquarters. By 19 September, the encirclement was complete, and the siege officially began. Responsible for the direction of the siege was General (later Field Marshal) von Blumenthal.

Prussia's chancellor Otto von Bismarck suggested shelling Paris to ensure the city's quick surrender and render all French efforts to free the city pointless, but the German high command, headed by the king of Prussia, turned down the proposal on the insistence of General von Blumenthal, on the grounds that a bombardment would affect civilians, violate the rules of engagement, and turn the opinion of third parties against the Germans, without speeding up the final victory. It was also contended that a quick French surrender would leave the new French armies undefeated and allow France to renew the war shortly after. The new French armies would have to be annihilated first, and Paris would have to be starved into surrender.

Trochu had little faith in the ability of the National Guards, which made up half the force defending the city. So instead of making any significant attempt to prevent the investment by the Germans, Trochu hoped that Moltke would attempt to take the city by storm, and the French could then rely on the city's defenses. These consisted of the 33 km (21 mi) Thiers wall and a ring of 16 detached forts, all of which had been built in the 1840s. Von Moltke never had any intention of attacking the city and this became clear shortly after the siege began. Trochu changed his plan and allowed Vinoy to make a demonstration against the Prussians west of the Seine. On 30 September Vinoy attacked Chevilly with 20,000 soldiers and was soundly repulsed by the 3rd Army. Then on 13 October the II Bavarian Corps was driven from Châtillon, but the French were forced to retire in face of Prussian artillery.

Kompagnie des Kaiser-Alexander-Garde-Grenadier-Regiments Nr. 1 attacking near Le Bourget, on 30 Oct 1870, painting by von Carl Röchling.

General Carey de Bellemare commanded the strongest fortress north of Paris at Saint Denis. On 29 October de Bellemare attacked the Prussian Guard at Le Bourget without orders and took the town. The Guard actually had little interest in recapturing their positions at Le Bourget, but Crown Prince Albert ordered the city retaken anyway. In the battle of Le Bourget the Prussian Guards succeeded in retaking the city and captured 1,200 French soldiers. Upon hearing of the French surrender at Metz and the defeat at Le Bourget, morale in Paris began to sink.

The people of Paris were beginning to suffer from the effects of the German blockade. Hoping to boost morale Trochu launched the largest attack from Paris on November 30 even though he had little hope of achieving a breakthrough. Nevertheless, he sent Auguste-Alexandre Ducrot with 80,000 soldiers against the Prussians at Champigny, Créteil and Villiers. In what became known as the battle of Villiers the French succeeded in capturing and holding a position at Créteil and Champigny. By 2 December, the Württember Corps had driven Ducrot back into the defenses and the battle was over by 3 December.

On 19 January, a final breakout attempt was aimed at the Château of Buzenval in Rueil-Malmaison near the Prussian Headquarters, west of Paris. The Crown Prince easily repulsed the attack inflicting over 4,000 casualties while suffering just over 600. Trochu resigned as governor and left General Joseph Vinoy with 146,000 defenders.

During the winter, tensions began to arise in the Prussian high command. Field-Marshal Helmuth von Moltke and General Leonhard, Count von Blumenthal who commanded the siege, were primarily concerned with a methodical siege that would destroy the detached forts around the city and slowly strangle the defending forces with a minimum of German casualties.

But as time wore on, there was growing concern that a prolonged war was placing too much strain on the German economy and that an extended siege would convince the French Government of National Defence that Prussia could still be beaten. A prolonged campaign would also allow France time to reconstitute a new army and convince neutral powers to enter the war against Prussia. To Bismarck, Paris was the key to breaking the power of the intransigent republican leaders of France, ending the war in a timely manner, and securing peace terms favourable to Prussia. Von Moltke was also worried that insufficient winter supplies were reaching the German armies investing the city, as diseases such as tuberculosis were breaking out amongst the besieging soldiers. In addition, the siege operations competed with the demands of the ongoing Loire Campaign against the remaining French field armies.

(Braquehais, Bruno)
French gunners during the siege of Paris, 1870.

On 5 January, on Bismarck's advice, the Germans fired some 12,000 shells into the city over 23 nights in an attempt to break Parisian morale. About 400 perished or were wounded by the bombardment which, "had little effect on the spirit of resistance in Paris." Due to a severe shortage of food, Parisians were forced to slaughter whatever animals were at hand. Rats, dogs, cats, and horses were the first to be slaughtered and became regular fare on restaurant menus. Once the supply of those animals ran low, the citizens of Paris turned on the zoo animals residing at Jardin des plantes. Castor and Polux, the only pair of elephants in Paris, were slaughtered for their meat.

On 25 January 1871, Wilhelm I overruled von Moltke and ordered the field-marshal to consult with Bismarck for all future operations. Bismarck immediately ordered the city to be bombarded with large-caliber Krupp siege guns. This prompted the city's surrender on 28 January 1871. Paris sustained more damage in the 1870–1871 siege than in any other conflict.

Balloon mail was the only means by which communications from the besieged city could reach the rest of France. The use of balloons to carry mail was first proposed by the photographer and balloonist Felix Nadar, who had established the grandiosely titled *No. 1 Compagnie des Aérostatiers*, with a single balloon, the *Neptune*, at its disposal, to perform tethered ascents for observation purposes. However the Prussian encirclement of the city made this pointless, and on 17 September Nadar wrote to the Council for the Defence of Paris proposing the use of balloons for communication with the outside world: a similar proposal had also been made by the balloonist Eugene Godard.

Construction of balloons at the Gare d'Orleans, 1870, engraving by Louis Figuier;
and the departure from Paris of Leon Gambetta on the balloon l'"*Armand-Barbès*" on 7 Oct 1870,
painting by Jules Didier and Jacques Guiaud.

The first balloon launch was carried out on 23 September, using the *Neptune*, and carried 125 kg (276 lb) of mail in addition to the pilot. After a three-hour flight it landed at Craconville, 83 km (52 mi) from Paris. Following this success, a regular mail service was established, with a rate of 20 centimes per letter. Two workshops to manufacture balloons were set up, one under the direction of Nadar in the Elyse-Montmartre dancehall (later moved to the Gare du Nord and the other under the direction of Godard in the Gare d'Orleans. Around 66 balloon flights were made, including one that accidentally set a world distance record by ending up in Norway. The vast majority of these succeeded: only five were captured by the Prussians, and three went missing, presumably coming down in the Atlantic or Irish Sea. The number of letters carried has been estimated at around 2.5 million. Some balloons also carried passengers in addition to the cargo of mail, most notably Leon Gambetta, the minister for War in the new government, who was flown out of Paris on 7 October. The balloons also carried homing pigeons out of Paris to be used for a pideon post. This was the only means by which communications from the rest of France could reach the besieged city. A specially laid telegraph cable on the bed of the Seine had been discovered and cut by the Prussians on 27 September. Couriers attempting to make their way through the German lines were almost all intercepted and although other methods were tried including attempts to use balloons, dogs and message canisters floated down the Seine, these were all unsuccessful.

The French defeat was followed by a popular uprising and the establishment, in March 1871, of the Paris Commune, a revolutionary government formed in accordance with anarchist and socialist principles. The Commune was bloodily suppressed in May 1871 by French troops under the government of Adolphe Thiers. During the brief period in which the communards controlled Paris, they dismantled the imperial column in the Place Vendôme. The suppression of the Commune resulted in further extensive damage to the city, as the communards set fire to the Tuileries Palace, the Louvre, and other buildings, and as desperate fighting between the communards and counter-revolutionary forces destroyed or damaged many other structures.

BATTLE OF RORKES DRIFT, 1879

The South African landscape has seen more than its share of battles and sieges. On 22 January 1879, the Battle of Rorke's Drift was fought during the Zulu-British War. Chief Cetewayo with more than 4,000 Zulus attacked northern Natal. Lt John Chard of the Royal Engineers with 140 troops fought off Cetewayo's tribesmen killing 400 and taking 25 casualties of his own. As a result, eleven Victoria Crosses were awarded, more than for any other single action ever fought.[280]

---

[280] The Victoria Cross, the Commonwealth's highest military decoration for bravery, is founded by Queen Victoria in 1856 to award outstanding gallantry in the Crimean War. The decoration, a bronze cross pattee with, in relief, the Royal crest, bears the simple words: "For Valour." It is suspended from a ribbon that was formerly blue for the navy and red for the army. The ribbon is now red (dull crimson) for all services.

Painting by Alphonse de Neuville of the Battle of Rorke's Drift which took place in Natal during the Anglo-Zulu War in 1879.

BOER WAR, 1899-1902

Firepower alone was rarely sufficient to protect or defeat a fortress. During the Boer War in 1899-1902 both sides brought heavy long-range guns into the field. The British eventually won the war by carrying out punitive expeditions based on chains of blockhouses, although the firepower of modern arms enabled the Boers to resist for two and a half years.[281]

---

[281] Lynn Montross, op. cit., p. 676.

General Piet Cronje's 94-pounder Creusot *Long Tom* gun, in service during the siege of Mafeking, South Africa, in 1899; and, General Piet Cronje's 94-pounder Creusot *Long Tom* gun firing on the British forces during the siege of Mafeking, South Africa, in 1899.

In 1899, the town of Mafeking in South Africa held by British forces came under siege by the Boer army.[282] Mafeking is situated upon the long line of railway, which connected Kimberley in the south with what was then known as Rhodesia (now Zimbabwe) in the north. It served as the main depot for the western Transvaal on one side, and the starting point for all attempts to cross upon the Kalahari Desert on the other, with the Transvaal border sited within a few miles of it. It was not clear to the defenders why the town should have been held since it had no natural advantages to aid in its defense and lay exposed in a widespread plain. Looking at a map, an attacker would quickly determine that the rail lines could easily be cut in places both north and south of the town, and the garrison was isolated some 250 miles from any reinforcements. The Boers clearly had the strength in men and guns to seize the town if and when they chose to do so. The unanticipated variable would be the extraordinary tenacity and resourcefulness of the defending commander, Colonel Baden-Powell. "Through his exertions the town served as a bait to the Boers and occupied a considerable force in a useless siege at a time when their presence at other seats of war might have proved disastrous to the British cause."

---

[282] The British had expanded into large portions of Central and Southern Africa just before the turn of the century. Cecil Rhodes, a British "diamond king" developed part of this territory and gave it his name "Rhodesia" (now Zimbabwe) in 1895. He clashed with President Kruger of the Transvaal Republic; just as major deposits of gold were discovered launching a destabilizing rush to the area. A Briton named Jameson led a disastrous and unsuccessful raid into the Transvaal which began much of the trouble leading up to the war. Jameson, a friend of Rhodes was captured and the German Kaiser, William II, telegraphed his congratulations to Kruger. Although William was Queen Victoria's grandson, the British were outraged. Relations between the Boer Republics and Great Britain deteriorated further because of the poor treatment of foreign miners and prospectors who had flooded into the Transvaal in the Gold Rush. War broke out in 1899. The skill and tenacity of the Boer farmers had been seriously underrated and the Boers under the command of men like General Cronje who led the Transvaal forces at the sieges of Mafeking and Kimberly, inflicted a number of serious defeats on the British forces with heavy losses. The arrival in early 1900 of Lord Roberts, who had conquered Afghanistan, and Lord Kitchener who had conquered the Sudan, improved the British situation, but the war did not end until May 1902. Though the Boers were granted the same civil liberties as those in effect throughout the British Empire, the two small farmer republics of the Transvaal and the Orange Free State disappeared, and the British dominated all of South Africa. *Larousse Encyclopedia of Modern History from 1500 to the Present Day*, Ed Marcel Dunan, Paul Hamlyn, Singapore, 1973, pp. 335-336.

Lieutenant-Colonel Robert S.S. Baden-Powell, South Africa, 1896.

Colonel Baden-Powell was the kind of soldier who was exceedingly popular with the British public. A skilled hunter and an expert at many games, there was always something of the sportsman in his keen appreciation of war. In the Matabele campaign he had out scouted the opposition's scouts and enjoyed himself tracking them through their native mountains, often alone and at night, trusting to his skill to save him from their pursuit. He would prove to be as difficult to outwit, as it was to outfight him. He was also blessed with a curious sense of humor, meeting the Boers head on with bluffs and jokes which were as disconcerting to them as his wire entanglements and his rifle-pits. It has also been said that he had that "magnetic quality by which the leader imparts something of his virtues to his men."

Even before the formal declaration of war, Baden-Powell had been well aware of the precarious state of defenses at Mafeking and had taken steps to prepare for the worst by provisioning the town. The garrison of the town consisted of irregular troops, 340 of the Protectorate Regiment, 170 Police, and 200 volunteers, as well as the Town Guard, who included the able-bodied shopkeepers, businessmen, and residents, numbering 900 men. Their artillery consisted of just two 7-pounder guns and six machine guns. Under the able direction of Colonel Vyvyan and Major Panzera who planned the defenses, Mafeking soon began to take on the appearance of a fortress.

The Boers arrived on 13 October and were met by two truckloads of dynamite sent out by Baden-Powell. The attackers fired on them blowing them to pieces. By 14 October, British pickets, which had been sited around the town, were driven behind their defenses. As they began their withdrawal, the defenders sent out an armored train and a squadron of a unit known as the "Protectorate Regiment," to support the pickets and drove the Boers way from them. A few of the Boers later doubled back and interposed themselves between the British and Mafeking. In response, two fresh troops were sent out from the garrison equipped with a 7-pounder cannon which was used to effectively fire enough high-explosive shrapnel to drive them off. The garrison lost two killed and fourteen wounded, but they inflicted considerable damage on the Boers.

On 16 October, the Boers stepped up their siege efforts and brought two 12-pounder guns to bear on Mafeking. They also managed to seize the garrison's outside water supply, although in anticipation of this, the garrison had already dug wells. Before 20 October, 5,000 Boers, under their formidable leader, General Cronje, had surrounded the town. He sent the garrison a message, which read, "Surrender to avoid bloodshed." In response, Baden-Powell asked, "When is the bloodshed going to begin?" After the Boers had been shelling the town for some weeks the light-hearted Colonel sent out another message telling Cronje, "if the shelling went on any longer he should be compelled to regard it as equivalent to a declaration of war." (Cronje's reply has not been reported).

The town's defenses contained some major drawbacks. For one, there were only about 1,000 men to defend a protective wall of five or six miles in circumference against a determined attacker who could assault at any point and time at his convenience. To cope with this, the defenders devised an ingenious system of small forts, each of which held from ten to forty riflemen, protected with bomb-proof shelters and covered ways. The central bomb-proof shelter was connected by a telephone line, which ran out to all the outlying forts, which reduced the risk and manpower in the form of runners. An alarm system was rigged using a system of bells within each quarter of the town. These were rung when an incoming shell was observed in time to enable the inhabitants to get to shelter. The defenders also made use of an armored train, which they camouflaged with green paint, covered it with scrub, and kept hidden in the clumps of bushes which surrounded the town.

The Boers began a heavy bombardment of the town on 20 October and kept it up with brief intervals for seven months. The Boers had brought an enormous gun across from Pretoria, which fired a 96-pound shell, and this, with many smaller pieces, kept up a nearly continuous fire on the town, although little was achieved. As the Mafeking guns were too weak to adequately return the Boer fire, Colonel Baden-Powell determined that a more suitable response would be to conduct a fighting patrol or sortie. On the evening of 27 October, about 100 men under Captain Fitz Clarence moved out against the Boer trenches with instructions to use only their bayonets. The mission was successful, and the Boer position was overrun with many of the Boers being bayoneted before they could disengage themselves from the tarpaulins, which covered them. The British lost six killed, eleven wounded, and two prisoners, with the Boer losses slightly higher.

On 31 October, the Boers launched an attack on Cannon Kopje, a small fort and eminence to the south of the town defended by Colonel Walford, of the British South African Police, with 57 of his men and three small guns. The attack was repelled with heavy loss to the Boers. The British casualties were six killed and five wounded.

This experience seems to have caused the Boers to rethink their strategy, and no further expensive attempts were made to rush the town. For the next few weeks, the siege degenerated into a blockade. About this time, Cronje was recalled to deal with a more important task, and the siege was taken over by Commandant Snyman. The Boers continued to use their great gun to fire its huge shells into the town, but the defenders boardwood walls and corrugated iron roofs reduced the impact of the bombardment. On 3 November, the garrison sent out a sortie to storm a position called "the Brickfields," which had been held by the enemy's sharpshooters. Another small harassing sally ventured out on 7 November.

On 18 October, Colonel Baden-Powell sent a message to Commandant Snyman that he could not take the town by biting and looking at it. At the same time, he dispatched a message to the Boer forces generally, advising them to return to their homes and their families. Some of the commandos had gone south to assist Cronje in his stand against Methuen, and the siege stagnated until 26 December when the garrison launched a casualty intensive sortie against the Boers. This attack was made against one of the Boer forts on the north. The Boers may have had some idea of what was coming, because the fort had been strengthened to the point where it could not be taken without the use of scaling ladders. The attacking force consisted of two squadrons from the Protectorate Regiment and one of the Bechuanaland Rifles, backed up by three guns. 53 out of the 80-man attacking force were killed and wounded, (25 killed, 28 wounded).

Such losses could not be sustained, and from then on, Colonel Baden-Powell chose to hold on until he could be relieved by the British forces under Plumer who could arrive from the north, or under Methuen who could drive up from the south. The siege settled down into a monotonous series of sporadic shelling by the Boers through the months of January and February. A truce was usually observed on Sunday, and the snipers who had exchanged rifle-shots all week gave only catcalls and occasionally good-humored chaff. In spite of the humor, however, there was no neutral camp for women or sick, and the Boer guns kept up their fire against the inhabitants inside Mafeking in order to bring pressure upon the defenders to surrender.

In the midst of the siege, the defenders held a Jubilee ball, presided over by the Colonel, which was briefly interrupted by a Boer attack. The defenders also endeavored to keep up sports matches to maintain morale. (Apparently their Sunday cricket matches so shocked Snyman that he threatened to fire upon it if they were continued).

In spite of limited resources, an ordnance factory was put into operation in Mafeking, formed in the railway workshops, and conducted by two men named Connely and Cloughlan, of the Locomotive Department. Daniels, of the police, supplemented their efforts by making both powder and fuses. The factory turned out shells, and eventually constructed a 5.5-in. smooth-bore gun, which fired a round shell with great accuracy to a considerable range.

(Firepower Museum Photo)
British 5.5-inch Smoothbore "Wolf" Gun built during the Siege of Mafeking.

The Boers constructed a series of trenches, which moved forward through the month of April 1900. When the trenches came within range, both sides resorted to throwing hand-grenades on each other, with a number being launched by Sergeant Page of the Protectorate Regiment. At times, the numbers of the besiegers and their guns diminished, due to forces being detached to prevent the advance of Plumer's relieving column from the north. The Boers who remained held their counterforts, which the British defenders were unable to storm.

The northern British force had a difficult task fighting the Boers, but they were eventually strengthened by the relieving column, and began making their way to Mafeking. This force was originally raised for the purpose of defending Rhodesia (now Zimbabwe), and it consisted of pioneers, farmers, and miners and other volunteers, many of whom were veterans of the native wars. The men of the northern and western Transvaal whom they were called upon to face, the burghers of Watersberg and Zoutpansberg, were tough frontiersmen living in a land where a "dinner was shot, not bought." Sir Arthur Conan Doyle described them as "shaggy, hairy, half-savage men, handling a rifle as a medieval Englishman handled a bow, and skilled in every wile of veldt craft, they were as formidable opponents as the world could show."

When the war first broke out, the British leadership in Rhodesia sought to save as much as possible of their railway line, which had kept them in contact with the south. For this reason, an armored train was dispatched just three days after the expiration of the Boer ultimatum to the British, to a point four hundred miles south of Bulawayo, where the frontiers of the Transvaal and of Bechuanaland join. Colonel Holdsworth commanded this small British force. About 1,000 Boer commandos attacked the train but were driven back with a number being killed. The train then pressed on as far as Lobatsi, where it found the bridges destroyed. At this point the commander directed it to return to its original position. As it did so, it was attacked again by the Boer commandos, but escaped capture and destruction a second time. From then until the New Year the line was kept open by an effective system of patrolling to within a hundred miles or so of Mafeking. Skirmishes continued with a successful British attack on a Boer laager at Sekwani being carried out on 24 November. Colonel Holdsworth approached the Boer laager and attacked in the early morning with a force of 120 frontiersmen, killing or wounding a number of the Boers and scattering the rest. Other British forces were engaged in similar tactics elsewhere on the northern frontier.

About this time, Colonel Plumer had taken command of the small army, which was operating from the north along the railway line with Mafeking for its objective. Plumer was an officer with considerable experience in African warfare. Conan Doyle described him as, "a small, quiet, resolute man, with a knack of gently enforcing discipline upon the very rough material with which he had to deal." With his weak force, which never exceeded a thousand men, and was usually from six to seven hundred, he had to keep the long line behind him open, build up the besieged railway in front of him and gradually creep onwards in face of a formidable and enterprising enemy. He kept his headquarters for some time at Gaberones, about 80 miles north of Mafeking, and kept up precarious communications with the besieged garrison. In the middle of March he advanced as far south as Lobatsi, which is less than fifty miles from Mafeking; but the Boers proved to be too strong for him, and Plumer had to drop back again with some loss to his original position at Gaberones.

Gathering his forces for another push, Plumer again came south, and this time made his way as far as Ramathlabama, within a day's march of Mafeking. Unfortunately, he only had 350 men with him, which was not enough to press through to the garrison. Plumer's relieving force was fiercely attacked by the Boers and driven back on to their camp with a loss of 12 killed, 26 wounded, and 14 missing. Although some of Plumer's men were dismounted, he managed to extricate them safely while under attack by an aggressive mounted enemy. His force withdrew again to near Lobatsi and collected itself for another effort.

While this was taking place, the defenders of Mafeking kept up a spirited and aggressive defense. Its riflemen maintained an accurate and deadly fire on the Boer gun crews, forcing them to move their biggest gun further away from the town. The siege had now dragged on for six months. In spite of being a small tin-roofed village, Mafeking had become a prize of victory, a symbol that would become a necessity for one side or the other to gain in order to demonstrate its supremacy in the South African conflict. Something had to be done to break the stalemate.

The Boer besiegers increased their ranks and added to the number of guns laying fire on Mafeking. On 12 May the Boer's launched a dawn attack with about 300 volunteers under Commander Eloff. They had crept around to the west side of the town at a point furthest the lines of the besiegers. At the first rush they penetrated into the native quarter, which they immediately set on fire. The first large building they seized was the barracks of the Protectorate Regiment, which was held by Colonel Hore and about 20 of his officers and men. The Boers quickly sent an exultant message by telephone to Baden-Powell to tell him that they had it. The Boers held two other positions within the lines, one a stone kraal and the other a hill, but their reinforcements were slow in arriving, and they were immediately isolated by the defenders and cut off from their own lines.

The Boers had successfully penetrated the town but were still far from being able to take it. The British for their part spent the day squeezing a cordon around the Boer positions, hemming them in without rushing them and incurring casualties, but making it impossible for the Boer commandos to escape from them. Although a few burghers slipped away in twos and threes, the main body found itself trapped in a fire-sack swept with rifle fire. Recognizing the hopelessness of their position, at seven o'clock in the evening Eloff with 117 men laid down their arms. Their losses had been 10 killed and 19 wounded. It is not known why these men were not reinforced once they had gained entry, but if they had been, it is possible the attack would have been successful. Colonel Baden-Powell, with his characteristic sense of humor introduced himself to Commander Eloff, saying, "Good evening, Commandant, won't you come in and have some dinner?" The prisoners, who were comprised of burghers, Hollanders, Germans, and Frenchmen, were apparently then treated to as good a supper as the destitute larders of the town could furnish.

Eloff's attack was the last, though by no means the worst of the attacks, which the garrison had to face. The siege ended with the British having lost six killed and ten wounded. On 17 May 1900, five days after Eloff's unsuccessful assault, the defenders of Mafeking were relieved. Colonel Mahon, a young Irish officer who had made his reputation as a cavalry leader in Egypt, had started early in May from Kimberley with a small but mobile force consisting of the Imperial Light Horse (brought in from Natal for the purpose), the Kimberley Mounted Corps, the Diamond Fields Horse, some Imperial Yeomanry, a detachment of the Cape Police, and 100 volunteers from the Fusilier brigade, with M battery horse artillery and pom-poms, some 1,200 men in all.

Mahon with his men struck round the western flank of the Boers and moved rapidly to the northwards. On 11 May, he had fought a short engagement with the Boers who had opened fire at short range on the Imperial Light Horse, who led the column. A short engagement ensued, in which the casualties amounted to 30 killed and wounded, but which ended in the defeat and dispersal of the Boers, whose force was certainly very much weaker than the British. On 15 May the relieving column arrived without further opposition at Masibi Stadt, twenty miles to the west of Mafeking.

In the meantime, Plumer's force in the north had been strengthened by the addition of C Battery of four 12-pounder guns of the Canadian Artillery under Major Eudon and a body of Queenslanders. These forces had been part of the small army which had come with General Carrington through Beira, and after a detour of thousands of miles, arrived in time to form a portion of the relieving column. These contingents had been assembled after taking long railway journeys, and then being conveyed across thousands of miles of ocean to Cape Town. From here they had covered enormous additional distances by rail and coach to Ootsi, and then conducted a 100-mile forced march to their battlefield positions. With these reinforcements and with his own hardy Rhodesians, Plumer pushed on and the two columns reached the hamlet of Masibi Stadt within an hour of each other. Their united strength was far superior to anything which Snyman's force could place against them.

Although the Boers put up a stiff resistance, they were eventually forced to withdraw past Mafeking and took refuge in the trenches on the eastern side. At this point, Baden-Powell sallied out of the garrison, and supported by the artillery fire from the relieving column, drove them from their shelter. The Boers still managed to escape with all of their guns except for one small cannon. They did leave a number of wagons and a considerable quantity of supplies.

The relieving force ended a siege of an open town which contained no regular soldiers and inadequate artillery against a numerous and enterprising enemy with very heavy guns. The defense of Mafeking took place during the opening months of the war and held up a Boer force of between 4,000 and 5,000 commandos. If these forces had been available at other points in the British line, the losses might well have been unsustainable. The Boers kept 2,000 men and eight guns, (including one of the four big Creusots in their arsenal) on the siege lines. It prevented the invasion of Rhodesia, at a cost of 200 British lives, with Boers taking an estimated 1,000 casualties. In Arthur Conan Doyle's words, "critics may say that the enthusiasm in the empire was excessive, but at least it was expended over worthy men and a fine deed of arms."[283]

BATTLE OF LIÈGE, 1914

The Battle of Liège (*Bataille de Liège*) was the opening engagement of the German invasion of Belgium and the first battle of the First World War. The attack on Liège, a town protected by the Fortified position of Liège, a ring of fortresses built from the late 1880s to the early 1890s, began on 5 August 1914 and lasted until 16 August, when the last fort surrendered. The siege of Liège may have delayed the German invasion of France by 4–5 days. Railways in the Meuse river valley needed by the German armies in eastern Belgium were closed for the duration of the siege and German troops did not appear in strength before the Fortified Position of Namur at the confluence of the Sambre and Meuse rivers until 20 August.

Belgian military planning assumed that other powers would expel an invader. Belgian troops were to be massed in central Belgium, in front of the National redoubt of Belgium ready to face any border, while the Liège fortress ring and the Namur fortress ring were left to secure the frontiers.

---

[283] Arthur Conan Doyle, The Siege of Mafeking; *The Great Boer War: A Two-Years' Record, 1899-1901*, London, Smith, Elder & Co., 1901. Internet: http://www.pinetreeweb.com/conan-doyle-mafeking.htm.

Belgian troops in top hats, defending a Herstal suburb, just north-east of Liège, Belgium, August 1914.

On 2 Aug 1914, the German government sent an ultimatum to Belgium, demanding passage through Belgian territory (in order to outflank French defences), as German troops crossed the frontier of Luxembourg. On 3 August, the Belgian Government refused German demands and the British Government guaranteed military support to Belgium, should Germany invade. Germany declared war on France and the British government ordered general mobilisation. On 4 August, the British government sent an ultimatum to Germany and declared war on Germany at midnight on 4/5 August. Belgium severed diplomatic relations with Germany and Germany declared war on Belgium. German troops crossed the Belgian frontier and attacked Liège.

LIÈGE FORTS

Liège is situated at the confluence of the Meuse River, which at the city flows through a deep ravine and the Ourthe River, between the Ardennes to the south and Maastricht, in the Netherlands, and Flanders to the north and west. The city lies on the main rail lines from Germany to Brussels and Paris, which Schlieffen and Moltke planned to use in an invasion of France. Much industrial development had taken place in Liège and the vicinity, which presented an obstacle to an invading force. The main defences were a ring of twelve forts 6–10 km (3.7–6.2 mi) from the city, built in 1892 by Henri Alexis Brialmont, the leading fortress engineer of the nineteenth century. The forts were sited about 4 km (2.5 mi) apart to be mutually supporting but had been designed for frontal, rather than all-round defence.

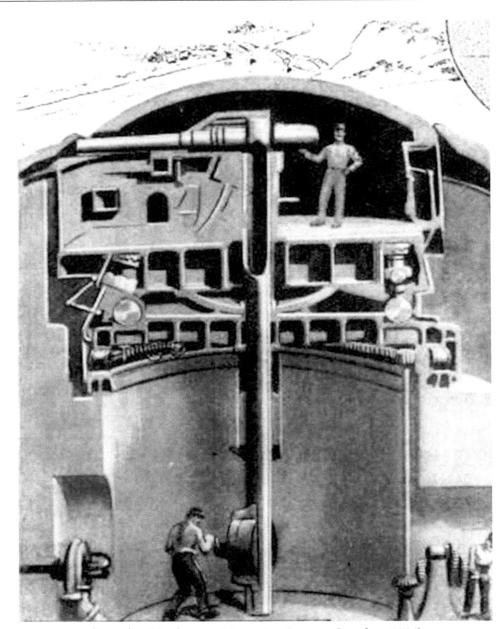

(Popular Mechanics Magazine Image, October 1914)
Drawings of Belgian Cupola Forts.

There were five large triangular forts, (Barchon, Fléron, Boncelles, Lancin, and Pontisse), four small triangular forts, (Evegnée, Hollogne, Lantin and Liers) and two small square forts (Chaudfontaine and Embourg). These forts were built of concrete, with a surrounding ditch and barbed-wire entanglements; the superstructures were buried and only mounds of concrete or masonry and soil were visible. The large forts had two armoured turrets with two 210 mm (8.3 in) guns each, one turret with two 150 mm (5.9 in) guns and two cupolas with a 210 mm (8.3 in) howitzer each. Four retractable turrets contained a 57 mm (2.2 in) quick firer each, two before the citadel and two at the base. A retractable searchlight was built behind the 150 mm turret with a range of 2–3 km (1.2–1.9 mi). Small forts had a 210 mm (8.3 in) howitzer cupola and three of the quick firers. The heavy guns and quick firers used black powder ammunition, long superseded in other armies, which raised clouds of smoke and obscured the view of the fortress gunners. The 150 mm (5.9 in) guns had the greatest range at 8,500 m (9,300 yd) but the black powder smoke limited the realistic range to about 1,500 m (1,600 yd). The forts contained magazines for the storage of ammunition, crew quarters for up to 500 men and electric generators for lighting. Provision had been made for the daily needs of the fortress troops but the latrines, showers, kitchens and the morgue had been built in the counterscarp, which could become untenable if fumes from exploding shells collected, because the forts were ventilated naturally.

The forts could communicate with the outside by telephone and telegraph, but the wires were not buried. Smaller fortifications and trench lines in the gaps between the forts had been planned by Brialmont but had not been built. The fortress troops were not at full strength and many men were drawn from local guard units, who had received minimal training due to the reorganisation of the Belgian army begun in 1911, which was not due to be complete until 1926. The forts also had c26,000 soldiers and 72 field guns of the 3rd Infantry Division and 15th Infantry Brigade to defend the gaps between forts, c.6,000 fortress troops and members of the paramilitary Garde Civique, equipped with rifles and machine-guns. The garrison of around 32,000 men and 280 guns, was insufficient to man the forts and field fortifications. In early August 1914, the garrison commander was unsure of the troops which he would have at his disposal, since until 6 August it was possible that all of the Belgian army would advance towards the Meuse.

The terrain in the fortress zone was difficult to observe from the forts because many ravines ran between them. Interval defences had been built just before the battle but were insufficient to stop German infiltration. The forts were also vulnerable to attack from the rear, the direction from which the German bombardments were fired. The forts had been designed to withstand shelling from 210-mm (8.3 in) guns, which in 1890, were the largest mobile artillery in the world but the concrete used was not of the best quality and by 1914 the German army had much larger 420-mm howitzers, (L/12 420-mm (17-in) *M-Gerät* 14 *Kurze Marine-Kanone*) and Austrian 305-mm howitzers (*Mörser* M. 11). The Belgian 3rd Division (Lieutenant-General Gérard Léman) along with the attached 15th Infantry Brigade defended Liège. The division comprised five brigades and various other formations with c.32,000 troops and 280 guns.

In the morning of 5 August, Captain Brinckman, the German Military Attaché at Brussels, met the Governor of Liège under a flag of truce and demanded the surrender of the fortress. Léman refused and an hour later, German troops attacked the east bank forts of Chaudfontaine, Fleron, Evegnée, Barchon and Pontisse, while an attack on the Meuse, below the junction with the Vesdre, failed. A party of German troops managed to get between Fort de Barchon and the river Meuse but was forced back by the Belgian 11th Brigade. From the late afternoon into the night, the German infantry attacked in five columns, two from the north, one from the east and two from the south. The attacks were supported by heavy artillery, but the German infantry were repulsed with great loss. The attack at the Ourthe forced back the defenders between the forts, before counterattacks by the 12th, 9th and 15th Brigades checked the German advance. Just before dawn, a small German raiding party tried to abduct the Governor from the Belgian headquarters in Rue Ste. Foi. Alarmed by gunfire in the street, Léman and his staff rushed outside and joined the guard platoon fighting the raiding party, which was driven off with twenty dead and wounded left behind.

German cavalry moved south from Visé to encircle the town; German cavalry patrols had been operating up to 20 km (12 mi) west of Liege, leading Léman to believe that the German II Cavalry Corps was encircling the fortified area from the north, though in fact the main body of that force was still to the east and did not cross the Meuse until 8 August, when the reservists had arrived. Believing he would be trapped, Léman decided that the 3rd Infantry Division and 15th Infantry Brigade should withdraw westwards to the Gete, to join the Belgian field army.

(Library and Archives Canada Photo, MIKAN No. 5013167)
German Zeppelin L-53 shot down on 11 August 1918, by Stuart Douglas Culley.

On 6 August, the Germans carried out the first air attack on a European city, when a Zeppelin (LZ 21 Class N, Z VI) airship bombed Liège and killed nine civilians. The airship's inadequate lift kept it at low altitude so that bullets and shrapnel from defending fire holed the gasbags. The ship limped back to Cologne but had to be set down in a forest near Bonn, completely wrecking it.

Léman believed that units from five German corps confronted the defenders and assembled the 3rd Division between forts Loncin and Hollogne to begin the withdrawal to the Gete during the afternoon and night of 6/7 August. The fortress troops were concentrated in the forts, rather than the perimeter and at noon, Léman set up a new headquarters in Fort Loncin, on the western side of the city. German artillery bombarded the forts and Fort Fléron was put out of action when its cupola-hoisting mechanism was destroyed by the bombardment. On the night of 6/7 August German infantry were able to advance between the forts and during the early morning of 7 August, Ludendorff took command of the attack, ordered up a field howitzer and fought through Queue-du-Bois to the high ground overlooking Liège and captured the Citadel of Liege. Ludendorff sent a party forward to Léman under a flag of truce to demand surrender but Léman refused.

Bülow gave command of the siege operations at Liège to General Karl von Einem, the VII Corps commander with the IX and X Corps under his command. The three corps had been ordered to advance over the Belgian border on 8 August. At Liège, on 7 August, Emmich sent liaison officers to contact the brigades scattered around the town. The 11th Brigade advanced into the town and joined the troops there on the western fringe. The 27th Brigade arrived by 8 August, along with the rest of the 11th and 14th brigades. Fort Barcheron fell after a bombardment by mortars and the 34th Brigade took over the defence of the bridge over the Meuse at Lixhe. On the southern front the 38th and 43rd Brigades retreated towards Theux, after a false report that Belgian troops were attacking from Liège and Namur. On the night of 10/11 August Einem ordered that Liège be isolated on the eastern and south-eastern fronts by the IX, VII and X corps as they arrived and allotted the capture of forts Liers, Pontisse, Evegnée and Fléron to IX Corps and Chaudfontaine and Embourg to VII Corps as X Corps guarded the southern flank.

Before the orders arrived, fort Evegnée was captured after a bombardment. IX Corps isolated fort Pontisse on 12 August and began a bombardment of forts Pontisse and Fléon during the afternoon, with 380-mm (15- in) coastal mortars and Big Bertha 420-mm (17-in) siege howitzers. The VII Corps heavy artillery began to fire on fort Chaudfontaine, fort Pontisse was surrendered and IX Corps crossed the

Meuse to attack fort Liers. Fort Liers fell in the morning of 14 August and the garrison of fort Fléron surrendered in the afternoon, after a *Minenwerfer* bombardment. The X Corps and the 17th Division were moved to the north and VII Corps to the south of the Liège–Brussels railway and on 15 August, a bombardment began on the forts to the west of the town. Fort Boncelles fell in the morning and fort Lantin in the afternoon; fort Loncin was devastated by the 420-mm guns and Léman was captured. Forts Hollogne and Flémalle were surrendered on the morning of 16 August after a short bombardment.

German soldiers in a car wait for Belgian attack, on the streets of Liège, Aug 1914; and German troops at Place Saint Lambert, Liège, Aug 1914. (Bibliothèque Ulysse Capitaine Photo)

By the morning of 17 August, the German 1st Army, 2nd Army and 3rd Army were free to resume their advance to the French frontier. The Belgian field army withdrew from the Gete towards Antwerp from 18–20 August and Brussels was captured unopposed on 20 August. The siege of Liège had lasted for eleven days, rather than the two days anticipated by the Germans. For 18 days, Belgian resistance in the east of the country had delayed German operations, which gave an advantage to the Franco-British forces in northern France and in Belgium.

Big Bertha (*Dicke Bertha*), 'Fat (or heavy) Bertha', was the name of a type of super-heavy siege artillery developed by the armaments manufacturer Krupp in German and used in both the First and Second World Wars. Its official designation was the L/12, Type *M-Gerät 14* (M-Equipment 1914) *Kurze Marine-Kanone* ("short naval gun", a name intended to conceal the weapon's real purpose). Its barrel diameter calibre was 420-mm (16.5-in)

The *M-Gerät 14* howitzer was a road-mobile weapon mounted on a two-wheeled field type carriage of conventional construction. It used a conventional Krupp sliding-wedge breech and fired shells of around 830 kg. Fully assembled it weighed 43 tons. Special steel "mats" were developed, onto which the wheels were driven, with a steel aiming arc at the rear of the carriage that allowed limited traverse. This aiming arc was fitted with a massive "spade" that was buried in the ground and which helped anchor the weapon. To prevent the weapon bogging down in muddy roads the guns were equipped with *Radgürteln*, feet attached to the rim of the wheels to reduce ground pressure. Krupp and Daimler developed a tractor for the Bertha, though Podeus motor ploughs were also used to tow the guns, which were broken down into five loads when on the road.

Only two operational M-Gerät were available at the beginning of the First World War, although two additional barrels and cradles had apparently been produced by that time. The two operational M-Geräte formed the Kurze Marine Kanone Batterie (KMK) No. 3; the 42 cm contingent contained four additional Gamma Geräte organized in two batteries, and one more Gamma became operational two weeks into the war as "half-battery". They were used to destroy the Belgian forts at Liège, Namur and Antwerp, and the French fort at Maubeuge, as well as other forts in northern France. Bertha proved highly effective against older constructions such as the Belgian forts designed in the 1880s by Brialmont, destroying several in a few days. The first wartime shot of an M-Gerät was fired against Fort Pontisse on the outskirts of Liege on 12 August 1914. The most spectacular success was against the nearby Loncin, which exploded after taking a direct hit to its ammunition magazine. The concrete used in the Belgian forts was of poor quality, and consisted of layers of concrete only, with no steel reinforcement.

Big Bertha gained a strong reputation on both sides of the lines due to its early successes in smashing the forts at Liege. The German press went wild with enthusiasm and declared the Bertha a Wunderwaffe. Later during the German assault upon Verdun in February 1916, it proved less effective, as the newer construction of this fort, consisting of concrete reinforced with steel, could mostly withstand the large semi-armour-piercing shells of the Berthas. Only Fort Vaux was severely damaged during this event, when the shells destroyed the fort's water storage supply, leading to the surrender of the fort.

A total of 12 complete M-Gerät were built; besides the two available when the war started, 10 more were built during the war. This figure does not include additional barrels; two extra barrels were already available before the war started, and possibly up to 20 barrels were built, though some sources state 18. As the war ground on, several Berthas were destroyed when their barrels burst due to faulty ammunition. Later in the Great War, an L/30 30.5-cm barrel was developed and fitted to some Bertha carriages to provide longer-range with lighter fire. These weapons were known as the *Schwere Kartaune* or *Beta-M-Gerät*.

(Österreichische Nationalbibliothek Photo)

The Škoda 30.5 cm Mörser M.11 was a siege howitzer produced by Škoda Works and used by the Austro-Hungarian Army during the First World War and by the German Army in the Second World War. The weapon was able to penetrate 2 m (6 ft 7 in) of reinforced concrete with its special armour-piercing shell, which weighed 384 kg (847 lb). The weapon was transported in three sections by a

100-horsepower 15-ton Austro-Daimler road tractor M.12. It broke down into barrel, carriage and firing platform loads, each of which had its own trailer. It could be assembled and readied to fire in around 50 minutes.

The mortar could fire two types of shell, a heavy armour-piercing shell with a delayed action fuse weighing 384 kg, and a lighter 287 kg shell fitted with an impact fuze. The light shell was capable of creating a crater 8 meters wide and 8 meters deep, as well as killing exposed infantry up to 400 m (440 yd) away. The weapon required a crew of 15–17 and could fire 10 to 12 rounds an hour. After firing, it automatically returned to the horizontal loading position.

Eight Mörsers were loaned to the German Army and they were first fired in action on the Western Front at the start of the First World War. They were used in concert with the Krupp 42-cm howitzer (Big Bertha) to destroy the rings of Belgian fortresses around Liège, Namur, and Antwerp (Forts Koningshooikt, Kessel and Broechem). While the weapon was used on the Eastern, Italian, and Serbian fronts until the end of the war, it was only used on the Western front at the beginning of the war.

Photograph of the destroyed fortification at Liège after it was struck by a shell from the Krupp siege gun. ("Popular Mechanics" Magazine Photo, November 1914)

The effect of German and Austrian super-heavy artillery on French and Belgian fortresses in 1914, led to a loss of confidence in fortifications; much of the artillery of fortress complexes in France and Russia was removed to reinforce field armies. At the Battle of Verdun in 1916, the resilience of French forts proved to have been underestimated.

SIEGE OF NAMUR, 1914

On 5 August 1914, the 4th Division at the Fortified Position of Namur, received notice from Belgian cavalry that they were in contact with German cavalry to the north of the fortress. More German troops appeared to the south-west on 7 August. *OHL* had, on the same day, ordered the 2nd Army units assembled near the Belgian border, to advance and send mixed brigades from the IX, VII and X corps to Liège immediately. Large numbers of German troops did not arrive in the vicinity of Namur until 19–20 August, too late to forestall the arrival of the 8th Brigade, which having been isolated at Huy, had blown the bridge over the Meuse on 19 August and retired to Namur. During the day, the Guards Reserve Corps off the German 2nd Army arrived at the north of the fortress zone and the XI Corps of the 3rd Army, with the 22 Division and the 38th Division, arrived to the south-east.

A siege train including one Krupp 420 mm (17- in) howitzer and four Austrian 305 mm (12- in) mortars, accompanied the German troops and on 20 August, Belgian outposts were driven in; next day the German super-heavy guns began to bombard the eastern and south-eastern forts. The Belgian defenders had no means of keeping the German siege guns out of range or engaging them with counter-battery fire, by evening two forts had been seriously damaged and after another 24 hours the forts were mostly destroyed. Two Belgian counterattacks on 22 August were defeated and by the end of 23 August, the northern and eastern fronts were defenceless, with five of the nine forts in ruins. The Namur garrison withdrew at midnight to the south-west and eventually managed to rejoin the Belgian field army at Antwerp; the last fort was surrendered on 25 August 1914.[284]

---

[284] Edmonds, J.E. (1926). *Military Operations France and Belgium, 1914: Mons, the Retreat to the Seine, the Marne, and the Aisne August–October 1914.* History of the Great War Based on Official Documents, by Direction of the Historical Section of the Committee of Imperial Defence. II (2nd ed.). London: Macmillan.

VERDUN, 1916

During the First World War, Germany's General Falkenhayn drafted a plan designed to indirectly strike at Britain by striking a blow at one of her allies.[285] He examined France, and looked for a seemingly impregnable place that could be assaulted on a narrow front with powerful artillery support. He chose the fortress of Verdun. It had originally served as a barrier across the wooded valley of the river Meuse, and Vauban had designed its enceinte. It was strengthened in the 1870s when a circle of forts was erected, and 1855 when another fort was built about five miles outside of town. Subsequently reinforced with steel and concrete, these detached forts put a strong defensive ring around Verdun itself, making it a fairly difficult fortress to assault. For this reason, the allies had great difficulty determining what Falkenhayn's intentions were, as he assembled a huge force on the western front in 1916. 32 divisions were arrayed against the British lines, and another 14 (later increased to 30) divisions were placed opposite Verdun.

It was Falkenhayn who had sanctioned the first use of gas at Ypres, advocated unrestricted submarine warfare and promiscuous bombing of built up areas in reprisal for Allied air raids. Ruthless he may have been, but his strategic appreciations were said to have been brilliant, and much of the credit for bringing Germany up out of the low point of disaster on the Marne belongs to Falkenhayn. He had a seemingly limitless capacity for work and drove himself and his staff to great lengths. He would prove to be a formidable opponent.[286]

Marshal Petain who commanded the 2nd French Army organized the defense of the fortress. Generals Nivelle and Mangin led the defenders, although the actual commander of Verdun was General Herr. The French forces were aware that something was coming on 16 January 1916, but apart from moving reserve forces forward, took no action. The Germans put in a dummy attack at Lihons, but the real assault was preceded by a prolonged bombardment by German batteries east, west, and north of the Verdun salient shelling the French positions along a 25-mile front. With only two army corps to hold back seven, the French had to take advantage of the ground. The engineers had added a number of protecting tunnels where the defenders could keep out of range of flame-throwers, deep saps in the woods with reliable cover against flying shrapnel, wire entanglements, land mines and forbidding barriers loaded with high explosive ready to go off at the first intruders touch.

Both sides in the battles at Verdun used extensive sapping in their operations. Sapping is a term used in siege operations to describe any trench excavated near an attacked, defended fortification, under defensive small arms or artillery fire. The trench, referred to as a "sap", is intended to advance a besieging army's position in relation to the works of an attacked fortification. The sap is excavated by brigades of trained soldiers, often called sappers. The sappers dig the trenches or specifically instruct the troops of the line to do so.

By using the sap (trench) the besiegers could move closer to the walls of a fortress, without exposing the sappers to direct fire from the defending force. To protect the sappers, trenches were usually dug at an angle in zig-zagged pattern (to protect against enfilading fire from the defenders) and at the head of the sap a defensive shield made of gabions (or a mantlet) could be deployed.

---

[285] On 28 June 1914, the Austrian Arch-Duke Franz Ferdinand was assassinated at Sarajevo in Bosnia. Austria held Serbia responsible, and William II promised his support to the Austro-Hungarians in case of war. On 28 July 1914 Austria-Hungary declared war on Serbia. Shortly afterwards, on 1 August, Germany declared war on Russia, and on 3 August Germany declared war on France and entered Belgium. On 4 August 1914, Great Britain declared war on Germany. As a British Colony, Canada was automatically at war as well.

[286] Alistair Horne, *The Price of Glory, Verdun 1916*, Macmillan and Co Ltd., London, 1962, p. 33.

Once the saps were close enough, siege engines or guns could be moved though the trenches and got closer to the fortification. From this closer firing point, to fire at the fortification. The goal of firing is to batter a breach in the curtain walls, to allow attacking infantry to get past the walls . Prior to the invention of large pieces of siege artillery, miners could start to tunnel from the head of a sap to undermine the walls. A fire or gunpowder would then be used to create a crater into which a section of the fortifications would fall creating a breach.

(Bundesarchiv Photo)
German soldiers with periscope in a trench on the Western Front, ca 1916.

After the heavy bombardment, the Germans concentrated heavy howitzers on a small sector of entrenchments near Brabant and the Meuse. 12" shells exploding fairly close together quickly blasted the trenches out of existence. Then the other end of the front was subjected to the same bombardment, followed next by the target of Cannes wood in the center of the Verdun salient. The Germans were attempting to capture the first lines of trenches without using infantry until they could move reconnaissance patrols forward. The French however, had sited their machine-gunners and a number of light guns in concealed positions some distance away from the front-line trenches. The German patrols were mown down, and the main attack made very little progress.

Through persistent attacks, the Germans gradually wore down the French opposition and broke up their defensive works for a depth of three or four miles, driving the defenders out of Brabant and Haumont. The French lost Herbois wood on the right of the line but managed to hold on to Hill 351. The slaughter in the Maucourt sector was particularly appalling, with large numbers of dead and wounded between Ornes and Vaux.

After heavy fighting on the left and in the center of the salient, the French forces near the Meuse attempted a counterattack but were forced to withdraw under accurate German shellfire. They withdrew to the Cote du Poivre (Pepper Hill), generally acknowledged to be the key to the defense system of Verdun. At this point, if the Germans had been able to advance to a position parallel to the Meuse, thousands of French troops would have been surrounded. French artillery fire under the command of General Herr halted the German advance at Vacherauville, just below the vital Pepper Hill.

More troops from both sides were moved up to reinforce their forward positions under the cover of February snows and mists. In spite of General Herr's successful defense on Pepper Hill, he was relieved of his command on the recommendation of General Castelnau, the French Chief of Staff, by Joffre. An engineering officer expert at the handling of heavy artillery, Henri Philippe Petain, replaced him. Petain took on the task of reorganizing the defenses of Verdun.

The Germans managed to capture the great armoured fort of Douaumont, the north-eastern pillar of the defenses of Verdun without having to fight for it, opening the way to Verdun itself. Not anticipating this "gift" the Germans did not follow up the initial opportunity it presented, and the delay allowed the French forces to throw extra bridges across the Meuse and to bring in relief divisions and more guns. Petain rotated his fresh troops, placing them where and when they could do the most good rather than jamming them into the congestion of Verdun all at once.

The Germans now held up on the Douaumont plateau, exerted pressure on their right, attempting to capture "The Mort Homme," (Dead Man Hill). The French forces held on. At great cost, the attackers took Forges, Bois des Corbeaux and Cumieres wood. Petain in turn hurled in more reinforcements and strengthened his positions on the long ridge of Dead Man Hill. In the lull that followed, Petain was promoted and transferred, being replaced at Verdun by General Nivelle.

Over the battlefield an enormous air battle was kept up. Outmatched 5 to 1, the French lack of air superiority over Verdun contributed to enormous losses sustained on the ground. The technology of airpower was beginning to exert its first great effect on fortification. Although the Germans had air superiority, they failed to cut the French supply lines, which would have sealed Verdun's fate.[287]

---

[287] Alistair Horne, op. cit., p. 205-206.

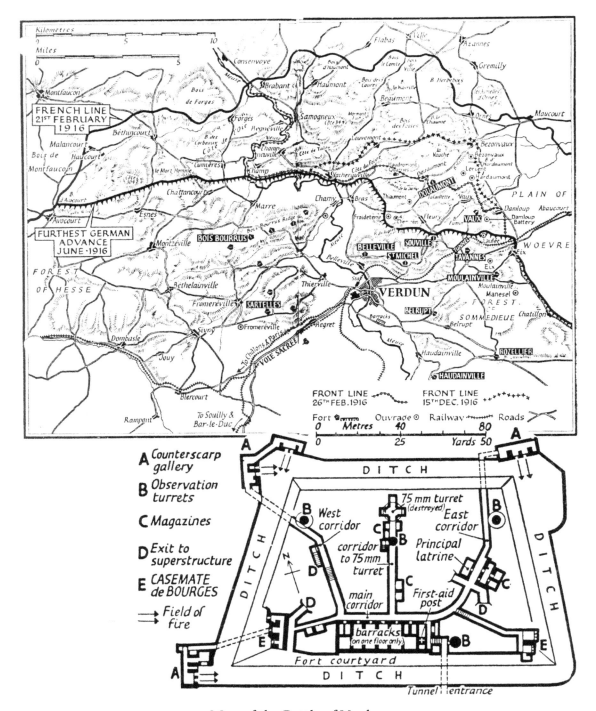

Map of the Battle of Verdun.

Sometimes the bravest efforts are overcome by the severest privations. Fort Vaux was one of the last forts to fall, in an isolated and heroic action. Shelled by heavy long range artillery known as Big Berthas, besieged, attacked by gas and fire, cut off from France, with nothing more imposing than machine guns for its defense, it had held off the weight of the Crown Prince's army for a week. Even after the Germans had actually penetrated the fort, they had been unable to advance more than thirty or forty yards underground in five days of fighting. The garrison had suffered about 100 casualties against the

German losses of 2,678 men and 64 officers. The men had fought well, but the fort had simply run out of water. A nearly impregnable fort had in the end been defeated by thirst.[288]

Falkenhayn continued to withdraw divisions from other theaters of war, especially the Russian front, in spite of recommendations that the German losses be cut, and the remaining troops withdrawn. Unfortunately, Falkenhayn realized that if he broke off the engagement, the reinforced French armies, now over 500,000 strong, would immediately switch over to the offensive. If he persisted however, there was a strong chance that he would fail. The steady drain on German military strength therefore continued until it was obvious that the breakthrough attempts at Verdun had failed. The Germans losses eventually totaled 337,000 men including 100,000 killed, and for France 377,231 of which 162,308 were killed or missing. The figures have varied, but the generally accepted figure for the combined casualties of both sides is over 700,000.[289]

Neither side "won" at Verdun. Horne summed it up as an indecisive battle in an indecisive war, both of which were unnecessary. Neither the French nor the German army would ever fully recover from this battle, and from this point forward the main burden of the war on the Western Front fell on Britain.[290]

An indirect effect of Verdun on siege warfare was the lasting impression of the survivability of the French forts against heavy artillery. This in turn led France to develop a new wall, its famous Maginot Line. The misplaced idea of putting the nation's complete trust in this wall led directly to the downfall of France in 1940.[291]

MAGINOT LINE, 1939-1940

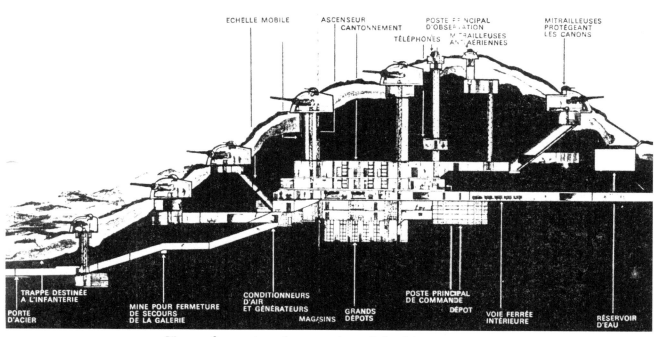

Turret formations in a portion of the Maginot Line.

---

[288]   Alistair Horne, *The Price of Glory, Verdun, 1916*, MacMillan and Co Ltd., London, 1962, p. 263.
[289]   Alistair Horne, op. cit., p. 304.
[290]   Charles Connell, op. cit., p. 196-202.
[291]   Alistair Horne, op. cit., p. 338.

The end of the First World War saw the diminishing of experimentation and innovation in France as technology became increasingly more costly. Marshal Petain and General Debeney influenced their officer corps by their advocacy of the dogma of static prepared defenses. "Continuous prepared battlefields" on the frontiers and massed defensive artillery replaced maneuvers set around fortified regions. This new mode was systematized and symbolized by the construction of fixed fortifications from Switzerland to Luxembourg. This line was decided on by military commissions between 1922 and 1927, but always attributed to the war minister, Andre Maginot, who piloted the laws for its finance through parliament. Permanently garrisoned, the line was politically uncontentious by virtue of appearing strictly defensive. It was a prudent investment, for it afforded not only security to vulnerable industrial regions only recently recovered from Germany, but also protection for the two-week process of mobilization and concentration of the army's reserves.[292]

Verdun may therefore have served its purpose in spite of the losses. Dupuy stated for example, that a defender's chances of success are directly proportional to fortification strength, although he noted that others assert that like Verdun, defenses are attractive traps to be avoided at all costs. One of his key observations, however, is that never in history has a defense been weakened by the availability of fortifications, and that defensive works always enhance combat strength. At the least they will delay an attacker and add to his casualties; at the best, fortifications will enable the defender to defeat the attacker. He noted that although the Maginot Line, the Mannerheim Line, the Siegfried Line, and the Bar Lev Line were overcome in battle, it was only because a powerful enemy was willing to make a massive and costly effort. In 1940, the Germans were so impressed by the defensive strength of the Maginot Line, that they bypassed it.[293]

To further illustrate how quickly the times changed, Verdun fell in less than 24 hours on 14 May 1940, to the German Panzers, costing them less than 200 dead. Airborne forces had also played a key role in the German invasion, particularly in the attack launched against the Dutch fortress of Eban Emael and the Albert Canal bridges on 10 May 1940.[294]

EBAN EMAEL, 1940

The German invasion of the Low Countries required that the Albert Canal and its extensive fortifications be captured in order to convince the Allies that the main German attack was to come through Belgium. The Belgians had built the canal after the First World War in order to deter any repetition of the 1914 German invasion.

[292] Peter Paret, *Makers of Modern Strategy from Machiavelli to the Nuclear Age*, Princeton University Press, Princeton, New Jersey, 1986, p. 604-605.

[293] Trevor N. Dupuy, *The Evolution of Weapons and Warfare*, Hero Books, Fairfax, Virginia, 1984, p. 330-331.

[294] Michael Hickey, *Out of the Sky, A History of Airborne Warfare*, Mills & Boon Limited, London, 1979, p. 51

(Romaine Photo)

The key to this defensive system was the fortress of Eben Emael. Considered impregnable, and set on the west bank of the Canal, its guns were capable of dominating all crossing sites on the Mass river and the Albert Canal out to a range of 16 kilometers. Surrounded by carefully sited moats and anti-tank ditches, it had four rooftop casemates which could retract into the ground. The guns of the fortress were only part of the fort's elaborate system of fire control, in which the firepower of Eben Emael was interlinked with the neighboring field works. The fortress was garrisoned with approximately 1200 officers and men, safely housed under 25 meters of concrete, and well supplied with food, water, and ammunition sufficient to withstand an indefinite siege.

More importantly, the fort commanded the three bridges the Germans would need in their drive to outflank the French Maginot Line which lay to the north, and the complex of Belgian forts around Liege. The bridges over the canal at Canne, Vroenhofen and Veldwezelt were well defended, each having a garrison of an officer and 11 men with anti-tank guns and automatic weapons. Reinforcements were also close at hand.[295]

The Germans studied this formidable defensive system carefully, accumulating and collating detailed intelligence and interpreting the data with an eye to minute details. They built models and used them to devise special methods for its conquest. On the advice of Hanna Reitsch, a well-known aviatrix, Hitler agreed to the recommendation for a silent assault using troop-carrying gliders. Lieutenant-General Student confirmed the plan's feasibility and nominated Hauptmann Walter Koch to carry it out.[296]

---

[295]   Michael Hickey, op. cit., p. 52.
[296]   Ibid, p. 53.

(Bundesarchiv Bild 101I-567-1519-18)
German DFS 230 Troop carrying gliders and German paratroops.

Hauptmann Walter Koch of the 1st Parachute Regiment made extensive use of a DFS-230 glider developed by General Student in training exercises, while a replica of the fortress at Eben Emael was constructed and subjected to different methods of demolition. Special 50 kg hollow charges were developed for piercing the reinforced concrete of the fortress. These charges would be placed by a team of 100 glider-borne sappers, who would land on the grassy roof of the fortress. Codenamed Granite, they were commanded by Lt Rudolf Witzig. Three assault groups codenamed Iron, Concrete and Steel were assigned to glide in and capture the key Albert Canal bridges. They were equipped with flamethrowers, machine guns, anti-tank sections, mortars, and demolition teams. Trained to fight in small groups, Koch's force was well prepared for the attack, which was set to go in one hour before dawn to achieve surprise.

Aircraft allocated to Assault Group Koch comprised 42 Ju-52 transports and glider tugs, and 42 DFS 230 gliders. Early on the morning of 10 May, the assault group set off from Koln-Wahn towards Maastricht, carrying a total of 493 officers and men.[297] Because surprise was essential, the operational plan called for the glider tugs to climb to a height over 8,200' and release their gliders over Germany, allowing the gliders to fly silently to their objectives. Most of the gliders cast-off from their tugs over the fortress. Accurate landings at two of the bridge sites, Veldwezelt and Vroenhofen, resulted in total surprise and success, but at the third bridge at Canne, the German gliders had landed slightly too far away, and the Belgian defenders were able to hold off the attackers just long enough to obtain permission to destroy the bridge. The garrison blew it in the face of the German's as they arrived.

Surprise was crucial at Eban Emael, and it was also successfully gained. The nine gliders, streaming brake parachutes, skidded to a rest within 20 meters of landing. The sappers dashed out and began placing their deadly explosive charges on the inconspicuous roofs of the six most important casemates and 12-gun emplacements that threatened them and the bridges, detonating them as dawn came. The German engineers then entered and secured the top level of the fortress, effectively trapping the majority of the garrison in the rest of the fortress, from where they could do little damage.[298]

At first light, swarms of Luftwaffe dive-bombers appeared overhead, sealing off all reinforcement routes to the stricken fortress. Paratroops arrived in the daylight to reinforce the assailants. Swarms of dummy parachutists were also dropped to the west to further confuse the defense.

Elements of the 4th Panzer Division fought across the Mass River and contacted the paratroopers and glider infantry at Veldwezelt at 1430. All through the night of 10 May, the Germans continued to batter away with their explosives, and at 1230 hours of the 11th of May 1940, the fort surrendered. Sixty of its garrison had been killed and 40 wounded and over 1,000 men marched out to be taken prisoner. The entire German force had lost only 6 men killed and 19 wounded. Hitler personally decorated Hauptman Koch's special force, and the unit was later expanded into an airborne assault regiment.[299]

The loss of this "impregnable" fortress, led to the subsequent German successes against the Belgian army and its capitulation on 28 May 1940.[300] Dutch, French and British forces were then driven into the sea, which in turn led to an armistice with France on 17 June 1940. Airborne forces had made a difference, and they would see more use as the war progressed, particularly during the Normandy invasion of 6 June 1944.

SIEGE OF TOBRUK, 1941

During the Second World War, Allied forces, mainly the Australian 6th Division, captured the Libyan port city of Tobruk on 22 January 1941. The Australian 9th Division ("The Rats of Tobruk") pulled back to Tobruk to avoid encirclement after actions at Er Regima and Mechili and reached Tobruk on 9 April 1941 where prolonged fighting against German and Italian forces followed. Although the siege was lifted after 241 days by Operation Crusader in November 1941, a renewed offensive by Axis forces

---

[297]   James Lucas, *Storming Eagles, German Airborne Forces in World War Two*, Arms and Armour Press, London, 1988, p. 22.

[298]   Philip de Ste Croix, *Airborne Operations, An Illustrated Encyclopedia of the Great Battles of Airborne Forces*, Salamander Books, London, 1978, p. 43.

[299]   Philip de Ste Croix, op. cit., p. 44.

[300]   The Belgian Ministry of Foreign Affairs, *Belgium, The Official Account of what happened*, 1939-1940, 1941, p. x.

under General Erwin Rommel the following year resulted in Tobruk being captured in June 1942 and held by the Axis forces until November 1942, when it was recaptured by the Allies.

(IWM Photo, E4792)

Australian troops occupy a front-line position at Tobruk, 13 Aug 1941. Between April and December 1941, the Tobruk garrison, comprising British, Australian, and Polish troops, was besieged by Rommel's forces. It fell to the Germans after the battle of Gazala on 21 June 1942 but was recaptured five months later.

SIEGE OF LENINGRAD, 1942

Medieval sieges tended to last less than 40 days (the length of service owed by serfs to their overlords). In later years, a determined attacker would stay until the fort, castle or city either fell or was relieved. During the Second World War, German forces kept the city of Leningrad under siege for 900 days. For the people of this city, today known once again as St. Petersburg, the *Blokada* (the Siege) of Leningrad is an important part of their heritage and for the older generations it brings memories that they will never forget.

(Soviet Army Photo)
Russians soldiers in the trenches, defending Leningrad with a 7.62-mm DP-27 machine gun.

German troops approached Leningrad within two and a half months of their invasion of the Soviet Union on 22 June 1941.[301] By 8 September 1941 they had outflanked the Red Army and had fully encircled

---

[301] On 22 June 1941, Adolf Hitler launched Operation Barbarossa, the greatest ground attack in history, with 138 divisions, (including 19 armoured divisions). On the left, Field Marshal Wilhelm von Leeb's Army Group "C" with 30 divisions attacked from East Prussia through the Baltic States toward Leningrad. On the right, Field Marshal Karl von Rundstedt's Army Group "A" with 57 divisions drove southeast from southern Poland and Rumania into the Ukraine. In the center, Field Marshall Fedor von Bock's Army Group "B" with 51 divisions, carried the heaviest weight of the German armor and with four armies in the van press north of the Pripet Marshes straight towards Moscow. To defend against this onslaught, the Soviet Union had 148 divisions spread along the 1,500-mile long frontier from the Baltic to the Black Sea. The Russian army groups were commanded by General Kliment Voroshilov in the north, General Semën Timoshenko in the center, and General Semën Budënny in the south. The ensuing combat is now known to history as the world's greatest land battle. In the north, Field Marshall von Leeb's forces advanced rapidly through the

Leningrad, at which point the siege began. The siege lasted from 8 September 1941 through to 27 January 1944, roughly 900 days. (In contrast, the siege of Moscow lasted only from 2 October to 5 December 1941).

The city held a civilian population of 2,887,000 (including about 400,000 children) and troops and was stocked with minimal supplies of food and fuel (1-2 months at the beginning of the siege). All public transport was brought to a standstill, and by the winter of 1941-42 heating and water supplies had ceased to exist, there was almost no electricity and very little food. The winter month of January 1942 was unusually cold, and food rations were reduced to only 125 grams (about 1/4 of a pound) of bread per person each day. More than 200,000 people died in Leningrad of cold and starvation during the months of January and February 1942 alone. The city did not surrender and continued to maintain some of its war industry production throughout the siege.

Several hundred thousand people were evacuated from the city across Lake Ladoga via the famous "Road of Life" ("*Doroga Zhizni*"), the only route that connected the besieged city with the mainland. When the weather warmed, people were ferried to the mainland, while in the winter they were carried by trucks that drove across the frozen lake under constant air attack and artillery bombardment. The city continued to function while preserving the treasures of the Hermitage and the suburban palaces of Petrodvorets, Pushin which were hidden in the basements of the Hermitage and St. Isaac's Cathedral. Many students continued their studies and even passed their final exams. Dmitry Shostakovich wrote his Seventh "Leningrad" Symphony and it was performed in the besieged city.

The German siege was broken in January 1943, but it was not fully lifted until a year later on 27 January 1944. At least 641,000 people died in Leningrad during the siege (some estimates are higher and place the losses at 800,000). Most lie buried in massed graves in different cemeteries, although almost 500,000 lie in the Piskariovskoye Memorial Cemetery, one of the most impressive national war memorials in present-day Russia.[302]

Continuing on the theme of airborne forces, the next operation to be reviewed is the siege of Dien Bien Phu.

BATTLE OF DIEN BIEN PHU, 1953-1954

When Japan surrendered to the Allied forces on 14 August 1945, the Indochinese colony of Vietnam technically reverted to French control. Unfortunately for France, Ho Chi-Minh, a veteran Marxist, proclaimed a Communist-dominated Vietminh republic as the legal government. Communist China and the Soviet Union supported the Vietminh, while France organized its own government headed by Emperor Bao Dai. Within a year, the country was torn by civil war. From 1946 to 1953 France fought a difficult campaign against the Vietminh guerrilla forces, who received much of their aid from Communist China on their northern border. In November of 1953, the French Commander-in-Chief General Henri Navarre prepared a plan to lure the guerrillas into a major pitched battle in which he believed European heavy weapons would prove decisive. Navarre chose to make his stand at Dien Bien Phu (which roughly translated means, "big frontier administrative center"), in a three-mile wide valley, which extended 11 miles from north to south.[303]

Baltic States to close in on Leningrad within 10 weeks of the initial invasion. David Eggenberger, *An Encyclopedia of Battles, Accounts of Over 1,560 Battles from 1479 BC to the Present.* Dover Publications, Inc., New York, 1985, p. 411.

[302] Internet: http://www.cityvision2000.com/history/900days.htm.

[303] David Eggenberger, *An Encyclopedia of Battles, Accounts of Over 1,560 Battles from 1479 BC to the Present.* Dover Publications, Inc., New York, 1985, p. 121.

The French had been fighting the Viet Minh for seven years in 1953 when General Harry Navarre, age 55, arrived in Saigon to take command of an army of 375,000 men. Not knowing that his own government had all but given up the cause of hanging on to Viet Nam, General Navarre was about to find himself up against General Vo Nguyen Giap, who had a determined army of 125,000 regulars, 75,000 regional troops and 150,000 guerrilla soldiers under his command.[304]

General Navarre set out a policy of mobility and aggressiveness for his conduct of the war in Indochina. He wanted to seek out the enemy, destroy him, and then gradually hand over the pacified areas to the Vietnamese army. His aim was to destroy Viet Minh attacks before they were launched, and to avoid involvement in a general battle.

Navarre put forward the concept of an air-land base at Dien Bien Phu, a district covering some thirty square miles up in the mountainous zone of Thai country. Situated in the middle of a formidable circle of hills, some as high as 2000', Dien Bien Phu was of immense strategic value. A force occupying such a natural administrative center would be in a position to control the whole region, as well as part of South-east Asia. Two problems had to be dealt with first. The French forces would have to be firmly established both in the basin and on the ring of heights. Secondly, good roads and airstrips would have to be constructed to the site. The French government had no money to spare for the scheme and refused to send reinforcements. Navarre pressed ahead anyway, giving the operation the code name "Castor," and setting the stage for the siege of Dien Bien Phu.

General Giap's forces were closing in on Laos at this time, and Navarre argued that the French occupation of Dien Bien Phu would effectively block such an advance. Navarre clearly did not fully understand the strong capability of Giap's forces to sustain itself in operations against the unsupported French army. The French orders for Castor were hammered out on 17 November 1953 against the advice of Navarre's own Staff officers, who objected on technical grounds. Major General René Cogny felt that there would not be enough troops to support the operation, and he believed that intelligence reports were correct in that at least two Viet Minh divisions would be in the region by Jan 1954. Colonel Jean Nicot, the officer commanding air transport, stated that it would be impossible to deliver a steady flow of supplies into Dien Bien Phu. Then, on 20 November 1953, General Navarre received instructions from the Committee for National Defense in Paris that he was to limit any operations to the means currently at his disposal.[305]

General Navarre believed that Giap could not maintain for very long the possible four divisions he was now estimated to have in the field. His staff also believed that the Viet Minh could not get artillery over the mountains and so would have to fire from reverse slopes at considerable distances. They also thought that French air strikes would destroy any artillery emplacements the Viet Minh could establish. Navarre concluded that Giap would not attack, and therefore pressed on in spite of the opposition.[306] Three days later on the morning of 20 November 1953, 65 twin-engine Dakota (DC-3/C-47) transport aircraft loaded with six battalions of paratroopers flew out of Hanoi.[307]

The initial landings of the 1st, 2nd and 6th Colonial battalions at Dien Bien Phu met with very little resistance and the first 5000 men to land began to dig in. The next day large twin-engined Fairchild C-119 Flying Boxcars dropped in bulldozers followed by other heavy equipment. The remaining garrison, eventually numbering 13,500 men including four battalions of the Foreign Legion, the 3rd Battalion of Moroccan Tirailleurs, the 2nd Battalion Vietnamese Infantry and the 3rd battalion Thai Infantry,

[304] Bruce A. Watson, op. cit., p. 149.
[305] Bruce A. Watson, op. cit., p. 149.
[306] Bruce A. Watson, op. cit., p. 150.
[307] Bernard B. Fall, *Hell in a Very Small Place, The Siege of Dien Bien Phu*, J.B. Lippincott Company, Philadelphia, New York, 1967, p. 1-3.

together with 10 M-24 Chaffee tanks, four 155 mm guns and 24 105-mm for artillery support, were then airlifted to the site.[308]

Air support was provided in the form of reconnaissance aircraft, four engine Privateer bombers, five Curtis SB2C Helldiver dive-bombers, DouglasB-26 Invader attack-bombers, Grumman F8F Bearcat, and Vought F4U Corsair fighter-bombers, four Douglas C-47 Dakota transports and a Sikorsky S-51 Dragonfly helicopter for casualty evacuation. The men on the ground found themselves in a valley about 12 miles long and between four and five miles wide with a winding river running along the valley floor. The hills varied in elevation from 700' to 1,400' and were covered with dense jungle. Dien Bien Phu was the largest settlement in the valley, with 112 houses.

General Giap was confident that even if the French persisted with their buildup at Dien Bien Phu, they would be overcome. He did not underestimate his enemy, and therefore brought all available force to bear before putting in his attack. On 29 November, another cavalry officer named Colonel Christian de Castries was placed in command of the Dien Bien Phu garrison. More stores and provisions were dropped onto the site, as General Giap's soldiers moved into position, well prepared for the coming battle. The Viet Minh worked indefatigably, bringing forward guns, ammunition, provisions and supplies of every description, building up a vast reserve. Supplies also continued to arrive for the French. The French Airforce had promised a daily delivery of 100 tons and fire support for the ground troops.

Within the town were the command post, the main hospital, and mortar emplacements. Ringing this center, an all-around defense perimeter was established with protective strongpoints including bunkers, dugouts, trenches, machine gun and mortar emplacements, each surrounded by barbed wire and minefields. These strongpoints were codenamed, on the west side, Claudine, Francoise, and Huguette and, on the east side, Elaine, and Dominique. The airfield angled northwest from the center. Strongpoint Anne-Marie, almost a mile from the center protected the field's wet flank, and strongpoint Beatrice, quite isolated and about another mile from the center, covered the field's east flank. Gabrielle, like a cork in a bottle, was over two miles north of the center. Isabelle was located about two miles south of the center. Numbers, such as Dominique 1, 2, and 3, and Claudine 1 identified the various peaks and the high ground within each strongpoint through 5.[309]

The French had twenty-four 105 mm guns and 16 heavy mortars, none of which were dug in. The entire complex was constructed with dirt and logs and there were no concrete bunkers. When General Navarre flew into the entrenched camp during the Christmas period, he found the situation alarming. He was well aware that the fate of the garrison depended entirely on ground-air cooperation. This could only work if Dien Bien Phu had a fully serviceable landing strip and there were no enemy anti-aircraft batteries.

By 5 December, four Viet Minh divisions were marching toward Dien Bien Phu, and by 31 December the position was surrounded. Giap kept adding men and equipment, eventually assembling 27 infantry battalions supported by twenty 105-mm guns, eighteen 75-mm guns, eighty 37-mm guns, one hundred 12.7-mm anti-aircraft machine guns and mortars varying in size up to 120-mm. All of it was brought in at night, and the French Airforce observed none of this. Giap prepared to do battle at Dien Bien Phu knowing he would be bringing some 70,000 Viet Minh troops including the 304th, 308th, 312th and 316th Infantry Divisions and the 351st Artillery Division as well as a regiment of engineers, against a French force of 15,000 men. In the end the battle would result in the combined deaths of over 10,000 of them.[310]

---

[308] Philip de Ste Croix, op. cit., p. 176.
[309] Bruce A. Watson, op. cit., p. 150.
[310] Bernard B. Fall, op. cit., p. 52-53.

As Navarre became aware of the seriousness of the situation, he decided to prepare an evacuation plan. His second in command, General Cogny disagreed and argued that the 13,500 men on site should stay put. Although Dien Bien Phu was surrounded, Navarre's greatest disadvantage was that he still underrated the enemy, believing that a Viet Minh victory over the French was inconceivable.

Vietminh soldiers in trenches at Dien Bien Phu, 1954.

Viet Minh artillery began shelling the airfield from the north-east. On 12 and 13 March, the enemy registered hits on four French aircraft. Next, all the strongpoints around the perimeter were attacked, and one of them, Beatrice, was captured and occupied with a 75% loss of men of the 13th Demi-Brigade of the Foreign Legion. The Viet Minh had dug approach trenches by night, cut the perimeter wire, and cleared paths through the minefields. Bangalore torpedoes were shoved under the remaining wire and exploded as the infantry rose to the attack. The assaults were launched from 200 yards, and one by one the French emplacements were overwhelmed.

On the 14 March, the 5th Vietnamese Parachute Battalion was dropped in to reinforce the garrison. At the same time the Viet Minh began an assault on strongpoint Gabrielle. The French fired some 6,000 rounds of 105 mm ammunition to stop the attacks, to no avail. Gabrielle fell to an attack by 8 Viet Minh battalions, in spite of a French counterattack supported by six tanks without artillery cover. Only 150 men escaped. The French gunner, Colonel Piroth committed suicide, distraught over the failure of his gunners to locate the

Viet Minh artillery emplacements, and for having left his own guns unprotected. Strongpoint Dominique was surrounded by 15 March, followed by Huguette and Claudine within four days. The Thai's abandoned Anne Marie on the 16th. In spite of the losses, reinforcements continued to be dropped in between 16 and 27 March, including 400 volunteers making their first jump. Parachute drops were only mildly successful, because anti-aircraft fire pushed drops up to 6000', causing many loads to land in the Viet Minh lines.

Two days later, all the strongpoints were either in enemy hands or in a state of siege and Giap's troops were in the process of tightening their stranglehold on the garrison.

The principal Viet Minh offensive came on 30 March. After exploding a mine beneath Elaine and firing a heavy preliminary bombardment, men of the 312th and 316th Divisions assaulted the five hills that made up the positions of Dominique and Eliane.[311] By 12 April, the dead numbered in the thousands, and Dien Bien Phu had become a charnel house. The combatants were often less than 30 yards apart. Navarre and Cogny blamed each other for the catastrophe. At this point, only outside intervention could have saved the situation. Unfortunately, this did not materialize before the conditions at Dien Bien Phu had deteriorated beyond salvage.

By the 14th the site was in a shambles, and towards the end of the month the Viet Minh captured the whole of the airstrip. This disaster was followed by days of heavy rain, which reduced the basin area to a sea of mud. Although the garrison could not hope to resist much longer, reinforcements in the form of the 1st Battalion Colonial Paratroops flew in at night and made a successful landing, heartening the defenders, even though the end was obviously in sight.

By 23 April, most of strongpoint Huguette had been lost to the Viet Minh. The airfield was overrun on the 25th, and on 4 May, Huguette, Dominique, Claudine, and Elaine collapsed. A plan was prepared to form three columns to smash through the ring of attackers at different points, each group to follow its own track. As this would have proved to be suicidal, the plan was abandoned.

During the next few days, the strongpoints outside the perimeter changed hands several times, with the Viet Minh attacking in waves with shock troops. The battlefield became one vast killing-ground. At midnight on the 6/7 May, five Dakotas attempted to drop reinforcements, but were forced to turn back to Hanoi without completing the operation, because they couldn't risk dropping into the battle with the light from flares exposing them to ground fire. The defenders on the ground had to choose between keeping the battlefield illuminated to give maximum effectiveness to the machine guns and recoilless rifles laying down final protective fires and accepting the risk of running out of defenders later. For immediate survival, the illuminating "fireflies" had to be given priority.[312]

As the battle continued, the Viet Minh set off a huge mine under strongpoint Elaine and followed up the blast with a heavy assault. The few French survivors continued to inflict terrible casualties on the attackers, but by morning they had been overwhelmed.

When 7 May dawned over the valley of Dien Bien Phu a heavy French air attack was launched, but it was too late to do much to relieve the beleaguered defenders, as the Viet Minh forces swarmed across the plain towards the severely reduced garrison. De Castries contacted Cogny and told him that Dien Bien Phu was finished. He requested permission for the main force to withdraw to the south, while he and a handful of men would stay behind and keep firing to cover the retreat. Aerial photographs dropped by a French Navy Vought F4U Corsair fighter flying low over the camp however, revealed that all avenues for possible escape were now too heavily defended by the Viet Minh to attempt a breakout and that it was now too late to escape.[313]

---

[311]   Philip de Ste Croix, op. cit., p. 177.
[312]   Bernard B. Fall, op. cit., pp. 381-382.
[313]   Bernard B. Fall, op. cit., p. 399.

As the garrison was hammered into submission, stores, arms, ammunition, vehicles, and everything of value was destroyed. De Castries had just been promoted to brigadier general, as he surrendered the defenders of Dien Bien Phu. When the Viet Minh took over on 7 May, he was taken away for interrogation and ten thousand Frenchmen were herded together to be marched off to the prisoner-of-war camps in Tonkin. Only 3000 men survived from the total of 16,544. Over 3000 died in the battle, and a further 10,000 in the march to the prison camps and the period of re-education in the camps. The Viet Minh lost 8000 dead and 15,000 wounded.[314]

The results of the decision to mount operation Castor cause it to be ranked as one of the greatest strategic blunders in history. The loss of Dien Bien Phu however, can be blamed on the combination of flagrant errors of judgment, the enemy's will to win, and in no small part, France's indifference and complacency.[315]

Although the United States was later to win every major battle that it fought in Viet Nam, including the siege at Khe Sanh, it too would find the enemy's will to win insurmountable. The Americans would lose the next war against the same Vietnamese forces that defeated General Navarre, for many of the same reasons.

CANADIAN AIRBORNE REGIMENT TRAINING OPERATION, 1988

(RCAF Photo)
RCAF Lockheed CC-130 Hercules dropping Canadian paratroopers, ca 1966.

---

314   Philip de Ste Croix, op. cit., p. 177.
315   Charles Connell, op. cit., pp. 257-264.

A typical airborne operation begins with the Commander's O-group. The Hercules aircrews, the Company/Commando Commanders and all support staffs are briefed on where, when, and how the operation will take place. The objectives are defined, the drop points selected for the first group of pathfinders who will go in to mark the drop zone and a plan presented on how it will be defended etc. Men and equipment are "cross-loaded." The loading is planned and mounted to ensure that not all the personnel from any one unit are placed on the same aircraft. This is to ensure that if an aircraft breaks down or crashes, there will be enough troops spread out among the other aircraft to enable the survivors to continue the mission. For example, the mortar platoon is split into two fighting elements; the tube-launched, optically-tracked wire-guided anti-tank (TOW) platoon is split in two fighting teams; even the Intelligence platoon with four people went on three different aircraft; the regiment's commander is on one aircraft and his deputy (the DCO) is on another etc.[316]

As members of the Headquarters and Signals Squadron Intelligence platoon, we built terrain models and assembled maps and briefings to cover the objectives. In preparation, the Company Commanders would gather their Commandos (about 250 to a Company, about 650 to a Battalion, close to 2000 for a Regiment) together for a collective briefing on the operation to come. Each unit Commander would brief his individual Commando/Company with all 250 men seated in front of the terrain model.

Every man is required to know every detail of the plan, because if some of them don't make it to the drop-zone or the objective, others will have to fill in the gaps or carry out alternate plans. Some will have the task of covering the drop zone with heavy weapons, some will be designated to take out guard towers, sentries, control, and access points, while others cover the entrances and exit or extraction points. Some will destroy buildings, aircraft, fuel and supply dumps and power sources, others may be designated to take prisoners, release hostages, carry out medical evacuations (Medevac) etc. If it is to be a combat extraction, the operation on the ground will last no more than two hours. Every man participating in the briefing is expected to understand the plan, and if only a few get through, the plan still goes ahead.

For a night drop, the Battalion turns up at the "nose dock" (a hangar big enough for the entire front end of a Hercules except for the tail), early in the evening, with their small-arms (rifles, Karl Gustav and M-72 anti-tank weapons etc.), rucksacks and equipment ready to go. The order to get dressed is given, and the buddy system is applied as each paratrooper dons his parachutes and mounts his rucksack and any special equipment he may have to carry (extra mortar rounds, fuel, water, extra ammunition, radios and so on). Each jumper is then checked by a rigger, who examines the paratrooper's main and reserve parachutes, rigs his static-line and after his inspection is complete, declares him ready to go (usually with a solid slap on the butt of the jumper's parachute harness and container). When all are dressed, the senior jumpmaster (JM) or his deputy will then order, "Listen up for the JM briefing." He will then brief the sticks of men who have been prepared for their specific "chalk" load on the jump procedures appropriate to the type of aircraft they are using, such as the Hercules or Buffalo transports or Griffon helicopters, and one where, when and how the drop will take place, at what altitude, the likely wind conditions and potential hazards they may encounter on the drop zone, and a reminder of emergency procedures in the event of a hang-up (being towed behind the aircraft if the static-line doesn't separate etc.) The JM will then complete his orders by stating, "You have now been manifested and will jump in accordance with these orders and instructions," at which point all will shout "HuaaH!" in response.

---

[316] The Author earned his military jump wings in 1975 at CFB Edmonton, Alberta, and later served as a member of the Canadian Forces Parachute Team (CFPT), the Sky Hawks from 1977 to 1979. From 1986 to 1989 he served as the Regimental Intelligence Officer for the Canadian Airborne Regiment (CAR) within the First Special Service Force (FSSF) based at CFB Petawawa, Ontario, when the training exercise described here took place. He also jumped with the German, French and British forces. He continued to serve as an active military parachutist until his retirement at CFB Gagetown, New Brunswick, in August 2011. The CAR motto is "Ex Coelis" (from the skies).

For a 12-plane drop, we have used fourteen Lockheed C-130 Hercules aircraft standing by with the props churning (two are back-up aircraft in case any break down or otherwise become unserviceable). The order to embark is given, and you may imagine the picture of long lines of double rows of men marching out across the tarmac runway to board twelve separate aircraft. (Actually, waddling would be a better description than marching, as they are heavily weighed down with parachute equipment and their rucksacks mounted in front). The Pathfinder reconnaissance team will have flown out earlier, as they will be jumping in freefall from a higher altitude (about 10,000' to 12,000'), and their rucksacks are mounted behind them. Their primary job is to mark the drop zone and to secure it with their weapons.

Once onboard the aircraft, all put their seatbelts on, white lights are extinguished, and the interior aircraft red lights are turned on to preserve night vision. The aircraft all taxi out in a long convoy-like line and take off in "trail" formation. To prevent one long line of continuous targets presenting itself over the drop zone, the entire flight of Hercules transports is split into four separate flights of three, which will approach the drop zone from different directions each flying in a finger-three formation.

Each separate flight of Hercules will proceed to fly cross-country at a very low level until just before the run-in for the drop, and then ramp-up to the pre-determined jump altitude (1000 feet to 1,200 feet in training, 650 feet to 700 feet over hostile terrain).

About ten minutes before the drop takes the jumpmaster (JM) on board each separate aircraft will issue the first of a sequence of commands, beginning with the attention-getting words, "Look this way!" Each paratrooper is anticipating this command and is particularly "focused" at this point, and on all succeeding commands given by the JM, which are shouted back, word for word, to ensure no one has missed hearing them. The next command shouted out by the JM is, "Seat belts off!" Every paratrooper reacts and complies in a coordinated and concerted action, and when ready, turns in his seat to face the JM again.

The next command is, "Stand Up!" at which point each jumper stands up and then removes his static line snap from where it had been stowed by the Rigger in an elastic band on his reserve takes one step towards the heavy steel static line cable strung overhead and holds the snap up to the cable and prepares to hook on. On the command, "Hook Up!" – the jumper snaps his static line onto the overhead cable which runs the length of the aircraft's interior, and slides it to the rear for the person behind him to double check, at which point the JM shouts "Check Static Line!" Each jumper examines the snap and static line of the person in front of him to see that it is secure, then he traces a path with his hand down the yellow nylon cord to the back of the parachute on the man in front and tightens up the slack in the elastic bands holding the remaining static line stows in place. The second last and last men in the line make a half turn so they can check each other.

The next command is, "Check your equipment!" This is when a jumper takes the opportunity to move his testicles and other private parts out from underneath the leg straps and double checks every snap and strap from helmet to equipment that he is wearing. The JM then double checks the snaps and kit of every single man in the line, then returns to his position near the exit door and shouts, "Sound off for equipment check!" Starting with the last man, each man shouts out in succession, "1 OK, 2 OK" and so on, with the last man standing closest to the exit door pointing to the JM and shouting, "All OK," when all have sounded off. About this time the red warning light over the jump door comes on. The JM and his deputy slide the doors up on each side of the Hercules, and stamp on the jump steps to ensure they are secure for "double-door exit." In some cases, the rear ramp may be lowered instead.

By now the three Hercules in each formation are in the process of moving from a line astern or "trail" formation into the finger-three formation. It is a spectacular sight if you are number one on the ramp of the lead Hercules watching the other two aircraft lined up behind you as they slide over to the left and right wings parallel with your aircraft.

The JM shouts, "Stand By!" and all jumpers step forward, sliding their static lines with them. When the green light flashes on, the JM shouts, "GO!" At this moment each and every paratrooper immediately steps forward in a one-two movement (known as the mambo step), and as he reaches the door or the end of the ramp, he throws his static line forward, stamps down hard on the jump step to get a good "launch," and exits smartly out the door, head down, feet together, hands on each side of his reserve, ready for the worst, hoping for the best, sounding out the count, "1,000, 2,000, 3,000, 4,000, 5,000, check canopy!"

The heat and the prop wash from four churning propellers hits the jumper just as he drops below the aircraft and the big round green T-10 parachute seems to explode off his back (many times harder than the gentle openings one experiences from a helicopter jump). The tightened harness straps keep him from being squeezed the wrong way, and after his count he will immediately look up to check for a properly open canopy. It is extremely rare that it does not open properly, primarily due to the Canadian invention of netting that runs around the skirt of the canopy which prevents partial malfunctions. The jumper then quickly grabs his rear risers and begins looking sharply around him all directions to watch for other jumpers and to avoid a canopy collision. If necessary, he will slip in the opposite direction by pulling down on the pair of suspension risers in the direction he needs to steer. If it is as dark as the inside of a monkey's nether end, he will look, listen, and feel for the wind on his face to get an idea of which way it is taking him. If it is a moonlit night, he will watch for the wind blowing along the grass or snow which looks like waves of fur fluttering along the back of a woolly bear, to get an idea of where to land and what obstacles to avoid.

About 300 above the ground, each jumper lowers his rucksack by pulling a special release tab, which lets it drop to hang about 15 feet below him. It will swing somewhat, but if it is really dark, he will feel it thump first and have some warning of when he needs to prepare to make contact with the ground. He keeps his feet and knees together and his elbows in tight as he prepares to hit and roll, arcing his body in the direction he is swinging and hopefully not landing too hard or on anything sharp.

Once the jumper has completed his "parachute landing fall" (PLF) on the ground he has to quickly deflate his chute to keep from being dragged by pulling on of the risers towards himself, then quickly undo his reserve, punch his quick release system to get out of the harness, and very quickly extricate his weapon. If it is his rifle, he may have to remove it from his snowshoes, and if it is a Sterling Sub-machinegun (SMG), from under his reserve. To reduce his outline as a potential target, the paratrooper keeps low to the ground as he gathers the chute and stuffs it into the built-in bag it comes with, then dons his rucksack and he prepares to move off the Drop Zone to meet the rest of his section at a pre-determined rendezvous (RV) point. At all times he must keep a watchful eye out for other jumpers and their equipment as they descend above him from the following waves so they don't land on him, particularly if they are dropping a platform with one of the Regiment's Airborne Artillery Battery guns, or an M113 A & R Lynx armoured reconnaissance vehicles, M113 armoured personnel carriers (APC), or a tube-launched optically-tracked anti-tank missile system (TOW) mounted on a jeep, or ambulance etc.

Each Commando team is watching for the pathfinder's markers. A soldier may have to wave a small blue, green, or red light on a pole for a few seconds every few minutes to guide each group into their RV point if it is really dark. If there is moonlight, the jumper can use his compass to get to an observable RV. As soon the majority of each assault team is in place, they move on to the objective. Time is of the essence, and it is very hard to recover when it has been lost. In a hostage-freeing scenario, the terrorists are hit according to the plan. Sometimes changes have to be made on the spot, and paratroopers have a ready instinct for an alternate but workable plan when necessary. In this exercise, the enemy force was taken out or neutralized, the hostages were freed and collected along with the wounded, and all injured were brought to a pre-planned collection point.

If it is a long-range operation, the paratroopers walk out. If it is a combat extraction operation, all assemble at pre-determined points on a designated runway. Each aircraft will roar into land, and taxi to the end of the runway lowering its ramp as it reaches the turn-around point to prepare for take-off. In the few seconds, the non-stop turn around takes place, each stick will re-board an incoming aircraft. When the Hercules has turned 180° and is facing the opposite end of the runway, the ramp is raised whether all are on board or not, and the aircraft takes off.

Each empty aircraft will take a turn coming in until all on the ground have been collected. It gets trickier loading the wounded with all due care and assistance, and no dead are left behind, so the body bags must be carried on board as well as the extra people including hostages and prisoners. On this exercise, which took place at CFB Borden, Ontario, more than 200 additional people were flown back, while a number on the ground made their way to vehicles hidden off-site. In spite of the hasty activity, no one wants to be left behind to hike 25 kilometres north to an alternate ground collection point, and in this last mission, everyone and everything except those role-playing the enemy force was onboard the tenth aircraft to land, leaving the last two pilots severely annoyed because they still had to practice their rapid extraction skills minus live bodies on the ground to load.

While airborne on the flight back, medics were very busy working to plant IV s, treat the wounded and manage triage. Everyone helped. Within an hour or two, all were back on the ramp at CFB Petawawa, and very shortly afterwards slid into a debriefing room to go over what has been collected and what took place during the operation. We will have gotten in, done the job, and gotten out, as close to schedule and plan as possible. We will also have proven once again; the Airborne gets the job done.

Ex Coelis!

TAIWAN STRAIT CRISIS, 1958

Also known as the Second Taiwan Strait Crisis, the 1958 Taiwan Strait Crisis, was a conflict that took place between the People's Republic of China (PRC) and the Republic of China (ROC). In this conflict, the PRC shelled the islands of Kinmen and the Matsu Islands along the east coast of mainland China in the Taiwan Strait, to "liberate" Taiwan from the Chinese Nationalist Party, also known as the Kuomintang (KMT); and to probe the extent of the America's defence of Taiwan's territory. A naval battle also took place around Dongding Island when the ROC Navy repelled an attempted amphibious landing by the PRC Navy.

In the 1930s, a civil war took place in China, that lasted until the Japanese invaded in 1937. The warring factions agreed to a truce to fight their common foe, but following the Japanese surrender in September 1945, the two sides (one led by Chairman Mao Tse-tung, the other by Chiang Kai-shek), went back to their civil war. The USA's General Marshall attempted to mediate but could not get the hardliners on either side to come to a resolution. Massive battles took place in 1948 and 1949 with Mao's Communists driving Chiang's Nationalists off the mainland and to the island of Formosa.

Most of the major nations of the world recognized communist China, but the US continued to recognized Chiang as the legitimate leader. Mao began to talk about invading and conquering Taiwan in 1954. The US signed a mutual defence treaty with the Nationalists on 2 Dec 1954. Shortly afterwards, the Communists launched their first offensive on 18 January 1955, on islands north of what is now named Taiwan, killing 720 men. Chiang responded by launching raids against communist ports.

The US Congress authorized the president to employ US manpower and weapons to defend Taiwan and its islands. It then made open threats to use nuclear weapons against China's major cities. On 23 April, the Communists announced they were willing to negotiate, and their assaults on the Nationalists ceased. On 23 August 1958, the Communists began the attacks on Nationalist forces again, with aim of "liberating" Taiwan.

The Soviets, led by Premier Nikita Khruschev, initially declined to back Chairman Mao, but in the end, Khruschev wrote to President Eisenhower to warn him that an American attack on China would be considered an attack on the Soviet Union. Eisenhower responded by sending the US Seventh Fleet to the Straits of Taiwan. Nationalist fighter jets equipped with American experimental air-to-air missles knocked down considerable numbers of Chinese MiG fighters. The US Joint Chiefs of Staff began planning nuclear strikes against China's mainland cities, including Shanghai and Canton. Beijing leadership took a step back, and on 6 September 1958, Chinese Premier Chou-en-Lai proposed peace talks.[317]

The two Presidents issued a Joint Communique reaffirming solidarity, stating that, according to the 1954 Sino-American Mutual Defense Treaty, Kinmen and Matsu islands were closely related to the defense of Taiwan, and condemning the Communist China's artillery bombardment against Kinmen. Chiang was the Supreme Commander of Allied forces in the China war zone while Eisenhower was the Supreme Allied Commander Europe. Chiang met President Franklin D. Roosevelt and British Prime Minister Winston Churchill at the Cairo Conference in 1943 while Eisenhower also attended the meeting.

BATTLE OF KHE SANH, 1968

The Battle of Khe Sanh (21 January - 9 July 1968) was conducted in the Khe Sanh area of northwestern Quảng Trị Province in the Republic of Vietnam (South Vietnam), during the Vietnam War. The main US forces defending Khe Sanh Combat Base (KSCB) were two regiments of the United States Marine Corps (USMC) supported by elements from the US Army and (USAF), as well as a small number of Army of the Republic of Vietnam (ARVN) troops. These were pitted against two to three divisional-sized elements of the North Vietnamese People's Army of Vietnam (PAVN).

The US command in Saigon initially believed that combat operations around KSCB during 1967 were part of a series of minor PAVN offensives in the border regions. That appraisal was later altered when the PAVN was found to be moving major forces into the area. In response, US forces were built up before the PAVN isolated the Marine base. Once the base came under siege, a series of actions was fought over a period of five months. During this time, KSCB and the hilltop outposts around it were subjected to constant PAVN artillery, mortar, and rocket attacks, and several infantry assaults. To support the Marine base, a massive aerial bombardment campaign (Operation Niagara) was launched by the USAF. Over 100,000 tons of bombs were dropped by US aircraft and over 158,000 artillery rounds were fired in defense of the base. Throughout the campaign, US forces used the latest technology to locate PAVN forces for targeting. Additionally, the logistical effort required to support the base once it was isolated demanded the implementation of other tactical innovations to keep the Marines supplied.

In March 1968, an overland relief expedition (Operation Pegasus) was launched by a combined Marine–Army/ARVN task force that eventually broke through to the Marines at Khe Sanh. American commanders considered the defense of Khe Sanh a success, but shortly after the siege was lifted, the decision was made to dismantle the base rather than risk similar battles in the future. On 19 June 1968, the evacuation and destruction of KSCB began. Amid heavy shelling, the Marines attempted to salvage what they could before destroying what remained as they were evacuated. Minor attacks continued

---

[317] Walter Lefeber, *The American Age* (New York, Norton, 1989)

before the base was officially closed on 5 July. Marines remained around Hill 689, though, and fighting in the vicinity continued until 11 July until they were finally withdrawn, bringing the battle to a close.[318]

In the aftermath, the North Vietnamese proclaimed a victory at Khe Sanh, while US forces claimed that they had withdrawn, as the base was no longer required. Historians have observed that the Battle of Khe Sanh may have distracted American and South Vietnamese attention from the buildup of Viet Cong (VC) forces in the south before the early 1968 Tet Offensive. Nevertheless, the US commander during the battle, General William Westmoreland, maintained that the true intention of Tet was to distract forces from Khe Sanh.[319]

(United States Army Heritage and Education Center Photo)
2nd Battalion, 173rd Airborne Brigade, destroying enemy bunkers after assault on Hill 875,
near Dak To, Vietnam, 1967.

SIEGE OF BEIRUT, 1982

The Siege of Beirut took place in summer 1982, as part of the 1982 Lebanon War, which resulted from the breakdown of the ceasefire effected by the United Nations. The siege ended with the Palestinian Liberation Organization being forced out of Beirut and the rest of Lebanon.[320]

---

[318] Michael Maclear, *The Ten Thousand Day War* (New York, St. Martin's, 1981)
[319] Phillip Davidson, *Vietnam at War* (New York, Oxford University Press, 1991)
[320] Rashid Khalidi, Under Siege, PLO Decision-making During the 1982 War (New York, Columbia University Press, 1986)

SIEGE OF BASRA, 1987

The Siege of Basra, code-named Operation Karbala-5, or The Great Harvest, was an offensive operation carried out by Iran in an attempt to capture the Iraqi port city of Basra in early 1987. This battle, known for its extensive casualties and ferocious conditions, was the biggest battle of the war and proved to be the beginning of the end of the Iran-Iraq War. The Iranians failed to reach their objective.

Operation Karbala-5 began midnight 8 January 1987, when a strike force of 35,000 Revolutionary Guards infantrymen crossed Fish Lake, while four Iranian divisions attacked at the southern shore of the lake, overrunning the Iraqi forces, and capturing Duaiji, an irrigation canal. They used their bridgehead at Duaiji as a springboard to recapture the Iranian town of Shalamcheh. Between 9-10 January, the Iranians broke through the first and second defense lines of Basra south of the Fish Lake with tanks. The Iranians rapidly reinforced their forces with 60,000 troops and began to clear the remaining Iraqis in the area.

As early as 9 January, the Iraqis began a counterattack, supported by newer Sukhois Su-25 Frogfoot and MiG-29 Fulcrum aircraft and by 10 January the Iraqis were throwing every available heavy weapon in a bid to eject the Iranians. Despite being outnumbered 10-1 in the air, Iran's air defenses downed many Iraqi aircraft (45 jets in total), allowing Iran to provide close air support with their smaller air force, which also proved superior in dogfighting, causing the Iraqis to temporarily stop providing their troops air support. Iraqi tanks floundered in the marshland and were defeated by Cobra helicopters and TOW missile-equipped anti-tank commandos. Later in the battle, after their ground forces took heavy losses due to the lack of air support, the Iraqi aircraft came back to the battlefield once again, facing their Iranian counterparts.

Despite superior Iranian infantry tactics, it was the depth of the Iraqi defences that prevented the Iranians from achieving a victory. On 19-24 January, Iran launched another infantry offensive, breaking the third line and driving the Iraqis across the Jasim river. The battle became a contest of which side could bring more reinforcements. By 29 January, the Iranians launched a new attack from the west of the Jasim river, breaking through the fourth line. They were within 12 km (7.5 mi) of the city. At this point, the battle became a stalemate. Iranian television broadcast footage of the outskirts of Basra but the Iranians pushed no further. Iranian losses were so severe that Iraq took the offensive and pushed them back, containing the Iranians to the Shalamjah area. The fighting continued while 30,000 Iranians continued to hold positions around Fish Lake. The battle bogged down into a trench war, where neither side could displace the other. Iran attacked several more times but without success. Karbala-5 officially ended by the end of February, but the fighting and siege of Basra continued.

Among those killed was Iranian commander Hossein Kharrazi. Roughly 65,000 Iranians and 20,000 Iraqis became casualties because of Operation Karbala-5. Basra was largely destroyed, and Iraq's army had taken many material losses. The fighting during this operation was the heaviest and bloodiest during the war, with the area around Shalamcheh becoming known as the "Somme of the Iran-Iraq War". At one point, the situation had deteriorated to the point that Saddam ordered several of his officers to be executed. With Iranian aircraft concentrated at Basra, the Iraqis bombed Iranian supply routes with chemical weapons, as well as Iranian cities with conventional bombs, including Tehran, Isfahan, and Qom. It is believed that around 3,000 Iranian civilians were killed in these attacks. Iran retaliated by firing eleven long-range SCUD missiles at Iraqi cities, inflicting heavy casualties among civilians, and killing at least 300.[321]

---

[321] William Yengst, *The Iran-Iraq War: The Siege of Basra*, (Command No. 28, May-June 1996)

SIEGE OF SARAJEVO, 1992 - 1996

The Siege of Sarajevo was carried out on the capital of Bosnia and Herzegovina in what is recorded to be the longest siege of a capital city in the history of modern warfare. After being initially besieged by the forces of the Yugoslav People's Army, Sarajevo was besieged by the Army of Republika Srpska from 5 April 1992 to 29 February 1996 (1,425 days) during the Bosnia War.

When Bosnia and Herzegovina declared independence from Yugoslavia after the 1992 Bosnian independence referendum, the Bosnian Serbs, whose strategic goal was to create a new Bosnian Serb state of Republika Srpska (RS) that would include Bosniak-majority areas, encircled Sarajevo with a siege force of 13,000 troops positioned in the surrounding hills. From there they assaulted the city with artillery, tanks, and small arms fire. From 2 May 1992, the Serbs blockaded the city. The Bosnian government defence forces (ARBiH) established inside the besieged city, consisted of approximately 70,000 troops. They were poorly equipped and unable to break the siege.

A total of 13,952 people died in the city during the siege, including 5,434 civilians. The ARBiH suffered 6,137 fatalities, while Bosnian Serb military casualties numbered 2,241 soldiers killed. After the war, the International Criminal Tribunal for the former Yugoslavia (ICTY) convicted four Serb officials for numerous counts of crimes against humanity committed during the siege, including terrorism.[322]

Twin apartment buildings burning in the centre of Sarajevo
after being hit by Serbian gunfire during the siege in 1992.

---

[322] Connelly, Charlie. *The new siege of Sarajevo*, (The Times, UK, 8 October 2005)

BATTLE OF GROZNY, 1994-1995

The First Battle of Grozny was the Russian Army's invasion and subsequent conquest of the Chechen capital, Grozny, during the early months of the First Chechen War. The attack lasted from December 1994 to March 1995 and resulted in the military occupation of the city by the Russian Army and rallied most of the Chechen nation around the separatist government of Dzhokhar Dudayev.[323]

The initial assault resulted in very high Russian Army casualties and an almost complete breakdown of morale in the Russian forces. It took them another two months of heavy fighting, and a change in their tactics, before they were able to capture Grozny. The battle caused enormous destruction and casualties amongst the civilian population and saw the heaviest bombing campaign in Europe since the end of the Second World War. Chechen separatist forces recaptured the city in August 1996, ending the war.[324]

Russian tanks destroyed during the battles in Grozny in 1996. (i.redd.it Photo)

ALLIANCES

Underestimating one's opponent is not the newest self-defeating tactic in siege warfare, but as has been shown, it is certainly one that was often repeated. The complacency of people who think that they are safe behind their walls continues. There are many in North America today for example, there are those who believe that there is no further need for a large army, nor a requirement to be part of the NATO, NORAD and UN alliances. In effect, since the house hasn't burned down, canceling the insurance policy can save money. I believe it has been shown that a country's best fortress continues to be its maintenance of an effective and combat ready offensive force in concert with solid alliances. The threat of weapons

---

[323]   (John B. Dunlop, Russia Confronts Chechnya (New York: Cambridge University Press, 1998)

[324]   Carlotta Gall and Thomas de Waal, *Chechnya: Calamity In The Caucasus*, (New York University Press, 1998)

of mass destruction in the hands of nations such as Korea, Iraq, Iran, or any rogue state has been an impending problem since these weapons were first developed.[325]

Walls are no longer effective. The Berlin wall was erected between 2 August and 20 November 1961 during the Cold War to keep its citizens in, rather than to keep an enemy out. It fell not to a siege, but to a change in political reality in October 1989. The North American fortress, in the form of its present coalition of armed forces, is far from impregnable. We stand behind our past service records and hope that it will be the same in the future, without the upgrading and maintenance required to stay ahead of the pendulum. The next conflict any of us becomes embroiled in, be it counter-terrorism or conventional war, will be a "come as you are" affair, as there will be no time to expand or build on our existing "fortress."

The technological pendulum is swinging faster in each direction as opposing forces seek to out-think each before trying to out-fight each other. The length of time it takes for a strategic, tactical, or technological idea to become obsolete is now being measured in nanoseconds. The ultimate stage of the technological pendulum may be infinite. The SDI Star Wars program put into effect under President Reagan was a counter missile program designed to render the offensive missiles of the former Soviet Union completely ineffective. Sometime in the not so distant future, a potential adversary will develop a method to overcome such advanced technology. Even though it was never implemented, Star Wars ideas implied we could have an aerial defence that would create form of "Fortress North America." Sooner or later the system would have been rendered obsolete. The recognition and implementation of a better idea that improves on the last good idea is the next (and possibly only) best defense.

By the landmarks of history included in this volume, it has been shown that no fortress is impregnable. Aristotle noted that walls should always be kept in good order, and be made to satisfy both the claims of beauty and the needs of military utility.[326] It would not be safe then, to say that the walls presently employed to protect North America, are in good order. The morale effect of fortification is often forgotten, but it has a great influence on the development of defensive systems and the thinking behind their construction. We would do well to remember this and take steps to ensure our "walls" in the form of forward-looking solutions to sound defenses, are in good order.

---

[325] On 6 and 9 August 1945, Atomic bombs were dropped on Hiroshima and Nagasaki, Japan, following the first atomic bomb exploded at Alamagordo in the United States. A non-nuclear explosive charge is used to bombard fragments of fissile material which thus reach a critical mass and spark off a chain reaction in a fraction of a second. Other countries quickly followed with nuclear devices of their own: the USSR on 14 July 1949, Great Britain in 1952, France on 13 February 1960, China in 1964, India in 1974, Pakistan more recently and certainly Israel, South Africa and soon others. On 1 November 1952, the first thermonuclear H-bomb was exploded in the USA. The A-bomb uses the fission of heavy nuclei, while the H-bomb uses light nuclei. The USSR quickly followed with an H-bomb device of its own on 12 Aug 1953, Great Britain in 1957, China in 1967 and France in1968. The detonation of the first atomic bomb in modern times marked 1945 as year one of the atomic era.

[326] Anthony Kemp, op. cit., p. 14.

Epilogue

"Innovation within the armed forces will rest on experimentation with new approaches to warfare, strengthening joint operations, exploiting...intelligence advantages, and taking full advantage of science and technology...While maintaining near-term readiness and the ability to fight the war on terrorism (it is necessary to have) a wider range of military options to discourage aggression or any form of coercion against (our homeland), our allies, and our friends."[327]

---

[327] The White House, Washington, 20 September 2002, W01081-02: *The National Security Strategy of the United States of America*, p.22.

Afterword

"The gravest danger to freedom lies at the crossroads of radicalism and technology. When the spread of chemical and biological and nuclear weapons, along with ballistic missile technology – when that occurs, even weak states and small groups could attain a catastrophic power to strike great nations. Our enemies have declared this very intention and have been caught seeking these terrible weapons. They want the capability to blackmail us, or to harm us, or to harm out friends – and we will oppose them with all our power."

President George W. Bush
West Point, New York
1 June 2002

Conclusions

The examples of siegecraft in this book have been used to demonstrate that no matter how invincible a fortress was thought to have been, sooner or later a determined enemy will devise a way to overcome it. When technology is not available, ideas take their place. These have included deception, imaginative and effective use of time and resources, innovation, bold and courageous application of strategy, and on occasion, the seizing of an unexpected opportunity and making the most of it. It has been demonstrated that, more often than not, the overcoming of a so-called impregnable fortress was often due to good planning to ensure the defenses had out-thought, long before they had been outfought.

The implications for our own future, and in particular for that of North America must therefore be viewed against this background. The future plans for defense must viewed in the light of the fact that one day soon, we will more than likely find ourselves again under some form siege, as has been effectively demonstrated on 11 September 2001. The siege will not necessarily limit itself to terrorism, or war and its technological means, but could include such factors as attempts by a foe to dominate our ideas, purchasing power, natural resources and our economy- in short, our very way of life.

In the introduction to this paper a siege was described as an assault on an opposing force attempting to defend itself from behind a position of some strength. It has been observed in this book that whenever the pendulum of technology swings against the "status quo," the defenders of a fortification were usually compelled to surrender. Sieges often take time to produce results, but in this day and age North America has very little time to develop its protective insurance policy in terms of preparing for an adequate defense for siegecraft of the future. We must stay ahead of the pendulum, and not be out-thought long before we are out-fought, for, as it has been shown here, "no fortress is impregnable."

About the Author

Former Honorary Lieutenant-Colonel Harold A. Skaarup

Born in Woodstock, New Brunswick, Canada, in 1951, Harold (Hal) Skaarup was privileged to serve 40 years with the Canadian Forces. He initially enrolled with the 56 Field Squadron, Royal Canadian Engineers, based in St. John's, Newfoundland in Feb 1971 and served with several Reserve units before transferring to the Regular Force in 1982. He is an experienced parachutist and skydiver, having served with the Canadian Forces Parachute Team (CFPT), the Sky Hawks, based in Edmonton, Alberta from 1977-1979. His overseas service began with a Class C Reserve deployment as an Intelligence Officer at HQ Canadian Forces Europe, CFB Lahr, Germany, 1981-1983.

In July1983, he transferred to the Regular Force Intelligence Branch and attended the Basic Intelligence Officer Course (BIOC) at the Canadian Forces School of Intelligence and Security (CFSIS), CFB Borden, Ontario. On graduation, he was retained at CFSIS as an instructor, until he was posted to Ottawa in 1984 where he trained CF Attachés and worked as Intelligence Analyst. His parachute experience caught up with him again when he was called to serve with the Canadian Airborne Regiment (CAR), at CFB Petawawa, Ontario from 1986 to 1989. He was immediately deployed to Cyprus, serving with the United Nations (UN) until Feb 1987. He graduated from the Canadian Forces Staff School (CFSS) in Toronto and the Canadian Land Forces Command and Staff College (CLFCSC) in Kingston, Ontario, and completed a number of military courses during his service. The courses provided unexpected golden opportunities, and in June 1989 he won the lottery, with a second posting to CFB Lahr, this time with the HQ and Signals Squadron, 4 Canadian Mechanized Brigade Group (4 CMBG), where he served as the Deputy Intelligence Officer.

Rotating back to Canada in 1992, he returned to CFSIS, where he served as an instructor, and on promotion to Major a year later, took charge of the Intelligence Training Company. In 1994, he was posted to the Tactics School at the Combat Training Centre (CTC), based at 5 Canadian Division Support Base (5 CDSB) Gagetown, New Brunswick, where he served as the Intelligence Directing Staff officer. In support of his interest in continuing education, and with the assistance of the CF education program, he graduated with a Master's degree in War Studies at the Royal Military College (RMC), Kingston, Ontario in May 1997. A month later, he deployed to Sarajevo, Bosnia-Herzegovina, where he served as the Commanding Officer of the Canadian National Intelligence Centre (CANIC) with the NATO-led Peace Stabilization Force (SFOR) until Dec 1997 .

On his return to Gagetown, the Army again sent him back to school, this time to attend the Land Forces Technical Staff Officer's Course at RMC in Kingston. There are always surprises when you have an extra check mark in one's military service tool box, and this course led to an immediate posting to North American Aerospace Defence (NORAD) HQ, at Cheyenne Mountain Air Force Station, Colorado Springs, Colorado, from 1999 to 2003. The 9/11 terrorist attacks on the World Trade Towers and the Pentagon took place in the middle of this tour – a most interesting time to be part of NORAD, to say the least.

Although posted to Land Forces Atlantic Area (LFAA) in Halifax, Nova Scotia, as the Area Intelligence Officer, the direct effect of 9/11 on the Major and his family, came in the form of a tasking to serve as the

Deputy Intelligence and Chief Assessments Officer, with the Kabul Multinational Brigade (KMNB), in Kabul, Afghanistan, from Jan to Aug 2004. He returned to Gagetown (now 5 Canadian Division Support Base Gagetown (5 CDSB)) in 2006, where he served as the Deputy Operations Officer and Commander's Intelligence Advisor.

Harold is married to Faye. Their son Jonathan and his wife Jocelyn have provided grandchildren Cole and Ashley and their son Sean and his wife Melyse have provided granddaughters Owen and Auli and grandson Bauer. Harold and Faye live in Fredericton, New Brunswick.

Harold is active as a member of the Friends of the New Brunswick Military History Museum at 5 Canadian Division Support Base Gagetown, providing guided tours to visitors and historical lectures on New Brunswick Military History. He is also a member of the Board of Directors for the Fredericton Region Museum. He is the author of several books including four volumes of "Out of Darkness - Light, a History of Canadian Military Intelligence", and continues to write with a focus on military history.

On 1 Feb 2015 Harold was appointed Honorary Lieutenant-Colonel for 3 Intelligence Company, Halifax, Nova Scotia, serving to 1 Feb 2018. He is immensely proud of this unit.

That's all!

Appendix A: The Crusades

1096-1099 First Crusade. This was essentially successful, and basically due to a backlash of Christendom against Islamic conquests in the Middle East. The Byzantines wanted Western assistance, and the Holy Roman Emperors needed some measure of unity. Knights and separate contingents of simple people were led by itinerant preachers such as Peter the Hermit. Many pogroms against the Jews took place during the course of this movement. The First Crusade reached Constantinople in 1097. A seven-month siege was mounted against Antioch in 1098, followed by the fall of Jerusalem on 15 July 1099, after a siege which had taken 40 days. The Kingdom of Jerusalem was then created and governed by Godfrey of Bouillon, Duke of Lower Lorraine, along with the Principality of Antioch and the Counties of Edessa and Tripoli. The 1st Crusade Battles of Nicaea, Dorylaeum I, and Tarsus were fought in 1097. The Battle of Antioch I was fought 1097-1098; the Battles of Jerusalem and Ashkelon I were fought in 1099.

Duke Godfrey of Bouillon was a tall red-bearded man and reputedly one of the hardest fighting knights of the Crusade. He captured Jerusalem in 1099, and eight days after the fall of the city he was elected the first Christian King of Jerusalem. He refused to take the title however, and instead chose to be named "the Defender and Baron of the Holy Sepulchre." He died of a fever a year and three days later and was buried in the Holy Sepulchure. During his short reign, he consolidated the new kingdom, and Outremer was founded for half a century. He was succeeded by Baldwin I on 18 July 1100.

Four Leaders of the First Crusade, engraving by François Guizot.

Four main crusader armies left Europe in August 1096, taking different routes to Constantinople. They gathered outside the city's walls of what is now Istanbul sometime between November 1096 and April 1097. Hugh I, Count of Vermandois arrived first, followed by Godfrey of Bouillon, Raymond IV, Count of Toulouse, and Bohemond I, Prince of Taranto.

The numbers estimated for the Crusader armies vary in the eyes of the historians. Some estimate there were 70,000 to 80,000 who left Western Europe between 1096 and 1111. Estimates for the number of Knights range from 7,000 to 10,000; 35,000 to 50,000 foot soldiers; and including non-combatants a total of 60,000 to 100,000.

Godfrey de Bouillon enters Jerusalem, engraving.

Duke Godfrey of Bouillon was a tall red-bearded man and reputedly one of the hardest fighting knights of the Crusade. He captured Jerusalem in 1099, and eight days after the fall of the city he was elected the first Christian King of Jerusalem. He refused to take the title however, and instead chose to be named "the Defender and Baron of the Holy Sepulchre." He died of a fever a year and three days later and was buried in the Holy Sepulchure. During his short reign, he consolidated the new kingdom, and Outremer was founded for half a century. He was succeeded by Baldwin I on 18 July 1100.

1147-1149 Second Crusade. The second major expedition to the "Holy Land" was prompted by the loss of Edessa to the Muslims and preached by St Bernard at Vezelay in 1146. Louis VII of France and the Emperor Conrad II took part. The Battle of Dorylaeum was fought 1147; the Battles of Edessa II and Damascus were fought in 1148.

On 4 July 1187, the **Battle of the Horns of Hattin** was fought near the shores of the Sea of Galilee. The armies of Jerusalem were defeated by Saladin and the true cross was captured by the Muslims. The cities and fortresses of the kingdom, denuded of their garrisons, could offer no serious resistance, and on 2 October 1187 the Holy City of Jerusalem was captured by Saladin. This action prompted the Third Crusade.

1189-1192 Third Crusade. This was a multi-national expedition which was mounted following the recapture of Jerusalem by Salah ed-Din Yusuf (Saladin) in 1187. Emperor Frederick Barbarossa took the cross, but while leading a major Germanic force, he drowned in Anatolia, Cilicia, on 10 June 1190. His forces melted away. Richard the Lionheart left England in 1190 and fought on the island of Cyprus until 8 June 1191. Philip Augustus, King of France left France in 1190 and arrived in the Holy Land 20 April 1191. Both took part in the Battle at Acre, from 1189-1191. Richard won a battle at Arsouf in 1191 but was not able to free Jerusalem. The Muslims capitulated on 12 July 1191 after a two-year siege. Leopold Duke of Austria sailed for Europe (after an altercation with Richard, for which he was later taken prisoner). Conrad of Montferrat (Italy) sulked in Tyre, and King Guy of Lusignan was installed as the Crusader ruler.

1202-1204 Fourth Crusade. This expedition was essentially an act of plunder on an ally, rather than an assault on the Holy Land. It was instigated by Pope Innocent III. The demands of the Venetians, who provided the Crusaders with sea transport, lead to the capture of the Byzantine town of Zara, then of Constantinople itself in 1204. A Latin empire replaced the Byzantine empire, and its capital was established at Nicaea. Frankish nobles carved out fiefs for themselves in Greece. The Crusaders launched an attack on the city of Constantinople on 7 April 1203. When the city walls were breached a year later (1204), the Byzantine Empire fell, and the establishment of a Latin Empire followed. Baldwin I was established as Emperor. Related Crusader Battles were fought at Adrianople in 1205; and at Philippoplis in 1208.

1208-1213 Albigensian Crusade. Crusade conducted in southern France against the Cathars. The Cistercian battles against Cathar heretics centered around Albi and Carcassonne. The Treaty of Paris ended the Crusade although the Cathar stronghold of Montsegur did not fall until March 1244.

Château de Montségur, France. In 1233 the site became "the seat and head" (*domicilium et caput*) of the Cathar church. It has been estimated that the fortified site housed about 500 people when in 1241, Raymond VII besieged Montségur without success. The murder of representatives of the inquisition by about fifty men from Montségur and faidits at Avignonet on 28 May 1242 was the trigger for the final military expedition to conquer the castle, the siege of Montségur,

In 1242 Hugues de Arcis led the military command of about 10,000 royal troops against the castle that was held by about 100 fighters and was home to 211 Perfects (who were pacifists and did not fight) and civilian refugees. The siege lasted nine months, until in March 1244, the castle finally surrendered. Approximately 220 Cathars were burned en masse in a bonfire at the foot of the pog when they refused to renounce their faith. Some 25 actually took the ultimate Cathar vow of consolamentum perfecti in the two weeks before the final surrender. Those who renounced the Cathar faith were allowed to leave and the castle itself was destroyed.

In the days prior to the fall of the fortress, several Cathars allegedly slipped through the besiegers' lines carrying away a mysterious "treasure" with them. While the nature and fate of this treasure has never been identified, there has been much speculation as to what it might have consisted of — from the treasury of the Cathar Church to esoteric books or even the actual Holy Grail. The siege itself was an epic event of heroism and zealotry, akin to that of Masada, with the demise of the Cathars symbolized by the fall of the mountain-top fortress (although isolated Cathar cells persisted into the 1320s in southern France and northern Italy)

The present fortress ruin at Montségur is not from the Cathar era. The original Cathar fortress of Montségur was entirely pulled down by the victorious royal forces after its capture in 1244. It was gradually rebuilt and upgraded over the next three centuries by royal forces. The current ruin so dramatically occupying the site, and featured in illustrations, is referred to by French archeologists as "Montsegur III" and is typical of post-medieval royal French defensive architecture of the 17th century. It is not "Montsegur II," the structure in which the Cathars lived and were besieged and of which few traces remain today.

1217-1221 Fifth Crusade. This was a failed expedition which was originated by Pope Innocent III. The crusaders took Cyprus, Acre and Egypt. Damietta in Egypt was taken between 1218 and 1221, but then lost. This expedition was preceded by the Children's Crusade, which in reality was composed of young people, the majority of whom died on the journey.

1228-1229 Sixth Crusade. This expedition was organized by Frederick II, even though he had been excommunicated at the time. He succeeded in capturing Jerusalem after negotiating a truce with the Sultan for the right to reoccupy the city, which was finally lost in 1244. The Crusade was relatively successful.

1248-1254 Seventh Crusade. Louis IX of France lead this expedition to Egypt. He succeeded in taking Damietta but was defeated and captured at Mansourah. After he was freed on payment of a ransom, he spent another four years in the Holy Land.

1270 Eighth Crusade. This expedition was led to Tunisia by Louis X of France, who died outside the city of Tunis. This is also the time of the earliest record of a sea chart, which was shown to Louis IX, King of France.

Appendix B: American Forts

The numerous forts constructed in the New World were used to command coastlines, protect frontiers and to serve as trading posts in times of peace or for protection during the multiple wars that followed the arrival of the Europeans. Many underwent storm and siege, and a few have remained intact for the present-day historian to examine archaeologically. The frontier forts remain alive in imagination through films and television depiction of the western theme, but there are many others with considerable historical significance. Of particular note are the 30-plus forts built after the War of 1812 to provide a "Third System" of protection for seaports along the Atlantic and Gulf coasts. The introduction of rifled cannon during the American Civil War rendered most of these fortifications obsolete, although many have survived to become tourist attractions. The following is a brief listing of a few of the major forts by state:

The Presidio of San Francisco, California, is the only "Third System" fort on the West Coast and stands intact beneath the south anchorage of the Golden Gate Bridge. It was the base of operations for the building of the bridge and a backdrop for many Hollywood movies.

Bent's Old Fort National Historic Site in La Junta, Colorado, is a reconstructed adobe trading post, which bustled as a commercial center on the Santa Fe Trail between 1833-1849. Its furnishings made it the "Castle of the Plains."

Castillo de San Marcos National Monument in Florida was designed to fend off pirates. The Castillo survives as the only intact 17th century fort in the continental U.S. and the larger of only two forts built anywhere using coquina stone.

Fort Pulaski National Monument in Savannah, Georgia is surrounded by a moat. The fortress took 18 years to complete, beginning in 1829. Considered invincible, its 7.5-foot-thick walls were breached by rifled artillery in 1862.

Fort Lamed National Historic Site in Lamed, Kansas has nine restored buildings, and is one of the best surviving outposts from the Indian Wars era. It functioned both as a guardian of the Santa Fe Trail and as an Indian Bureau Agency.

Fort McHenry National Monument and Historic Shrine in Baltimore, Maryland is the site of the historic star-shaped fort (built 1799-1805) whose garrison repelled an intense British attack in September 1814. Commander Armistead wanted the post's flag "large enough that the British will have no difficulty in seeing it," resulting in the inspired composition of America's national anthem.

Fort Mackinac, Mackinac State Historic Parks, located on Mackinac Island, Michigan has a military outpost with 14 structures whose initial construction was begun by the British in 1780. A sister fort, **Colonial Michilimackinac**, is located near the Mackinac Bridge in Mackinaw City. On the site of a 1715

French fort and fur-trading village are 18 reconstructed buildings and an underground archaeological exhibit.

Fort Atkinson State Historical Park, at Fort Calhoun, Nebraska was the first post west of the Missouri River from 1820 to 1827 and was built to protect the Western fur trade. Local concern resurrected the fort in the 1960s, leading to its substantial reconstruction.

Fort Union National Monument, at Watrous, New Mexico has a number of ghostly ruins still standing which give testimony to the military outpost and supply depot that flourished here alongside the Santa Fe Trail in the mid-1800s. A tour trail winds through the adobe ruins of the largest fort in the Southwest, built to protect settlers and travelers from Indian raids. Nearby is the largest network of wagon ruts from the Santa Fe Trail.

Fort Stanwix National Monument at Rome, New York is a Revolutionary War-era fort, which has been almost completely reconstructed.

Fort Ticonderoga, near present-day Ticonderoga, New York overlooks Lake Champlain and controlled the connecting waterway between Canada and the American Colonies. Originally built by the French in 1755, it saw battles between the French and British, and during the Revolutionary War.

Aerial view of the fort. (Mwanner Photo)
The storming of Fort Ticonderoga, 1775, by Frederick Remington.
(Mid-Manhattan Picture Collection)

Fort Fisher Historic Site at Kure Beach, North Carolina was the largest Confederate earthwork fortification during the Civil War and kept the seaport of Wilmington open to receive foreign supplies for Confederate armies. Less than 10% of the fort remains.

Fort Union Trading Post National Historic Site at Williston, North Dakota was built by the American Fur Company in 1828. Fort Union was the center for trading on the Upper Missouri.

Fort Sumter National Monument on Sullivan's Island, South Carolina was a "Third System" fort in Charleston Harbor, and the target of the first engagement of the Civil War. Later, Confederates held it through a 22-month siege that nearly destroyed it.

Fort Davis National Historic Site, Fort Davis, Texas guarded the San Antonio-El Paso Road from 1854 to 1891, garrisoned the famed Buffalo Soldiers, and tested the use of camels for the military. This site is considered the best-preserved fort in the Southwest.

Fort Vancouver National Historic Site, at Vancouver, Washington was an outpost created by the Hudson's Bay Company and became the fur trade capital of the Pacific Coast from 1825 to 1849, making it a political and cultural hub.

Glossary

Abacus	The flat portion on top of a capital.
Abatis	An obstacle made by placing cut trees or pointed poles lengthwise at a 45° angle to the ground in front of a defensive position, with sharpened ends pointed towards the attacker.
Aisle	The space between an arcade and an outer wall.
Allure	Wall-walk, or passage behind the parapet of the battlements on a castle wall.
Ambulatory	The aisle around an apse.
Approach	A trench, at least 10 feet in depth and width, dug toward a fortress. Approaches were intended to shield the besieger from the fortress's fire and served as communications trenches for the movement of wagons and guns to the more advanced positions.
Apse	The rounded end of a chancel or chapel.
Arcade	A row of arches, free-standing and supported on piers or columns. A blind arcade is known as a dummy.
Arch	Round-headed, pointed, two-centered or drop, which is an arch struck from center on the springing-line. An ogee is a pointed arch with double-curved sides, upper arcs convex, lower concave. A lancet is a pointed arch formed on an acute-angle triangle. A depressed arch is flattened or elliptical.
Archère	An arrow-slit or loophole in castle walls for archers to fire through.
Arquebus	An early hand-held matchlock firearm.
Arrow Slit	A narrow slit in towers or curtain walls which allowed archers to shoot through. They were carefully spaced to avoid weakening the castle's masonry. There were generally two kinds: the single, upright slit and the cross-shaped slit for use with a crossbow. Also called an Arrow Loop.
Ashlar	A block of dressed or worked stone or masonry with a flat surface, or squared stone in regular courses.
Aumbry	A recess in a wall used to hold sacred vessels, often found in castle chapels.
Bailey	A courtyard, specifically the area enclosed within a curtain wall or palisade. It would provide space for outbuildings such as the kitchen and stables. The term is applied to any court within a series of walls. Also known as a Ward.
Ballista	A Roman siege engine resembling a crossbow, which uses tension to throw projectiles, hurl missiles or fire large arrows.
Baluster	A short shaft, such as is used in balustrades, usually thicker in the middle than at the ends.

Banquette	A step or ledge behind the parapets of a rampart, a covered way, or of a trench, to enable soldiers to fire over them at attackers.
Barbican	A masonry outwork built to protect the approach to a castle. It was primarily a form of protective stonework for a gateway used to defend the approaches to a bridge or gatehouse.
Barmkin	Outer fortification of a castle. Also, a siege tower, known as a Belfry.
Barrel Roof	A roof shaped like a covered wagon or inverted ship's hull.
Barrel Vault	A plain vault with a uniform cross-section.
Bartizan	A small overhanging turret projecting from the top of a wall or tower, also known as an Eschaugette. Often an overhanging battlemented corner turret, corbelled out. Common in France and Scotland.
Bascule	A gate at the entrance of a fort, raised and lowered by counterweights.
Bastide	Military settlements laid out in a Roman pattern in southern France, 14th Century.
Bastille	Redoubt or outwork.
Bastion	A small tower at the end of a curtain wall or in the middle of the outside wall. It is usually a four-sided projection from the main rampart in an enceinte of a fortress, consisting of two faces and two flanks. Also, a fortified projection occurring at intervals in a castle wall. These were usually a low, solid masonry projection, generally sharp-angled and designed to provide the maximum amount of flank protection to the curtain walls and to its neighbouring bastions, while at the same time providing as small a target as possible to the attackers. "Tours bastionées" were bastions with two or more stories introduced by Vauban in the 17th century.
Batter	A strong sloping or scarped side of a curtain wall thicker at the base. The sharp angle at the base of all walls and towers along their exterior surface. Also known as a Talus. Inclined face of a wall, therefore "battered."
Battlement	Narrow wall built along the outer edge of the wall walk An indented parapet with a series of openings originally designed for shooting through and to protect archers with raised parts in between known as "merlons" or crenellations.
Bays	A constituent portion or compartment of a building, complete in itself and corresponding to other portions. Also refers to internal divisions of a building marked by roof principals or vaulting piers.
Belfry	A siege tower, also called a Beffroi.
Bergfried	A tall, narrow tower similar to a keep, found in many castles in Germany and German speaking countries.
Berm	A flat space between the base of the curtain wall and the inner edge of the moat. It is also a narrow ledge between the ditch and the base of the parapet next to a moat or ditch, designed to prevent earth and debris from falling into the ditch when the parapet was struck by projectiles.
Berquil	A large outdoor reservoir found in Crusader and Muslim castles.
Bivalate	A hillfort defended by two concentric ditches.
Bombard	A heavy 14th to 15th century siege cannon that fired stones or other projectiles.
Boyau	A communication trench.

Bracket	A piece of stone or wood projecting from a wall, used to support hoarding or machicolation. Also known as a Console.
Brattice	A timber tower or projecting wooden gallery. An open-floored latrine or machicolation over a gate, also called a Bretèche.
Breach	A hole or gap blown in the rampart or wall of a fortification by projectiles or mining, wide enough for a body of troops to enter the inner works of a fortress.
Brown Bess	British musket, 1750, caliber .75.
Burgh	A fortified Anglo-Saxon township.
Buttery	Room for the service of beverages.
Buttress	A projection from a wall for additional support.
Cannon	Long-barreled artillery piece firing solid round shot on a flat trajectory.
Caponnière	A covered passage from the main wall of a fortress with firing ports for muskets, intended to provide communication with the outworks. It is also a strong casemated work of 6 or 7-foot parapets sloping perpendicularly down to the ditch in order to provide additional flanking fire for the ditch.
Cascane	A hole sunk by the defenders in the platform of the rampart to provide an escape for mines or made by the attackers as a way up from mines made below the moat.
Casemate	A bombproof chamber or gallery generally built into the thickness of the ramparts and used as barracks or for firing positions. Early versions were normally fitted with loopholes for archers. Later versions housed cannons that fired through embrasures in the scarp. Vaulted in permanent fortifications, casemates also appeared in tiers in seacoast defences of the 19th century. They were often sighted in the base of a tower from which flanking fire could be given.
Castellan	The governor, commander, or officer in charge of a castle, also known as a Constable.
Castellation	Battlements used as a decorative feature.
Cat	A nickname for an assault tower or penthouse, which is used as a moveable shelter for miners, sappers, and ram operators. Also called a Sow or Mouse.
Catapult	Stone-throwing engine, usually employing torsion.
Catapulta	Roman catapult designed to fire arrows.
Cavalier	A raised work built on the rampart, terreplein of a bastion, or of a curtain wall where an artillery battery could be placed.
Cesspit	The opening in a wall in which the waste from one or more garderobes (toilets) was collected.
Chamfer	A masonry surface made by smoothing or paring off the angle between two stone faces.
Chandelles	Posts set up to provide a concealing screen for the defenders.
Chemin couvert	A level walk on the far side of the moat, protected by the parapet formed by the higher portion of the glacis, with "places d'armes" at intervals.
Chemin de ronde	The rounds, a narrow walkway or passage on top of the scarp wall at the base of the exterior slope of a rampart. It was protected by a small parapet, and was used by soldiers to make their rounds, to observe the glacis at close range, and to defend against attempts at escalade.

Chemise	An inner walled enclosure of a castle built closely around a Donjon or Keep protecting it. The wall either completely surrounds it or joins on to it.
Chevaux-de-frise	Defensive obstructions generally used in field fortifications to check cavalry charges, but also used to close breaches. These consisted of large pieces of timber, 10-12 feet long, into which were driven many long wooden pins tipped with iron points or sharp blades to impale attackers.
Chevron	Zigzag moulding generally found in 12th century castles.
Circumvallation	A line of entrenchments cut by besiegers in the surrounding country to prevent a relieving force's surprising of the besieger's camp.
Citadel	A small but strong work of four to six bastions or sides, usually at one corner within a fortified town, intended to dominate and protect the town if the main works fell.
Clunch	Hard chalk material.
Cob	Unburnt clay mixed with straw.
Composite bow	A bow made of three basic layers of dissimilar materials, usually wood, horn, and sinew. This combined the best features of each to yield a bow that was stronger and more resilient than the simple bows of just wood. It also meant that a much shorter bow could be much stronger than the longer simple bows.
Concentric Castle	A central fortress ringed by a series of outer curtain walls. This design of castles dates from the late 12th century onwards and generally consists of two or more complete circles of walls within one another. The ground plan gives all sides equal stength against an attacker, while simultaneously permitting the defenders to respond more quickly to an attack on any part of the garrison.
Contravallation	A line of entrenchments made at the beginning of a siege facing the fortification that is under attack in order to prevent a sortie or assault from the fortification.
Console	A bracket, generally describing the supports from which machicolations were built out from a wall.
Constable	The officer or official in charge of a castle in the owner's absence.
Contregardes	Protective works in front of the bastions.
Contrescarpe	The sloping outer side of the moat next to the covered way, usually revetted.
Corbel	A stone, brick, or timber bracket supporting a projection from a wall to provide a horizontal support.
Cordon	The rounded stone moulding or band below the parapet of the revetment of the rampart going all around the fort.
Cornes	Hornwork (ouvrage à conres), a work outside the fort and detached from it, with two half bastions ending in acute angels on the front facing the attacker.
Cornice	A decorative projection along the top of a wall.
Corve'e	Unpaid or lowly paid labour, rendered to a lord by a vassal or as a substitute for taxes.
Corvus	The word means crow or raven in Latin, for a Roman naval boarding device used in sea battles against Carthage during the First Punic War.

Cour d'honneur	The reception courtyard of a Château.
Countercastle	A castle or defence-work erected by besiegers to protect their operations.
Counterfort	Interior buttresses built behind scarp walls in order to strengthen them.
Counterscarp	The outer wall or slope of a ditch, the side away from the body of the position. The counterscarp was usually faced with stone or brick to make the besieger's descent into the ditch more difficult and might also be used to support the covered way.
Counterscarp gallery	A work situated behind the counterscarp from which the ditch could be enfiladed with reverse fire.
Covered Way	A broad road extending around the counterscarp of the ditch and protected by the parapet from enemy fire, intended to form a "communication" around the position. At its foot was the banquette, used to cover the glacis with musket fire to prevent the enemy from approaching the counterscarp of the ditch. It also functioned as a place of assembly for sorties. Also known as the via coperta.
Course	A level layer of stones or bricks.
Coursière	A wooden roof erected over a wall-walk.
Courtine	Curtain, the long straight front of the rampart from the re-entering angles of the junction of the bastions with the front of the rampart.
Crenellation	A notched battlement made up of alternate crenels (openings) and merlons (square saw-teeth) in battlements. Embrasures or gaps in a parapet through which archers or musketeers could fire. Crenellate means "to fortify."
Crosswall	An interior dividing wall of a castle.
Crownwork	An outwork similar in shape to a crown, with two fronts and two branches. The fronts were composed of two half-bastions and one whole one and were generally placed in front of the curtain or bastion. They were intended to enclose buildings that could not be brought within the body of the place, to cover the town gates, or to occupy ground that might be advantageous to the attacker.
Crupper	Strap going from saddle around the backside and under the tail of the horse. The combination with the breast and girth straps gave some support for steadying the rider (especially valuable if an archer) but was not even close to the steadiness gained with the later arrival of real saddles with stirrups.
Crusades	Holy Wars. There are many that took place in the Middle Ages. The most important were the First 1096-1102; Second 1147-1149; Third 1189-1192; Fourth 1202-1204; Fifth 1218-1221; Sixth 1228-1229; Seventh 1248-1254; and Eighth 1270. (For more details see Appendix A).
Curtain Wall	The main outer defence wall of a castle's fortifications, which connect adjacent flanking-towers, bastions, or gates. A length or portion of connecting wall hung between two towers or bastions. Also known as a Courtine.
Cuvette	A narrow secondary trench or ditch sunk in the center of the moat or the bottom of a dry ditch for drainage purposes. Also known as a Cunette.

Daub	A mud and clay mixture applied over wattle to strengthen and seal it.
Dead Angle	An angle of view where thee ground can't be seen by the defenders and is therefore indefensible.
Dead Ground	Any area at the base of fortifications where the attackers cannot be reached by the arrows or projectiles launched by the defenders.
Demilune	A detached triangular work built in the moat. It is also a work constructed to cover the curtain and shoulders of the bastion. It was composed of two faces forming a salient angle toward the country. It had two demigorges formed by the counterscarp and was surrounded by a ditch. The demilune was also called a ravelin.
Diaper Work	Castle decorations using squares or lozenges.
Ditch	A dry wide, and deep trench around a defensive work designed to either stop the attacker from crossing, or at least hampering them in doing so. The dirt from its excavation was used to form the rampart and parapet, and when it was filled with water it was known as a wet ditch.
Dogtooth	A design or decoration in the form of diagonal indented pyramids.
Donjon	The inner stronghold of a castle, usually found in one of the towers. Donjon is the French word for a castle's Keep (not a dungeon). The word is derived from the Latin "dominus" which means "lord." It indicates the dominion of the keep-holder, but was later changed into "dungeon," which means prison. In Germany it is known as a Burgfried, and in Italy it is called a Mastio.
Dormer	A window placed vertically in a sloping roof.
Drawbridge	A heavy timber platform built to span a moat between a gate house and surrounding land that could be raised when required to block an entrance. It was a moveable bridge generally hinged at one end and free at the other, that can be drawn up to prevent an attacker crossing a ditch or moat in front of the gate. It could be in the form of a simple moveable plank, while others were pulled up by chains mounted on pulleys. More elaborate versions utilized a counter-poise system in which the chains were suspended from beams which fitted into recesses provided for them above the entrance to house them when they were drawn up. Others worked on a pivot so that the inner part of the bridge fell into a pit, while the outer part completely covered the entrance.
Dressing	Carved stonework around openings.
Drum Tower	A large circular tower, typically low and squat.
Drystone	Unmortared masonry.
Embattled	Battlemented walls.
Embrasure	The low segment of the alternating high and low segments of a battlement. It is a small opening cut through a parapet or wall sighted between the merlons, forming crenellations through which cannon or other weapons could be fired. The sides of the embrasure usually splayed or flared on the inside of the wall to protect the defenders from attacking fire and to provide a broader sweep or range of fire.
Enceinte	An enclosing wall, usually exterior, of a fortified place. It also comprised the full circuit of curtain walls, ramparts, parapets, and towers that formed the main enclosure around a fortification or castle.

Enfilade fire	Artillery or musket fire that swept a line of troops or the length of a defence work from one end to the other. The equivalent naval term would be "to rake."
Epaule	A rectangular recess at the junction of the flanks of bastions with the courtine.
Escalade	The assault of a castle by climbing or scaling its walls.
Eshaugette	A turret projecting from the top of a wall or tower, also know as a Bartizan.
Face	In a bastion, this is the exposed outer wall between the flanked angle and the shoulder angle. It is also one of the two sides of the bastion that converged to a salient angle pointing outwards toward the country and was situated on the line of the defense. The sides of bastions facing the attacker and meeting at an angle at the salient point of the bastion.
Fascine	A long cylindrical bundle of sticks or brush firmly bound together at short, regular intervals, and used in building earthworks and batteries and in strengthening ramparts. Fascines were also used to fill ditches during a siege or assault on a fortified position.
Fausse-braye	A low, outer rampart usually built of earth, which stood in front of the curtain wall. It provided shelter for troops firing against the besiegers before they entered the ditch. Under bombardment, debris from the wall behind tended to wound its defenders, and by the <u>end</u> of the 17th century, its use was largely abandoned by engineers.
Fieldwork	Temporary fortifications constructed in the field.
Fillet	A narrow flat band for decoration.
Finial	A slender piece of stone used to decorate the tops of the merlons.
Firepot	An early form of incendiary grenade, usually ceramic or glass.
Firing step	A ledge for defenders along the inside top of a wall.
Flanc Fichant	Fire given from a flank to the bastion opposite.
Flanc Rasant	Fire that passes the "face" of the bastion opposite.
Flank	The section of a bastion between the face and the curtain, from which the ditch in front of the adjacent curtain and that flank and face of the opposite bastion were defended.
Flanking	The design of fortifications is such a way as to ensure that the approaches to each tower are covered by neighbouring towers. Flanking eliminates dead ground in order to ensure that no approach is safe for an attacker.
Flanking fire	Weapons fire from one or both sides of an attacker, rather from straight ahead.
Flèche	A simple V-shaped fieldwork with two faces that formed a salient angle. Usually used in the fortification of walls where it was not necessary to build bastions. Also known as a Redan, the Flèche pointed toward the attacker and was open to the rear.
Flintlock	An ignition system for firearms of the 17th to 19th centuries, utilizing a spring-loaded flint wedge to strike sparks on a steel surface above a pan of gunpowder.
Fluting	Concave mouldings arranged in parallel lines.
Foliated	Castle decorations carved in stone in the form of leaves.
Footings	The bottom part of a wall.

Forebuilding	A projection in front of a keep or donjon, containing the stairs to the main entrance. Also, a block-built n front of a keep to form a lobby or a landing.
Fossé	A moat or ditch, dry or wet.
Fraises	Palisades of pointed timbers 5 » square and 7 to 8 feet long, fixed horizontally between the main wall and the ditch or other earthwork, and in some cases slightly inclining toward the attackers. Their purpose was to hinder an assault while at the same time avoiding the provision of the kind of protection an abatis could offer. Also known as storm poles.
Freestone	High-quality sandstone or limestone.
Fresco	A painting on a wet-plaster wall.
Gabion	A cylindrical wicker basket filled with earth and used during sieges to form temporary defenses or parapets and to reinforce fieldworks.
Gable	A wall covering the end of a roof-ridge.
Gallery	A long passage or room.
Ganerbenburg	A German term for a castle under the mutual ownership of several heirs.
Garderobe	Small latrine or toilet, either built into the thickness of the wall or projected out from it.
Gatehouse	The complex of towers, bridges, and barriers built to protect each entrance through a castle or town wall. Essentially the fortifications specifically designed to guard the main or other points of entry into a castle.
Glacis	A gentle (less that 45°) bank, sloping away from the parapet of the covered way. Its purpose was to expose an attacker to fire from the defenders. Since considerable time and labour went into removal of trees and scrub growth, and grading the soil, glacis were normally found only around permanent fortifications.
Gorge	The neck or the open rear portion of a bastion or other outwork.
Grapeshot	Many small projectiles fired simultaneously from a cannon in a single, shotgun-like discharge. Generally used against troops.
Great Chamber	The overlord's Solar, or his bed-sitting room.
Greek fire	An ancient flame-throwing weapon, developed by the Byzantine Greeks.
Great Hall	The building in the inner ward that housed the main meeting and dining area for the castle's residents.
Grenadoe	An early term for an explosive shell.
Groining	The angular edges formed by the intersection of cross-vaults in a ceiling.
Guerite	A sentry-box corbelled out from the angles of ramparts, also known as an echaugette.
Gunloop	An aperture for firing handguns through, similar in use to the Arrow Slit. There are many varieties, with some consisting of a round hole for the barrel of the gun, and a slit, sometimes vertical, often in the shape of a cross (making the cross and orb pattern), for sighting and to allow the gases to escape.
Halberd	A pole weapon combining a spike and an axe-blade. Useful for pulling knights off their horses.

Half-shaft	Roll-moulding on either side of an opening.
Half-timber	The common form of medieval construction in which walls were made of a wooden frame structure filled with wattle and daub.
Hall	Principal living quarters of a medieval castle or house.
Hall for hynds	Servants' hall.
Herringbone pattern	The placing of stones aslant in a wall so that each two rows form a succession of angles resembling the backbone of a herring.
Hillfort	A bronze or Iron Age earthwork made of ditches and banks.
Hoarding	A temporary covered wooden gallery or balcony suspended from the tops of walls and towers to provide vertical defense before a battle. Hoarding enabled defenders to see the base of a wall and to drop or accurately fire objects on the attackers below.
Hood	An arched covering. When used to throw off rainwater, it is called a hood-mould.
Hornwork	An important outwork made up of a bastioned front with two demibastions and a curtain, and two long sides called branches.
Howitzer	A short-barreled artillery piece used to fire explosive shells on a high trajectory to enable plunging fire on an enemy position.
Impost	A wall bracket used to support an arch.
Inner Curtain	The high wall that surrounds the inner ward.
Inner Ward	The open area in the center of a castle.
Investment	The process of isolating a fortress at the beginning of a siege by cutting off roads and taking control of all routes around it, so that it could not be relieved.
Jamb	The side of an arch, door, or window.
Janissary	Member of an elite corps of the Ottoman Turkish Army, raised mainly from captive Christian boys.
Joist	Timber which is laid from wall to wall to support floorboards.
Keep	English term for the donjon, or final redoubt, usually the strongest and often the biggest tower or building within a castle. It was often used as the place of last refuge and in later ages, as a residence.
Lancet	A long, narrow window with a pointed head.
Lantern or louvre	A small open turret placed on a roof as an outlet for smoke.
Light	The spaces between the mullions and transoms of a window.
Line of defence (Ligne de defense)	A theoretical line extending from the flanked angle of a bastion along a face to the point of the adjacent bastion. This line of fire determined the position of the face of the bastion relative to the flank that would defend it.
Lintel	A horizontal stone or beam bridging opening.
Lists	A term for the area designated for jousting. A few authors also use the word list to describe the spaces between two lines of towers and curtain walls in concentric castles.
Loophole	A hole, slit or narrow opening through a wall, allowing defensive fire with small arms.
Louvre	An opening in a roof, often vented to allow smoke to escape from a central hearth.
Lunette	A defensive position set outside the main walls of a defended fortress. Originally crescent-shaped, lunettes later became pointed in shape.

Machicolation	A stone projection or gallery mounted on brackets on the outside of castle walls with floor holes through which projectiles, missiles, molten lead, and other hot liquids could be dropped vertically onto attackers at the base of the wall. Wooden hoardings served the same purpose.
Madrier	A long plank.
Mangonel	A siege engine in the form of a catapult using torsion for flinging its missiles.
Mantlet	A moveable shield or mobile protective screen consisting of 3-inch planks, 5 feet high, sometimes covered with tin and mounted on wheels for use by besiegers as covering protection.
Matchlock	An ignition system for firearms of the 14th to 17th centuries, utilizing a smouldering cord thrust into a pan of gunpowder.
Merlon	The high part of the square "sawtooth" between crenelles in a battlement, and the solid part of masonry or brick parapets between the embrasures in a wall.
Meurtrière	An arrow loop, slit in battlement or wall to permit firing of arrows, or for observation. Also, a loophole in a castle or fortification sited over a passageway to permit defenders to drop objects on the attackers below and known in English as "murderholes."
Mine Gallery	Siegeworks designed to cause a wall to collapse.
Moat	A water-filled ditch surrounding a castle, sometimes completely artificial, often partly natural in origin. The word is derived from "motte," originally meaning the highest part of the castle, which was transformed to name the ditch from which it was excavated. It could be either left dry or filled with water.
Mortar	A short, large calibre smoothbore artillery piece for firing explosive or incendiary projectiles over obstacles at a high angle of elevation.
Motte	An artificial earth-mound for Norman and English keeps of 11th and 12th century castles.
Motte-and-Bailey	A steep artificial hillock or natural mound of earth often mounting a wooden or stone keep surrounded by a ditched and palisaded enclosure or courtyard.
Moulding	Decorative masonry.
Moulinette	A turnstile.
Mullion	The vertical divisions of stone or wood between the lights of windows.
Multivallate	A hillfort with three or more concentric lines of defence.
Mural	A wall.
Murderhole	Openings in the floors of rooms in gatehouses above the passageway from the entrance to the castle or other important access routes.
Nailhead	Decorative pyramid moulding.
Neolithic	Of or relating to the last period of the Stone Age, with polished stone tools, bows and arrows, domestic animals, cultivated crops, wheels, weaving, and village life.
Newel	The centre-post of a circular staircase.
Nookshaft	A shaft set in the angle of a jamb or pier.

Onager	A heavy catapult. Over the history of the Roman Empire the onager, catapult, and ballista changed in appearance, due to design changes, gradual technology improvements, and intended uses (such as for a lengthy siege or for a mobile attack). The catapult which could throw large spears looked at times like the ballista, which could be configured to throw small stones or wood or metal bolts (much like the later crossbow).
Oolite	Granular limestone.
Open Joint	A wide space between the faces of stones.
Oratory	A private chapel in a house or castle.
Orgues	A defence for the entrance to forts consisting of long heavy pieces of wood covered with iron, hung singly, and dropped separately to block entrance.
Oriel	A projecting window in a wall on an upper floor. Originally a form of porch, often made of wood.
Orillon	A curved or rounded projection (also known as an epaule, or "ear") placed at the shoulder of a bastion, designed to cover a retired flank from fire.
Oubliette	A secret dungeon or prison whose opening was a trap door from above.
Outer Curtain	The wall which enclosed the outer ward.
Outer Ward	The area around the outside of and adjacent to the inner curtain.
Outwork	A work inside the glacis but outside the body of the fortification.
Ouvrages de couronnement	Crown works, fortifications supplementary to the hornwork.
Palisade	A sturdy wooden fence usually built to enclose a site until a permanent stone wall could be erected. They were usually constructed with sharpened wooden stakes or posts 9 feet long, 6" or 7"square and fixed 3 feet in the ground in rows with 3" spaces between the posts surrounding a castle or defensive position. Also set in the covered way at a distance of 3 feet from the inner face of the glacis.
Parados	A low wall on the inner side of the main wall.
Parallel trench	A wide and deep trench dug by besiegers parallel to the fortress under attack. From it, zigzag approaches were dug to the next,more forward, parallel as the siege progressed.
Parapet	Protective wall at the top of a fortification, around the outer side of the wall-walk. Usually a low wall or earth or masonry on top of the rampart providing protection behind which troops could fire. Often found on the outer side of the main wall or tower, it forms a protective screen of Crenelles and Merlons, also known as Battlements.
Paté or Patée	A small outwork of earth well rammed, usually horseshoe shaped in plan.
Pediment	A low-pitched gavle over porticos, doors, and windows.
Pier	The mass of masonry between arches and other openings. A pier served as a support base for an arch, usually square rather than pillar (round).
Pike	A long thrusting spear.
Pilaster	A square or rectangular pillar, engaged in, and projecting slightly from, a wall, in order to buttress the wall.
Pinnacle	An ornament crowning a spire or tower.
Piscina	A handbasin, usually set in or against a wall, with a drain attached.

Pipe-rool	Exchequer accounts rolled on narrow wooden cylinders.
Pitch	The slope of a roof.
Pitching	Rough cobbling.
Place d'Armes	Spaces left at intervals in the covered way and other outworks for soldiers to assemble.
Plinth	The projecting base of a wall.
Polygonal trace	A fortification design devised by Montalembert consisting of faces forming salient angles (the outward points of a bastion) or re-entering angles (angles pointing toward the interior of a fortification) of small depth, flanked by a powerful caponnière.
Pont-levis	The drawbridge of a castle.
Portcullis	Vertical sliding wooden grille shod with iron suspended in front of a gateway, let down to protect the gate. Usually a heavy wood and metal grating suspended on chains worked by winches which could be dropped quickly down vertical grooves in the gatehouse or at other important entrances.
Postern or sally-port	Small secondary exit gate used as the "backdoor" of a castle.
Putlog Hole	A hole intentionally left in the surface of a wall for insertion of a horizontal pole.
Quadrangle	The inner courtyard of a castle.
Queue d'Aronde	An outwork shaped in panform like a swallow's tail.
Quoins	Dressed decorative cornerstones.
Ram	Battering-ram.
Rampart	A thick defensive stone or earth wall often formed from the dirt excavated from the ditch to protect the enclosed area from artillery fire and to elevate defenders to a commanding position overlooking the approaches to a fortification. Usually, a rampart was capped with a stone or earth parapet. Its presence signified a permanent defence.
Rath	A low, circular ringwork.
Ravelin	A low V-shaped or triangular-shaped outwork consisting of two faces that formed a salient angle, sited outside the ditch of a fortification to cover the portion of a curtain wall between two bastions.
Redan	A simple V-shaped fieldwork with two faces that formed a salient angle. Usually used in the fortification of walls where it was not necessary to build bastions. Also known as a Flèche, a Redan was shaped like a saw pointed toward the attacker and was open to the rear.
Re-entrant	A recessed angle pointing toward the interior of a castle or fortification.
Redoubt	A small work in a bastion or ravelin. A redoubt is also a small independent outwork, usually an earthwork of square of polygonal shape, with little or no means of flanking defence. Redoubts were used to fortify a hilltop or pass, or any other main avenue of enemy approach.
Re-entering place of arms	A larger space in the covered way, found at the re-entering or salient angles of the covered way, designed for troops to assemble and engage in a sortie.
Refectory	A communal dining hall.
Relieving arches	Tiers of arches built in the rear of the scarp wall and between the counterforts, intended to make it more difficult for attackers to make breaches in the wall.

Revetment	A facing of earth, sandbags, or stone built to protect an embankment (such as the sides of the ditch or parapet), against bomb splinters and shell fragments. Essentially a protective retaining wall.
Rib	Raised moulding dividing a vault.
Ricochet fire	The art of firing projectiles so that the missiles drop over the parapet of a fortification bounce along its length. The ricochet was intended to wreak havoc among the defenders in a fortification as it skipped along the ground.
Ring-work	A circular earthwork combing a bank and a ditch. Also used to describe any defensive enclosure, regardless of period, size, or function.
Romanesque	An architectural style in use from the 8th to 12th centuries, with rounded arches.
Roofridge	The summit line of a roof.
Round shot	A solid cannonball, initially made of stone, later made of cast iron. Round shot could be heated in a mobile furnace before being fired into the hull of a wooden ship, making it difficult to remove and extinguish.
Rubble	Unsquared stone that has not been laid in courses. A random mixture of rocks and mortar.
Rustication	Worked ashlar stone, with the faces left rough.
Salient	Two lines of works meeting and pointing toward the country, away from the center of fortification.
Salient angle	An angle pointing out toward the field.
Sally port	An opening or underground passage that led from the inner to the outer works. Cut into the glacis, it was a gateway through which many troops could pass when making a sortie.
Saltire	A diagonal, equal-limbed cross.
Sap	A narrow trench cut by besiegers to protect their approaches toward a fortification.
Sapping	Undermining, as of a castle wall.
Scaffolding	The temporary wooden framework built next to a wall to support both workers and materials.
Scarp	The slope on the inner side of a ditch. Also known as "escarp," it is part of the facing of a fortification that fronts the exterior, from the bottom of the ditch to the parapet of that wall.
Schildmauer	A particularly strong wall guarding the only line of approach to a castle built on a mountain or on a spur in certain parts of Germany.
Screens	Wooden partition at the kitchen end of a hall, protecting a passage leading to the buttery, pantry, and kitchen.
Scutum	Roman battle shield.
Semi-detached Scarp	A scarp wall with loopholes constructed in its upper part so that soldiers can fire into the ditch or across the ditch toward the covered way and the glacis.
Sepoy	Indian infantryman of the British East India Company's army, later of the Indian Army of Great Britain.
Shaft	A narrow column.
Shell-keep	A circular or oval wall surrounding the inner portion of a castle.
Shoulder angle	The interior angle formed by the meeting of a flank and a face of a bastion. An orillon sometimes supported the shoulder.

Soffit	The underside of an arch or opening.
Solar	Originally a room above ground level, but commonly applied to the great chamber or a private sitting room off the great hall. It was a private room for a lord or his family, generally with windows facing sunlight.
Sortie	A raid outwards by defenders of a besieged position.
Splay	A chamfer, or sloping face.
Springald	War engine of the catapult type, employing tension.
Spur	An angular projection applied, for example, to the base of a drum tower to hinder mining operations. It served the same purpose as a Talus.
Squint	An observation hole in a wall or room.
Star fort	An enclosed work with a trace made up of a series of salient and re-entering angles.
Stele (stela)	A slab, column, pillar, or wall erected for commemorative purposes, with pictures and/or text carved on it.
Steward	The man responsible for running the day-to-day affairs of the castle in the absence of the lord.
Storm poles	Palisades of pointed timbers between the main wall and the ditch or other earthwork, directed horizontally or slightly inclining toward the attackers. Their purpose was to hinder an assault while at the same time avoiding the provision of the kind of protection an abatis could offer. Also known as Fraises.
Stringcourse	A continuous horizontal moulding on a wall face.
Talus	A strong sloping or scarped side of a wall thicker at the base. Also known as a Batter.
Tenaille	A small low-lying work, placed in a main ditch between adjoining bastions to provide cover from the curtain wall.
Tenaille trace	A succession of redans (V-shaped works, open to the rear) joined at right angles to form a front of defence that resembles the teeth of a saw.
Terreplein	The top or horizontal surface of the earthen rampart, situated behind the parapet and used as a support for the cannon.
Testudo	A protective screen (usually of overlapping shields) held overhead or in front of attacking soldiers. In some cases (such as Roman) it was even in the form of a protective "house" on wheels, which the soldiers rolled forward from inside.
Tire-à-Ricochet	Plunging fire.
Tour bastionnée	A masonry tower, several stories high, with gun platforms higher than the curtain ramparts.
Tourelle	A turret projecting from a larger tower which was used either as a watchtower or, if constructed with machicolation, for vertical defence. Also used for decoration.
Towerhouse	Residential towers of the 14th and 15th centuries.
Trace	The plan on which fortifications are arranged on the ground.
Tracery	Intersecting ribwork in the upper part of a window.
Transitional Keep	French and English polygonal Keeps of the 12th century designed to overcome the disadvantages of the square or rectangular Keep.
Transom	The horizontal division of a window.

Traverse	A barrier (earthen bank or wall) constructed across a covered way, a terreplein or other defensive work, to protect troops and guns from flanking fire (enfilade).
Trébuchet	A siege engine developed in the Middle Ages which relied on an unequal counterpoise arm to launch its missiles.
Trefoil	Three-lobed, or three sided.
Trous de loup	Field fortifications comprised of a series of pits designed to hold pointed stakes projecting from the bottom.
Truss	One of the timber frames built to support the roof over the Great Hall.
Turret	A small slim tower or a tourelle, round or polygonal, projecting from a larger tower, usually used as a lookout point.
Vault	Stone roofing.
Via coperta	A broad "road" extending around the counterscarp of the ditch and protected by the parapet from enemy fire, intended to form a "communication" around the position. At its foot was the banquette, used to cover the glacis with musket fire to prevent the enemy from approaching the counterscarp of the ditch. It also functioned as a place of assembly for sorties. Also known as a covered way.
Vice	A spiral stairway in the thickness of a wall.
Vitrified	Material reduced to glass by combustion.
Voussoir	Wedge-shaped stone in an arch.
Wall-stair	A staircase built into the thickness of a wall.
Wall-walk	A passage along a castle wall.
Ward	The courtyard or bailey of a castle.
Wattle	A mat of woven sticks and weeds.
Weathering	Sloping surfaces designed to throw off rainwater.
Wing-wall	A wall down slope of a motte to protect a stairway.
Yett	The Scottish word for an iron gate.

Bibliography

ADCOCK, F.E. *The Greek and Macedonian Art of War.* University of California Press, Berkley, 1957.

ANDERSON, William. *Castles of Europe, from Charlemagne to the Renaissance.* Ferndale Editions, London, 1980.

ASHWORTH, G.J. *War and the City,* Routledge, London, and New York, 1991.

BACHRACH, Bernard S. "Medieval Siege Warfare: A Reconnaissance." *The Journal of Military History,* 58, 1994.

BARNES, Leslie W.C.S. *Canada's Guns: an Illustrated History of Artillery.* Canadian War Museum, National Museums of Canada, Ottawa, 1979.

BLOOMFIELD, Reginald. *Sebastien le Prestre de Vauban, 1633-1707.* Methuen & Company Ltd., London, 1938.

BORNHEIM, Werner et al. *Burgen un Schlosser, Kunst und Kultur in Rheinland-Pfalz, (Fortresses and Castles, Art and Culture in the Rhineland-Pfalz Region),* Ahrtal-Verlag, Bad Neuenahr-Ahrweiler, 1981.

BRADBURY, Jim. *The Medieval Siege.* The Boydell Press, Woodbridge, Suffolk, 1992.

BRAUN, *G. Stauferburgen am Oberrhein (Staufer Castles on the Upper Rheinland),* G. Braunsche Hofbuchdruckerei un Veerlag, Karlsruhe, 1977.

BRICE, Martin H. *Stronghold, A History of Military Architecture,* B.T. Batsford Ltd., London, 1984.

BLOOMFIELD, Reginald. *Sebastien le Prestre de Vauban 1633-1707.* Methuen & Company Limited Publishers, London, 1938.

BROWN, R. Allen et al. *Castles, A History and Guide.* Blandford Press, Poole, Dorset, 1980.

CAESAR, Julius. *The Conquest of Gaul,* translated by S.A. Handford from *The Gallic War* (52 BC), Penguin Books, Harmondsworth, Middlesex, England, 1967.

CHARBONNEAU, Andre, DESLOGES, YVON and LAFRANCE, Marc, QUÉBEC, *The Fortified City: From the 17th to the 19th Century,* Parks Canada, Ottawa, 1982.

CHANDLER, David. *The Campaigns of Napoleon.* Macmillan, New York, 1966.

CLARKE, Dale. *British Artillery 1914-1919. Field Army Artillery.* Osprey Publishing, Oxford, UK, 200.

CLAUSEWITZ, Carl von. *On War, (Vom Kriege, 1832).* translated by Routlege & Kegan Paul 1908, Penguin Classics, London, 1982.

CONNELL, Charles. *The World's Greatest Sieges.* Odham Books Limited, Long Acre, London, 1967.

CONNELL, Robert L. "The Roman Killing Machine," *Quarterly Journal of Military History* Vol. 38, Autumn, 1978.

CONNOLLY, Peter. *Greece and Rome at War.* Prentice-Hall, Englewood Cliffs, New Jersey, 1981.

COTTRELL, Leonard. *The Warrior Pharaohs.* G.P. Putnam, New York, 1962.

CORFIS, Ivy A., and WOLFE, Michael, eds. *The Medieval City under Siege.* Woodbridge, Boydell & Brewer, Suffolk, Rochester, 1995.

CRAIG, Philip. *Last Stands, Famous Battles Against the Odds.* Bison Books Ltd., Kimbolton House, London, 1994.

CREVELD, Martin van. *Technology and War, From 2000 BC to the Present.* The Free Press, Collier MacMillan Publishers, London, 1989.

CRON, Herman. *Imperial German Army 1914-1918: Organization, Structure, Orders of Battle.* Hellion & Company Limited, Solihull, England, 2002.

DÉCHENE, Louise. *la correspondance de Vauban relative au Canada.* Ministere des affaires culturelles, Paris, 1968.

DELBRUCK, Hans. *The History of the Art of War.* University of Nebraska Press, Lincoln, Nebraska,1990.

DENNIS, George T. *Three Byzantine Military Treatises.* Dunbarton Oaks, Washington, D.C., 1985.

DOLLAR, Jacques, *Vauban a Luxembourg, Place Forte de l'Europe (1684-1697),* RTL Edition, Luxembourg, 1983.

DOOLY, William G. Jr. *Great Weapons of the First World War.* Bonanza Books, New York, 1969.

DUFFY, Christopher. *Siege Warfare: The Fortress in the Early Modern World.* Routledge and Paul Kegan, London, 1969.

DUPUY, Trevor N. Colonel. *The Evolution of Weapons and Warfare,* Hero Books, Fairfax, Virginia, 1984.

EDWARDS, Robert. *The Fortifications of Armenian Cilicia.* Dumbarton Oaks Institute, Washington, D.C., 1987.

EGGENBERGER, David. *An Encyclopedia of Battles, Accounts of Over 1,560 Battles from 1479 BC to the Present.* Dover Publications, Inc., New York, 1985.

ELLIOT, Major S.R. *Scarlet to Green, A History of Intelligence in the Canadian Army, 1903-1963* , CISA, Hunter Rose Company, Toronto, 1981

ENGELS, Donald W. *Alexander the Great and the Logistics of the Macedonian Army.* University of California Press, Berkeley, California, 1978.

FAULKNER, R.O. "Egyptian Military Organization," *Journal of Egyptian Archaeology* , Vol. 39, 1953.

FALL, Bernard B. *Hell in a Very Small Place, The Siege of Dien Bien Phu*, J.B. Lippincott Company, Philadelphia, New York, 1967.

FERRIL, Arther. *The Origins of War.* Thames and Hudson, London, 1985.

FORD, Roger. *The World's Great Military Guns, from 1860 to the Present Day.* Brown Books, London, 1999.

FRY, Bruce W. *"An Appearance of Strength", The Fortifications of Louisbourg,* Volume One and Volume Two. Canadian Government Publishing Centre, Supply and Services Canada, Hull, Quebec, 1984.

FULLER, J.F.C. Major General. *The Conduct of War, 1789-1961,* Lyre and Spottiswoode, London, 1962.

GABRIEL, Richard. *The Culture of War.* Greenwood Press, Westport, Connecticut, 1991.

GABRIEL, Richard and METZ, Karen. *From Sumer To Rome: The Military Capabilities of Ancient Armies* . Greenwood Press, Westport, Connecticut, 1992.

GAEL, Anne and CHIROL, Serge. *Châteaux et Sites de La France Medievale,* Hachette Realites, Paris, 1978.

GIES, Joseph and Frances. *Life in a Medieval Castle.* Harper Colophon Books, New York, 1979.

GOFFART, Walter. *Barbarians and Romans: The Techniques of Accommodation.* Princeton University Press, Princeton, New Jersey, 1980.

GOODSPEED, LCol D.J. *The Armed Forces of Canada 1867-1967.* Directorate of History, Canadian Forces Headquarters, Ottawa, Ontario, 1967.

GOSSELIN, Daniel, LCol. CFCSC, Toronto, RMC War Studies 500 Program, 1994.

GRAHAM-CAMPBELL, James, and KIDD, Dafydd. *The Vikings.* The British Museum Publications, London, 1980.

GRANT, Michael *The Army of the Caesars.* Charles Scribner, New York, 1978.

GURNEY, O.R. *The Hittites.* Penguin Books, Baltimore, Maryland, 1962.

HACKETT, General Sir John, *The Profession of Arms,* Sidgwick & Jackson Ltd., Great Britain, 1983.

HALBERSTADT, Hans. *The World's Great Artillery, from the Middle Ages to the Present Day,* Barnes & Noble Books, New York, 2002.

HAMLYN, Paul. *Larousse Encyclopaedia of Modern History, from 1500 to the Present Day.* Hamlyn Publishing, 1973.

HANNON, Leslie F. *Forts of Canada, The Conflicts, Sieges, and Battles that Forged a Great Nation.* McClelland and Stewart Ltd., 1969.

HAYES, Carlton J.H. Hayes et al. *History of Western Civilization,* The MacMillan Company, New York, 1964.

HEATH, Ian. *The Vikings.* Osprey Publishing, London, 1985.

HERMAN, Marguerita Z. *Ramparts, Fortifications from the Renaissance to West Point.* Avery Publishing Group Inc., Garden City Park, New York, 1992.

HICKEY, Michael. *Out of the Sky, A History of Airborne Warfare.* Mills & Boon Limited, London, 1979.

HOGG Ian. *The History of Fortification,* Orbis Publishing Ltd., New York, 1981.

HOGG, Ian V. Hogg & THURSTON, L.F. *British Artillery Weapons & Ammunition 1914-1918.* Ian Allan, London, UK, 1972.

HOGG, Ian V. *German Artillery of WWII.* Arms and Armour Press, London, 1975.

---. *German Artillery of WWII.* 2nd corrected edition. Stackpole Books, Mechanicsville, PA, 1997.

HORNE, Alistair. *The Price of Glory, Verdun, 1916.* MacMillan and Co Ltd., London, 1962.

JÄGER, Herbert. *German Artillery of WWI.* Crowood Press, Ramsbury, Marlborough, Wiltshire, UK, 2001.

JOHNSON, Anne. *Roman Forts of the First and Second Century AD in Britain and the German Provinces.* St. Martin's, New York, 1983.

JOHNSON, Paul. *Castles of England, Scotland, and Wales.* Weidenfeld and Nicolson, London, 1989.

JONES, Archer Jones. *The Art of Warfare in the Western World.* University of Illinois Press, Chicago, 1987.

KOCH H.W. *History of Warfare,* Bison Books Ltd., London, 1987.

KOCH, H.W. *Medieval Warfare,* Bison Books Limited, London, 1982.

KOCH, H.W. *The Rise of Modern Warfare.* Prentice-Hall, Englewood Cliffs, New Jersey, 1981.

KEMP, Anthony. *Castles in Colour,* Blandford Press, Poole, Dorset, 1977.

KRAMER, Samuel Noah. *The Sumerians: Their History, Culture, and Character.* University of Chicago Press, Chicago, Illinois, 1963.

LAFFRONT, Robert. *The Ancient Art of Warfare* (2 vols.) Time-Life Books, New York, 1966.

LAWRENCE, A.W. *T.E. Lawrence by His Friends,* Jonathan Cape, London, 1954.

LAWRENCE, T. E. (of Arabia). *Crusader Castles* (1936). Edited by PRINGLE, Denys. Clarendon Press, Oxford, 1988.

LAZENBY, J.F. *The Spartan Army.* Aris and Philip, Wiltshire, England, 1985.

LUCAS, James. *Storming Eagles, German Airborne Forces in World War Two,* Arms and Armour Press, London, 1988.

LUTTICHAU-BARENSTEIN, Hannibal von. *Alte Burgen-Schone Schlosser, Eine romantische Deutschlandreise, (Old Fortresses and beautiful Castles, a romantic German tour),* Verlag Das Beste GmbH, Stuttgart, 1980.

MACK, John E. *A Prince of Our Disorder, The Life of T.E. Lawrence,* Mack, London, 1976.

MARSHALL, Christopher. "Castles and Strongpoints" and "Sieges." *Warfare in the Latin East.* Cambridge University Press, Cambridge, 1992.

MCCONNELL, David. *British Smooth-Bore Artillery: A Technological Study to Support Identification, Acquisition, Restoration, Reproduction, and Interpretation of Artillery at National Historic Parks in Canada.* Minister of Supply and Services Canada, 1988.

MCNEILL, William H. *The Pursuit of Power.* University of Chicago Press, Chicago, Illinois, 1982.

MEYER, Werner and LESSING, Erich. *Deutsche Ritter, Deutsche Burgen,* Orbis Verlag, 1990.

MONTGOMERY of Alamein, Field-Marshal Viscount Bernard L. *A History of Warfare.* Collins, London, 1968.

MONTROSS, Lynn. *War through the Ages.* Harper & Brothers Publishers, New York, and London, 1946.

NEWARK, Tim. *The Barbarians: Warriors and Wars of the Dark Ages.* Blanford Press, London, England, 1985.

NORMAN, A.V.B. and WILSON, G.M. *Treasures from the Tower of London,* Lund Humphries, Bradford, 1982.

NOSSOV, Konstantin. *Ancient and Medieval Siege Weapons, A fully illustrated guide to siege weapons and tactics.* The Lyons Press, Guilford, Connecticut, 2005.

OLMSTEAD, A.T. *The History of the Persian Empire.* University of Chicago Press, Chicago, Illinois, 1948.

OMAN, C.W.C. *The Art of War in the Middle Ages*. Cornell University Press, Ithaca, New York, 1953.

PALUZIE DE LESCAZES, Carlos. *Castles of Europe*, Crescent Books, Barcelona, 1982.

PARET, Peter. *Makers of Modern Strategy from Machiavelli to the Nuclear Age*. Princeton University Press, Princeton, New Jersey, 1986.

POUNDS, N. J. G. *The Medieval Castles in England and Wales: A Political and Social History*. Cambridge University Press, New York / Cambridge, 1991.

PRITCHETT, W. Kenrick. *The Greek State At War*. University of California Press, Berkeley, California, 1971.

RICE, Tamara Talbot. *Everyday Life in Byzantium*. Dorset Press, New York, 1967.

ROGERS, R. *Latin Siege Warfare in the Twelfth Century*. Oxford Historical Monographs. Clarendon Press, Oxford, 1992.

ROUX, Georges. *Ancient Iraq*. Penguin Books, New York, 1964.

RUNCIMAN, Steven. *The Fall of Constantinople, 1453*. Cambridge at the University Press, 1965.

SAGGS, H.W.F. *The Might That Was Assyria*. Sidgwick and Jackson Ltd., London, England, 1984.

SARTY, Roger F. *Coast Artillery, 1815-1914*. Museum Restoration Service, Bloomfield, Ontario, 1988.

SCHUERL, Wolfgang F. *Medieval Castles and Cities*. Cassell Ltd., London, 1969.

SEYMOUR, William. *Great Sieges of History*. Brassey's (UK), Oxford, 1991.

SKAARUP, Harold A. *Vauban: His Fortifications and Methods of Siege*. RMC War Studies 500 paper, 1994.

SKAARUP, Harold A. *Siegecraft – No Fortress Impregnable*. iUniverse.com, Lincoln, Nebraska, 2003.

---. *Out of Darkness – Light, a History of Canadian Military Intelligence, Volume 1, Pre-Confederation to 1982*. (iUniverse.com, Lincoln, Nebraska, 2005).

---. *Out of Darkness – Light, a History of Canadian Military Intelligence, Volume 2, 1983-1997*. (iUniverse. com, Lincoln, Nebraska, 2005).

---. *Out of Darkness – Light, a History of Canadian Military Intelligence, Volume 3, 1998-2005*. (iUniverse. com, Lincoln, Nebraska, 2005).

---. *Canadian Warplanes*. ((iUniverse.com, Bloomington, Indiana, 2009).

---. *Ticonderoga Soldier – Elijah Estabrooks, 1758-1760*. (iUniverse.com, Lincoln, Nebraska, 2000).

---. *Whiz Bangs and Woolly Bears - Walter Ray Estabrooks and the First World War.* (iUniverse.com, Lincoln, Nebraska, 2000).

---. *New Brunswick Hussar.* (iUniverse.com, Lincoln, Nebraska, 2001).

---. *Ironsides - Canadian Armoured Fighting Vehicle Museums and Monuments.* iUniverse.com, Bloomington, Indiana, 2011.

---. *Shelldrake – Canadian Artillery Museums and Gun Monuments.* iUniverse.com, Bloomington, Indiana, 2011.

STE. CROIX, Philip de. *Airborne Operations, An Illustrated Encyclopedia of the Great Battles of Airborne Forces.* Salamander Books Ltd., London, 1978.

STEWART, Desmond. *T.E. Lawrence,* Paladin, Granada Publishing, London, 1979.

THE BELGIAN MINISTRY OF FOREIGN AFFAIRS, *Belgium, The Official Account of What Happened, 1939-1940,* Evans Brothers Limited, London, July 1941.

THE HOLY BIBLE, King James Version, Thomas Nelson Inc., Camden New Jersey, 1970.

THOMPSON, Michael Welman. *The Decline of the Castle.* Cambridge University Press, New York / Cambridge, 1987.

THOMPSON, Michael Welman. *The Rise of the Castle.* Cambridge University Press, New York / Cambridge, 1991.

TITCHMARSH, Peter and Helen. *Exploring France.* Warwick, 1990.

TIME Canada Ltd., Toronto, Ontario, 1994.

Treatise on the Manufacture of Guns and Text-Book of Service Ordnance, Third Edition. Printed by Order of the Secretary of State for War. (Harrison and Sons, St. Martin's Lane, London, 1886).

TUCHMAN, Barbara. *A Distant Mirror, The Calamitous 14th Century.* Ballantine Books, New York, 1978.

WARNER, Philip. *Sieges of the Middle Ages.* G. Bell and Sons Ltd., London, 1968.

WARNER, Philip. *The Medieval Castle: Life in a Fortress in Peace and War.* Taplinger Publication Company, New York, 1971.

WATSON, Bruce A. *Sieges, A Comparative Study.* Praeger Publishers, Westport, Connecticut, 1993.

WATSON, G.R. *The Roman Soldier.* Cornell University Press, Ithaca, New York, 1969.

WEBSTER, Graham. *The Roman Imperial Army.* Barnes-Noble, Toronto, Ontario, 1985.

WEIGLEY, Russell F. *The Age of Battles: the Quest for Decisive Warfare from Breitenfeld to Waterloo.* Indiana University Press, Bloomington, and Indianapolis, 1991.

WINDROW, Martin. *The Great Sieges.* Quercus Publishing Plc, London, 2009.

YADIN, Yigael. *The Art of Warfare in Biblical Lands.* McGraw-Hill, New York, 1963.

ZEWEN, Luo, et al. *The Great Wall.* McGraw Hill Book Coy, Maidenhead, England, 1981.

ZINK, Robert D. *Forts of Everywhere - Northern Frontier (U.S.), Southern Frontier (Canada),* (Coast Defense Study Group Journal, Vol. 8, No. 4, November 1994).

ZOKA, Yaha. *The Imperial Iranian Army from Cyrus to Pahlavi.* Ministry of Arts and Culture Press, Teheran, Iraq, 1971.

Index

The expansion of the mind in search of new information rests ultimately with the individual.

Lightning Source UK Ltd.
Milton Keynes UK
UKHW051225110123
415109UK00013B/747